Planning Ideas That Matter

Planning Ideas That Matter

Livability, Territoriality, Governance, and
Reflective Practice

Edited by Bishwapriya Sanyal, Lawrence J. Vale, and
Christina D. Rosan

The MIT Press
Cambridge, Massachusetts
London, England

© 2012 Massachusetts Institute of Technology

All rights reserved. No part of this book may be reproduced in any form by any electronic or mechanical means (including photocopying, recording, or information storage and retrieval) without permission in writing from the publisher.

MIT Press books may be purchased at special quantity discounts for business or sales promotional use. For information, please email special_sales@mitpress.mit.edu or write to Special Sales Department, The MIT Press, 55 Hayward Street, Cambridge, MA 02142.

This book was set in Sabon by Toppan Best-set Premedia Limited. Printed on recycled paper and bound in the United States of America.

Library of Congress Cataloging-in-Publication Data

Planning ideas that matter : livability, territoriality, governance, and reflective practice / edited by Bishwapriya Sanyal, Lawrence J. Vale, and Christina D. Rosan.
    p.   cm.
Includes bibliographical references and index.
ISBN 978-0-262-01760-2 (hardcover : alk. paper)—ISBN 978-0-262-51768-3 (pbk. : alk. paper)
1. City planning—Social aspects. I. Sanyal, Bishwapriya. II. Vale, Lawrence J., 1959– III. Rosan, Christina D. IV. Title: Livability, territoriality, governance, and reflective practice.
HT166.P533   2012
307.1'216—dc23
2011045433

10 9 8 7 6 5 4 3 2 1

Contents

III Ideas about Governance

IV Ideas about Professional Reflection

Acknowledgments

This book originated in a weekly symposium held as part of the events commemorating the seventy-fifth anniversary of the course in city planning at the Massachusetts Institute of Technology. We are grateful for the support of Adèle Naudé Santos, dean of MIT's School of Architecture and Planning, and the school's Bemis Funds, which enabled us to commission the papers that became the basis for this book. We also greatly appreciate the assistance of Karen Yegian, Janice O'Brien, Sandra Elliott, Nimfa de Leon, Patti Foley, Chandan Deuskar, Janine Marchese, and Ezra Glenn of MIT's Department of Urban Studies and Planning. At the MIT Press, Clay Morgan expressed sustained enthusiasm for this project and solicited two anonymous reviews of the manuscript, which helped us improve it significantly. We have also been ably assisted in manuscript editing and production by Marjorie Pannell and Deborah Cantor-Adams.

At base, however, this book exists because of the patience and intellectual energy of the contributing authors, and we each gained a tremendous amount from joining them on our collective quest to understand planning ideas.

Contributors

Timothy Beatley, Teresa Heinz Professor of Sustainable Communities, University of Virginia

Neil Brenner, Professor of Urban Theory, Harvard Graduate School of Design

Raphaël Fischler, Associate Professor and Director of the School of Urban Planning, McGill University

Robert Fishman, Emil Lorch Professor of Architecture and Urban Planning, University of Michigan

Merilee Grindle, Edward S. Mason Professor of International Development, Harvard University

Patsy Healey, Professor Emeritus of Town and Country Planning, Newcastle University

Gary Hack, Dean and Paley Professor, Emeritus, University of Pennsylvania

Mohammad A. Qadeer, Professor Emeritus, Queen's University, Canada

Christina D. Rosan, Assistant Professor of Geography and Urban Studies, Temple University

Lynne B. Sagalyn, Earle W. Kazis and Benjamin Schore Professor of Real Estate, Columbia University

Bishwapriya Sanyal, Ford International Professor of Urban Development, MIT

Michael B. Teitz, Professor Emeritus of City and Regional Planning, University of California, Berkeley, and Senior Fellow, Public Policy Institute of California

June Manning Thomas, Centennial Professor of Urban and Regional Planning, University of Michigan

Lawrence J. Vale, Ford Professor of Urban Design and Planning, MIT

David Wachsmuth, Department of Sociology, New York University

Peter M. Ward, Professor of Public Affairs and Sociology, University of Texas

Robert D. Yaro, Professor in Practice of City and Regional Planning, University of Pennsylvania, and President, Regional Plan Association

1

Four Planning Conversations

Bishwapriya Sanyal, Lawrence J. Vale, and Christina D. Rosan

This book was crafted as an effort to understand the core sentiments and sensibilities that undergird the field of urban and regional planning, and to spark discussions about the evolution of the field over the last one hundred years. We conceptualize these discussions as "planning conversations," building on a style of scholarly inquiry initiated by the urban historian Robert Fishman's writing on "urban conversations" (Fishman 2000). The conversations in this book are a form of professional discourse and are presented by academics who have participated in discussions on four key questions that have shaped the evolving intellectual identity of the field of urban and regional planning: Why are some places more livable than others? Which structuring of territorial jurisdictions contributes to both economic growth and social equity? What form of governance is necessary to create synergistic relationships across state, market, and civil society? What kinds of professional knowledge and expertise are necessary to enhance the quality of lives in cities and regions? To be sure, these questions do not exhaust the list of concerns voiced over the last century by the many actors who influenced the trajectory of the field of urban and regional planning, nor are they meant to generate definitive answers based on detailed historical accounts of planning endeavors around the world. The planning conversations included in this book focus on those issues with which the authors have concerned themselves, as academic observers and, sometimes, as practitioners. We hope their developed understandings will generate further conversations, thereby enriching the field of urban and regional planning.

We acknowledge previous efforts to record the historical evolution of the field (Ward 2002; Hall 1988), and such studies deeply influenced our own thinking about the geographic breadth of the planning conversations. Such conversations, conducted across great distances, have often entailed different forms of borrowing of planning ideas—at times quite undiluted, but more often selective or synthetic in spirit. As Stephen Ward (2002) observes, planning ideas have sometimes been exported from one setting to another and imposed by authoritarian means (under conditions of colonialism or postwar reconstruction efforts), sometimes deployed in more negotiated and contested ways (especially following World War II in Europe), and sometimes deployed consensually (as in the case of the European Union, or as evidenced by the aspirations of global environmental summits). But in general, professional conversations are rarely an egalitarian dialogue among the participants. All sorts of biases, interests, and preconceived notions influence the propagation of ideas. The contributors to this book take into account the unequal social terrain of planning conversations. They are often critical of how such conversations have been influenced by dominant nations, institutions, and individuals.

In describing the evolution of planning ideas, we have not attempted to follow a chronological approach, as in Peter Hall's *Cities of Tomorrow* (1988), nor do we limit ourselves to physical planning in the West. Our mode of inquiry is interpretive: we seek the essence of conversations, wherever they may have originated and wherever they may have traveled. Many of these conversations originated in the West but have leapt across geographic boundaries to pass from the highly urbanized to the newly urbanizing nations. Our interpretation of such conversations across the globe is, however, not all-encompassing and comprehensive. We asked the contributors to provide their understanding of why some elements of the collective conversation have endured while others have withered away.

Since most of the contributors are planning academics teaching in U.S. or Canadian planning programs, their interpretations are influenced by the conversations "at home." More important, what emerges from their reconstructions of planning conversations is the dominant role of U.S. institutions, including universities, in shaping planning ideas, particularly over the last fifty years. This is true not only in the field of urban and regional planning. *Time* publisher Henry Luce coined the phrase "American Century" in 1941 to describe and predict the dominance of U.S. institutions in science, technology, business practices, and even political processes, particularly in the aftermath of World War II (Evans, Buckland, and Baker 1998). It should not be surprising that the contributors differ in their interpretation of whether and how planning conversations influenced planning outcomes even as they acknowledge, sometimes implicitly, that many of the post–World War II dominant planning ideas emerged in the United States and were exported abroad.

The process has been neither uncontentious nor predictable, however. Planning conversations, both within the United States and around the world, have been anything but homogeneous and hegemonic since the 1960s. There have been many arguments and counterarguments about substantive as well as procedural planning issues and few if any clear resolutions of arguments, unlike in the natural sciences. This is one reason why the term *planning conversations*, and not *planning doctrines*, better captures the essence of the evolving process. It also affirms that, despite all the arguments that mark the evolution of the field, a few overarching concerns have kept the conversations from degenerating into cacophony. We identify four such themes that have animated the conversation of planners and shaped the evolving identity of the profession. We consider these themes to be planning ideas that matter: they are centered on the livability of places, the management of territoriality at various spatial scales, the distribution of responsibility among key actors—state, market, and civil society—for governance, and the efficacy and proper exercise of professional authority.

The essays in this book scrutinize the nature of these conversations and why they matter. Where did such ideas come from? Who generated or imported them? How did they spread among planners? Were these ideas contested, and if so, why? Did such challenges alter these ideas, or reinvigorate their conceptual appeal? The answers to such questions illuminate how planning conversations have been shaped not only by ideas but also by institutions and the changing socioeconomic contexts of cities and regions worldwide. Such analyses also reveal the core beliefs and dominant patterns of reasoning that mark the relatively young field of urban and regional planning as compared to, say, law or medicine. The concerns, anxieties, hopes, and aspirations of planners affect the intentionality of their professional actions and thereby help define the boundaries of their professional mission. Planning conversations are more than just talk. We want to know how the intentions of planners have evolved since the early years of industrialization and urbanization to shape the meanings of today's profession.

These questions sparked the curiosity of faculty in the Department of Urban Studies and Planning (DUSP) at the Massachusetts Institute of Technology, so we invited a dozen prominent scholars of planning to help us identify key planning ideas. These individual ideas in turn revealed larger and longer conversations in the field, and eventually evolved into

the essays in this book. We launched the discussions as part of the cel-
ebratory events held in 2008 to mark the seventy-fifth anniversary of
one of the oldest and largest planning programs in the world, a department that has long engaged in planning efforts across the globe, not just
in North America. It was our hunch that many DUSP faculty members,
such as Kevin Lynch, Lloyd Rodwin, John Turner, Lisa Peattie, Bernard
Frieden, Lawrence Susskind, and Donald Schön, had played key roles in
influencing planning conversations over the last seventy-five years. We
wanted to understand better why such individuals were successful in
shaping planning conversations and how DUSP could continue to play
a role in advancing planning conversations that reflect our beliefs, sensibilities, and intellectual sympathies. We also wanted to look more
broadly at the persistent themes at the heart of urban planning debates
to shed light on how they continue to influence the profession in the face
of new challenges confronting urban regions.

The essays are organized according to four key topics that have generated sustained conversation in the planning field: livability, territoriality,
governance, and reflective practice. These categories are not exhaustive
but are intended to spur similar discussions about other planning conversations that can help the profession better understand its evolving
identity. *Livability* has always been a central preoccupation of planners:
making places that enhance the quality of life. The notion of *territoriality*
was introduced by John Friedmann and Clyde Weaver (1979) in writing
about regions and regional identities in Europe and North America. How
a place is experienced, remembered, and protected depends to a large
extent on inhabitants' sense of territoriality within and between city
regions. The focus on subnational regions in this book acknowledges an
important shift in planning conversations from cities to cities plus regions
by the second decade of the twentieth century. The third section of the
book focuses on *governance*. We use the term broadly to encompass
long-established city planning and management issues emerging from
the Progressive Era in the United States to more recent discussions of
good governance as a precondition for the development of newly industrializing nations. The essays in this section address a key question in
planning: what should the role of government be in creating places,
managing territorial regions, and fostering the development of newly
industrializing and urbanizing nations? The fourth section is devoted to
ideas regarding the styles of planning practice itself, in particular, the
need for professional *reflection*, an idea that was introduced into planning conversations by our late colleague, Donald Schön. Together, these

four planning conversations—concerned with ideas about livability, territoriality, governance, and professional reflection—provide a glimpse into what city and regional planners have cared for and argued about as the world has passed through a century of urbanization and suburbanization, industrialization and deindustrialization, and economic growth and decline.

Ideas about Livability

For a profession rooted in efforts to transform physical spaces into places, perennial key concerns include issues of urban density, boundary setting between different land-use arrangements, and complex relations between the built environment and natural systems. These concerns are captured to some extent by the concept of zoning, an idea that has animated planning conversations since the early periods of urbanization. Zoning, however, is little more than a tool, a reactive practice rooted in the implementation of regulations, although as a practice it reflects deeper values about spatial hierarchy and social separation. It is more important to probe the underlying ideas and ideals that gave rise not only to tools such as zoning but also to more proactive planning efforts. To that end, the first group of chapters provides a historical account of how planners have addressed the issue of livability, more recent efforts to restructure the relationship between city and suburb, and the history of the sustainability movement.

Gary Hack in "Shaping Urban Form" revisits functional theories about why cities develop and normative theories about how they should be planned. He examines the long history of efforts to control urban development and argues that planners care about urban form because it affects the choices that individuals make regarding how they live, the societal allocation of resources, the provision and maintenance of infrastructure, and citizens' perceptions and values. Tracing the history of efforts to control the perimeter of the city from seventh-century Medina to nineteenth-century Europe to the present, Hack finds that the idea of the greenbelt has been particularly easy to transfer, citing successful adaptation in places as distant as Seoul and São Paulo. In the United States, the greenbelt idea has been reimagined as urban growth limits or boundaries. The most celebrated U.S. example is Portland, Oregon. In 1973, Oregon's state legislature required all cities to adopt urban growth boundaries. But such boundary setting has faced stiff political opposition, even in Portland. Hack argues that without appropriate governance by institutions capable of administering these boundaries, and facing significant political pressure from developers, the United States has had only limited success in channeling urban growth into desirable patterns.

Hack then explores whether cities in Canada, where every major city-region has a metropolitan-level government, have been more successful than the U.S. cities in controlling growth. He finds many of the same planning conversations about greenbelts. In Ottawa, for example, the greenbelt was established much earlier, in 1950, but has subsequently been bypassed. By contrast, Vancouver has successfully managed to balance agricultural and urban land development for the past thirty-five years. Toronto, too, has developed an eighty-five-mile regional greenbelt despite political opposition.

Hack argues that the power of the greenbelt idea lies in its adaptability. Greenbelts have served to protect rural and agricultural lands, the food supply, and an agrarian way of life. They have also served as security barriers for cities. The concept has been adapted to fit areas with varying local and national political systems, geographies, and resource availability, as well as different constellations of local interest groups. The ability to fit the varying needs of diverse locations and political conditions has been critical to the success of this planning.

Ideas about how to control urban form have also mutated as they have moved from place to place and responded to different challenges over time. Hack anticipates that the challenge of climate change, by calling attention to the need for cities to reduce their carbon footprints, will continue to influence planning conversations regarding urban form. Planners understand that cities will need to become denser, and will have to provide alternative means of transportation to reduce vehicle miles traveled. In fact, many cities are currently implementing policies of transit-oriented development, where higher-intensity development takes place around transit nodes. Hack suggests that efforts such as PlaNYC and the London Plan are important steps in the right direction. He credits planners in Vancouver for heavy investment in public transit in preparation for the 2010 Olympics. Hack anticipates that such planning efforts will influence urban form and provide confidence to both planners and citizens that planning ideas matter. In other words, while controlling urban density has long been a topic for discussion, climate change may introduce a new foundational rationale into the conversation.

Next, in chapter 3, Robert Fishman explores the idea of New Urbanism, a term coined in the late twentieth century but rooted in earlier ideas about Garden Cities and garden suburbs, and also linked to ideas from Jane Jacobs about mixed use urban vitality. Fishman argues that a group of outsiders—mainly architects practicing in the field of urban design—revived many of the forgotten ideas of the Garden City movement and reintroduced these old ideas into contemporary planning conversations. Raymond Unwin's (1911) "garden suburb" idea, originally conceived to address overcrowded cities through strategic decentralization, is now being applied to the opposite problem of urban sprawl. The garden suburb has reemerged in twin guises: a West Coast version rooted in transit-oriented development and an East Coast variant characterized by neotraditional towns, intended to control sprawl in regions where population has already dispersed. The power of New Urbanism as a planning idea derives from its capacity to revitalize neglected themes in the planning tradition, such as streetcar suburbs, and present them as solutions to contemporary problems. In this instance, West Coast New Urbanists have coined new terminology to refresh an old conversation about walkable communities organized around the availability of transit.

Timothy Beatley in chapter 4 traces the history of the idea of sustainability and its implications for urban planning. It originated as a way of considering how best to exploit the world's resources. Beatley notes that the early advocates of sustainability, such as Gifford Pinchot, defined sustainability as the wise use and management of nature. In that sense, it was not an urban concept at all. Over time, however, scholars, activists, organizations, and initiatives adapted the concept and helped popularize it; their numbers include Rachel Carson, Carleton and Jerry Ray, Gro Brundtland, Dana Meadows, and William Rees. As a result, there is growing recognition of how serious our environmental problems really are, and a clearer mission for cities in promoting sustainability.

The challenge of sustainability has evolved, Beatley argues: "It is about cities and the built environment; it is about the social and the economic as much as the ecological; and it is now permeating and penetrating cultural consciousness in a way earlier versions did not." Much of this new consciousness is bubbling up from the bottom, he notes, and sustainability is no longer an issue confined to conversations among experts in state and federal offices. Even the vocabulary and the language of sustainability have changed, and the concept has seeped into many aspects of how planners think about the world. There is a growing acknowledgment that the way cities are built dramatically affects sustainability. There is also a growing interest in understanding how building types affect urbanism, as exemplified in the work of both thinkers and practitioners, such as William McDonough, Richard Register, Janine Benyus, Thomas Bender, and Gary Lawrence. Expanding grassroots involvement in sustainability initiatives in major cities is another influence on contemporary planning conversations. As evidenced in the work of Majora Carter, Los Angeles mayor Antonio R. Villaraigosa, and PlaNYC, concern for sustainability now pervades conversations about the design and management of both cities and regions.

In 1987, the report from the UN World Commission on Environment and Development, *Our Common Future*, had only one chapter on cities. Now, Beatley notes, the conversation about global sustainability has taken an "urban turn," translating "broad sustainability goals and aspirations into tangible physical and social outcomes." Conversations about sustainability in cities range from utopian ideas for ecocities to model ecological cities, green planning, and even urban gardening. The U.S. Mayors' Climate Protection Agreement, launched in 2005, has influenced a growing number of cities to construct politically backed sustainability plans, signaling a firm commitment to a new approach to urban development. The sustainable city movement has created important alliances with partners in public health, merging green and social justice agendas and thereby created a new alliance for social sustainability. This too has influenced new ways of designing cities and is evidence that the idea of sustainability is now a key concept in most planning conversations.

Ideas about Territoriality

What is the appropriate scale at which problems of human settlement should be addressed? This question has animated planning conversations for nearly one hundred years, generating a large body of literature on regionalism and metropolitanism and a relatively recent argument regarding territorial competition. The chapters in this section, on regional development planning, metropolitanism, and territorial competition, highlight both the agreements and the disagreements among planners engaged in this conversation. Taken together, these chapters trace the evolution of the idea of territoriality. More important, however, they describe the many challenges planners have faced in implementing regional initiatives when appropriate governing institutions are lacking and global competition for investment is intense.

Michael B. Teitz in chapter 5 argues that the concept of regional development planning draws on deeply rooted intellectual currents. He traces the history of the idea back to the eighteenth-century Enlightenment in Europe and North America. According to Teitz, the tension between rational self-interest and the need to belong to a community has been a hallmark of planning conversations since well before the planning profession gained formal recognition. The concept of region embodies this duality. Teitz divides the history of the idea of regionalism into four periods: (1) the utopian era, from the mid-nineteenth century up to 1930, (2) the heroic era, from 1930 to 1945, (3) the development era, from 1945 to 1985, and (4) the global era, from 1985 on. Spanning these four periods, the history of the idea is a continuing flow of historic change, albeit punctuated with specific thinkers and events that stand out as markers, Teitz proposes. He concludes by arguing that even though the concept of regional planning appears to be at an ebb at the moment, it "has proved itself to be a resilient idea, and it should not simply be written off as part of a discarded past."

Robert D. Yaro in chapter 6 examines the origins and development of metropolitanism and regional planning in the United States. Yaro defines metropolitanism as an awareness that the economies of large cities extend beyond their political jurisdictions into surrounding areas, serving as nodal zones within larger regional territories. Using the case of the Regional Plan Association (RPA) of New York, the oldest independent regional planning agency in the nation, Yaro explores how this planning idea survived despite many opposing ideas such as anti-urbanism, federalism, entrenched localism, and the city-suburb divide. He describes how the opposition of powerful intellectual traditions and political interests was ultimately overcome by a range of planning initiatives, some currently under way in many parts of the United States. He argues that the concept of metropolitanism was inspired and shaped by the work of the RPA and its ad hoc predecessor group, the Committee on the Regional Plan of New York and Its Environs. "New York has always been in the vanguard of urban and metropolitan development and planning," Yaro writes, "because urban problems emerge in New York early and at a scale that requires metropolitan-scale solutions." In many cases, the innovations that emerged from the RPA's plans and actions have inspired similar thinking and actions in regions around the world.

Yaro describes RPA's three regional plans, completed in 1929, 1968, and 1996, to demonstrate how the idea of metropolitanism influenced planners. All three plans covered a range of issues and concerns, including transportation and mobility, urban form, economic structure, environmental and open space protection, housing, social equity, and workforce skills development. Yaro examines how these plans shaped planning practice and theory, then speculates about where metropolitan planning may now be heading. He contends that "for nearly a century the RPA has both influenced and mirrored the thinking of metropolitan planners and theorists in New York, across the United States, and around the world." This is an upbeat assessment of subnational planning efforts at a scale larger than that of a city. Some would argue that it is also wishful thinking on the part of planners (Harvey 2006) and that such thinking has become pronounced with the rapid globalization of economies and the lack of appropriate planning institutions that could tame globalization for the benefit of national or subnational territories (Soja 2000). These debates about the effectiveness of planning and its ability to adequately address the political and economic realities of our times offer an important critical lens with which to scrutinize planning practice. They demonstrate that planning ideas are not always shared and can be in conflict with one another. However, through this dialogue, planning research and practice evolve to better meet urban and regional challenges.

Neil Brenner and David Wachsmuth in chapter 7 agree that planning has its limits; they argue that so far, planning has not been able to channel private investment for the benefit of territories. Brenner and Wachsmuth attribute this adverse outcome to the ascendancy of the idea of territorial competition, which has pervaded planning discourse since the neoliberal period of the 1980s. According to Brenner and Wachsmuth, beginning in the 1980s, territorial competitiveness has gradually become one of the dominant ideas in mainstream approaches to local economic development. The idea rests on the assumption that territories—whether national economies, regions, or cities—must compete with one another to attract mobile capital investment. Concomitantly, various institutional reforms and policy reorientations are required to create location-specific socioeconomic assets that would attract private capital. Brenner and Wachsmuth investigate the conceptual lineages of such assumptions, evaluate their validity, and trace their impact on public policies designed to promote local economic development. Drawing on a historical analysis of territorial planning under modern capitalism, the authors explore why earlier policies of "balanced urbanization" and "endogenous growth" were eventually abandoned as planners became preoccupied with territorial competition.

Next, Brenner and Wachsmuth summarize contemporary planning discourses and evaluate policies motivated by the idea of territorial competitiveness, particularly in the industrialized nations. They argue that the neoliberal preoccupation with competitiveness followed closely the transition from the Keynesian "welfare state" to post-Keynesian "competition states" and the increased neoliberalization of interlocality relations across the world economy. They assert that the notion of territorial competitiveness is based on deeply flawed intellectual assumptions and serves primarily as a means of ideological mystification. Instead of initiating local economic development, it obfuscates the capitalist restructuring process that is under way and leads to the formulation of incoherent, wasteful, or self-undermining policies, which are then adopted by territories. The widespread adoption of such policies, motivated by territorial competitiveness, hurts those cities and regions that attempt to forge alternative policy approaches to local economic development. Insofar as most localities in any interurban system adopt policies for territorial competitiveness, those localities that try to opt out of such policies experience significant disadvantages. The chapter concludes by exploring possible escape routes from this "competitiveness trap."

Ideas about Governance

What are the appropriate roles of the state, market institutions, and civil societies in fostering urban and regional development? This has been a central question animating planning conversations in both industrialized and industrializing nations, and in theoretical terms it can be framed as a matter of governance. This question emerged as far back as the seventeenth century with the formation of nation-states (Blockmans and Tilly 1994). It was introduced into planning conversations by the beginning of the nineteenth century in Europe, around the 1870s in the United States, and by the early 1950s in newly decolonized developing nations (Friedmann 1987). The planning conversations have changed and evolved in all three settings, but by the beginning of the twenty-first century they were more alike than different (Wade 1990; Walzer 1995). Like all planning conversations, the discussion of governance has been influenced by concepts borrowed from other disciplines, and also by historical events such as wars, market depressions, decolonization, and the urban protests of the 1960s (Unger and West 1998). Not surprisingly, the specific impacts of such events on planning practices have varied in different planning contexts (Berger and Dore 1996). What's intriguing, however, is how contemporary events are creating a convergence of views about the appropriate roles of the state, markets, and civil society in urban and regional development (Stiglitz 2006). The very use of the term *governance* to refer to the tripartite relationship is a sign of this convergence in planning conversations (Danson, Halkier, and Cameron 2000). Along with other concepts, such as private-public partnerships, decentralized development, and urban management, the frequency of use of the term governance has increased since the collapse of communism after 1989 (Grindle 2007). The four chapters on urban development, private-public engagement, good governance, and self-help housing in this section are attempts to understand the changing nature of planning conversations about the roles of states, markets, and civil society at the urban, regional, and national levels.

Mohammad Qadeer in chapter 8 argues that urban development is primarily a Western idea and that the shift in conversations from urban planning to urban development in the 1960s was externally induced by Western planners who had rejected traditional master plans as effective tools for planning Western cities. The idea was then propagated by bilateral and multilateral aid agencies to newly decolonized nations. Compared to the earlier period of colonial rule, when Western political power was used directly to construct segregated colonial cities, the new flow of ideas from the West in the 1960s may appear to be less authoritarian at first glance, but it drastically altered planning practice in developing nations. Qadeer argues that Western advice on how to address urban planning problems in developing nations lacked consistent logic because such advice changed periodically along with changing views of Western planners about how best to address urban problems in their own cities.

In Qadeer's analysis, planning conversations failed to vary despite differing planning contexts. Rather, dominant ideas—first from Europe, and later, after World War II, from the United States—were imposed by agencies that provided funds for the implementation of such ideas. Qadeer provides many examples of these shifts in dominant ideas from the West: the change from urban planning based on architecture and engineering to policy efforts driven by social science; the odd juxtaposition of social policies with physical planning, as in the Model Cities program in the United States; the transfer of Jane Jacobs's ideas of "livable neighborhoods"; the notion of the private-public partnership; and more recently an idea pushed most forcefully by the World Bank, that urban planners should reduce the regulation of markets and instead "enable" private agents to provide public goods and services. Similarly, there has been a surge in the popularity of the idea that "civil society," "self-help," and "social capital" are essential for the management of "megacities"—yet another term coined in the West. With regard to megacities, Qadeer states that Western advice about cities has also changed drastically over the years, from the recommendation that city size be controlled to the proposal that slums and squatter areas be developed to, now, the idea that "good urban management" should be used to reap the benefits of large-scale urban agglomerations. Such policy changes have made Qadeer skeptical about the rigor as well as the relevance of Western advice about urban problems in newly industrializing nations. He predicts that a new cycle of ideas regarding how to address climate change will also soon spread from the West to the rest.

The essence of Qadeer's chapter is that Western ideas have controlled development discourse. Implicit in his argument is a plea for more intellectual autonomy of indigenous planners in newly industrializing nations. This is an intellectual position that has received some attention, from macroeconomists more than urban planners, since the early 1970s. Starting with Raúl Prebisch (1984) and including contemporary economists such as Dani Rodrik (1999), some have persuasively argued that the imposition of orthodox Western theories of economic growth has slowed the pace of industrialization by less-developed nations. There are examples, however, of developing nations industrializing quietly by relying on heterodox policies they crafted themselves (Tendler 1997). At the city level, too, there are some signs of successful indigenous planning efforts; Jaime Lerner's planning and urban design interventions in Curitiba, Brazil, are especially inspiring (Rabinovitch 1996). Similarly, there are signs that some cities in India, such as Ahmedabad and Hyderabad, have been able to craft good urban planning efforts on their own (Misra and Misra 1998). These cities did not shield themselves from external ideas, however; instead, they modified external ideas to fit their specific contexts and, in the process, innovated new approaches, often unexpectedly (Borja et al. 1997). The lesson to draw from these few inspiring examples is that planners in newly industrializing nations can self-assess the usefulness of all ideas, including those that have been manufactured abroad.

One such idea is probed in chapter 9 by Lynne B. Sagalyn—the public-private partnership (PPP), initiated in the United States but later exported to many nations, both developing and developed. Sagalyn focuses on the impact of this idea on planning conversations and practices in the United States, but her critical arguments are relevant for developing countries as well. As she shows, the PPP is viewed as an efficient means of leveraging private capital for urban development that cannot be accomplished by government alone. Sagalyn interprets the growing interest in PPPs since the early 1980s as a desire for "reform of urban governance at a time when direct government action needs both a new cloak of political optimism and a deep source of capital funding." The emphasis on PPPs is often a rallying cry for reforms of prevailing policy regions, Sagalyn argues. This is evident in the propagation of such slogans as "partnerships for progress," "a new framework for infrastructure," "a tool for economic modernization," "helping to address urban environmental crises," and "meeting the investment challenge."

According to Sagalyn, PPPs have been widely adopted around the world because of the "particular political pliability inherent in the public-private strategy." She writes that the "open character, flexible format, and customization of project-specific business terms and conditions for the private-public sharing of risks and responsibilities make the PPP model highly adaptable." In addition, the actual meaning of the public-private label remains ambiguous—and this can be useful for developing public support. PPP could mean many different things: "informal collaboration, formal organizational alliance, and contractual business venturing, if not an exactly equal sharing of risks and rewards as commonly connoted by the word 'partnership.'" The PPP represents a new way of responding to the old question of who should do what. By seeking common ground and a mutually reinforcing relationship between the state and the market rather than the traditional adversarial role of the state as market regulator, the PPP suggests a fundamental change in approach to problem solving by planners. However, the ambiguity of the concept also makes it a somewhat imprecise tool for addressing complex urban problems.

It is not simply the impreciseness of the idea that worries Sagalyn. She argues that the PPP's increasing popularity among planners blurs the line between private and public actors, undermining public agencies and generating a host of "vexing governance questions." Sagalyn is skeptical about whether the PPP is appropriate as a governance reform tool because it reduces accountability and increases political risks. Also, its effectiveness has rarely been tested rigorously. In other words, Sagalyn is perplexed by the growing popularity of this imprecise planning idea, and wishes that planning conversations would be more demanding of such politically trendy ideas.

Along the same lines, Merilee Grindle analyzes the concept of good governance, which also influenced planning conversations during the

1980s, when newly industrializing nations grappled with declining growth rates, accumulating debt, and severe fiscal and monetary problems. Like Sagalyn, Grindle is skeptical about conceptually fuzzy ideas and their effectiveness as policy tools. She acknowledges that the idea of governing institutions and practices that are "fair, judicious, transparent, accountable, participatory, responsive, well-managed, and efficient" is certainly appealing. There is at least one historical precedent of a similar idea working reasonably well in the United States during the Progressive Era (Sandel 1996). Yet Grindle is doubtful whether the recent upsurge of support for good governance in developing nations will really improve government performance. She argues that the good governance agenda is so "seductive" that the popularity of the idea has "far outpaced its capacity to deliver." Grindle writes, "In its brief life, it has also muddied the waters of thinking about the development process." True, this idea encouraged some institutional reforms of governmental agencies, but on the whole, it did not address the economic problems of newly industrializing nations.

What would explain the growing popularity of the idea of good governance? Grindle argues that the idea had broad appeal across the political spectrum because of its wide-ranging goals, couched in a rhetoric that signaled positive moral values that were hard to dispute. She attributes the popularity of the idea to the kind of research that ranked nations by scoring factors such as transparency, accountability, responsiveness, and so on, and then produced composite indices of good governance. These indices were portrayed as objective and rigorous measures of government performance (World Bank 1997). Grindle argues that this type of broad-brush research is not as useful to planners as rigorous case studies are.

Multilateral agencies, such as the World Bank, popularized the idea of good governance, Grindle points out, because such ideas introduced a technical quality to an initiative that was, in reality, a political effort to restructure governance systems. Good governance acted as "an umbrella concept to describe a wide variety of 'good things,'" she writes. "The popularity of the idea has been more of a problem than one that serves as an impetus for better understanding of the development process." The idea seems to explain away the intricacies of the development process with an all-embracing slogan. The large-N studies of governance that supported the idea did not account for the real, complex nature of the development process. These studies produced blueprints and "best practices" of good governance that are not usually replicable. Finally, good governance has been posed as a precondition for development when in fact it is an outcome. Grindle concludes her analysis by proposing the idea of "good enough governance" that would provide "the minimal conditions necessary to allow political and economic development to occur."

Peter M. Ward's chapter, "Self-Help Housing," analyzes yet another way planners have dealt with governance-related issues—in particular, how to house the urban poor in newly industrializing nations. The idea of self-help housing is older than that of good governance. It was formulated in the late 1940s by Jacob Crane at the U.S. Housing and Home Finance Agency to address housing shortages in Puerto Rico. Later, after a hiatus of almost twenty years, John Turner reintroduced the idea into planning conversations as a way to respond to the growth of unregistered housing settlements on the peripheries of cities in Latin America and elsewhere. Turner's advice, that such settlements should be considered not as a problem but as a solution, coincided with the general sense of intellectual and political crisis during the 1960s as established modernization theories of development lost their earlier punch (Ingham1993). Turner argued that larger scale modernist housing schemes and the eviction of squatters had substantially failed, leaving the poor with no option but to build their own housing, incrementally, in unauthorized areas. Turner's criticism had two purposes. One was to dismiss the conventional wisdom that governments can increase housing supply by directly building housing. More important, however, it praised the poor for devising innovative solutions to the problem despite governmental opposition, and for creating a decentralized, flexible process of incremental housing improvements in which the poor no longer needed to depend on the government.

Turner's criticism of government and his simultaneous celebration of self-help housing by the poor are precursors to two strands of ideas that ultimately influenced planning conversations about governance in the 1980s. First, Turner's famous verdict, "governments have done so little with so much, while poor people have done so much with so little" (Turner 1979), laid the conceptual groundwork for the severe criticism of the state that soon followed from both the right and left of the ideological spectrum (Sanyal 1994). The idea of good governance began to emerge out of this broad-ranging criticism only after international agencies had grudgingly acknowledged the limits of self-help and the government's role in the delivery of goods and services, including housing for the urban poor (World Bank 1997).

The second idea—which eventually came to be described as leveraging social capital—was implicit in Turner's explanation of why the poor are capable of self-help. Even though Robert Putnam (Putnam, Leonardi, and Nanetti 1993) popularized the phrase "social capital" later, Ward argues that fragments of the concept were in circulation as far back as the 1950s during community planning efforts in London. Ward attributes the origins of the idea of self-help housing, usually associated with cities in poor countries, to earlier planning conversations in wealthy countries. He then puzzles over a paradox: given its Western gestation, why is self-help housing not considered seriously in current thinking about housing problems in developed nations such as the United States?

In pondering this paradox, Ward highlights the role that international organizations such as the World Bank and the UN played in promoting Turner's idea and, in the process, associating it with housing problems only in developing nations. Ward argues that the concept eventually influenced a broad range of development ideas, from theories of modernization to those of structuralism, interdependency, globalization, and even recent efforts in decentralization and urban management. Why are Western planners reluctant to acknowledge the extent of self-built and informally produced housing in the cities of developed nations? Drawing on his extensive research in Texas, Ward argues that even though self-built housing is widespread in many periurban areas, planners and public officials do not notice such efforts, and even when they do notice them, they are reluctant to transfer ideas and best practices from less-developed nations to support such efforts in the United States. Ward concludes that even though the idea of self-help has been exported widely around the world, it is rarely acknowledged as useful to address problems in the United States or other developed nations.

Ideas about Professional Reflection

A fourth enduring area of conversation within the planning profession has been an inward-facing one, full of persistent reflexive questions about planning practice itself. Why do planners resist changing the ways they usually address problems? Why are some planners able to learn on the job and modify their practice accordingly, while others continue to operate in old ways, even when faced with new problems and changing planning contexts? Which models of planning do planners currently use to frame problems and make decisions? Which ideas underlie such professional action? Where did such ideas come from? Have these ideas evolved over time, particularly since the 1960s, when planners' conventional values, beliefs, and modes of professional practice were subjected to serious scrutiny? What was the impact of the civil rights movement and other social change movements that demanded wider participation in planning decisions? Which people should be empowered to take greater roles in planning conversations, either as planners or as part of an engaged public? The three chapters in this section, on reflective practice, communicative planning, and social justice, address these questions. They analyze the altered conversations and planning practices that emerged from the social and conceptual turmoil of the 1960s.

Raphaël Fischler, writing in chapter 11 on the idea of reflective practice, describes the nature of practice before the formal inception of this idea. He argues that until the 1960s there were two sorts of planners: master consultants, who wanted to construct general principles on which to base city planning; and technicians, who were charged with implementing these principles at the local level. The upheavals of the 1960s unnerved both types of planners because the previously generalized principles lost their relevance in the rapidly changing context. Lacking formulaic prescriptions, the technician-planners were at a loss in seeking to address urban problems. The deepening uncertainty and instability of the moment were compounded by sharp value conflicts, making traditional planners question what they had taken for granted as useful knowledge. It also made them question the efficacy of how they made decisions, shaking their confidence in modern professionalism and its central idea of technical rationality. The nature of planning conversations changed dramatically in content and tone.

Fischler proposes that the key individual who directly addressed this crisis of professional competence was Donald Schön with his call for reflective practice. Schön's call was not aimed only at urban planners. Trained as a philosopher but coming from the business world to teach in the DUSP at MIT, Schön was concerned about conventional professionalism in general during an unstable time. He proposed, that to be effective, professionals needed to abandon conventional and general metatheories of good practice and instead learn from their own actions, particularly when the outcomes of such actions were surprising. Until then, surprising outcomes were treated as anomalies to be disregarded, but Schön proposed that they be cherished as windows offering new insights into the complexity of the problems planners were trying to address. This required reflection "in action" and "on action," as Fischler notes, and it entailed a different approach to problem framing in which goals are discovered, determined, and modified along the way.

If pursued by organizations as well as individuals, the reflective approach could create "learning systems," Schön suggested. Under such systems, individuals and organizations would continuously assess their own actions and those of others with curiosity and as experiments. Such experiments would reveal no general principles but only finely tuned, context-specific insights into how to modify action under changing circumstances. Fischler scrutinizes this vision of the planner as a reflective practitioner rather than as a grand theorist or a technocrat and poses an interesting paradox: why is it that the idea of reflective practice is widely respected by planners when very few actually follow its planning style? Perhaps it is more an irony than a paradox that the idea of reflective practice, which rejects "espoused theories" (what planners say they do) and valorizes "theories in use" (what they actually do), has itself become an espoused theory. Reflective practice may be more interesting than earlier espoused theories of action, but it may not be any more widely practiced—at least not yet.

Patsy Healey in chapter 13 takes the conversation forward. She describes how some ideas not only influenced normative planning conversations about what planning should be but also altered actual practice on the ground. The notion of communicative planning, which also emerged in response to the 1960s crisis of professional legitimacy, is one such idea. Healey situates the idea of communicative planning within "a broad movement in social theory and philosophy that has helped shift political and practical attention to the significance of the micropolitics of collective action and, in particular, the potentialities of active agency within and around formal government organizations." In its emphasis on the microlevel, communicative planning is similar to reflective practice. Also, both ideas reject technocratic planning of the kind that preceded the 1960s. Yet there are significant differences between communicative planning and reflective practice. For one, communicative planning focuses not on individual planners and their learning trajectories but on the collective behaviors of communities in which the planners are facilitators and consensus builders. Second, communicative planning explicitly acknowledges the influence of micropolitics and uneven power distribution on planning decisions. It is not Marxian, however, in the way it situates planners amid conflicting interests. In fact, communicative planning—which Healey describes as being practiced increasingly in developed, democratic nations—has gained popularity precisely because it does not cast all conversations in the rigid terms of classic class antago-nism. Conflicts of interests and views among members of communities are acknowledged, but with the hope that planners can help set a process for deliberations and dialogue that will eventually lead to some conver-gence of views and social learning, ideas developed by planners such as Lawrence Susskind and John Forester.

The idea of communicative planning is now "an idea in good cur-rency," but, as Healey describes, the idea had lain dormant for a while after its inception in the late 1970s. Planning conversations then were influenced by a range of ideas, from neo-Marxism to postmodernism to multiculturalism, each with its supporters and critics. From this intel-lectual turmoil, however, the idea of neoliberalism emerged, put in prac-tice initially by Ronald Reagan and Margaret Thatcher. The neoliberals' attack on planning is well known by now (Sanyal 2005a). What has been relatively unknown is that communicative planning as an idea not only survived the attack but even flourished, as neoliberalism has in turn come under attack for its post–cold war "triumphalism," ill-advised financial speculations, and resurgence of religious and political fundamentalism (Lechner 1992; Killick 1989). Communicative planning did not propose any megatheory as an alternative to neoliberalism; it simply remained focused at the ground level, on what Healey calls "micropractices," to augment democracy, which ultimately curbed neoliberalism.

Planners cannot yet declare victory, however. Racial and ethnic preju-dices exposed by the civil rights movement of the 1950s and 1960s in the United States remain major obstacles on the road to social justice. As June Manning Thomas observes in chapter 14 while tracing the history of planning conversations about racial and ethnic justice from the 1960s to the present, the nature of the conversation has indeed evolved. Planners' awareness of racial and ethnic injustices has grown, and this has altered planning style from the so-called rational model of the 1950s to advocacy planning in the 1960s and now to communicative planning, which has indeed expanded citizen participation in planning decisions. And yet, Thomas argues, such procedural changes have not significantly reduced power imbalances, seen as a necessary precursor to achieving social justice. Thomas worries that as planning conversations evolved from advocacy planning to radical planning and then to other planning styles, the concern for process—particularly regarding citizens' participation—somewhat overshadowed concerns regarding actual plan-ning outcomes. In particular, she questions whether new planning ideas have created a more level playing field, politically and racially.

Thomas's analysis is based on a systematic study of the proceedings of annual conferences held by the American Society of Planning Officials (ASPO) and articles published in the *Journal of the American Planning Association*. Combing through these papers, she noticed that advocacy planning emerged as two streams of ideas, one legalistic and the other focused on social inequalities. Paul Davidoff amalgamated these using the legal system and the historical moment to push for progressive social reforms. By the mid-1970s, however, the pace of change had begun to slow, and the ideas that had provided intellectual and emotional vigor for advocacy planning had dissipated. True, the general awareness of social justice issues among planners had increased, but simultaneously the sharpness of the argument for advocacy planning, as initially formulated by Davidoff, had dulled (Peattie 1978). Eventually, new offshoots from the original idea emerged in the form of arguments for "equity planning" and "radical planning." In Thomas's assessment, though, it is the original idea and the ideals of advocacy planning that have had the greatest impact on planners' thinking about how to address social injustices. Much work still needs to be done, Thomas points out, to rebalance power relationships in a meaningful way and redefine race relationships. This will require American planners to be not only self-reflective and participatory but also critical of the status quo.

The Meaning of Planning Conversations

The conceptual tent for planning conversations has been quite large, with room not only for architects and urban planners but also for concerned individuals from many other disciplines and professions: economists, sociologists, political scientists, geographers, engineers, environmentalists, real estate developers, bankers, lawyers, and social activists, to name a few. Conversations among these individuals, all of whom care about urban and regional issues, have been influenced over the years by their different disciplinary training, but also by the diverse range of institutions they represent, from local municipal departments to academia to international organizations. Moreover, interactions between individuals and institutions have been influenced, not surprisingly, by historical moments and specific urban settings, creating a large web of beliefs, aspirations, methods of thinking, and, of course, plans for action. In other words, planning conversations have been strikingly open to all sorts of ideas, but more important, the nature of such conversations has continuously evolved as planners have willingly embraced the intractable challenges of urban poverty, racial segregation, urban sprawl, and now climate change.

The ideas planners have drawn on in conversing and arguing (and the ideas that we suggest have held the profession together so far) have not been as tightly controlled as, say, in economics. The methodological rigor underlying some planning arguments has also been less stringent than in some other disciplines and professions. But there are benefits in opting for social relevance over methodological rigor, as comparative reviews of a variety of fields have demonstrated (Bender and Schorske 1998). And, certainly, relevance and rigor should not be assessed as an either/or proposition. What may be more useful is to understand the reasons for the variation in the way different disciplines and professions aim for both objectives. In the case of urban and regional planners, one must take into account their intellectual willingness and readiness to tackle multiple challenges, some of which are addressed in this book. Planners have been relatively more democratically open than, say, economists in conversing about such challenges; they have also been more self-critical than others, as Fischler notes in this book. This may at times give the impression that planning conversations lack coherence and have no basis in core beliefs or shared sentiments. But that would be a superficial and ahistorical assessment. It ignores the gradual maturing of planning conversations—and, also, their increasingly democratic tone, even though not everyone is included in the same way, as Thomas reminds us.

This book records the shared beliefs and aspirations, as well as the disagreements, that mark planning conversations. Among the shared sentiments, at least three stand out. First, the notion of progress—that the status quo need not be accepted as a fait accompli—is writ large in all planning conversations. Second, there is agreement that placemaking is to be preferred over what James Kunstler (1993) decried as "a geography of nowhere." Third, there is an acknowledgment that some form of governmental authority is necessary for reform. This is coupled with a sense that equitable governance is a shared responsibility, not simply the domain of public officials. Such sentiments are woven together by a set of progressive yearnings, but there are no definitive answers as yet on how to equalize life opportunities, how to steadily democratize decision making, and what form of community is necessary to counter isolation and exclusion amid unpredictable economic changes.

Planners have disagreed, too, but such disagreements have never stifled conversations. On the contrary, disagreements about how to frame and address problems have moved the profession forward to embrace new challenges, sometimes without a clear understanding of what such challenges might actually entail. Starting with the famous disagreement between Frederick Law Olmsted, Jr., and Benjamin Marsh that marked the inception of the profession in the United States in 1909 (Peterson 2009), planning conversations have periodically been stirred by disagreements about planning styles, such as the clash of views between Robert Moses and Jane Jacobs (Flint 2009); about the purpose of comprehensive planning, such as that between Alan Altshuler and John Friedmann (1965); about the centrality of private property values in placemaking, such as that between Harry Richardson and Peter Marcuse (Dear and Scott 1981); and about the appropriate role of government in furthering public interest, such as that between Rexford Tugwell and Friedrich Hayek (Klosterman 1985).

The debates continue, as the contributors to this book show, and criticality, not complaisance, remains a key attribute of planning conversations. Hack, for example, is ambivalent about the effectiveness of conventional mechanisms for growth control. Fishman suspects that old ideas are being repackaged under the label of "New Urbanism." Beatley, however, is more hopeful that the concern for sustainability is not a fleeting passion. By contrast, Grindle is concerned that the new emphasis on good governance may hinder a deeper understanding of the complexities of the development process. Likewise, Sagalyn is skeptical about terms such as private-public partnership and recommends that planners understand better the intricacies of risk- and profit-sharing arrangements. Qadeer, too, is apprehensive. He questions the staying power of fluctuating planning ideas shaped by international institutions with short attention spans.

Again, in contrast, while Yaro is relatively confident that metropolitanism as an idea is gaining deserved support despite opposition, Teitz is less sanguine about the prospects for regional planning at the moment, even though he remains hopeful that as an idea that has lasted for well over a hundred years, regional planning will continue to inspire planners, even if it is not fully implemented. Brenner and Wachsmuth are critical of the trajectory of planning ideas regarding territoriality from the earlier beliefs in the "balanced growth of regions" to more recent endorsements of regional competition. They blame the regressive impact of neoliberalism on a failure of planning imagination and lament the loss of progressive ideals, such as equality and balanced growth, in shaping planning conversations.

Why are there such disagreements about the power of urban and regional planning as an instrument for enhancing the quality of life in cities and regions? For one, the contributors to this volume are not ideologically homogeneous. Each author's interpretation of planning conversations and outcomes is influenced by his or her ideology, practical experience, and disciplinary lens, ranging from architecture to political sociology. While this variation may be seen as a source of weakness, it is also a source of strength for a relatively young and lively field. Second, the scale of inquiry varies considerably among the authors. Even though individual neighborhoods and the global economy are deeply connected, as the literature on shrinking cities documents so vividly (Pallagst et al. 2009), the varying spatial scales of social inquiries often lead to dissimilar interpretations. To put it differently, just because micro- and macroeconomics are usually portrayed as complementary by economists, that does not mean they are experienced as such by all observers of economic processes. Then there are differences in methods of analysis. It is possible to differ productively over where to draw the conceptual boundary, how to analyze causalities, and what inferences, if any, can provide generalizable insights about a sociospatial process with such variations, complexity, and uncertainty.

In light of the conceptual challenges that mark the field of urban and regional planning, it is heartening to realize that the vast and diffuse professional discourse over the last century is malleable enough to be grouped at all, let alone into four neat categories of planning conversations. Perhaps it is a sign of the editors' optimism, but it is not mere wishful thinking. After all, planning practices have evolved in some clearly discernible directions, even if this is not uniformly the case across the world: from being totally technocratic to relatively more politically conscious (Healey), from modernist government control of housing delivery to housing by the people (Ward), from the idea that nature needs to be conquered to an embrace of the value of natural systems (Beatley), from uncontrolled suburbanization to growth control (Hack), from the supremacy of the private automobile to renewed recognition of the importance of public transit (Fishman), and from physical determinism to a multidisciplinary understanding of cities and regions (Qadeer). This is not an exhaustive list of evolution in planning ideas. Others have noted similar changes in other aspects of planning ideas over the last one hundred years (Birch and Silver 2009).

There is one additional characteristic of planning conversations that is particularly relevant for the early twenty-first century and that finds widespread agreement: the productive globalization of discourse. Since the early days of the profession, at the beginning of the twentieth century, planning ideas have increasingly crossed national boundaries and have influenced planning conversations between and among nations, cities, and regions the world over. This is not to say that concerns for spatial, cultural, and institutional specificities are no longer an element of planning conversations. The focus remains on specific localities, cities, and regions, but the context in which such specificities are discussed has broadened significantly, acknowledging growing global interconnections in many ways, including in the flow of planning ideas (Sanyal 2005b). As Hack points out, the greenbelt idea traveled first from the UK to the United States and is now being used in the design of cities in the Middle East. Similarly, the idea of the master plan and its modified version, the urban development plan, has traveled from developed to developing nations, as Qadeer shows. Healey, too, observes how European philosophers such as Jürgen Habermas influenced the idea of communicative planning, which eventually flourished in the United States but is now practiced in the UK and other European nations, informed by planning conversations on both sides of the Atlantic. The idea of public-private partnerships spread rapidly from the United States not only to Europe but far beyond; and as Brenner and Wachsmuth describe, the idea of territorial competition is now influencing policies in both industrialized and industrializing nations. Beatley's description of the idea of sustainable development spreading across the globe and inspiring calls for a global consensus on sustainable practices is more uplifting than Brenner and Wachsmuth's description of the global contagion of neoliberal competition. Yet both interpretations of the impact of global conversations may be right. Like planning conversations at the local, state, or national level, conversations at the global level permit multiple strands of ideas to flourish. Some are ideologically progressive, while others may be relatively conventional and accepting of existing power hierarchies.

One aspect of the globally expanding planning conversation needs to be acknowledged explicitly because it is of concern to the contributors as well as to the editors of this book: the flow of planning ideas has never been dialogic in the sense that ideas traveled back and forth among all conversing individuals and institutions with equal powers of persuasion. As Qadeer, Ward, and Grindle describe vividly, ideas and ideologies have flowed mostly from the global North to the global South, not the other way around. We acknowledge this uneven and unequal nature of planning conversations, but we are also intrigued and inspired by the signs of a gradual shift toward a more egalitarian discourse and the collective deliberations Beatley's chapter documents. After all, if planning conversations can evolve within nation-states toward a more participatory approach, as Healey shows in discussing the idea of communicative planning, is it inconceivable to think that a similar push for inclusion may make some headway at the global level? True, we must appreciate June Thomas's concern: broadening citizens' participation in planning conversations is necessary but not sufficient for equalizing the life chances of all citizens. If this is true within any national jurisdiction, it must be even harder at the global level. But that should not deter us from our search for positive changes, however small, in the nature of global conversations about appropriate ways to plan cities and regions. Given that we are witnessing the consequences of a historic transition into a world where a majority of the global population now lives in urban areas (United Nations 2010), the dialogues of planners about cities and regions are sparking increased attention. As our life histories and life chances are increasingly influenced by global phenomena—by climate change, food insecurities, transnational migrations, and global banking—it is likely that the nature of planning conversations will change too. The trajectory of that change cannot be predicted with conventional social and political theories, which seem too deterministic for the level of uncertainty we collectively face.

And so the four planning conversations highlighted in this book are likely to continue, not only among planning academics, who are particularly good at scrutinizing and generating ideas, but also among practitioners and policymakers. We hope that the conversations will expand to include increasing numbers of concerned citizens of cities, nation-states, and those whose allegiances transcend traditional boundaries and consider themselves "rooted cosmopolitans" (Appiah 2006). We are optimistic that the core concerns of planners—the quality of life in city regions, the equitable development of territories, the shared responsibilities of governance, and the need for critical reflection on what constitutes professionalism—are taking on a greater urgency in the broader society. As the public at all levels, from local communities to global social movements, comes to appreciate the importance of these issues, it will look for good ideas, reflexive and reflective professionals, and innovative institutions. All of these are necessary for shaping the destiny of communities, regions, nations, and the world, and all affirm the need for planning. This is an optimistic and ambitious objective, and the pathway toward it can only be forged by steering planning conversations, not by foreclosing them.

References

Appiah, Anthony. 2006. *Cosmopolitanism: Ethics in a World of Strangers*. New York: Norton.

Bender, Thomas, and Carl Schorske, eds. 1998. *American Academic Culture in Transformation: Fifty Years, Four Disciplines*. Princeton, NJ: Princeton University Press.

Berger, Suzanne, and Ronald Philip Dore, eds. 1996. *National Diversity and Global Capitalism*. Ithaca, NY: Cornell University Press.

Birch, Eugenie L., and Christopher Silver. 2009. One Hundred Years of City Planning's Enduring and Evolving Connections. *Journal of the American Planning Association* 75 (2): 113–122.

Blockmans, Wim P., and Charles Tilly. 1994. *Cities and the Rise of States in Europe, A.D. 1000 to 1800*. Oxford: Westview Press.

Borja, Jordi, Manuel Castells, Mireia Belil, and Chris Benner. 1997. *Local and Global: The Management of Cities in the Information Age*. London: Earthscan..

Danson, Mike, Henrik Halkier, and Greta Cameron, eds. 2000. *Governance, Institutional Change and Regional Development*. Aldershot, UK: Ashgate.

Dear, Michael J., and Allen J. Scott. 1981. *Urbanization and Urban Planning in Capitalist Society*. London: Methuen.

Evans, Harold, Gail Buckland, and Kevin Baker. 1998. *The American Century*. New York: Knopf.

Fishman, Robert. 2000. *The American Planning Tradition: Culture and Policy*. Washington, DC: Woodrow Wilson Center Press.

Flint, Anthony. 2009. *Wrestling with Moses: How Jane Jacobs Took On New York's Master Builder and Transformed the American City*. New York: Random House.

Friedmann, John. 1965. A Response to Altshuler: Comprehensive Planning as a Process. *Journal of the American Planning Association* 31 (3): 195–197.

Friedmann, John. 1987. *Planning in the Public Domain: From Knowledge to Action*. Princeton, NJ: Princeton University Press.

Friedmann, John, and Clyde Weaver. 1979. *Territory and Function: Evolution of Regional Planning*. London: Hodder & Stoughton Educational.

Grindle, Merilee S. 2007. Good Enough Governance Revisited. *Development Policy Review* 25 (5): 553–574.

Hall, Peter. 1988. *Cities of Tomorrow: An Intellectual History of Urban Planning and Design in the Twentieth Century*. Oxford: Blackwell.

Harvey, David. 2006. *Spaces of Global Capitalism: Towards a Theory of Uneven Geographical Development*. London: Verso.

Ingham, Barbara. 1993. The Meanings of Development: Interactions between "New" and "Old" Ideas. *World Development* 21 (11): 1803–1821.

Killick, Tony. 1989. *A Reaction Too Far: Economic Theory and the Role of the State in Developing Countries*. London: Overseas Development Institute.

Klosterman, Richard E. 1985. Arguments for and against Planning. *Town Planning Review* 56 (1): 5–20.

Kunstler, James H. 1993. *Geography of Nowhere: The Rise and Decline of Americas Man-Made Landscape*. New York: Touchstone.

Lechner, Frank J. 1992. Global Fundamentalism. In *Future for Religion: New Paradigms for Social Analysis*, ed. William H. Swatos. Thousand Oaks, CA: Sage.

Misra, Kamlesh, and R. P. Misra, eds. 1998. *Million Cities of India: Growth Dynamics, Internal Structure, Quality of Life and Planning Perspectives*. New Delhi: Sustainable Development Foundation.

Pallagst, Karina, Terry Schwarz, Frank J. Popper, and Justin B. Hollander. 2009. Planning Shrinking Cities. *Progress in Planning* 72 (4): 223–232.

Peattie, Lisa R. 1978. Politics, Planning and Categories Bridging the Gap. In *Planning Theory in the 1980s: A Search for Future Directions*, ed. George Sternlieb and Robert W. Burchell, 83–94. New Brunswick, NJ: Rutgers University Center.

Peterson, Jon A. 2009. The Birth of Organized City Planning in the United States, 1909–1910. *Journal of the American Planning Association* 75 (2): 123–133.

Prebisch, Raúl. 1984. Five Stages in My Thinking on Development. In *Pioneers in Development*, ed. Gerald M. Meier and Dudley Seers, 173–204. Oxford: Oxford University Press.

Putnam, Robert D., Robert Leonardi, and Raffaella Y. Nanetti. 1993. *Making Democracy Work: Civic Traditions in Modern Italy*. Princeton, NJ: Princeton University Press.

Rabinovitch, J. 1996. Innovative Land Use and Public Transport Policy: The Case of Curitiba, Brazil. *Land Use Policy* 13 (1): 51–67.

Rodrik, Dani. 1999. *The New Global Economy and Developing Countries: Making Openness Work*. Washington, DC: Overseas Development Council.

Sandel, Michael J. 1996. *Democracy's Discontent: America in Search of a Public Philosophy*. Cambridge, MA: Harvard University Press.

Sanyal, Bishwapriya. 1994. *Cooperative Autonomy: The Dialectic of State-NGOs Relationship in Developing Countries*. Geneva: International Institute for Labor Studies.

Sanyal, Bishwapriya. 2005a. Planning as Anticipation of Resistance. *Planning Theory* 4 (3): 225–245.

Sanyal, Bishwapriya. 2005b. *Comparative Planning Cultures*. New York: Routledge.

Soja, Edward W. 2000. *Postmetropolis: Critical Studies of Cities and Regions.* Malden, MA: Blackwell.

Stiglitz, Joseph E. 2006. *Making Globalization Work.* London: Allen Lane.

Tendler, Judith. 1997. *Good Government in the Tropics.* Baltimore, MD: Johns Hopkins University Press.

Turner, John. F.C. 1979. Housing in Three Dimensions: Terms of Reference for the Housing Question Redefined. In *The Urban Informal Sector: Critical Perspectives on Employment and Housing Policies,* ed. Ray Bromley, 1135–1146. Oxford: Pergamon Press.

Unger, Roberto M., and Cornel West. 1998. *The Future of American Progressivism: An Initiative for Political and Economic Reform.* Boston: Beacon Press.

United Nations. 1987. *Our Common Future.* Oxford: Oxford University Press.

United Nations. 2010. *World Urbanization Prospects: The 2009 Revision.* New York: United Nations, Department of Economic and Social Affairs, Population Division.

Unwin, Raymond. 1911. *Town Planning in Practice: An Introduction to the Art of Designing Cities and Suburbs.* London: Fisher Unwin.

Wade, Robert. 1990. *Governing the Market: Economic Theory and the Role of Government in East Asian Industrialization.* Princeton, NJ: Princeton University Press.

Walzer, Michael, ed. 1995. *Toward a Global Civil Society.* Providence, RI: Berghahn Books.

Ward, Stephen. 2002. *Planning the Twentieth Century City: The Advanced Capitalist World.* Chichester: Wiley.

World Bank. 1997. *World Development Report 1997: The State in a Changing World.* New York: Oxford University Press.

I
Ideas about Livability

2

Shaping Urban Form

Gary Hack

Shaping the form of cities has been a central preoccupation of city building from the dawn of civilization. The purposes and values of settlements
have varied considerably over the centuries, as have theories of good
urban form, but the importance of designing settlements has never
flagged. Even in current times, heralded as an era when place and location matter little, decisions about urban form remain critically important,
and hotly contested.

The term *urban form* encompasses the location, shape, geometry, and
spatial relationships between and among streets, buildings, occupied
spaces, and open land; the pattern of infrastructure that allows urbanized
places to function; and the social conventions or legal regime created to
determine who has access to collective resources. Ideas about urban form
exist at a variety of scales, ranging from the overall shape of the urbanized region to the layout of neighborhoods and districts to the three-
dimensional character of streets and public spaces. As a way of limiting
the discussion, this chapter focuses mainly on the form of the metropolitan region. Undeniably, the internal structure of an urban area also affects
the quality of life of those who inhabit it. Nonetheless, there has been a
remarkable continuity of ideas about urban form at the regional scale,
even in the face of dramatically changing social and economic patterns.

What difference does urban form make? The pattern of settlement has
immediate human consequences, affecting the choices individuals make
in organizing their lives. Common sense suggests that a sprawling metropolitan area requires more travel to maintain the same level of face-
to-face contact as in a more compact area. But does this matter? What
if communications advances allow many tasks to be handled vicariously,
reducing the need for travel, as seems to have been the case in the recent
past? Ironically, there has been a steady increase in vehicle miles traveled
in U.S. metropolitan areas[1] even as alternative forms of communication

(the Internet, mobile phones, networks, multiple-channel television) make remote access easier and cheaper (Newman and Kenworthy 1999). With rising incomes, people may be prepared to allocate more of their time and resources to travel, and those who choose not to spend their time that way may locate in the densest parts of metropolitan areas. But many others do not have this choice; the jobs may be in one place and the individuals in another, without easy access to jobs except by traveling. This is the second reason why urban form matters: it affects individuals in a society differentially, and it particularly affects those who have fewer resources to make location choices.

A third reason why urban form matters is that it affects the societal allocation of resources. In a metropolitan area spread over many miles, it intrinsically costs more to build and maintain infrastructure than in a more compact area. It is impractical to provide some services. such as mass rapid transit or elementary schools within walking distance of every home, in a spread-out urban area. Sprawling metropolitan areas are more vulnerable to price rises in fuel, which affects households but also the cost of services provided by local governments. Metropolitan form can dramatically influence the carbon emissions of an urban area. The consequences of urban form persist from one generation to the next. It is not easy to alter the pattern of a built-up urban area since infrastructure, buildings, land ownership, and habits of life are durable. They change slowly, and often at great cost.

Moreover, the form of a metropolitan area has social implications beyond economic resources. It affects the perception and values of residents, ultimately shaping location decisions. When unique resources, such as the edges of rivers, are developed for the public rather than held in private hands, they can become a matter of collective pride and the setting for events, celebrations, and shared activities. A dense urban center with parks and walkable streets can become the showplace of an area's possibilities for both residents and visitors. Cities with magnificent public buildings—city halls, libraries, court facilities, social spaces, educational institutions, art museums, sports stadiums, and the like—emphasize the collective values of a place. Sports teams can come to symbolize the spirit of places, but in cities that have unique environments, persona and place become one and the same.

Values and Urban Form

Throughout much of recorded history, concern over the spatial form of settlements was dominated by a single overriding value—defense. Cities were sited in defensible locations, walls were created, gates were erected, and the internal pattern of the settlement was structured to allow quick mobilization of troops in the face of threats. As threats diminished in the nineteenth century and trade and industrialization changed the nature of the city, the form of cities began to reflect values other than defense: making room for expansion, protecting against diseases and pestilence, facilitating the movement of goods and people to workplaces, creating harbors and facilities for importing resources and exporting products, and creating places for social interchange, enjoyment, and rituals. New cities built to exploit natural resources or to express national aspirations, such as state or national capitals, needed to incorporate other values, and had greater degrees of choice in urban form.

In his seminal work, *Good City Form*, Kevin Lynch (1984) catalogues at least thirty values that are typically in play in decisions about the form of urban areas, grouping them loosely into five categories: strong values (such as increasing mobility, providing space for wanted uses, and reducing pollution), wishful values (including improving equity, conserving material and energy resources, and increasing amenities), weak values (including increasing social integration and increasing choice and diversity), hidden values (including maintaining political control and prestige, making a profit, and removing unwanted people and activities), and neglected values (e.g., increasing the symbolic and sensory experience of cities and user control). Lynch illustrates how all theories of urban form are rooted in values, contrary to widely accepted beliefs at the time that urban areas grow through inevitable "natural processes" of ecological succession. While recognizing the complexity of urban evolution and change, Lynch's alternative theory is the creation of an evolving "learning ecology." "To the familiar ecosystem characteristics of diversity, interdependence, context, history, feedback, dynamic stability and cyclic processing, we must add such features as values, culture, consciousness, progressive (or regressive) change, invention, the ability to learn, and the connection of inner experience and outer action."

Good City Form is an analytic tour de force, integrating a world of social, physical, and design theories and placing them within a framework of values and criteria for planning the form of urban areas. The importance of the book needs to be seen in the context of the 1960s, when Lynch began collecting his thoughts in manuscript form. Over the previous decade, massive interventions in urban areas—urban renewal, highway building, suburbanization—had been justified by biological and ecological analogies—the cores of cities are rotten and need to be carved out, the arteries are clogged and need to be expanded, room is needed for expanding downtowns or they will choke to death, cities need to grow or they will die, and the like. Lynch argued that nothing was inevitable in urban change, and that it had to be informed by experience and values. His propositions were a departure from the ecological theories of the Chicago School of social geography that had dominated the field of urban development since the 1920s.

In place of all-encompassing theories of urban form, Lynch offered a set of performance dimensions that bridge between values and policies carried out on the ground. They provide ways of judging the quality of proposals aimed at shaping urban form:

1. *Vitality* The degree of support offered by a settlement for the biological and survival requirements of a society.

2. *Sense* The degree to which the settlement can be clearly perceived and mentally differentiated, and the degree to which it matches the values and concepts of the society.

3. *Fit* The degree to which a pattern satisfies the needs for space and places and for social interaction.

4. *Access* The ability to reach other people and places, and to transport the goods needed for urban living.

5. *Control* The ability of those most affected by places to control those places' character and use.

To these, Lynch added two metacriteria, which are always present:

6. *Efficiency* The optimal use of resources in meeting the other criteria.

7. *Justice* Fairness in the distribution of benefits and costs (Lynch 1984, 121–235).

These criteria remain useful for evaluating many ideas about how to reshape the form of urban regions.

Contrarians on Urban Form

While there is a great deal of consensus among most planners on the performance dimensions just cited, not everyone believes it is either possible or desirable to shape the form of urban areas. In *Good City Form*, Lynch lists eight commonly cited objections. These range from the notion that "physical form plays no significant role in the satisfaction of important human values" to the belief that "physical form is not critical at the scale of a city or a region" to the view that "city form is intricate and complex" and hence "cities are vast natural phenomena, beyond our ability to change, and beyond our knowing how we ought to change them." Echoes of these views persist in design and planning culture today. They have gained considerable currency as part of a broader critique of the role of government in shaping private decisions and the role of designers in ordering urban life.

The following assertions are often made:

The market is capable of reflecting human values and complex choices better than political decisions This point has been argued by Peter Gordon and Harry W. Richardson, among others (Gordon and Richardson 1998, 2004). As they point out, it is not an accident that cities have sprawled. Sprawl is the outcome of individual choices in favor of lower densities, preferred locations of businesses, reactions to deteriorated inner cities, and a host of other factors. Moreover, they claim that the result does not automatically result in inefficient land-use patterns. As evidence, they point to Los Angeles' gross residential densities, which they claim are among the highest in the United States, far higher than those of many tightly planned and regulated cities.

Efforts to shape urban form are likely to be counterproductive The process of urban development is complex, and one cannot anticipate all the consequences of intervening in local land markets. Randal O'Toole (2001) makes this case looking at Portland, Oregon, and the city's growth boundaries, intended to decrease travel, protect valuable agricultural lands, promote mass transit, and make public service delivery more cost-effective. O'Toole argues that the real results have been rapidly escalating property values, highly subsidized and underutilized mass transit, and a development environment that drove growth even further afield (O'Toole 2007). Planners and politicians, according to O'Toole, have insufficient understanding of urban development to be able to predict the consequences of their actions.

Orderly urban form is likely to distill the life out of urban areas From a wholly different perspective, designers, including Rem Koolhaas, have argued that the chaos of loosely planned development is likely to produce the richest urban fabric, filled with accidents and surprises (Koolhaas 1995, 959–971). Critics such as Herbert Muschamp regularly argue that controls on development stifle creativity, both at the scale of individual buildings and at the scale of city and regional planning (Muschamp 2009). These arguments mirror the notions of development economists that over the long term, uneven development may produce the greatest amount of initiative and entrepreneurial activity.

It is difficult to validate or disprove such broad assertions since much of the case hinges on judgments about what constitutes the good city and how equitably the costs and benefits of urban life are distributed among an area's residents. For every example of a city stifled by overly rigid land use regulation, another example may be found of truly horrific urban development created without any effective controls. And in the rapidly developing cities of the world, the choice of whether to guide development to conform to some conscious notion of urban form has direct and immediate consequences.

Bangkok may be the poster child for the problems created by the absence of accepted notions of urban form. In many ways, it matches Koolhaas's notion of a rich and unpredictable urban fabric—Bangkok is all fabric and no form. It has no discernible land-use pattern, with sprawl in all directions and infrastructure that lags well behind urbanization. Massive commercial development has occurred in central areas with minimal transport access, and on the perimeter, urbanization is fast destroying the city's prime food production areas. Bangkok has legendary traffic congestion, with commuting time averaging two hours in each direction and terrible air quality that results largely from vehicles stuck in traffic. Flooding and public health issues stem from the inability to provide sewers to all areas of the city owing to ground subsidence because of pumping for industrial and potable water and to the lack of planning of drainage patterns. The poor are disproportionately affected by each of these issues. And it is extraordinarily difficult and costly to provide infrastructure and services to a dispersed metropolitan area that has developed reflecting only the logic of large-scale property ownership and entrepreneurship. In recent years, the introduction (at great human and economic costs) of elevated expressways and mass transit lines has begun to ease the most serious congestion, but the city remains largely out of control.

Bangkok's problems were not inevitable, and other cities faced with a similar population and industrial growth trajectory have managed to avoid the worst of them through considered planning of major infrastructure and by guiding development into areas capable of being served by public investments. Taipei, Singapore, Seoul, and dozens of Chinese cities come to mind. Their metropolitan plans prescribed armatures for public transportation, infrastructure, and facilities projects. In turn, regulation of the development pattern was critical to ensuring that investments on the ground were used to capacity.

It seems overly detached to argue that the market should be left to make the choices about urban patterns when public choices need to be made about where and when to construct roads, mass transit systems, and other public service systems. Ultimately, urban form matters because there are decisions to be made, and because the public (or public officials or legislators) demands a logic for collective action. In many cases, the public (or special interest groups) helps give form to an urban area through the projects it advocates, such as placing agricultural land in reserves, preserving greenways, or setting aside large forest preserves at the perimeter of metropolitan areas. Such efforts often find broad support at the ballot box when posed as referenda questions or through bond issues tied to larger environmental objectives. And responding to global climate change and increased energy costs today provides a new imperative for collective action to shape urban form.

Controlling the Perimeter

Many public policies shape metropolitan form, including those having to do with the layout of infrastructure, land-use controls, prescribed densities, direct acquisition of land for development, and restrictions on land development through conservation actions. But to succeed over time—and to be accepted by the public—policies need to be driven by easily explained ideas about good urban form. Widely accepted ideas have a habit of persisting, even if they reappear in different guise during different eras.

One abiding preoccupation has been exercising control over the perimeter of urban areas. It has found expression in various strategies, but especially in the creation of urban limits and greenbelts that define the edge of urbanization. The reasons for creating greenbelts have been quite varied but generally include a combination of wanting to limit the spread (or sometimes the population) of a city, promote higher density development, preserve the countryside, reserve high-value agricultural lands, provide a recreation resource, clean the air, and improve the efficiency of infrastructure by delimiting the area served. In Lynch's terms, greenbelts particularly address the needs for *vitality* (by maintaining natural systems to support urban life), *sense* (by helping form clearly identified urban units), and *fit* (by supporting the recreational and social needs of dense urban areas), and they do so by promoting the *efficiency* of the urban pattern and *justice* through offering open access to these common lands. The power of the idea has all to do with the many purposes greenbelts serve.

One of the earliest greenbelts is said to be the seventh-century decision by Mohammed to prohibit the cutting of trees in a twelve-mile-wide band around Medina (Iqbal 2005). Contemporary greenbelts, however, have their origins in nineteenth-century Europe. The idea has diffused across the world, with resonance in widely different circumstances.

When defensive walls were needed, settlements remained compact, and the important functions of cities were located within an easy walk of each other. The boundary between settlement and countryside was sharp, and the commercial interface of urban and rural uses often developed near the main gates to the city, where food markets and other commercial activities clustered. Occasionally these spilled out beyond the walls. Berlin's Potsdamer Platz, Moscow's Red Square, Beijing's Tiananmen Square (before it was eradicated for the massive public square of today), and New York's Wall Street each originated in clusters of commercial activity at the edge of a walled city. In some cities, areas outside the gates were reserved as places of recreation; Berlin's Tiergarten, designed in 1830 as the pleasure and hunting grounds of the electors of Brandenburg, is one early example.

By the nineteenth century, most European countries enjoyed comparative peace, and defensive perimeter walls became irrelevant. Trade exploded, and both European and American cities became manufacturing centers. The need for sites for industrial enterprises, particularly flat sites for ever larger factories, fueled an outward expansion of cities. To mobilize workers and materials and distribute the goods required railroads, and ultimately mass transit lines. Inner-city areas continued to grew more crowded even as cities doubled and tripled in area. Railroad companies promoted new lifestyles set in open countryside and benefited not only from the patronage of the new suburbanites but also from the rapid increases in value of the lands they owned along the right-of-ways. But by the 1880s a backlash had begun, with cries that cities were sprawling across the countryside in uncontrolled ways, destroying agricultural lands, polluting rivers, and scattering the detritus of industrialization in the form of slag heaps, garbage mounds, and extraction pits.

The notion of controlling the spread of cities first took root in England. Utopian experiments, spawned by John Ruskin and the Arts and Crafts movement, sought new ways of integrating city and country and a return to handcraft and artistic values. Industrial patrimony offered another alternative, with Bourneville, begun in 1879 by the Cadbury brothers, and Port Sunlight, constructed by William Lever beginning in 1889, as examples. These model towns were planned with open spaces, gardens, commerce, institutions, and healthful housing all located within a short walk of the workplace. The first compelling image of how such planned settlements might be scaled up to a metropolitan area was provided by Ebenezer Howard in his 1898 self-published book, *To-morrow: A Peaceful Path to Real Reform* (Howard [1902] 1946).

Howard's utopia promoted a new confluence between city and countryside by restraining city growth within a fixed perimeter and locating new settlements in planned towns each limited to 32,000 residents, separated from the central city by agricultural and open lands. He envisioned the lands between settlements as a working landscape that included allotment gardens, smallholdings, fruit farms, new forests, cow pastures, and agricultural colleges, but also brickfields, farms for epileptics, convalescent homes, asylums for the blind and deaf, and children's cottage homes. He suggested that the land surrounding the city be owned by the public and leased to a variety of private farmers and operators, noting that "the natural competition of these various methods of agriculture, tested by the willingness of occupiers to offer the highest rent to the municipality, tend . . . to bring about the best system of husbandry, or, what is more probable, the best systems adapted for various purposes." In arguing his case for limiting the growth of metropolitan areas, Howard pointed to Adelaide, Australia, which in 1837 set aside 2,300 acres surrounding the town to limit its growth, possibly the first planned urban greenbelt in the world (figs. 2.1 and 2.2).

The idea of constructing freestanding new towns took root in England sooner than the proposal to create greenbelts around existing cities. The site for Letchworth, Ebenezer Howard's first Garden City, was purchased in 1903. Designed by Raymond Unwin and Barry Parker, it included housing, shops, parks, and the full range of activities of a town. As Howard prescribed, industry (the Spinella factory, which manufactured women's undergarments) was located at the edge of the town, and a generous greenbelt was reserved around the entire perimeter of the new town.

Establishing more extensive greenbelts around England's cities, however, would require a national movement to overcome the hurdles of property owners who wished to benefit from urban growth, developers, and industrialists. Patrick Abercrombie's influential book, *The Pres-*

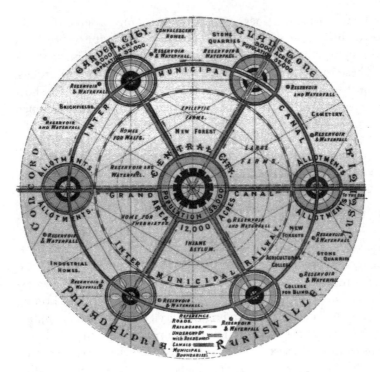

Figure 2.1
The Ideal Metropolitan Pattern. *Source*: Howard (1902).

ervation of Rural England (1926), became the rallying point and resulted in the creation of the Council for the Preservation of Rural England (CPRE), which exists to this day. Its first target in limiting sprawl was "ribbon" development along major motorways out of cities, which saw success in 1935 with the passage of the Restriction of Ribbon Development Act. In 1933, Raymond Unwin proposed a more dramatic move, the "Green Girdle for London," which the CPRE quickly adopted and championed. It would take the intervention of a war and a massive reconstruction commitment to move England toward a national policy of creating greenbelts around London and other cities.

Since the 1950s, fourteen greenbelts have been created around cities in the UK, comprising 16,716 sq km, or 13 percent of England, and 164 sq km of Scotland. In addition to London's metropolitan greenbelt, large greenbelts have been established around Liverpool and Manchester, Leeds and York, Birmingham, and other cities. Areas designated as greenbelts have been restricted from development by a combination of regula-

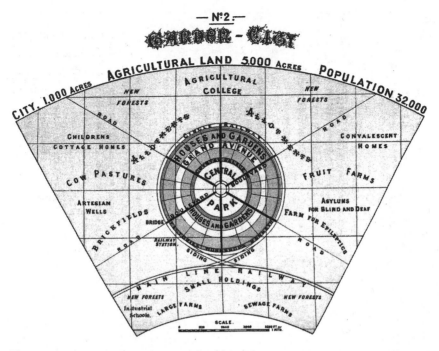

Figure 2.2
The Garden City and Its Surroundings. *Source*: Howard (1902).

tions and governmental purchases. These moves have been complemented by the creation of twenty-eight New Towns beyond the greenbelts, beginning in 1946 with the development of Stevenage in Hertfordshire. Not all of the New Towns have been successful—and the government formally wound up the New Towns development corporations in the 1990s—but the greenbelts remain in place, although under constant threat of invasion by public and commercial uses (fig. 2.3).

The UK policy of maintaining greenbelts remains rooted in its original objectives: to "check the unrestricted sprawl of large built-up areas; prevent neighbouring towns from merging into one another; assist in safeguarding the countryside from encroachment; preserve the setting and special character of historic towns; and assist in urban regeneration, by encouraging the recycling of derelict and other urban land" (Department for Communities and Local Government [England] 2007). At the same time, there are recurring pressures to expand communities, particularly New Towns bordering on greenbelts, and public facilities such as Heathrow Airport and Olympic venues into greenbelt lands. While

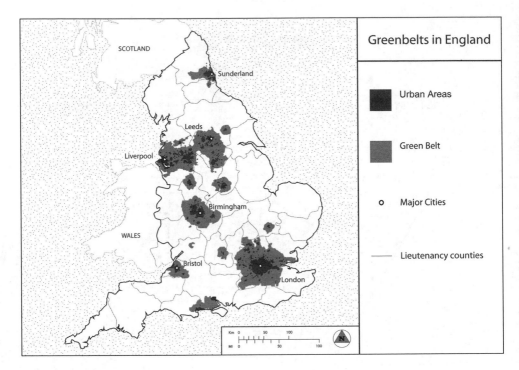

Figure 2.3
Greenbelts in England.

summer camps for children were originally permitted in the greenbelts, there has been an increasing number of proposals for large-scale recreational developments. The growth of intensive agriculture (e.g., greenhouse gardening and feedlots) also forces a rethinking of the kinds of uses that will be permitted in the future. And there is a persistent argument about whether greenbelts have pushed up housing costs and contributed to greater commuting times for those who must locate beyond them. Nonetheless, the UK greenbelt policy has been widely supported by the public and by influential environmental and heritage preservation groups. Greenbelts have proved popular recreation areas for urbanites and have received broad public support. Perhaps it is their intrinsic value that appeals to so many, or their popularity may reveal a deep-seated desire to limit urban areas to a scale that is comprehensible. Greenbelts must be counted as among the most important planning successes in UK over a period of more than half a century. And they have been emulated in countries throughout the world.

Greenbelts in Rapidly Developing Cities

The idea of creating greenbelts and new communities has been transported literally to other countries faced with rapid urbanization. Korea,
as an example, established a greenbelt around Seoul and thirteen other
cities in 1971 as part of a national comprehensive development plan that
also mandated the construction of a number of New Towns to absorb
the rapidly urbanizing population (Bengston and Youn 2004, 27–35).
Referred to as a Restricted Development Zone, Seoul's greenbelt now
consists of 1,567 sq km, about 13 percent of the metropolitan area.
About 80 percent of the land remains privately owned, and two-thirds
of it consists of forests and mountains, which provide a valuable recreation resource to the twenty million residents of metropolitan Seoul. In
addition to reducing sprawl, eliminating the shantytowns that had grown
up around the city, and protecting the food supply and sensitive environmental areas, Seoul's greenbelt had an overriding purpose—providing a
10 km security belt around the city in the event of invasion from North
Korea. The greenbelt retains high public support, even in the face of
vigorous lobbying by landowners who feel they have been unfairly prevented from realizing the true value of their lands.

New development has gone far beyond the Seoul greenbelt, particularly in the five new satellite cities that were part of the 1975 metropolitan plan and are now largely complete, and in the several new peripheral
cities that have been initiated over the past ten years. Studies of the
economic impacts of Seoul's greenbelt have focused largely on the price
impacts of constrained land supply, and at least one study suggests that
it may have contributed modestly to land costs across the city. However,
land for development is highly constrained by other regulations as well,
and it is difficult to disentangle the precise role of the greenbelt (Choi
1994). There is little dispute that the presence of the greenbelt has
increased densities in historic Seoul (Bae and Jun 2003, 380). Studies
have also noted a modest increase in travel costs of metropolitan residents as a result of the need of increased distances to work, although
these studies were done before the rapid growth of tertiary employment
in outlying areas (Kim 1993).

As the Seoul greenbelt land has become more valuable, its functions
have changed, and it has been used more intensively. It has become the
storehouse for the city—for vehicles, inventories of building materials,
and similar uses. Hundreds of square kilometers of greenhouses have
been created for fruit and vegetable production. Some Seoul residents

suggest that the greenbelt be relabeled the "city under plastic"—or perhaps the "greenhouse belt."

São Paulo, Brazil, is quite the opposite of Seoul: it has little capacity to regulate land development and urban form. It is perhaps surprising to find that it has implemented a successful program of creating a greenbelt around the city. Many of the poorest residents of São Paulo live at the periphery of the city, and with massive growth of the population, issues of periurban development are sharply contested. In the thirteen-year period from 1986 to 1999, 30 percent of the green tissue of the region was lost, with the worst affected areas consisting of water catchment areas and mountainsides, where at least 140 illegal land settlements had grown up (Moraes Victor et al. 2004).

Changes to São Paulo's development pattern were triggered by a citizens' environmental movement that arose in reaction to the construction of a peripheral highway (the Rodoanel project) and a variety of other projects that would displace settlements and destroy environments. The state government acted by creating the São Paulo City Green Belt Biosphere Reserve (Reserva da Biosfera do Cinturão Verde da Cidade de São Paulo) in 1995. Ultimately, four municipal nature parks were created as compensation for the revised Rodoanel project, along with a broad forest buffer zone on each side of the highway.

The São Paulo greenbelt reserve currently encompasses 16,117 sq km and is part of a larger ecological reserve, the Atlantic Forest Biosphere Reserve, recognized by UNESCO (fig. 2.4). Substantial portions of the greenbelt are set aside for ecological tourism and recreation, and the creation of the greenbelt has had the impact of reining in urbanization. A highly successful program of engaging youth in forestry and other projects has grown up as several powerful interest groups, aided by multinational NGOs, have gained influence. Development is not strictly prohibited in the greenbelt, but all projects are subjected to an overlay of codes that promote sustainable uses and social practices. Regulations focus on preventing climate change (preventing heat islands), soil protection and runoff regulation, and water purification.

Other cities in the world, including Tokyo, have instituted partial greenbelts by restricting development from agricultural lands, on the grounds of national security of the food supply. In Tokyo's case, however, many of the rice lands have found more profitable open space uses, including as golf courses. Hundreds of golf courses today ring the city 25–40 km from the center—a unique form of greenbelt, or "greensbelt."

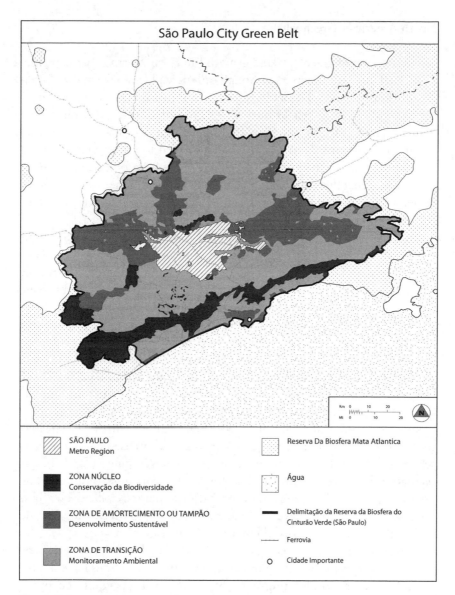

Figure 2.4
São Paulo City Green Belt Biosphere Reserve.

North American Greenbelts

The discussion of greenbelts and growth limits for North American cities dates back at least a century, although only few places have realized their greenbelt aspirations. Daniel Burnham and Edward H. Bennett proposed a metropolitan greenbelt in their 1909 *Plan of Chicago* (Burnham and Bennett [1909] 1991), along with fingers of open space that would extend into the city. Cook County has managed to put in place a decidedly more modest version of the greenbelt in the form of a string of forest preserves, generally following the Fox River and other watercourses. Development over the years has leapfrogged the open spaces, but they remain important recreation resources.

Other American cities have attempted to set aside large areas at the metropolitan periphery as open spaces, with uneven success. They have faced many obstacles, including the real estate interests that control the land, agricultural interests that are threatened by regulations, the problem of multiple jurisdictions, which has made coordinated strategies difficult to implement, and conflicting interests of promoting growth, making adequate land available for housing, and protecting valuable ecological resources. Nonetheless, the New York region—quite possibly the most jurisdictionally divided metropolitan region in the world—has managed to set aside important open space resources at the urban fringe, largely because of the consistent and tireless advocacy by the Regional Plan Association. Watershed lands have been reserved or controlled to protect the region's water supply, unique environmental areas such as the New Jersey Pinelands have been protected from development, and unique recreation resources, including shorelines, river corridors, and mountain areas, have been designated state or national parks. Collectively, these areas structure urban development patterns only loosely, but they do ensure the presence of critical environmental resources.

In recent years, the preferred American strategy for shaping peripheral growth has been the adoption of urban growth limits. Cities have limited spread either by prohibiting entirely development beyond the urban growth boundary or by make it extremely expensive for the developer to pay for all infrastructure to support the development. Close to a dozen cities or counties have adopted urban growth boundaries, including the Twin Cities, Minnesota; Miami-Dade County, Florida; San Diego, California; and Lexington, Kentucky. Sometimes regulations limiting growth are accompanied by other incentives, such as the transfer of development rights, programs for the purchase of development easements, or tax incentives for land that remains in agricultural usage. Each city has responded to a unique imperative—protecting lakes and open areas in Minnesota or the dramatic hillsides of San Diego, respecting the ecosystem of the Everglades in Florida, and preserving the unique resource of the horse farms that give Lexington its special identity. The best-known example of implementing a U.S. urban growth strategy is Portland, Oregon. In 1973 the state legislature required all Oregon cities to create urban growth boundaries, and six years later Portland did so as part of a larger strategy of encouraging higher densities in the city and installing a mass transit system. An important motivation for the growth limit was to protect the valuable agricultural lands surrounding the city, including the wine lands of the Willamette Valley. The original state legislation assumed that the growth limits would be revised outward regularly to allow adequate lands for urban expansion, but this did not occur, and in 1995 the legislature passed a law requiring cities to provide enough land for a twenty-year supply of future housing. This did not end the controversy, however. It was kept alive by a coalition of property owners wishing to develop their exurban lands, developers with land in the line of development, and timber interests whose harvesting practices and other opportunities were severely constrained. Their cause was joined by several commentators and interest groups with an antiplanning bent, who argued that growth limits were costly to residents and did not represent the kind of community values most Portland residents shared (O'Toole 2007). Growth limits, they asserted, simply diverted growth to communities further away from Portland, increasing their travel times to downtown Portland (fig. 2.5).

Meeting little success in changing Portland residents' minds about urban growth boundaries, the law's opponents campaigned for statewide restrictions on the ability of cities to regulate land uses. After two failed efforts (one of which passed initially and was struck down by the courts), Measure 37 was adopted in 2004 by 61 percent of the voters in the state. It required that any landowner be compensated if his or her property values were adversely affected by environmental or land-use regulations passed subsequent to the purchase of the land. The measure threw the entire planning and regulatory system in Oregon into chaos since no municipality could afford the kind of compensation required, and no government was prepared to adopt plans or regulations with the financial consequences imposed by Measure 37. In 2007 Measure 49, a compromise measure, was passed, granting owners of land the right to build a personal house on restricted lands, to subdivide and pass

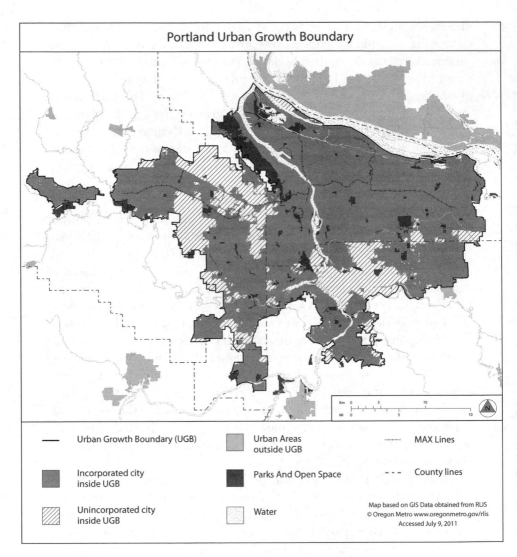

Figure 2.5
Portland, Oregon, Urban Limits.

along the rights to heirs, and to allow municipalities to waive the restrictions on commercial development in specific situations. At the same time, it continued to disallow subdivisions on high-value farmlands and groundwater-restricted lands, maintaining the intent of the growth boundaries.

The difficulty in maintaining the Portland urban growth boundary over time—in perhaps the most favorable public climate for planning—exposes the issues that makes controlling the perimeter of American cities extremely difficult: the absence of regional entities that develop traditions of governance of urban development, the powerful interests arrayed against restricting development, and the use of statewide ballot initiatives to overturn local interests. While there is no less pressure from developers and landowners in Canada, the activist stance of provincial governments toward urban development has resulted in greater acceptance of plans to restrict the spread of urbanization. Every major urban area in Canada has a metropolitan government, and several of them, including Toronto and Winnipeg, have had their area expanded and responsibilities fine-tuned every decade or so to reflect the new metropolitan spatial pattern.

Canada's first greenbelt was established around Ottawa, the national capital, as a key element in Jacques-Henri-Auguste Gréber's 1950 Plan for the National Capital (Gordon 2006) There was little support for the national government to impose land use regulations (this is a provincial responsibility), so beginning in 1958, it has purchased 20,000 ha of land to be maintained as an open space reserve and limit to development. Many of the lands were leased back to their original owners for farming, and other lands were used for parks and low-intensity national government purposes (the Dominion Experimental Farm, as an example). It was initially contemplated that it might be a "rolling greenbelt," expanded outward while lands on its inner edge were released as needed for development. However, by the 1960s, development had leapfrogged the greenbelt, with the construction of the New Town of Kanata, and two smaller towns became important development magnets. Other environmentally sensitive lands have been added to the greenbelt over the years (fig. 2.6).

Ottawa may be an extraordinary case, as national capitals often are, but other Canadian cities have followed suit in limiting their perimeter. Beginning in 1973 with the British Columbia Land Commission Act, an agricultural land reserve was created in the delta of the Frazer River surrounding Vancouver, based on the capability and suitability of the

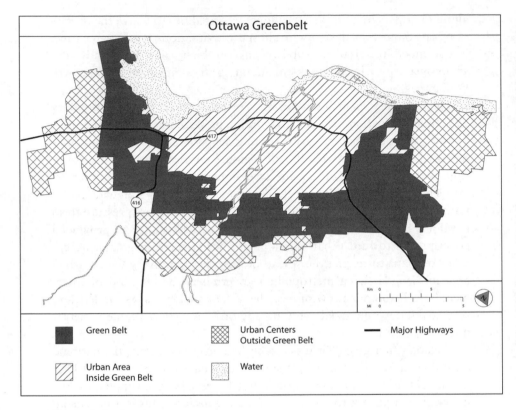

Figure 2.6
The Ottawa Greenbelt.

land for agriculture (Similar land reserves were created around other cities in the province as well.) In general, urban development was prohibited in areas with Class A or B farmland, which had the effect of diverting new development to hillsides and lands without agricultural potential. The attraction of the system was that it employed supposedly objective criteria—soils data, groundwater, and the like—that were closely coupled to its purposes, and limited discretion in establishing the growth boundary (Quayle 1998).

While the Agricultural Land Reserve (ALR) has maintained broad public support, it has not been without controversy. During the 1980s a number of controversial industrial developments on ALR lands were approved. Golf courses have proved particularly problematic: they consume large areas of land and a great deal of water, and often want to be accompanied by recreation or resort components. By 1991, 181 such proposals had been made, repeating the Tokyo experience. By 1996 it was clear that the ALR would need to be coupled with an urban growth strategy that promoted transit and higher densities in urban areas to relieve some of the pressures on the reserve. At the same time, the Farm Practices Protection Act, also known as the Right to Farm Act, was passed to help support the effective uses of reserve lands for agriculture. Vancouver stands as an example of successfully balancing urban and agricultural land interests for more than thirty-five years.

A startlingly ambitious greenbelt was created in the Toronto region in 1985 through a provincial act, over the objections of many developers and landowners (Ministry of Municipal Affairs and Housing [Ontario] 2005). Spanning almost 200 miles from the eastern edge of Toronto to Niagara Falls and extending northward to Lake Simcoe, it includes 1.8 million acres (2,813 square miles), an area roughly the size of the urbanized portions of the Greater Toronto region (fig. 2.7). Portions of the greenbelt were previously protected as natural features, including the Niagara Escarpment, the Oak Ridge Moraine, and the shores of Lake Simcoe. The sheer size of the area that is being controlled and the diversity of current uses make the task daunting.

The approach to managing the greenbelt involves dividing it into three "policy systems"—the agricultural system, the natural heritage system, and the settlement areas—each with different regulations that overlie municipal codes and requirements. Within the settlement areas, growth boundaries have been established, and local plans amended accordingly. A unique feature of the Greenbelt Act was the creation of the Greenbelt Foundation, with an endowment to promote use of the reserved lands and invest in the transition to value-added agriculture. The experience of the greenbelt will be reviewed after ten years, with modest expansions of the development area possible at that time, as long as such expansions do not overstress environmental and infrastructure capacity or erode natural heritage areas.

There has been plenty of opposition to the Ontario greenbelt, particularly from developers and think tanks associated with them (Cox 2004), not unlike the response in the Portland area. However, the strong traditions of provincial authority over local governments and the long-standing requirement that the province approve local plans and amendments make it unlikely that an assault on the regulations will be mounted soon. The Greenbelt Foundation has also been effective in building grassroots support for the virtues of reserving lands from development, which makes a repeal of the action highly unlikely.

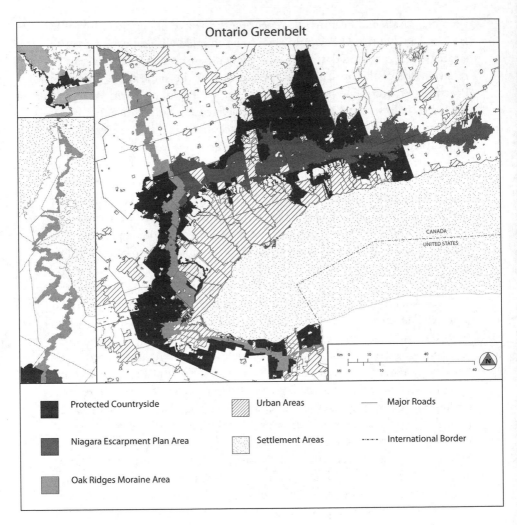

Figure 2.7
The Ontario Greenbelt.

The history of greenbelts over more than a century, on all settled continents, speaks to the diffusion of ideas in the planning field and the importance of being able to link concrete actions to quality-of-life concerns. Part of the power of the idea is its adaptability to varying concerns. Greenbelts were seen as the solution to maintaining agriculture and food supply systems and rural ways of life in the face of urbanization, protecting ecosystems, ensuring a water supply and other needs of urban life, providing recreation resources, and even serving as a security barrier for cities. Greenbelts have usually been coupled with strategies to increase densities within the buildable area or to create multiple centers well served by public transportation, as in Washington, D.C. The implementation of growth limits has had to take into account local and national political systems, the geography of the urban area, resources, and local interest groups, and in not every city are these factors aligned favorably. Nonetheless, the idea of shaping urban form by controlling the urbanization perimeter is a recurring theme with continued relevance for urban regions.

Shaping Urban Form in the Future

Urban regions across the globe are being forced to revisit the question of their urban form as a response to the dual (and linked) imperatives of rapidly escalating energy costs (and absolute shortages of petroleum) and the need to address climate change. Many areas are reviving efforts to control the perimeter and increase the densities of urban areas while ensuring the protection of local agriculture and forested areas at the perimeter. The new twist is that the worldwide imperative for change must be solved locally.

The issues in play are by now familiar: petroleum prices are likely to continue to climb as the supply of inexpensive carbon fuels is depleted, and all carbon fuels emit CO_2 into the atmosphere. Increases in atmospheric CO_2 in turn promote the long-term warming of the atmosphere and make shorelines vulnerable to sea-level rise. They also alter climate patterns, creating more frequent droughts, extreme storms, and year-to-year variation in temperature.

A promising way to look at these issues is by considering what it would take to eliminate the annual growth of emissions of greenhouse gases (stabilization) or to become carbon-neutral in our emissions (zero net carbon), or to roll back our emissions of greenhouse gases to 5–10 percent below 1992 levels, as mandated by the Kyoto agreements, or to be even more ambitious and aim for lower targets. The Obama administration has proposed a 83 percent reduction in carbon emissions by 2050, in line with the proposals of most European countries.

Stephen Pacala and Robert Socolow (2004) argue that no one step can accomplish the needed reductions, and they offer the idea of a series of "carbon wedges," each designed to assume a portion of the burden. Among the seven wedges they examine to reach stabilization are two that have significant impacts on urban form: increasing vehicle efficiency and reducing the number of miles traveled in private vehicles. Other wedges that have some relevance to urban form, such as improving the energy efficiency of buildings and energy sources, could affect locations and the cost of living and working in cities, but the precise implications for urban form are more difficult to predict (fig. 2.8).

A look at the impact on urban form of tackling the two key carbon wedges is instructive. The first—a doubling of the average mileage per unit of energy of every vehicle on the roads, say—could be met by hybrid technologies, although the energy needed to manufacture new vehicles that met the standard would somewhat offset the carbon reduction. Vehicles would need to be lighter and smaller, and there would undoubtedly be a shift to electric and fuel-cell technologies. Greater differentiation of vehicles and car share or other services could "right size" the vehicles in use. At the local scale, land currently used for parking would be freed up to be used more intensively, allowing higher population

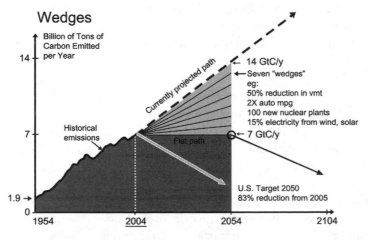

Figure 2.8
Carbon Emissions and Carbon Wedges. *Source*: Based on Pacala and Socolow (2004).

densities, and vast areas currently used for parking would be available for other purposes.

Addressing the second carbon wedge, which I will take here as reducing by one-half the miles traveled by all motorized vehicles (automobiles and trucks, principally), would also have a direct impact on densities. It is difficult to contemplate how this might be accomplished. In 2006, all vehicles in the United States traveled approximately 3,000 billion miles, an average of about 10,000 miles per capita. This figure has almost tripled since 1971, although it declined ever so slightly in 2008 (FHWA 2008). On average, Americans traveled 5,701 miles per capita in automobiles in 1996, a figure that is 2.4 times the average in Japan, 1.5 times that in most European countries, and 1.2 times that in Canada. To reduce by half the vehicle miles traveled, Americans would likely have to change travel patterns to more resemble those of Japan and Europe, which rely heavily on mass transit for work trips, walking and bicycles for everyday travel, and shorter commuting distances.

The challenge is being met by the large number of cities in the United States that have installed light- or heavy-rail systems over the past three decades. However, studies of commuting shifts do not make one optimistic. From 1960 to 1995 the U.S. transit work trip market share declined from around 12 percent to less than 4 percent. Cities that have added new transit systems have fared somewhat better, particularly as the systems have become large enough to offer travel options. However, in only a few cities did mass transit capture more than 1 percent of the increased travel during the 1990–1995 period, and those cities remain heavily automobile dependent. In Buffalo, for every new transit vehicle passenger mile, there were 828 miles traveled by automobile. Even in Washington, D.C, the most successful new public transit city, 226 new automobile vehicle miles were added for every transit passenger mile (Wendell Cox Consultancy 2003).

Clearly, creating new transit alone will not promote the kind of shift in behavior that will be necessary. Synchronizing transit and development has greater potential. Studies in Washington, D.C., have demonstrated that the probability of using transit increases dramatically if both residence and workplace are within walking distance of a Metro stop (Cervero 2004, 157). In the San Francisco region, three factors have been shown to be important in encouraging the shift to transit: the density of areas around transit stations, the diversity of uses and residents nearby, and the design of areas to create an easy flow between transit, housing, shopping, and workplaces (Cervero 2004, 148).

How Are Cities Responding to These New Imperatives?

Cities the world over are rushing to develop sustainability plans, climate change strategies, and urban strategy plans. The common denominator in these plans is the strategy of increasing densities and limiting the sprawl of metropolitan areas. Regions that girdle development through a greenbelt, urban limit line, or significant pattern of reserved lands on the perimeter have a distinct advantage over their counterparts that must rely on persuasion to attract residents to higher-density areas.

PlaNYC, New York City's long-range strategic plan, released in 2006 (City of New York 2006), is also rooted in the recognition that the city must address climate change issues—even though, as it notes, New Yorkers produce 71 percent less CO_2 per capita than the average American. Carbon emissions are projected to grow by 27 percent by 2030, while PlaNYC sets a target of reducing emissions by 30 percent. The strategy focuses on four carbon wedges: avoiding sprawl, creating cleaner power, mandating more efficient buildings, and expanding sustainable transportation (fig. 2.9). Each of these strategies has implications for urban form.

Since New York City represents less than half of the New York metropolitan region, it cannot rein in suburban development to avoid sprawl. Rather, PlaNYC proposes that land-use policies and regulations be

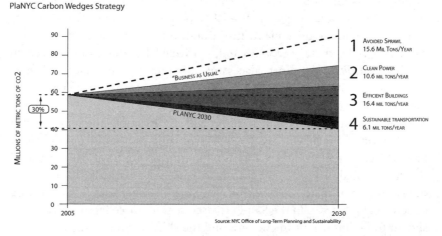

Figure 2.9
PlaNYC Carbon Wedges.

changed to attract 900,000 new residents, some to reside on reclaimed contaminated land, and to encourage higher densities in areas well served by mass transit. A transit-first policy of investing in mass transit and charging for road usage will encourage a shift in travel patterns in the city. New regulations and policies will encourage renewable power and clean distributed generation of the city's electric supply. An aggressive program of mandating energy-efficient buildings, beginning with the vast network of public buildings, will reduce the demand for energy and the resulting carbon discharges. In short, greater density, changes in transportation behavior, and efficiencies in energy generation and use could allow New York to achieve its carbon wedges.

The London Plan, published by the Greater London Authority in 2004 (Mayor of London 2004a), takes a similar approach, albeit with the advantages of a greenbelt that helps structure development. Its first objective is to "accommodate London's growth within its boundaries without encroaching on open spaces," which means accommodating an additional 700,000 people, largely within the city's greenbelt (Mayor of London 2004b, 9). The plan emphasizes the "Blue Ribbon Network," centered on the Thames River and its tributaries, as a prime corridor for intensifying development both within and beyond the greenbelt (Mayor of London 2004a). It offers an opportunity for new forms of transportation (ferries, freight barges, etc.) and an abundant set of sites ripe for conversion from docklands and industrial uses to mixed use housing, workplaces, shopping, and recreation areas.

Vancouver, also blessed with tight development controls that constrain fringe development, has opted for what it calls "eco-density," coupled with a massive program of investing in new mass transit lines, both above- and belowground (City of Vancouver 2008). The focus on changing urban form in Vancouver will be on restructuring densities and urban patterns in the built-up area of the city. The 2010 Winter Olympics provided an incentive for the transit investments, and the city has encouraged redevelopment and doubling of densities along bus (formerly streetcar) transit corridors and has taken actions to make obsolete industrial and rail yard areas into sites for new development. This is already bearing results, although not at the rate that will be required in the future: "As a result of building housing close to jobs in Vancouver and maintaining sites for services close to the core, emissions from cars and light trucks increased less than 6 percent from 1990 to 2000 despite a population increase of 18 percent and a shift toward less fuel-efficient

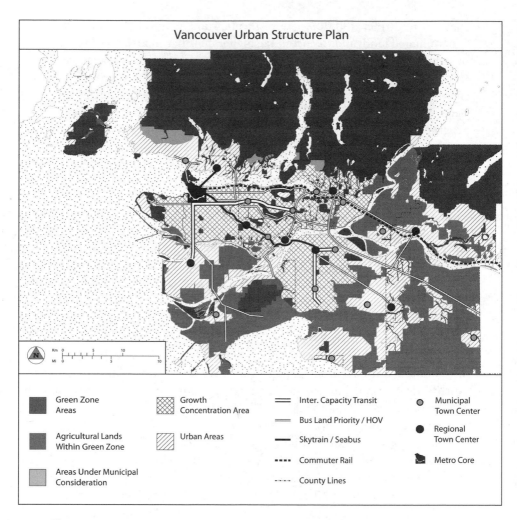

Figure 2.10
Vancouver Urban Structure Plan.

vehicles" (Cool Vancouver Task Force 2005, 19). Stepping up its efforts, the province has recently introduced a carbon tax, the first in North America, which serves as an incentive for energy efficiency in transportation, and is in the midst of debating a cap-and-trade system that would complement it (fig. 2.10).

Continuity of Planning Ideas

It is perhaps remarkable that the ideas of constraining the perimeter of urban areas and promoting clusters of higher-density, transit-oriented development have remained leading ideas for well over a century. Over that span, the ideas have been repurposed to accommodate shifts in attitudes, imperatives, and technology. The greenbelt, originally seen as a device to preserve a rural way of life and provide open spaces between cities, has been reframed as an environmental resource, an ecological preserve, a zone of defense, a protected area for urban-oriented agriculture, a recreation zone, a girdle for urban development that can promote higher urban densities and reduced travel distances, and most recently a zone for carbon sequestration. Robust ideas such as this have the capacity to evolve and be added to with each successive generation. They are also adaptable to varying cultures and development circumstances.

It is possible to reframe the rules of urbanization in even the most complex urban regions, as Kevin Lynch has argued. The recent emergence of climate change as a worldwide preoccupation has provided new impetus to policy debates over urban form. The atmosphere knows no jurisdictional boundaries, and this fact alone alters the dialogue between cities and suburbs and among cities across the globe. As national and state or provincial governments assume responsibility for setting targets for reduced carbon emissions, the geographic focus of policy will need to shift to regional patterns of urbanization. Addressing climate change may have made the difference in persuading the province of Ontario to create the ambitious Toronto greenbelt. Shaping urban form is likely to be more, not less, important in the future.

Note

1. Recently, vehicle miles traveled have leveled off in the United States and even declined slightly, as a result of the jump in gasoline prices and a weak economy, the first break in the long-term pattern of increased travel.

References

Abercrombie, Patrick. 1926. *The Preservation of Rural England*. London: Hodder and Stoughton.

Bae, Chang-Hee Christine, and Myung-Jin Jun. 2003. Counterfactual Planning. *Journal of Planning Education and Research* 22 (4): 374–383.

Bengston, David N., and Yeo-Chang Youn. 2004. Seoul's Greenbelt: An Experiment in Urban Containment. In *Policies for Managing Urban Growth and Landscape Change,* ed. David N. Bengston. Technical Report NC-265. St. Paul, MN: U.S. Department of Agriculture, Forest Service, North Central Research Station.

Burnham, Daniel H., and Edward H. Bennett. (1909) 1991. *Plan of Chicago*. New York: Princeton Architectural Press.

Cervero, Robert. 2004. *Transit-oriented Development in the United States*. Transit Cooperative Research Program Report No. 102. Washington, DC: Federal Transit Administration.

Choi, M. J. 1994. An Empirical Analysis of the Impacts of Greenbelt on Land Prices in the Seoul Metropolitan Area. *Korean Journal of Urban Planning* 29 (2): 97–111.

City of New York. 2006. *PlaNYC: A Greener, Greater New York*. New York: Mayor's Office of Planning and Sustainability.

City of Vancouver. 2008. *EcoDensity Charter: How Density, Design, and Land Use Will Contribute to Environmental Sustainability, Affordability and Livability*. Adopted by City Council, June 10. http://vancouver.ca/commsvcs/ecocity.

Cool Vancouver Task Force. 2005. *Community Climate Change Action Plan: Creating Opportunities*. http://vancouver.ca/sustainability/documents/CommunityPlan.pdf.

Cox, Wendell. 2004. Myths about Urban Growth and the Toronto Greenbelt, *Frazer Institute Digital Publication*, December. http://www.demographia.com/db-torgreenbelt.pdf.

Department for Communities and Local Government (England). 2007. Local Planning Authority Green Belt Statistics: England 2006. http://www.communities.gov.uk/publications/corporate/statistics/lagreenbelt2006.

Federal Highway Administration. 2008. Traffic Volume Trends: 2008. http://www.fhwa.dot.gov/policyinformation/travel_monitoring/tvt.cfm.

Gordon, David L.A. 2006. *Planning Twentieth-Century Capital Cities*. New York: Routledge.

Gordon, Peter, and Harry W. Richardson. 1998. Prove It: The Costs of Sprawl. *Brookings Review* 16 (3): 23–26.

Gordon, Peter, and Harry W. Richardson. 2004. Exit and Voice in Settlement Change. *Review of Austrian Economics* 17 (2/3): 187–202.

Howard, Ebenezer. (1902) 1946. *Garden Cities of To-Morrow*. London: Sonnenschein & Co. Reprinted, edited and with a preface by F. J. Osborn and introduction by Lewis Mumford. London: Faber and Faber.

Iqbal, Munawar. 2005. *Islamic Perspectives on Sustainable Development.* Palgrave Macmillan, University of Bahrain, and Islamic Research and Training Institute.

Kim, K. H. 1993. Housing Prices, Affordability, and Government Policy in Korea. *Journal of Real Estate Finance and Economics* 6:55–71.

Koolhaas, Rem. 1995. Whatever Happened to Urbanism? In *S, M, L, XL*, ed. Rem Koolhaas with Bruce Mau/OMA. New York: Monacelli Press.

Lynch, Kevin. 1984. *Good City Form.* Cambridge, MA: MIT Press.

Mayor of London. 2004a. *The London Plan: Summary*, February. London: Greater London Authority.

Mayor of London. 2004b. *The London Plan: Spatial Development Strategy for Greater London.* February. London: Greater London Authority.

Ministry of Municipal Affairs and Housing (Ontario). 2005. *Greenbelt Plan.* Toronto, ON: Ministry of Municipal Affairs and Housing.

Moraes Victor, Rodrigo Antonio Braga, Joaquim de Britto Costa Netto, Aziz Nacib Ab'Sáber, et al. 2004. Application of the Biosphere Reserve Concept to Urban Areas: The Case of São Paulo City Green Belt Biosphere Reserve, Brazil—São Paulo Forest Institute. A Case Study for UNESCO. *Annals of the New York Academy of Sciences* 1023:237–281.

Muschamp, Herbert. 2009. *Hearts of the City.* New York: Random House.

Newman, Peter, and Jeffrey Kenworthy. 1999. *Sustainability and Cities: Overcoming Automobile Dependence.* Washington, DC: Island Press.

O'Toole, Randal. 2001. *The Vanishing Automobile and Other Urban Myths: How Smart Growth Will Harm American Cities.* Camp Sherman, OR: Thoreau Institute. www.ti.org.

O'Toole, Randal. 2007. *Debunking Portland: The City That Doesn't Work.* Policy Analysis No. 596. Washington, DC: Cato Institute.

Pacala, Stephen, and Robert Socolow. 2004. Stabilization Wedges: Solving the Climate Problem for the Next 50 Years with Existing Technologies. *Science* 13 (August): 968–972.

Quayle, Moura. 1998. Provincial Interest in the Agricultural Land Conservation Act: A Report to the Minister of Agriculture and Food, British Columbia. www.agf.gov.bc.ca/polleg/quayle/stakes.htm.

Wendell Cox Consultancy. 2003. Urban Transit Fact Book. www.publicpurpose.com/ut-index.htm.

3

New Urbanism

Robert Fishman

In the genealogy of planning ideas, New Urbanism might best be defined as the unexpected synthesis of Jane Jacobs and Ebenezer Howard. New Urbanism learned from Jacobs the fundamental importance of "close-grained diversity," the energizing density that unites a full range of people and functions in lively public spaces. From Howard and his successors in the Garden City/New Town movement, New Urbanism took the idea that urbanism could not be limited to a single central city within a metropolitan region. The real challenge to planning lies in creating diversity, walkability, and sustainability throughout the metropolitan region in a network of carefully designed small communities that complements and supports the central city. If the urban crisis of the second half of the twentieth century had raised the threat of what Lewis Mumford termed "total urban disintegration" (Mumford 1968b, 133), New Urbanism sought to respond with a regionwide program of action that drew on what was strongest and most lasting in both Jacobs and Howard.

Neither Jacobs nor Howard could have anticipated—or indeed welcomed—this attempted synthesis. In the introduction to her highly personal history of planning ideas, *The Death and Life of Great American Cities* ([1961] 1993), Jacobs identified Howard and the Garden City/New Town movement he founded in 1898 as the leading source of what she termed "city-destroying" planning ideas. Howard's hopes for the planned decentralization of large cities, she charged, reflected a pathological hatred of urban density and diversity; he "simply wrote off the intricate, many-faceted, cultural life of the metropolis" and his beloved "Garden Cities" of 30,000 people set in greenbelts were "really nice towns if you were docile and had no plans of your own and didn't mind spending your life among others with no plans of their own" (Jacobs [1961] 1993, 26), 24).

Lewis Mumford, Howard's leading disciple, responded in 1962 with a scathing *New Yorker* review titled "Mother Jacobs' Home Remedies for Urban Cancer." Mumford argued that Jacobs "innocently believes that complexity and diversity are impossible without the kind of intense congestion that has in fact been emptying out the big city." Angrily dismissing Jacobs's critique of the Garden City ideal, Mumford insisted that "Instead of asking what are the best possible urban patterns today for renovating our disordered cities, Mrs. Jacobs asks only under what conditions can existing slums and blighted areas preserve their congenial humane features without any serious improvements in their physical structure or their mode of life" (Mumford 1968a, 202, 197). And "serious improvements" meant for Mumford the necessary decentralization of the great city into human-scale New Towns. In the end, Mumford's punishing review simply reinforced Jacobs's assertion in *Death and Life* that her approach to the city had nothing in common with Howard and the Garden City tradition.

It took the full force of the urban crisis of the 1970s and 1980s—a crisis profoundly devastating to both Jacobs's and Mumford's ideals—to impel a group of young urban designers to revisit this debate and see the possibilities of a synthesis that had eluded Jacobs and Mumford in the 1960s. If nothing else, the urban crisis profoundly altered the axioms of metropolitan form that had once defined both Jacobs's and Mumford's antagonistic positions. The decline of the central cities laid waste to many of the core neighborhoods that best fit Jacobs's ideal; simultaneously, frantic growth at the metropolitan periphery meant that the beautiful sites Mumford and other New Town enthusiasts had imagined for well-planned New Towns were already engulfed in sprawl. A rolling wave of abandonment and disinvestment coming out of the inner cities was already threatening the older, "first-ring" suburbs and small towns with their still surviving Main Streets. Indeed, anything public or urban seemed in crisis, and the American metropolis itself seemed doomed to Mumford's "total urban disintegration."

The worst years of the urban crisis were perhaps not the best time to found a design, planning, and social movement based on compact, walkable urbanism (Talen 2005). Nevertheless, the founders of New Urbanism not only saw the urgent need to reverse what threatened to be the inevitable metropolitan trends of their time, they also saw the possibility that elements in both Jacobs and Howard could be mobilized to combat "total urban disintegration" at all scales from the neighborhood to the region. Working mostly in modest, struggling urban design firms, the future leaders of New Urbanism developed their ideas through a mix of small commissions, competition entries, part-time teaching, and foundation grants. As such, they managed to be marginal at once to university-based planning departments, architecture schools, public sector policymakers, and private real estate developers. Ironically, their very marginality made it possible for them not only to escape from the ideological divisions of the past but to conceive a "movement" style of advocacy that could unite academics, practitioners, business leaders, and activists and even speak directly to the elusive "general public" (Brain 2005).

A key breakthrough came in 1982 when an untried developer, Robert Davis, commissioned two young Miami urban designers, Andres Duany and Elizabeth Plater-Zyberk (co-partners in the firm Duany Plater-Zyberk & Company who also happened to be married to each other) to design the master plan for a small north Gulf Coast resort community on an unfashionable stretch of the Florida Panhandle known as the "redneck Riviera" (Mohney and Easterling 1991). Davis wanted an alternative to the ugly sprawl that was disfiguring the Florida coast; Duany and Plater-Zyberk saw the opportunity in this eighty-two-acre project called Seaside to create a model community that would embody their hopes for a radical change in American development patterns (Duany and Plater-Zyberk 1991). Seaside's townscape of exuberantly traditional houses with porches fronting narrow streets that led to attractive public spaces seemed to promise a new era of compact, communitarian design. The development rapidly became a rallying point for like-minded designers who had been pursuing similar ideas, and a familiar image in architecture and planning periodicals.

In 1991, Judy Corbett and Peter Katz of the Sacramento-based non-profit Local Government Commission brought Duany and Plater-Zyberk together with some of their West Coast counterparts, including Peter Calthorpe, Stefanos Polyzoides, and Elizabeth Moule. The resulting Ahwahnee Principles (named for the Yosemite hotel where the document was presented) represented the first attempt to formulate the basic credo of the emerging movement (Local Government Commission 2008). From that meeting sprang the idea of a national design advocacy group that would unite a broad coalition of professionals, academics, environmentalists, and social activists around a common platform of "New Urbanism" (the competing term "neotraditionalism" having been rejected as too retrograde). The Congress for the New Urbanism (CNU) held its first meeting in Alexandria, Virginia, in 1993 with two hundred invited

participants (Lewis 1993). As co-founder Dan Solomon recalls, the original aim was to produce a definitive book whose impact might be comparable to that of the 1933 arch-modernist manifesto, the Congrès
Internationaux d'Architecture Moderne's "Charter of Athens" (Solomon
2003, 211). Although the CNU did publish its admirably brief, three-
page "Charter of the New Urbanism" in 1996, the organization soon
converted to a more permanent, open, and diverse advocacy group that
today numbers over 3,100 members.

As a planning doctrine, New Urbanism proceeds powerfully and
directly from Jane Jacobs's passionate defense of "close-grained diversity" as the essence of good urbanism. This means not only an intricate
mix of uses and incomes down to the block level but above all a lively
public realm, a carefully designed setting for the theater of urbanity built
around the pedestrian, the sidewalk, and enclosed public spaces. New
Urbanism, moreover, accepts Jacobs's assertion that such close-grained
diversity requires density, for only density can produce those intricate
and unexpected mixtures of people and functions that Jacobs famously
termed the "ballet of the good city sidewalk."

Jacobs had concluded in 1961 that good urbanism therefore requires
great cities, which alone can sustain the density of true urbanism. She
briskly dismissed the rest of the metropolitan region as "semisuburban-
ized and suburbanized messes" (Jacobs [1961] 1993, 581). But by the
1980s these "suburbanized messes" held most of the population of most
American metropolitan regions and the majority of retail stores, industrial production venues, and even class-A office space (Fishman 1990).
To write them off seemed at best an evasion of the main problem in
contemporary urban design and at worst a formula for failure even
within the central cities. For the essence of the urban crisis was precisely
the capacity of the sprawl dynamic to suck resources and population out
of the central cities and to consume ever-increasing tracts of open space
at the edge.

New Urbanists, to their credit, understood that no lasting defense of
urbanism even within the central city was possible without confronting
the power of sprawl and challenging conventional suburban development patterns directly. But how to tame the sprawl dynamic? Here New
Urbanism drew on—and effectively revived and reinterpreted—the great
"alternative tradition" for suburban planning, the Garden City/New
Town movement. As Mumford had reminded Jacobs in 1962, Ebenezer
Howard's true aim was not the simple dispersion of central-city populations throughout the region; he sought to guide this dispersion into a

network of walkable communities, each with a clear center and edge. These Garden Cities would be, as we say today, mixed use and mixed income; the pedestrian-oriented neighborhoods would be within easy walking distance of jobs, open space, and the town center. Within the scale of a small town, planning could provide at moderate densities the diversity and walkability that are the essence of traditional urbanism. In short, Howard's aim was to recreate urbanism at many points in the region—not just the central city (Fishman 1977).

Howard's immediate followers, especially Raymond Unwin, the co-designer with Barry Parker of the first Garden City at Letchworth, England (1903), and Hampstead Garden Suburb (1906), north of London, were remarkably successful in translating Howard's sweeping aims and geometric diagrams into actual places. Unwin borrowed heavily from traditional townscapes with their intricate mixtures of narrow streets and open courtyards to create moderate density and aesthetic variety without the drab monotony of so many nineteenth-century cities; he carefully mixed classes and functions to recapture a communitarian spirit lacking in the deeply divided industrial city. And his designs always had a clear town center and a green edge (Unwin [1909] 1994).

Unwin's designs were highly influential in the United States, where their moderate densities and picturesque planning reinforced trends emerging from the best American streetcar suburbs. In the hands of such expert designers as Grosvenor Atterbury (Forest Hills Gardens, 1912), Frederick Law Olmsted, Jr. (Rancho Palos Verdes, 1923), and John Nolen (Mariemont, 1918), the "garden suburb" reached a high level of sophistication by the 1920s (Stern and Massengale 1981). But this design vocabulary came under attack after Radburn, New Jersey (Clarence Stein and Henry Wright 1928), "a town for the motor age," replanned garden suburb design to make accommodating the automobile a primary goal (Schaffer 1982). Even Mumford bitterly complained in the 1960s that the vaunted English and Scandinavian New Towns of the postwar era were too dispersed to be genuinely walkable (Hughes 1971, 134–137). The American New Towns of the 1960s—Columbia, Maryland; Reston, Virginia; and Irvine, California—attempted to fight sprawl and cluster development, but their designs still embodied the compromise that Radburn began (Forsyth 2005).

But in the 1970s and 1980s, a whole group of urban designers began to look again at the early Garden Cities and suburbs of the Unwin era as possible models for disciplining sprawl and designing genuinely walkable communities. In 1981, Robert A. M. Stern and John Massengale put together a comprehensive exhibit titled *The Anglo-American Suburb* at the Cooper-Hewitt Museum in New York City. This display of plans and images of what Stern termed "the tradition of planned suburbs and planned suburban enclaves" paid special attention to Hampstead Garden Suburb and its immediate predecessors and successors, including Forest Hills Gardens, Mariemont, and the Unwin-inspired World War I–era workers' housing, done under the leadership of Frederick Law Olmsted, Jr. As published in *Architectural Digest*, the exhibit made this tradition not only newly available but newly relevant as a fully worked-out design language that could serve as a radical alternative to later automobile-dependent suburban development (Stern and Massengale 1981).

The early Garden City tradition provided another crucial concept for New Urbanism: the linkage between land use and transit that Peter Calthorpe would call Transit-Oriented Development. The early Garden Cities and suburbs were walkable because they had to be; before the automobile people required a full range of services in their neighborhoods, as well as a transit stop within walking distance. Howard as early as 1898 had generalized from the network of "streetcar suburbs" that were rapidly surrounding all large cities to conceive of what he called "the Social City," a network of Garden Cities linked to each other and to a central city by transit (Howard [1898] 1965, 23).

Raymond Unwin in the 1920s had translated this abstract suggestion into an ambitious vision of a "regional city" defined by rail lines running out from a central-city hub (Creese 1967). Each stop would be a separate mixed use, mixed income Garden City, tightly organized around its rail stop/town center to bring all its residents within walking distance of the stop and to ensure open space between the Garden Cities. As population left the overcrowded central cities, the "urbanism" of what Unwin now termed "the regional city" would no longer be concentrated at the core but located in the network that the Garden Cities formed. Unwin's regional city became the basis for such social democratic regional cities as the English New Towns around London; the Swedish New Towns around Stockholm; and the Danish "Finger Plan" around Copenhagen (Swenarton 2008).

Peter Calthorpe took this aspect of Garden City design—originally intended largely to get populations out of the central city—and grasped its new relevance in an age of sprawl (Calthorpe 1993). Even in a society with near-universal automobile ownership, a regional light-rail network could discipline sprawl by recentering development around its stops. If a light-rail stop became the town center for a New Urbanist community and if that community were limited in size to the quarter-mile radius within walking distance of the stop, then the basic framework would be in place for moderately dense neighborhoods, mixed use development, and communities with a clear center and edge.

Such a light-rail network would have the further benefit of recentering the metropolitan region on its core city, the regional "hub" where all the transit spokes converge. This would create the right conditions for the restoration of the regional downtown and the repopulation of devastated inner-city neighborhoods. This late twentieth-century version of Unwin's regional city would thus offer a range of urbanisms, from the high-density, twenty-four-hour core urban districts that Jacobs celebrated to the moderate-density Garden City neighborhoods that Mumford believed most Americans favored. With new development limited to land within walking distance of a transit stop, sprawl could be curtailed, open space preserved, and the region reconstituted as walkable, transit-friendly cities and towns from the core to the edge.

New Urbanism thus arrived at its unexpected synthesis of Jacobs and Howard. Compared to conventional suburban development, New Urbanism had set itself some very difficult tasks. Where the typical automobile-dependent suburb could be built in scattered fragments—the subdivisions, the strip mall, the regional mall, etc.—that by the 1980s were very well understood, New Urbanism required a virtuoso design performance even at the neighborhood level. Achieving walkability meant somehow orchestrating a harmonious built environment that would include the proper block size and densities, mixed use typologies, small lot sizes with houses oriented to the street, pedestrian-friendly streets and sidewalks, and convenient, well-defined open spaces. Moreover, providing the neighborhoods with a town center within walking distance meant adding yet another level of complexity, not only in designing a lively, pedestrian-oriented set of shopping streets but also in mastering the difficult economics of small retail businesses (Leinberger 2008). Finally, a public realm and transit-oriented development meant coordination with and dependence on a public sector that was radically shrinking in the age of Reagan.

All this had to be done in the face of lenders who simply did not understand mixed use development, developers whose success had come through accommodating the automobile, and, not least, local planners who found themselves administering regulations that mandated sprawl. As Alex Krieger has observed, "It is easier to sketch or even build a town fragment than it is to achieve an actual town" (Krieger 1991, 13).

Although there are literally hundreds of developments that could claim
to be New Urbanist, only a few so far have achieved the scale and design
integrity to demonstrate the movement's principles. These developments
include Kentlands in Gaithersburg, Maryland (master plan by Duany
Plater-Zyberk, 1988); Celebration, Florida (a Disney Corporation project
designed by a team of New Urbanists, including Robert A. M. Stern,
Cooper, Robertson, and Urban Design Associates, 1996); and Stapleton,
built on the site of Denver's former airport (master plan by Calthorpe
Associates 1999).

Indeed, even if more New Urbanist communities could be built exactly
as designed, there would still remain the fundamental issue that Jacobs
highlights in a long footnote in *Death and Life* directed at Lewis
Mumford. She remarks, "Some planning theorists call for urban variety
and liveliness, and simultaneously prescribe 'in-between' densities." She
respectfully quotes Mumford's comment that the "great function of a
city" is to provide "a stage on which the drama of social life may be
enacted," but then castigates his assertion that such drama could really
take place at Mumford's preferred density of twenty-five to fifty units
per acre. "Urbanity and in-between densities like this . . . are incompat-
ible," she states flatly, "because of the economics of generating city
diversity" (Jacobs [1961] 1993, 275). From Unwin to Duany, Plater-
Zyberk and Calthorpe, urbanists in the Garden City tradition have
struggled to find the right design for a new community that indeed combines urbanity and moderate densities. It remains elusive.

West Coast and East Coast New Urbanisms

As I hope to show in the rest of this chapter, there is no single New
Urbanism; it is rather the collective product of many different urban
designers, all adapting in different ways to the intense difficulties of
putting theories into practice. Moreover, both New Urbanist theory and
practice have necessarily changed as the urban crisis ran its course. For
purposes of convenience I discuss the varieties of New Urbanism under
two broad headings, West Coast New Urbanism and East Coast New
Urbanism. West Coast New Urbanism, the less familiar of the two,
emerged largely from the ecology movement of the 1970s, in particular
the passive solar movement (described in greater detail in chapter 4 of
this book, where it is linked to evolving ideas about sustainability). East
Coast New Urbanism owed more to internal debates within architecture
itself after the fall of high modernism.

If West Coast New Urbanism is more progressive and the East Coast variety more traditionalist in many respects, both groups were products of a unique moment in twentieth-century architecture's relationship to the past. The early 1970s, when so many future leaders were still studying architecture or just beginning their practice, saw the collapse of modernism's claim to define history as inevitable progress, a single track toward a future that rendered "historical" synonymous with "obsolete." Suddenly, a new generation found the past *available*, as architectural historian Vincent Scully observed, not just "as objects of interest and precursors of Modernism, but also as direct models for contemporary use" (Scully 1991, 18).

West Coast New Urbanism was dominated by the drama of discovering that a way forward out of the energy crisis was to go back to older technologies like the streetcar, just as the way out of the urban crisis was to go back to more traditional urban forms. This was largely the achievement of Peter Calthorpe, although other West Coast New Urbanists such as Elizabeth Moule and Stefanos Polyzoides, Douglas Kelbaugh, and Dan Solomon also made their own distinctive contributions (Farr 2008). In the 1970s, Calthorpe had rejected conventional architectural practice to concentrate on social and especially environmental issues. He came to urban design indirectly from the passive solar movement in architecture that took shape in the 1970s in opposition to the more technology-driven attempts to reduce energy consumption. As architect Don Prowler explains it, passive solar was "an exciting alternative to the neutrality of modern architecture in which they had been educated and the placelessness of the modern suburb in which they had been reared. Passive solar buildings had to be oriented to the sun . . . [and] by necessity, settled on their site. They were somewhere" (Prowler 1989, 101).

But passive solar buildings also tended to be stand-alone structures on large suburban or rural lots. When Calthorpe joined the California Energy Commission, a remarkable institution created by then governor Jerry Brown, he not only helped under the leadership of Berkeley professor Sim Van der Rijn to design a remarkable collection of energy-saving buildings, he began to think carefully about the neighborhood and urban scale and its impact on energy. Looking at the older neighborhoods near the California state capitol, he saw that the very form of Old Sacramento saved energy and promoted community. Not only did the row house party walls conserve energy in each unit but the intermingling of functions in older neighborhoods with jobs and services within walking distance was a more powerful "energy-saving device" than the best passive solar design (Calthorpe 1986).

Contrasting current building practice with the "sustainable patterns" of the past and the (hoped-for) future, he and Sim Van der Rijn wrote a brief summation that continues to define new urbanism as an architectural/environmental movement:

[Current] buildings ignore climate and place, uses are zoned into separate areas, and individuals are isolated by a lack of convivial public spaces. Sustainable patterns break down the separations; buildings respond to the climate instead of overpowering it, mixed uses draw activities and people together, and shared spaces reestablish community. (Van der Rijn and Calthorpe 1986, x)

Calthorpe thus began to set the "sustainability agenda" for New Urbanism. Perhaps more important, as California's growth exploded in the 1980s, he began to consider how the patterns of density he admired in Old Sacramento could be introduced into the rapidly expanding suburbs around the Bay Area. In 1972, the landscape architect Lawrence Halprin had proposed an ambitious plan to save the Willamette Valley in Oregon from sprawl by building new light-rail lines to concentrate development around its stops (Halprin 1972). But the plan was never implemented, and the concept receded from sight.

Fifteen years later, Calthorpe began to explore his own version of the concept under the rubric "pedestrian pockets." In 1988, he published a short article with Mark Mack in the *Northern California Real Estate Journal* proposing that the defunct Northwestern Pacific rail right-of-way that ran through Marin County north of San Francisco be re-equipped for light rail. Along its line he envisioned some twenty pedestrian pockets, mixed use developments covering about sixty acres each, tightly planned around the rail stop/town center, which would include both retail and office space. Closely clustered around the center would be housing for some five thousand people, all within easy walking distance of the stop. The pedestrian pocket would preserve the surrounding countryside from sprawl and cut down on automobile dependency yet provide rail-based mobility that would reconnect the region (Calthorpe and Mack 1988).

This brief article in an obscure publication outlines a regional vision that Calthorpe has been pursuing ever since, a vision that has become an integral part of New Urbanism and, increasingly, of national transportation and land-use policy. His goals went beyond energy efficiency or preserving open space. As he wrote, "The end goal of this tight mix of housing and open space is not just to provide appropriate homes for different uses, or to offer the convenience of walking, but hopefully to reintegrate the currently separated age and social types of our diverse culture. The shared common spaces and local stories may create a rebirth of our often lost sense of community and place" (Calthorpe and Mack 1988, 8). In some respects Calthorpe was doing nothing more than rediscovering the design logic of the early twentieth-century streetcar suburb. His originality was in seeing that this logic could be used to address the problem of late twentieth-century sprawl. Light rail—the streetcar—was, of course, one of the old-fashioned technologies that progressive modernism had declared obsolete. The residents of the pedestrian pocket would not necessarily live without cars, but the regional transit system would give them a vital alternative to the automobile, and one that promoted greater community and equity. With a more complex understanding of the relationship between past and present, Calthorpe made light rail the center of his sustainable "city of the future."

In 1989, Calthorpe teamed with Douglas Kelbaugh, a leader in the passive solar movement who was then chair of architecture at the University of Washington, Seattle, to put together a pedestrian pocket charrette. The charrette has been a favorite medium of production and communication for New Urbanism (Kelbaugh 1997). A multiday design exercise that brings together teams of architects, planners, and other design professionals with students and sometimes stakeholders from the community, the charrette makes possible a rapid communication among diverse firms and professions whose separation would otherwise hinder a total design effort. Moreover, by including community leaders, the charrette can address and focus on a broad range of social issues that have an impact on design. Calthorpe and Kelbaugh's pedestrian pocket charrette brought together a remarkable group of designers as charrette team leaders, including Dan Solomon, Harrison Fraker (later dean of architecture at both Minnesota and Berkeley), and Don Prowler. Published as *The Pedestrian Pocket Book* (Kelbaugh1989), this "new suburban design strategy" both revived the Garden Cities/New Town regional approach to transit and pointed forward to twenty-first-century needs.

Calthorpe cannot claim to be a brilliant formal designer, but he possesses another quality, rare in any field: *clarity*, and especially the ability to see clearly the strategic elements in a large, complex problem. The full development of this strategic vision came not in northern California, where Calthorpe had established his urban design firm, or in the Puget Sound, where the pedestrian pocket charrette was set, but in Portland,

Oregon. Since the 1970s, when the state of Oregon established an "urban growth boundary" around Portland and the city rejected an urban freeway in favor of a short light-rail line, Portland has been a national "capital of good planning," as Carl Abbott termed it (Abbott 2000). In the early 1990s another proposed freeway, this time running to the west of the city, again threatened to breach the urban growth boundary and accelerate sprawl. A remarkable citizens' activist group called 1000 Friends of Oregon turned to Calthorpe for an alternative. His LUTRAQ (Land Use, Transit, Air Quality) plan for Portland enabled him to develop the concept of the pedestrian pocket, now called transit-oriented development, into a genuine regional plan (Calthorpe 1993, 122–125). LUTRAQ envisions not only a single light-rail line replacing the controversial freeway but six new light-rail lines coming out of downtown Portland to create a regionwide network. Each of their stops would be a transit-oriented development, a mixed use, mixed income, walkable community. As administered by the nation's only elected regional government according to a comprehensive Portland 2030 Plan, LUTRAQ has become the national model for sustainable regionalism (Calthorpe and Fulton 2001, 141–151).

The distinctive character of West Coast New Urbanism came in large part from its collective strength, dominated as it was by such figures as Elizabeth Moule and Stefanos Polyzoides, Dan Solomon, and Douglas Kelbaugh, in addition to Calthorpe. East Coast New Urbanism, by contrast, is associated with a single firm and the couple who founded it, Andres Duany and Elizabeth Plater-Zyberk. Both are graduates of Princeton University and the Yale School of Architecture, and their work reflects more directly the debates that transfixed architecture during the transition years of postmodernism. The sudden collapse of high modernism with its urban design vocabulary based on Le Corbusier's concept of massive clearances to be replaced by "towers in the park" left a vacuum that was inevitably filled by a new appreciation of the older cities the modernists had despised. The Italian Neo-Rationalist architects, led by Aldo Rossi (1982), theorized that the great cities were not the creations of individual geniuses but were built up over time out of the repetition of certain standardized but highly flexible traditional building types such as the row house, whose ability to accommodate many different functions and classes provided the economic and social diversity that defines a city. In this urban typology, the constant repetition of the basic type creates an overall unity to the urban fabric of each city, while small variations in the design of each building introduce the needed measure of visual variety. Rossi was supplemented and supported by Leon and Rob Krier, two architects (and brothers) from Luxembourg whose passionate defense of the "European city" against modernism and industrialism was focused on the revival of traditional building practices and above all of traditional blocks, streets, and neighborhoods (Krier, 1991; Economakis 1992).

Yale in the early 1970s was, as Yale professor Vincent Scully puts it, "an intellectual environment where, in history at least, the vernacular and classical traditions of architecture were sympathetically studied" (Scully 1991, 17). Nevertheless, he remembers his surprise when two of his best students, Duany and Plater-Zyberk, began to explore the typical New Haven neighborhoods where Scully himself had grown up. In this "ordinary" environment, now threatened by disinvestment or by urban renewal, they discovered an "American city" with as rich and cohesive a set of typologies and neighborhood designs as the European city that Rossi and the Kriers had celebrated. To be sure, Robert Venturi and Denise Scott Brown had in their book based on their famous Yale studio on the Las Vegas strip in 1968 proclaimed, "Learning from the existing landscape is a way of being radical for an architect" (Venturi, Scott Brown, and Izenour [1972] 1977, 8). And Venturi himself, in *Complexity and Contradiction in Architecture,* had asked his famous rhetorical question, "Is not Main Street almost all right?" (Venturi 1966, 89). Nevertheless, Venturi and Scott Brown in their own work had treated Main Street and other historicist typologies ironically and abstractly. Duany and Plater-Zyberk looked at the close-knit houses, comfortable porches, and pedestrian-friendly streetscapes of New Haven and saw their "city of the future."

Despite these insights, Duany and Plater-Zyberk were still tempted by the prestige of the architectural avant-garde. After graduation they were among the founders of the Miami firm Arquitectonica, whose high-tech, high-gloss designs set the standards for hip Miami. As Duany has recently recalled, a lecture visit to Miami by Leon Krier reminded him and Plater-Zyberk of their earlier mission and ideals (Redmon 2010). In 1980 they resigned from Arquitectonica to found their present firm. By 1982 they had the commission for Seaside.

Duany and Plater-Zyberk are rightly regarded as the central figures in New Urbanism, a position they have earned through a remarkable creativity and productivity ranging from the aesthetics of urban design to the complexities of building codes and zoning. Duany is the more public figure, a charismatic speaker who has deeply engaged himself in such technical issues as form-based building and zoning codes. Plater-Zyberk has been dean of the School of Architecture at the University of Miami since 1996, in addition to her careers as designer and author. I know of no other two-person team that has been so influential in a creative field.

Compared to the West Coast New Urbanists, Duany and Plater-Zyberk are more focused on design per se. They share Calthorpe's ecological and social ideals, but they are more passionate about the urban experience, the way in which all the elements of a great neighborhood or city come together to produce "civic art." Ultimately they have faith in what they have termed traditional neighborhood design (their equivalent of Calthorpe's transit-oriented development) to create community, even in the absence of transit or mixed use purposes. Because they are deeply invested in making their own work reflect the best local traditions wherever they design, they have been among our most influential, if little acknowledged, historians of planning and urban design. They have made themselves experts in Savannah and Charleston for their southern projects, in the Middle Atlantic colonial town for Kentlands, and in the American small town generally. Duany wrote the preface for the 1994 reissue of Raymond Unwin's 1909 masterwork, *Town Planning in Practice,* and he has been instrumental in the rediscovery of such varied American "garden suburbs" as Yorkship Village, in Camden, New Jersey, a government project for shipyard workers (1918), and the affluent resort town of Coral Gables, Florida (1921). They have championed such diverse and neglected figures as John Nolen and Benton MacKaye, and in general, have recaptured a lost tradition of integrated urban design, planning, and landscape architecture that flourished in the 1910s and 1920s (Duany, Plater-Zyberk, and Alminana 2003).

Ironically, this very passion for design has isolated Duany and Plater-Zyberk from most schools of architecture, which have gone strongly in the avant-garde, Arquitectonica direction that they themselves rejected. Peter Calthorpe has insisted that New Urbanism "has become mostly known as a style . . . and I don't think style is what is at its heart" (Calthorpe 2005, 17). While Duany and Plater-Zyberk claim they would accept a modernism that accomplishes as much urbanistically as traditional styles, their loyalties are clearly with the neotraditionalist vision that Leon Krier has consistently championed. Their influence might therefore be greater in schools of planning, where style is indeed not an issue, than in schools of architecture.

If New Urbanism is a melding of elements from its West Coast and East Coast branches, we might now inquire specifically how the ideas of this hybrid movement have principally affected planning. The New Urbanist vision, deeply rooted in the Garden City/New Town alternative tradition of publicly directed development, posed a direct challenge to a profession whose aim was to serve the public good but whose actual practices, especially at the suburban fringe, degenerated into the technical administration of sprawl. New Urbanism offered a critique, a vision, and design framework at a time when suburban planners had largely ceded any directing role in the growth and structure of suburbia to highway engineers and subdivision developers.

New Urbanism not only reaffirmed an alternative tradition of civic action and leadership, the New Urbanists' training as architects restored to the growth debate that gift of vision that had been lacking since planning had shifted toward a more technical and policy-oriented discourse. Not only did New Urbanism argue strongly for radical changes in metropolitan form, but the movement was able to show these changes in dramatic imagery that had the capacity to communicate the New Urbanist message beyond professional policy circles and thus to mobilize a wide audience around planning issues. Working outside academia, the New Urbanists spoke out powerfully and directly to broad concerns about the devaluing of the "American dream" in the congestion and banality of the typical suburb (Duany, Plater-Zyberk, and Speck 2000). From this "outsider" position, New Urbanism outflanked academics and bureaucrats to change planning theory and practice in four different areas.

First, New Urbanism helped restore physical planning as an integral element in planning theory and practice. After decades when planning seemed to lose its physical dimension through a turn toward quantitative policy studies, New Urbanism's emphasis on creating a walkable urbanism meant the need to look closely at neighborhoods, Main Streets, and downtowns as physical environments. Without close attention to block size, street and sidewalk widths, the orientation of buildings toward the street, traffic patterns, transit stop locations, ground-floor retail establishments, and solid street walls uninterrupted by the voids of surface parking, walkability fails. As with so much of New Urbanism, the turn toward physical planning entailed a return to and a rediscovery of major figures like Unwin, Olmsted, Nolen, and Harland Bartholomew, all of whom fostered both education and practice that combined urban design, landscape architecture, and planning (Swenarton 2008).

Second, this return of physical planning led indirectly but necessarily to a fundamental challenge to the land-use regulations and traffic codes that are at the heart of planning practice (Ben-Joseph 2005). New Urbanists quickly realized that their cherished visions of walkable neighborhoods and diverse communities were blocked by the multitude of legal restrictions and "best practices" that mandated single-use and single-class neighborhoods and the "thin dispersions" that Jacobs had attacked in *Death and Life*. Andres Duany, who made the issue of regulation his special study and passion, was especially scathing when he pointed out in his frequent lectures that Savannah, Georgia; the Georgetown district of Washington, D.C.; Back Bay, Boston; and indeed all the historic districts we most admire today could not be built because they violate multiple land-use, street-width, and parking requirements (Duany, Plater-Zyberk, and Alminana 2003).

But Duany could not accept Jacobs's libertarian prescription of simply removing the offending regulations. He argued that with sprawl patterns so deeply engrained in the "best practices" of developers even when they build in cities, removing regulation would inevitably lead to worse sprawl and social segregation. To be sure, traditional townscapes were constructed with minimal regulation, but these emerged out of a shared, unspoken understanding of the built environment that has been lost; America today, Duany insists, needs Codes with a capital "C" (Duany and Plater-Zyberk 1991, 96–103). Where conventional zoning separates uses, limits density, and largely ignores built form, Duany and Plater-Zyberk provide detailed codes that require mixed use, mandate density, ensure orientation to the street, and provided detail architectural guidelines to maintain a harmony among buildings. The Seaside code famously requires porches, as well as stipulating building materials and massing. The aim of the codes is to ensure a coherent walkable environment where buildings, sidewalks, and streets all share in a harmonious relationship.

These codes accord, at least in their social aims, with the movement that Paul Davidoff and other equity planners launched in the 1970s to attack "snob zoning," which required the separation of functions and large houses on large lots throughout a suburban jurisdiction (Davidoff, Davidoff, and Gold 1970). But for Duany and Plater-Zyberk the aesthetic dimension of urban design cannot be separated from the social dimensions of equity planning. Duany has recently taken the lead in addressing the tendency of so many metropolitan regions to wind up with an undifferentiated sprawl landscape at every point from the core to the edge, a tendency aggravated by undifferentiated zoning regulations throughout the metropolitan area. To combat this tendency he has proposed what he calls "the transect," a cross section of a metropolitan area from the downtown to the rural outskirts. As one moves from the high-rise center to the rural edge, different codes come into force, each designed to preserve the appropriate form and density of the corresponding district (Duany and Talen 2002).

Third, New Urbanism has given new impetus to transportation planning, especially Calthorpe's transit-oriented development. Planners had of course been championing transit long before New Urbanism did so, but usually as part of a strategy to maintain the regional downtown (Cervero 1984). But precisely because they were focused on bringing commuters and shoppers downtown, planners had shown surprisingly little interest in what is now New Urbanism's main theme, the use of transit to create walkable neighborhoods and communities around every transit stop throughout the metropolitan region. In a remarkable 1958 article written in response to the 1956 Interstate Highway Act, Mumford had cautioned against any government policy that placed total reliance on the automobile and asked the critical question, "Transportation for what?" (Mumford 1963). New Urbanism has provided a comprehensive answer to Mumford's question and a regional vision of the benefits of a balanced transportation system.

Finally, New Urbanism, despite its reputation as "the New Suburbanism," has played a crucial role in the resurgence of a vital urbanism in our central cities, largely through leadership in the HOPE VI federal housing program to demolish failed high-rise (and low-rise) public housing projects and replace them with mixed income neighborhoods. Jane Jacobs made the failures of such projects perhaps her main theme, but she had little to say about how to replace them. In 1996, HUD secretary Henry Cisneros not only resolved to appropriate sufficient funds to demolish more than 60,000 units in more than 130 failed projects, he turned to the CNU to devise the design guidelines for their replacements (Weiss 2000).

Here again the design clarity and strategic vision were largely provided by Peter Calthorpe, whose plan to replace the Henry Horner Homes in Chicago helped popularize what has become a nationwide model. Instead of the now empty superblocks of demolished high-rises, he proposed reinstating the former grid of streets that used to run through the neighborhood. Such rethinking of project landscapes and city grids actually predates the New Urbanists and is rooted in ideas developed by Oscar Newman in the 1970s and applied in the early 1980s in Boston by firms such as Goody, Clancy and Lane Frenchman (Vale 2002). In the early 1990s, Ray Gindroz, principal of Urban Design Associates in Pittsburgh, showed in his rehabilitation of the low-rise Diggs Town project in Norfolk, Virginia, that public housing reoriented to a new street grid with traditional front yards and private entrances restored a sense of responsibility for and ownership of one's own front yard and immediate surroundings that the vaguely public but poorly maintained terrain of the housing project did not yield (Bothwell, Gindroz, and Lang 1998). For the community of Westhaven that replaced Henry Horner, Calthorpe incorporated such lessons into a row-house streetscape whose stoops, private entrances, and small front yards recreated the basic character of the surrounding neighborhood (Calthorpe and Fulton 2001, 243–270).

But behind the facades the social mix was anything but traditional. Some HOPE VI housing aimed for a mix of about one-third market-rate condominium ownership, one-third market-rate rentals, and one-third subsidized rentals to accommodate households from the old projects. Other HOPE VI mixes brought in a middle tier of apartments subsidized by low-income housing tax credits while skipping the ownership component. As developed by nonprofit cooperatives or for-profit developers, the housing would be highly competitive with the private market and would include such special features as day-care centers, health care clinics, and community rooms. The mixture of income groups would ensure that the tenants generated enough rent to enable management to maintain the new development.

HOPE VI has been controversial both on the streets and in academia (Popkin et al. 2004). Because of the planned mixture of incomes, very few HOPE VI projects can provide one-to-one replacements for the low-rent units that were demolished. This has made possible a careful screening of low-rent tenants for HOPE VI developments from among the former project residents, with those not selected finding what housing they can on the private market with HUD Section 8 vouchers. This has led scholars to argue that the success of HOPE VI owes more to the forced removal of the poorest and most problematic households than to any positive effect of the design and the income mix. HOPE VI has been less controversial, however, in proven capacity to provide its mixed income tenants with a well-designed living environment that has indeed often encouraged the wider rebuilding of surrounding neighborhoods. Although—to take two excellent examples—the Torti Gallas–designed brick row house project in South Philadelphia called Martin Luther King Plaza (Torti Gallas and Partners 1998) and Dan Solomon's wood-frame, Northwest-inflected Othello Station/NewHolly in Seattle (Solomon E.T.C. 2005) reflect very different regional typologies, both are outstanding for creating genuine neighborhood design that makes affordable housing a positive contribution to the district.

The rebuilding of so many inner-city neighborhoods reminds us that New Urbanism has managed to outlive the worst of the urban crisis that originally impelled its leaders to action, and the movement now operates in a very different context from the one that threatened "total urban disintegration" (Fishman 2008). When the charter of the New Urbanism called in 1996 for "the restoration of existing urban centers and towns," this modest wish for restoration appeared to be an almost utopian hope. By contrast, the charter's other principal goal—"the reconfiguration of sprawling suburbs into communities of real neighborhoods and diverse districts"—seemed a far more plausible aim in the context of a perpetual urban crisis.

Today, New Urbanism finds itself in unexpectedly strong competition with "old urbanism," that is, with existing center-city neighborhoods in the process of renovation that are already well served by transit lines, close to lively downtowns with well-paying jobs, and enjoying rapidly improving schools, public safety, and other services. Not surprisingly, these neighborhoods have attracted many of the young people who might have fueled the demand for greenfield New Urbanist projects. Meanwhile, the American suburb has proved to be highly resistant to extensive reconfiguration along New Urbanist lines. Despite the success of walkable neighborhoods in cities, developers on the periphery seem stuck in Jacobs's thin dispersions. During the recent bubble years, a massive misallocation of capital seeking quick profit inevitably favored the most conventional sprawl-type development on cheap land at the edge of automobile-dependent regions such as Las Vegas, Phoenix, or central California, places where regulation is weak and dispersion extreme.

With long-term housing demand shifting from the metropolitan edge to the core (U.S. Environmental Protection Agency 2010), the overhang of already built sprawl subdivisions will surely discourage the kind of slow, difficult development process that New Urbanist projects require. Witold Rybczynski's remarkable investigation in *Last Harvest* (2007) of a developer's attempt to build a New Urbanist community on a peripheral greenfield site in Chester County, Pennsylvania, during the boom years must now be read as more of a cautionary tale than perhaps

Rybczynski (and certainly the developer) intended. The book details the seemingly endless disappointments and delays that the Arcadia Land Company faced in developing "New Daleville" as a New Urbanist community. The book ends just as the boom collapsed, and New Daleville has remained an isolated fragment almost as auto dependent as the sprawl it was intended to replace (Inskeep 2008).

If, therefore, we can expect relatively few fully developed New Urbanist communities on greenfield sites, the movement will probably operate most effectively in suburbia on two very different scales: the regional plan and what Ellen Dunham-Jones and June Williamson (2011) have called "retrofitting suburbia." The regional plans embody not only the large-scale vision and ambitions of New Urbanism but also the impressive economic and ecological skills that the largest New Urbanist design firms have been able to master, from data collection to geological and ecological mapping to computer-aided visualizations of the future of entire regions. The model for these regional plans remains Calthorpe's LUTRAQ plan for Portland, as well as Calthorpe's subsequent work for Salt Lake City, "Envision Utah" (1999), and his "Southern California COMPASS Blueprint," which covers six counties, 184 cities, and more than 17 million people (Southern California Association of Governments 2005). Duany/Plater-Zyberk's "Miami 21" is important for reinterpreting the zoning code of a large city according to form-based code models (City of Miami 2010). In all these ways, New Urbanism might affect regional development far more deeply than a hundred isolated New Dalevilles.

Suburban retrofit, by contrast, refers to small-scale, highly focused attempts to bring walkability and mixed use to sites within an existing suburban fabric that was built on very different principles. Ideally, such retrofits seize on and complete regional initiatives, such as Moule & Polyzoides's Del Mar Transit Village, which takes a Pasadena transit stop on the new Los Angeles Gold light-rail line and creates a walkable center (Moule & Polyzoides 2003). In Bethesda, Maryland, planners are working to transform the underutilized area around the White Flint stop on the Washington, D.C., Metro into a compact transit village while converting the nearby traffic-clogged arterial, Rockville Pike, into a multiuse, walkable boulevard (Spivack 2009). Each revived light-rail line in older "first-ring" streetcar suburbs represents the possibility of multiple suburban retrofits along its line.

Other retrofits are more purely opportunistic, such as replacing a dead or dying mall (the supply of which should be ample in coming years) with a mixed use development that might grow into a viable town center. The model for these is Duany Plater-Zyberk & Company's Mashpee Commons, designed to replace a dead mall on Cape Cod with a New Urbanist community (Duany and Plater-Zyberk 1991, 74–76; Dunham-Jones and Williamson 2011, 95–107). The housing component has been slow to materialize, but their walkable town center was so convincing a reincarnation of the best New England village centers that it has flourished and inspired hundreds of pedestrian-oriented "lifestyle centers." Even in the most sprawled-out cul-de-sac subdivisions, there are possibilities for connecting the fragmented cul-de-sacs within a suburban superblock and thus creating a walkable environment where children especially can reach an elementary school, a park, and or local retail store without crossing a busy collector street or arterial (Duany, Plater-Zyberk, and Alminana 2003, 78). Compared to the larger hopes of fundamental suburban reconfiguration expressed in the 1996 CNU charter, these retrofits are necessarily modest; collectively, their impact could be significant.

New Urbanism, like all American reform movements, functions on the borderline of success and disappointment. New Urbanism has perhaps been most successful and lasting in the realm of organization. Its founders have built up a network of urban design firms that are crucial repositories of interdisciplinary skills and ideas, true successors to the Olmsted, Nolen, and Bartholomew firms that were responsible for so much that was best in early twentieth-century American urbanism. Like those firms, New Urbanism operates most successfully today when bringing together planning, urban design, and landscape architecture at scales from the neighborhood to the region. Moreover, the CNU, now headed by the former mayor of Milwaukee, John Norquist, remains a unique "public square" where the full range of actors responsible for our built environment can meet on equal terms. By contrast, New Urbanism, although founded by architects, has been most resisted as a style, especially in schools of architecture. Neotraditional design remains popular with the general public, but Krier's and Duany/Plater-Zyberk's hopes that it would replace modernism as the definitive style of our time have been disappointed.

Finally, New Urbanism as a movement in planning ideas faces an opposite challenge from what it faces in architecture. New Urbanism has become so intertwined with mainstream planning theory that the movement threatens to lose its identity among planners. New Urbanism's key ideas have been absorbed within such rubrics as "smart growth," "form-based codes," and "sustainable urbanism," and most recently by what HUD and DOT reports refer to simply as "livable communities" (U.S. Department of Transportation 2009). But planning *practice*, especially at the suburban fringe, has yet to change radically; exclusionary zoning, mandated sprawl, and subsidized automobility remain the rule. Still less has real estate development on the whole accepted the new paradigms that New Urbanism began advancing almost thirty years ago. New Urbanism is thus caught in a strange duality. Within planning theory, New Urbanism is close to achieving what is perhaps the ultimate accolade of any ideological movement: to be redundant. As a guide to action on the metropolitan scale, however, New Urbanism's work has only begun.

References

Abbott, C. 2000. The Capital of Good Planning: Metropolitan Portland since 1970. In *The American Planning Tradition: Culture and Policy*, ed. R. Fishman, 241–262. Baltimore, MD: Johns Hopkins University Press.

Ben-Joseph, E. 2005. *The Code of the City: Standards and the Hidden Language of Place Making*. Cambridge, MA: MIT Press.

Bothwell, S., R. Gindroz, and R. Lang. 1998. Restoring Community through Traditional Neighborhood Design: A Case Study of Diggs Town Public Housing. *Housing Policy Debate* 9 (1): 89–114.

Brain, D. 2005. From Good Neighborhoods to Sustainable Cities: Social Science and the Social Agenda of New Urbanism. *International Regional Science Review* 28 (2): 217–227.

Calthorpe, P. 1986. The Urban Context. In Van der Ryn and Calthorpe, *Sustainable Communities*, 1–33.

Calthorpe, P. 1993. *The Next American Metropolis: Ecology, Communities, and the American Dream*. New York: Princeton Architectural Press.

Calthorpe, P. 2005. New Urbanism: Principles or Style? In *New Urbanism: Peter Calthorpe vs. Lars Lerup*, ed. Robert Fishman, 16–39. Michigan Debates on Urbanism. Vol. 2. Ann Arbor: Taubman College of Architecture and Urban Planning, University of Michigan.

Calthorpe Associates. 1999. Stapleton. http://www.calthorpe.com/stapleton.

Calthorpe, P., and Mack, M. 1988. Pedestrian Pockets: New Strategies for Suburban Growth. *Northern California Real Estate Journal*, February 1, 1.

Calthorpe, P., and W. Fulton. 2001. *The Regional City*. Washington, DC: Island Press.

Cervero, R. 1984. Journal Report: Light Rail Transit and Urban Development. *Journal of the American Planning Association* 50 (2): 133–147.

City of Miami. 2010. Miami 21. http://www.miami21.org.

Congress for the New Urbanism. 1996. Charter of the New Urbanism. http://www.cnu.org/charter.

Creese, W., ed. 1967. *The Legacy of Raymond Unwin: A Human Pattern for Planning*. Cambridge, MA: MIT Press.

Davidoff, P., L. Davidoff, and N. Gold. 1970. Suburban Action: Advocate Planning for an Open Society. *Journal of the American Planning Association* 36 (1): 12–21.

Duany, A., and E. Plater-Zyberk, eds. 1991. *Towns and Town-making Principles*. New York: Rizzoli.

Duany, A., E. Plater-Zyberk, and R. Alminana. 2003. *The New Civic Art: Elements of Town Planning*. New York: Rizzoli.

Duany, A., E. Plater-Zyberk, and J. Speck. 2000. *Suburban Nation: The Rise of Sprawl and the Decline of the American Dream*. New York: North Point Press.

Duany, A., and E. Talen. 2002. Transect Planning. *Journal of the American Planning Association* 68:245–255.

Dunham-Jones, E., and J. Williamson. 2011. *Retrofitting Suburbia: Urban Design Solutions for Redesigning Suburbs*. Hoboken, NJ: Wiley.

Economakis, R., ed. 1992. *Leon Krier: Architecture and Urban Design, 1967–1992*. New York: St. Martin's Press.

Farr, D. 2008. *Sustainable Urbanism: Urban Design with Nature*. Hoboken, NJ: Wiley.

Fishman, R. 1977. *Urban Utopias in the Twentieth Century: Ebenezer Howard, Frank Lloyd Wright, and Le Corbusier*. New York: Basic Books.

Fishman, R. 1990. America's New City. *Wilson Quarterly* 14 (1): 24–55.

Fishman, R. 2008. New Urbanism in the Age of Re-Urbanism. In *New Urbanism and Beyond: Designing Cities for the Future*, ed. Tigran Haas. New York: Rizzoli.

Forsyth, A. 2005. *Reforming Suburbia: The Planned Communities Irvine, Columbia, and the Woodlands*. Berkeley: University of California Press.

Halprin, L. 1972. *The Willamette Valley: Choices for the Future*. Salem, OR: Willamette Valley Environmental Protection and Development Council.

Howard, E. (1898) 1965. *Garden Cities of To-morrow*. Cambridge, MA: MIT Press. First published as *To-morrow: A Peaceful Path to Real Reform*.

Hughes, M. 1971. *The Letters of Lewis Mumford and Frederic J. Osborn*. New York: Praeger.

Inskeep, S. 2008.The Exurbs: Houses, Cornfields, and Empty Lots. National Public Radio (transcript), August 22. http://www.npr.org/templates/story/story.php?storyId=93842128.

Jacobs, J. (1961) 1993. *The Death and Life of Great American Cities*. New York: Modern Library.

Kelbaugh, D. 1997. *Common Place: Toward Neighborhood and Regional Design*. Seattle: University of Washington Press.

Kelbaugh, D., ed. 1989. *The Pedestrian Pocket Book: A New Suburban Design Strategy*. New York: Princeton Architectural Press.

Krieger, A. 1991. Since (and before) Seaside, in Duany and Plater-Zyberk, *Towns and Town-making Principles*, 9–16.

Krier, L. 1991. Afterword to Duany and Plater-Zyberk, *Towns and Town-making Principles*, 117–119.

Lewis, Roger K. 1993, "New Urbanism" Congress Crusades for a Change. *Washington Post*, October 16, F4.

Leinberger, Christopher B. 2008. *The Option of Urbanism: Investing in a New American Dream*. Washington, DC: Island Press.

Local Government Commission. 2008. Original Ahwahnee Principles. http://www.lgc.org/ahwahnee/principles.html.

Mohney, D., and K. Easterling, eds. 1991. *Seaside: Making a Town in America*. New York: Princeton Architectural Press.

Moule & Polyzoides. 2003. Del Mar Station. http://www.mparchitects.com/projects/del_mar/index.html.

Mumford, L. 1963. *The Highway and the City*. New York: Harcourt. Title essay first published 1958 in *Architectural Record*.

Mumford, L. 1968a. Home Remedies for Urban Cancer. In *The Urban Prospect*. New York: Harcourt. First published 1962 as "Mother Jacobs' Home Remedies for Urban Cancer."

Mumford, L. 1968b. *The Urban Prospect*. New York: Harcourt.

Popkin, S., B. Katz, M. Cunningham, K. Brown, J. Gustafson, and M. Turner. 2004. *A Decade of HOPE VI: Research Findings and Policy Challenges*. Washington, DC: Urban Institute and Brookings Institution.

Prowler, D. 1989. Building with the Sun: An Architect Looks Back on the Rise and Fall of the Solar Movement and Reflects on Its Repercussions. *Metropolis* 8 (9): 74ff.

Redmon, K. 2010. The Man Who Reinvented the City: An Interview with Andres Duany. *Atlantic: Future of the City*, May 18. http://www.theatlantic.com/special-report/the-future-of-the-city/archive/2010/05/the-man-who-reinvented-the-city/56853.

Rossi, A. 1982. *The Architecture of the City*, trans. D. Ghirado and J. Ockman. Cambridge, MA: MIT Press.

Rybczynski, W. 2007. *Last Harvest: How a Cornfield Became New Daleville*. New York: Scribner.

Schaffer, D. 1982. *Garden Cities for America: The Radburn Experience*. Philadelphia: Temple University Press.

Scully, V. 1991. Seaside and New Haven. In *Towns and Town-making Principles*, ed. A. Duany and E. Plater-Zyberk, 17–20. New York: Rizzoli.

Solomon, D. 2003. *Global City Blues*. Washington, DC: Island Press.

Solomon E. T. C. 2005. Othello Station, Seattle, WA. http://www.wrtdesign.com/projects/detail/Holly-Park-Othello-Station/8.

Southern California Association of Governments. 2005. Southern California Compass Blueprint. www.Compassblueprint.org.

Spivack, M. 2009. High-Rise Hopes along Rockville Pike. *Washington Post*, March 19, B1.

Stern, R., and Massengale, J. 1981. The Anglo-American Suburb. *Architectural Design* 51 (10–11).

Swenarton, M. 2008. *Building the New Jerusalem: Architecture, Housing, and Politics 1900–1930*. Bracknell, UK: IHS BRE Press.

Talen, E. 2005. *New Urbanism and American Planning: The Conflict of Cultures*. New York: Routledge.

Torti Gallas and Partners. 1998. King Plaza Neighborhood Revitalization. http://www.tortigallas.com/project.asp?p=50202.

U.S. Department of Transportation. 2009. HUD and DOT Partnership. March 18. http://www.dot.gov/affairs/dot3209.htm

U.S. Environmental Protection Agency. 2010. Residential Construction Trends in America's Metropolitan Regions. http://www.epa.gov/piedpage/pdf/metro_res_const_trends_10.pdf.

Unwin, R. (1909). 1994. *Town Planning in Practice: An Introduction to the Art of Designing Cities and Suburbs*. London: Unwin.

Vale, L. 2002. *Reclaiming Public Housing: A Half-Century of Struggle in Three Public Neighborhoods*. Cambridge, MA: Harvard University Press.

Van der Ryn, S., and P. Calthorpe, eds. 1986. *Sustainable Communities: A New Design Synthesis for Cities, Suburbs, and Towns*. San Francisco: Sierra Club Books.

Venturi, R. 1966. *Complexity and Contradiction in Architecture*. New York: Museum of Modern Art.

Venturi, R., D. Scott Brown, and S. Izenour. (1972) 1977. *Learning from Las Vegas: The Forgotten Symbolism of Architectural Form*. Cambridge, MA: MIT Press.

Weiss, M. 2000. Within Neighborhoods . . . an Authentic Community. In *The Charter of the New Urbanism*, ed. M. Leccese and K. McCormick, 89–96. New York: McGraw-Hill.

4

Sustainability in Planning: The Arc and Trajectory of a Movement, and New Directions for the Twenty-First-Century City

Timothy Beatley

The Evolution of a Compelling Idea and Vision

There has been a remarkable global emergence of new commitments to sustainability since 2000, with sustainability taking center stage as a major new paradigm in planning. Andrés Edwards in his recent book calls it the "sustainability revolution," or "a pervasive and permanent shift in consciousness and worldview affecting all facets of society" (Edwards 2005, 2). He notes the similarities between the sustainability revolution and the Industrial Revolution, including the emergence of support for sustainability across diverse sectors of society and the involvement of a fast-growing set of organizations, interest groups, individuals working on behalf of sustainability under a decentralized leadership. Sustainability has also been described as the next wave of innovation, following on the heels of the information age and taking us in profoundly new directions in respect to renewable energy, green chemistry, and resource efficiency.

Arguably, there is nothing especially new about the core values of sustainability: thinking long term and many generations into the future, using caution and care in allocating resources, understanding that there are limits beyond which serious degradation and loss of productive capacity will occur, and living off the ecological interest (e.g., using renewable resources such as timber, some fish stocks, and replenished groundwater). Native American culture and history, for instance, show evidence of sustainable thinking and living (the Iroquois seventh generation rule[1]), as, later, do the conservation movement and national park movement. Early conservation leaders, such as Gifford Pinchot, the first director of the U.S. Forest Service, argued that forests should be managed and their harvesting carefully regulated to ensure production in perpetuity. This is a goal we still espouse, however hard it has been to put into practice. The perspective was (and is) highly anthropocentric, of course, and it is the human economic value of these resources that requires their long-term management and stewardship. As Pinchot eloquently wrote more than a century ago, "Are we going to protect our springs of prosperity, our raw material of industry and commerce and employer of capital and labor combined; or are we going to dissipate them? According as we accept or ignore our responsibility as trustees of the nation's welfare, our children and our children's children for uncounted generations will call us blessed, or will lay their suffering at our doors" (Pinchot 1908, 12). Exhausting or squandering our natural resources is wrong and unwise, and much of the armature of contemporary conservation and environmental management aims in one way or another to affect this conservation ethic. Our understanding of sustainable resource management has become more nuanced, then, and we now understand the need to look at forests as more than tree crops, preserve biodiversity as well as timber, and take into account new concerns about recreation, viewsheds, and other important values.

Sustainability, then, has been largely about how to wisely use natural resources of various kinds—forests, fisheries, productive soil. *Sustainable* is a modifier or adjective attached to a number of conventional and long-standing activities, done in a different way: sustainable fisheries management, sustainable forestry, sustainable agriculture. And here the operational meaning of sustainability has perhaps been the clearest: extract or harvest only that amount that will ensure the resource continues in perpetuity. Though the term sustainability is a more recent usage, emerging as these ideas began to find meaning applied more broadly to international and economic development projects, these early concepts of natural resource management represent the primary definition and one that continues today.

Legislation such as the U.S. Marine Mammal Protection Act of 1972 enshrined these concepts, in this case by seeking optimal sustainable populations, and the International Union for Conservation of Nature and Natural Resources (IUCN) in *World Conservation Strategy* put forth the notion of "sustainable utilization," which it defined as being "somewhat analogous to spending the interest while keeping the capital. A society that insists that all utilization of living resources be sustainable ensures that it will benefit from those resources virtually indefinitely" (IUCN 1980, 9). These basic conservation values continue to be important, but since the 1970s they have matured to offer a more capacious perspective on the natural environment, one that sees forests as complex ecosystems and thus must be managed to protect the larger interests and values they support, including recreation and biodiversity conservation (Lindenmayer and Franklin 2002).

Our more contemporary sustainability thinking has also recognized that the extent and severity of the ecological impacts of human action are much greater than was understood by the earlier conservationists. The sustainability literature and thinking that blossomed in the early 1970s introduced into popular culture the concept of limits and the possibilities of thresholds beyond which resource use, consumption, and population growth could result in crashes of these systems, a concept that built on the insights and research made available by biologists and ecologists. Donella Meadows and co-authors in *The Limits to Growth* (1974) saw the possibility of systemic limits, or limits to the ability of the larger global ecosystems to absorb and accommodate such extreme human pressures on planet Earth. Through these seminal studies, Meadows and her colleagues helped to apply ideas from biological and ecological thinking to the larger societal and economic systems (Meadows et al. 1974; Meadows, Randers, and Meadows 1993, 2004). That human action could result in global resource crashes was a relatively new idea, echoed by other writers of the time such as Paul Ehrlich, notably in *The Population Bomb* (1968), and while the specific predictions remain debated, the focus on limits and thresholds, and on living and designing within limits, whether designing a watershed, a groundwater aquifer, or global fisheries and food supply, along with the urgency of change, remains an important mental framework for planners.

Major international meetings and expressions of sustainability values include the 1972 UN Conference on the Human Environment (the Stockholm Conference), the World Commission on Environment and Development (the so-called Brundtland Commission, after its chair, Gro Brundtland, prime minister of Norway), the 1992 Rio Conference, and more recently the World Summit on Sustainability, held in Johannesburg in 2002. The Brundtland Commission and its 1987 report, *Our Common Future*, are viewed as especially influential and have produced what is perhaps the most commonly invoked definition: sustainable development is development that "meets the needs of the present without compromising the ability of future generations to meet their own needs" (World Commission on Environment and Development 1987, 8). As vague as this definition is, it embraces a profound ethical reorientation toward the future and has been something of battle cry and mantra over the past several decades.

That the world has changed in significant ways from the early heady period of optimism of the conservation movement is undeniable. The environmental problems we face today are more severe than ever before, and our understanding of them is much greater. Global climate change, loss of biodiversity, the global crash of fisheries, the continued loss of tropical rain forests, and the general downward slide of every major ecosystem type are all indicative of the seriousness of the problems faced today. It is important, nevertheless, to acknowledge that sustainability as a concept and practice exists in a political context, and that while most in the planning field recognize the importance of sustainability, this view is not universal. While there is much consensus on the need to tackle problems such as global warming, there is also much controversy and disagreement, even over the science and reality of this topic, and objections based on ideological grounds to sustainability projects and policies are now commonplace.

Despite these controversies and disagreements, sustainability has emerged as an important new lens through which to understand resource allocation and planning policy. What is different now about sustainability, and how has the concept evolved? To summarize: sustainability essentially began as a rubric for understanding and moderating the use and exploitation of exhaustible resources (forests, fisheries, soil), guided by a scientific understanding of limits from biology and ecology, but the concept has evolved to encompass much more in its twenty-first-century incarnation. Today, sustainability is understood as also being about cities and the built environment, about the social and the economic as much as the ecological; and it is now permeating and penetrating cultural consciousness in a way earlier versions did not. Much of the activity and activism is bubbling up from the bottom, and sustainability is no longer confined to the realm of experts in state and federal offices. The language of our society and culture has changed.

From Sustainable Development to Sustainable Cities

The sustainability agenda has been decidedly nonurban (and pertaining to the non-built environment) for much of its history. Since the late 1960s, however, the language of "sustainable communities" and "sustainable cities" has entered the collective lexicon. The 1987 Brundtland Commission's report, *Our Common Future*, includes a chapter on cities, emphasizing especially the urban challenges of the developing world. Little of the language of sustainable or ecological cities can be found here, though there is much discussion about the need to address urban poverty and housing inadequacy in cities in the developing world, problems that remain salient.

The interest in a more central role for communities and cities in the sustainability agenda is rooted in the activism and growing environmental awareness of the 1960s and early 1970s. Ernest Callenbach's profoundly prescient novel, *Ecotopia,* published in 1975, predicted many of the sustainability ideas for living and planning that we are still working hard to flesh out and implement: people living in mixed use, compact, car-free "mini-cities," whisked about by maglev trains, repairing and reinvigorating the green and natural within and around cities, profoundly rethinking material goods and consumption, and generally living richly with less (Callenbach 1975). While the premise of the novel—the prospect of the Northwest seceding from the United States—remains far-fetched, many of the ideas and technologies and new patterns of ecological living have come to fruition in one place or another. And the interest in bioregions remains a powerful prompt for reconnecting humans to culture and nature, and for organizing policy and settlement planning around units of nature that make more sense.

In constructing the family tree of sustainability, we see that key early thinkers who saw the city as an ecological system loom prominently. Richard Register has been a key proponent of ecological cities, and *EcoCity Berkeley,* first published in 1987, is an important aid to imagining what a sustainable urban future might look like. Register—and others—argues for ecocities, and the need to view cities as ecological systems. He has stimulated similar ecocity organizations and activities in other cities, from Cleveland to Adelaide, Australia, and has organized a series of yearly international ecocity conferences. Also a talented artist, Register has been able to visually articulate this ecocity vision. His depictions of "integral neighborhoods," with streams, nature, and food production integrated with other living structures in dense, walkable, built form (featuring solar panels and small wind turbines on the rooftops), have helped inspire the real thing in many cities (Register 1987, 2006). Rutherford Platt has also written about and passionately advocated for ecological cities, an essentially very similar agenda, and has organized or helped organize a series of public forums around the country to advance this agenda (Platt, Rowntree, and Muick 1994).

Antecedents of contemporary community sustainability owe much as well to the think of visionary Italian architect Paolo Soleri, who began building Arcosanti in 1970, in the high desert of Arizona. Meant to represent a prototype of what Soleri calls *arcology* (architecture plus ecology), Arcosanti is a physically small but important model of a compact pedestrian community, based on capturing sun and daylight. The buildings in Arcosanti have a distinctive apse design, a kind of dome sliced in half, capturing the sun, providing shade at important times, and establishing open connections to environment and sky (Soleri 2006). In harmony with the surrounding natural environment, producing much of its own food through greenhouses, gardens, and orchards, and pro-foundly connected to place (and the deep Native American history of settlement in the Arizona desert), Arcosanti inspires well beyond its modest physical dimensions. And the model continues to teach: on a recent visit I was suprised to discover that Soleri's vertical structures incorporate into their rooftop design angled seats for viewing the night-time sky (fig. 4.1).

One of the first applications of the language and thinking of sustain-ability to mainstream planning was Seattle's innovative 1994 com-prehensive plan. Subtitled "Toward a Sustainable Seattle," the plan was

Figure 4.1
Arcosanti. Paolo Soleri's ideas for merging architecture and ecology, what he calls arcology, found early tangible expression in Arcosanti, a green community in the high desert of Arizona. Arcosanti has been Soleri's laboratory for trying out and testing ideas for sustainable living and building. *Photo*: Timothy Beatley.

organized around three values: environmental stewardship, social equity, and economic opportunity and security, an early expression of the three E's—environment, economics, and equity—that has been a touchstone of sustainability, and its perceived advantage to many of expanding the scope beyond a single-minded focus on environment to consider the fairness of the distribution of resources and opportunities in society ("sustainable for whom") and the essential role of economics in any push in this direction. Gary Lawrence, then planning director for the city of Seattle and now director of corporate sustainability for Aecom, shepherded the plan along. It sought to capture much of the regional population growth, steering it into an innovative network (and hierarchy) of urban villages that reflects (still) many of the qualities we believe sustainable places should exhibit: access to transit, the mixing of uses and activities, and vibrant pedestrian-oriented places.

Cities and Buildings to the Fore

Many cities around the world have now developed comprehensive green plans, or sustainability plans, and recent history is impressive for the ambitious reach and scope of those efforts. Cities like Copenhagen have recently declared their intention to become "ecometropoles" and have laid out ambitious targets (e.g., the goal of 50 percent of home-to-work trips made by bicycle by 2015; City of Copenhagen 2007). London and may other cities have laid out impressive energy and climate change strategies. In the United States, almost every major city has developed or is in the process of developing an ambitious green plan and a sustainability plan, and there has emerged a friendly competition between cities such as Chicago and New York as to which will be the greenest. An agenda increasingly championed by mayors, it is testament to the gathering political and popular support these issues enjoy. New York's PlaNYC 2030, while experiencing some significant setbacks (including a state legislature that objected to congestion pricing), sets out an impressive agenda and a compelling vision for a (more) sustainable future (City of New York 2008). As of February 2009, more than nine hundred U.S. cities had signed on to the Mayors Climate Protection Agreement, indicative of the growing popular and political support for sustainable cities.

The last several decades have seen the emergence of new research and thinking that support the importance of urban form and city planning in reducing the extent of environmental damage and resource consumption (see Newman and Kenworthy 1999). Many in planning now commonly advocate the importance of investments in public transit (which is much more energy efficient on an energy per passenger mile basis) and the environmental benefits of walkable and bikeable cities and urban living environments (Beatley 2000; Girardet 2008; Newman and Jennings 2008). It is natural, then, that sustainability should take an urban turn, both because of the growing impact of built environments and because of the potential for urban design and planning, and urban lifestyles, to offer viable possibilities for sustainable living (fig. 4.2).

Sustainable cities, and ideas of green urbanism, have emerged as a compelling model for translating broad sustainability goals and aspirations into tangible physical and social outcomes. The trend has been in the direction of understating the need for more holistic urban strategies, and the best examples of sustainable cities, from Freiburg, Germany, to Curitiba, Brazil, are those that take this holistic and integrated approach. Their leadership recognizes the need to do many things at once—to address compact urban form, sustainable transport, energy efficiency and

Figure 4.2
Bicycles, Copenhagen. Cities are looking for ways to reduce dependence on cars and their emission of carbon dioxide. Copenhagen has worked hard to create a bicycle-friendly city and today nearly 40 percent of home-to-work trips are made by bicycle. The city is doing even more, recently declaring its bold intention to be the first carbon-neutral capital city. *Photo:* Timothy Beatley

green building, and recycling and zero-waste techniques, among many others—and to understand how each policy and planning sector can help strengthen and reinforce the other. They are, moreover, places where a new culture of green governance prevails, where the governing of the city itself, from its procurement policies to what it builds or commissions to be built to how it manages it buildings, parks, and streets, shifts to both reduce impacts and set the example and tone for other sectors in society. San Francisco has formally adopted the precautionary principle[2] as a specific expression of what sustainability requires, with serious implications for how it manages its parks and facilities (avoiding the use of pesticides and herbicides) and strong support for renewable energy and green building, sustainable transport (e.g., City Carshare), and ambitious recycling targets. Many cities, from Seattle to Melbourne to Den Haag, have adopted some form of sustainability indicators or "green accounts" that assess how well they are doing on a range of specific sustainability measures and help judge the extent of progress in meeting sustainability goals.

The sustainability movement builds on and gains strength and relevance from other social policy traditions, especially public health policies, and the goal of creating healthy cities, a vision that can certainly be seen in the sanitation-reform era and in efforts to create more healthful urban living conditions. The more recent concerns about sedentary lifestyles and increasing obesity rates reflect this synergy. Planners find strong endorsement from the public health community for compact, walkable communities that get people out of their cars. And sustainable communities that facilitate social interaction and extend and expand friendship networks are similarly supported by research findings on healthy behavior.

There is a helpful unity of purpose between designing healthier homes and buildings (e.g., structures with abundant daylight and natural ventilation) and those that are less energy and resource consumptive, and indeed, the arena of green building has been one of the emerging success stories. While principles and practices that we might think of as green design and green architecture have been around for a long time (e.g., designing pre-air-conditioned structures to take advantage of the stack effect and natural ventilation), an explicit, institutionalized interest in green building is relatively new. Milestones include the formation in 1989 of the AIA Committee on the Environment, and the nation's first local green building program—the Austin, Texas, Green Star rating system—in 1992. There is little doubt that popular interest in and governmental and political support for green building have risen dramatically in recent years, as evidenced by the interest in the LEED—Leadership in Energy and Environmental Design—certification programs of the U.S. Green Building Council. LEED certification began only in 2000, and already there are more than 2,200 structures certified, with the number growing each year. Membership in the U.S. Green Building Council has quadrupled since 2000, and each year the annual conference Greenbuild grows substantially in size. Growing interest in green building and sustainability has been accompanied by the birth of new public and private institutions and organizations, and new regulatory and planning requirements.

A number of cities have now established offices or agencies that carry the sustainability moniker in one way or another. Often they are within a mayor's office, as in the case of Oakland's Office of Sustainability. New York was one of the first cities to give sustainability practice and ideas clear visibility in its governance structure. It created the Office of Sustainable Design, housed within the City's Department of Design and Construction in 1997, on the leading edge. This office was instrumental in crafting the city's innovative High Performance Design Guidelines and jump-starting the impressive emphasis on green building that has taken place there. Strolling around Battery Park, it is hard to deny the green progress, and green appeals made to prospective condo buyers and renters—The Solaire, for instance, completed in 2003, touts its status as the country's first green residential office tower and integrates a number of impressive green features (fig. 4.3).

Expanding the Impact of Sustainable Design and Development

In places like Battery Park, there is a nagging concern that the agenda of sustainability is more about selling and marketing than reality. This remains a worry, probably an inevitable by-product of a diverse movement, early enough in its development that there is little professional agreement or standard setting (the U.S. Green Building Council's LEED standards notwithstanding) about what constitutes green buildings, or green *anything*. There also remains concern that sustainability and green urbanism are the domain of the affluent and wealthy. The new condos in Battery Park are perhaps more affordable than in many other parts of Manhattan, but they still assume a high degree of wealth and status. There is an understandable skepticism that green ideas and technologies may fail to be applied to improving the lives of the poor and less

Figure 4.3
The Solaire, NYC. The Solaire, located in Battery Park in New York, is purported to be the world's first green residential tower and is LEED-certified. The building incorporates a number of green features, including a green rooftop, facade-mounted photovoltaic cells, and a wastewater recycling system. *Photo:* Timothy Beatley.

affluent. This concern is born, perhaps, from the early application of environmental and conservation design principles most frequently to wealthy enclaves (e.g., coastal communities such as Sanibel, Florida) and more affluent liberal (often university) communities (e.g., Boulder, Colorado, and Burlington, Vermont). There are now, however, many good examples of green building and projects undertaken in the context of affordable housing and improving the livability of less affluent neighborhoods. Solara, near San Diego, boasts that it is the first affordable housing project in the country "fully powered by the sun," while Colorado Court, in Santa Monica, integrates impressive sustainability features into a single-room-occupancy (SRO) building (fig. 4.4). In Chicago, architect Helmut Jahn has designed a LEED-certified SRO building adjacent to the redevelopment site of the Cabrini-Green housing project, and several public housing redevelopment schemes under HUD's HOPE VI program have made use of green technologies, including green roofs in Milwaukee and a LEED-certified midrise residential building at Boston's Maverick Gardens development.

Figure 4.4
Colorado Court, Santa Monica. Colorado Court, located in Santa Monica, California, is a single-room-occupancy project and shows the possibilities of merging low-income housing and green design. The building produces almost all of its own energy, with much of it coming from visually dramatic, facade-mounted photovoltaic panels. *Photo:* Timothy Beatley.

Planners and others increasingly understand sustainability as an avenue for improving the quality of life of the most disenfranchised, most disadvantaged communities and neighborhoods, and if ever the need existed for housing and living environments with lower footprints, it is in these communities. Colorado Court produces almost all of its own power on-site through a combination of visually dramatic, facade-mounted photovoltaic cells and a small, natural gas–powered cogeneration plant, and residents pay no monthly utility bills. Car-free or car-limited housing projects, advocated by many in the sustainability community, are promising in part because they have the potential to profoundly lower the cost of living. While there are plenty of cars in Solara, this solar complex has been located near shopping, and all new residents are given a specially designed rollable shopping cart and encouraged to do their shopping without the car.

An optimistic shift has been an expansion of the base of green urbanism in cities to more communities of color and more disenfranchised neighborhoods and parts of cities. With guidance from urban leaders such as Van Jones and Majora Carter, the green urban agenda has been transformed, recast from a slightly elitist interest to one that understands the importance of green rooftops, rain gardens, and community farms as generators of employment and community vitality and renewal. The application of green design principles to affordable housing reflects a similar sentiment: part social justice, part pragmatism. The environmental justice movement has become more urban focused in recent years, with promising results. Carter founded the organization Sustainable South Bronx essentially to find ways to merge the green and the social equity agendas, and has taken on a host of green projects: creating jobs in this struggling borough by training residents to do urban greening, creating new parks and spaces that improve the quality of the living environment (e.g., the South Bronx Greenway), and organizing politically to resist land-use decisions that undermine the neighborhood (e.g., the imposition of new prisons or waste management facilities). The Bronx Environmental Stewardship Training (BEST) program exemplifies this push to train residents to assume "green-collar jobs," including such pursuits as urban horticulture, green rooftop installation, and remediation work on brownfield sites. The vision is to understand the imperatives of the new green urbanism as an opportunity to generate jobs and expand economic opportunity in economically challenged neighborhoods like the South Bronx.

The work of organizations like Sustainable South Bronx illustrate the emergence of a larger concern about the need to promote and advance *social sustainability*, a term increasingly invoked in many places, as well as the more common *ecological sustainability*. Some have bemoaned the creation of a yet more ambiguous notion of sustainability, but this does show the positive trend of giving importance given to the third E (or third leg of the stool in some sustainability models): the equity and the social dimension. Social sustainability generally encompasses efforts at promoting diversity in a community, facilitating engagement by all groups and sectors, systematically understanding the social impacts of projects and initiatives, overcoming economic and other inequities, and addressing the special needs of certain groups in the community, notably the young, the old, and the less able. Some communities have prepared social sustainability plans or special procedures and processes for taking social impacts into account. The city of Boulder, Colorado, for instance, adopted a Social Sustainability Strategic Plan in 2007 that identifies key social goals, strategies, and action items (City of Boulder 2007). Among the specific proposals are the creation of a social sustainability screen for evaluating proposed city projects, further underwriting of child care for low-income working families, and increasing the transportation options for the elderly.

The economic downturn of 2008 and high unemployment in the global North have raised new concerns about social equity and created new challenges to moving forward on sustainability. In some interesting ways, however, the economic crisis has helped shift some individual and household decisions in the direction of sustainability—more people using public transit, more regarding the home as a long-term residence than as a temporary investment, and a reduced consumption of some material goods—though the longer term staying power of these changes remains unclear. In the global South, alleviating poverty must remain a goal on par with sustainability. Improving jobs and livelihoods and providing food, water, and health care in informal settlements, where much of the population growth is and will be in the future, must be undertaken at the same time that the planet focuses on reducing the drawdown of global resources.

New Ways of Seeing Cities

Biophilic Cities
Another challenge is how we design and build and restore our cities in ways that incorporate nature. A growing chorus of voices points to the need for biophilic design and biophilic cities, building on the impetus

E. O. Wilson gave to the concept of biophilia—that we have coevolved for millennia to need direct contact with nature (Wilson 1984, 1993). The compactness and density that many argue are necessary for sustainable cities sometimes make integrating nature difficult. Nevertheless, progress in mainstreaming urban greening techniques and technologies has been impressive. Green rooftops have become a priority in many American cities. An example is Chicago, where former mayor Richard M. Daley's City Hall retrofit and support for green rooftops has yielded impressive results, with more than 450 green rooftops either built or in development. The urban greening ideas are both large and small: tree planting, converting turfgrass landscapes into native prairies, making green walls (such as Patrick Blanc's beautiful designs in Paris and elsewhere; fig. 4.5), creating rain gardens and bioswales, and even using urban stream daylighting, in which formerly piped underground streams are brought back to the surface and routed through urban neighborhoods.

In part, urban biophilic design entails restoring the habitats and environments already in place but degraded or overlooked, such as the restoration of the Los Angeles River, Jamaica Bay in New York, and the Buffalo Bayou in Houston. The agenda is difficult to execute, certainly, but proponents of biophilic design argue that there need be no conflict between the natural and the urban, and indeed, we increasingly acknowledge that a healthy urban life requires access to the natural world in all its forms. Along with this emerging sense of the importance (and feasibility) of urban nature is a reassessment of the very meaning of nature and natural wildness itself. The American conservation story was born from a myth of pristine, Arcadian nature, with at least a hidden bias in favor of natural features that fit this mental image. Increasingly we appreciate that there is also inherent worth in everyday or common nature, in the highly altered landscapes and features close to where most Americans live. We need to foster this different natural sensibility, to be sure, but there is little doubt that experience shows the value—psychological, social, even economic—of these smaller, less visually dramatic snippets of wildness.

The environmental movement has shown an anti-urban bias for much of its history, and this bias continues to haunt planning. Even today, most major books on the environment and environmental management and policy usually depict a more "natural" setting as the jacket image—a shot of a national park such as Yosemite, say, or of a pristine wetland or coastal marsh, usually without any apparent indication of human presence. This is changing with the emergence of grassroots sustainability

Figure 4.5
Patrick Blanc vertical garden, Paris. One of the Patrick Blanc's beautiful vertical gardens, at the Musée du Quai Branley, Paris. These green walls provoke a reconsideration of how and where nature might enter the city, and suggest there will be many creative and unusual opportunities for biophilic urbanism. *Photo:* Timothy Beatley.

organizations, such as Sustainable South Bronx, and some national environmental groups, such as the Trust for Public Land, now with a major focus on cities. Bette Midler's New York Restoration Project, the result of a fight to preserve small community gardens, is another example of the shift toward urban environmentalism.

Over time, planners began to realize that there were newer and more effective ways to garner popular and political support for planning conducted on the lines of urban ecological principles, and special value in emphasizing the important (and free) ecological services provided by natural systems. "Green infrastructure" and "ecological infrastructure" have become common terms in environmental planning, the new language in which to speak of wetlands, forests, and riverine systems. That nature needs protecting and restoring because of the many utilitarian benefits and values these systems provide—better air quality, water supply and water pollution amelioration, stormwater retention—remains a powerful conceptual framework. The utilitarian arguments in turn are increasingly expressed in terms of economic values, as organizations such as American Forests have developed economic models that can translate forest canopy cover into specific dollar estimates of the value of these otherwise free ecological services (e.g., American Forests 2001).

Understanding nature and natural systems as often viable and more effective substitutes for engineering and engineered structures is also part of this evolution. Wetlands are often more effective in controlling and retaining floodwaters than are engineered (and expensive) conventional flood control measures.

These promising trends can be seen in many specific planning tools, techniques, and ideas. Low-impact development, or essentially smaller, decentralized stormwater management techniques—including tree planting and installing green rooftops, but also creating rain gardens and bioswales and using permeable pavement techniques—emerged as a significant package of practice options and ideas in the 1980s. These modest, low-impact management techniques show a profoundly different way of thinking about urban infrastructure, one that questions the value and utility of large-scale solutions, notably centralized pipe and gutter stormwater collection.

And these new decentralized technologies and techniques in turn nurture (and are nurtured by) new aesthetic sensibilities. The centralized engineering attitude toward stormwater was always one that saw a problem, saw water as something that needed to be taken away, hidden from sight, collected, and transported, not unlike the prevailing view of cars and traffic—the faster the better, with efficiency and success measured in terms of gallons per minute flow and the absence of any standing (unsightly) water following rain events. That view has changed dramatically. Many planners, elected officials, and the general public now hold a different view: water in all its forms, including stormwater, can and should be celebrated. It should be made visible and be a visible part of neighborhoods. The rain garden becomes an important visual reference point and a connection to watershed and environment that is missing from the engineering approach.

Cities Inspired by Nature

Much of the new importance given to cities is a recognition of the ultimate source of environmental and resource consumption, as well as a recognition of where the real potential for a more sustainable future lies. Bill Rees and Mathis Wackernagel's work in developing the ecological footprint as an educational model has profoundly reshaped our perceptions of the problem (Wackernagel and Rees 1998). The connection between the modern lifestyle and the loss of tropical rain forests, increased carbon emissions, and the consumption of nonrenewable fuels to produce food and heat homes is now much more evident. The ecological footprint concept and method (what Rees originally called ecological footprint analysis) profoundly shifted our collective understanding of cities, which depend on an extensive hinterland, extracting and appropriating the carrying capacities of regions and countries far away. And, at least for northern industrial cities, this footprint is growing in both reach and size. A recent study of London's ecological footprint, for example, found that the land area needed to support this city of eight million was nearly three hundred times the size of the city itself. The numbers also offer hope and guidance for change, however: in the case of London, much of the footprint is associated with the importation of food over long distance, a boost to the efforts of advocates of local and regional food production.

The concept of the ecological footprint fosters a view of a city as an organic entity, analogous to the human body, requiring inputs and generating outputs. The last several decades have seen a rise in explicit efforts to apply organic or natural models of how nature works, and what might be learned from natural models, to the design of buildings and cities. Janine Benyus's groundbreaking book *Biomimicry* (1997) has been instrumental, as has been the inspiring design work of architect William McDonough (McDonough and Braungart 2002). McDonough is famous for imploring us to design "buildings like trees, cities like forests" (McDonough 2002). A city that functions like a tree is a model for our time, as we imagine cities that are carbon neutral and energy balanced (i.e., producing as much power as they need, and surviving within the limits of current solar income), that are zero waste, and that integrate and celebrate diversity (from which cities will become more resilient in the face of climate change and a highly dynamic world). McDonough and his colleagues have managed to build structures that, while not perfect examples, do almost function as trees do. The Environmental Studies building at Oberlin College, for instance, produces more energy than it needs, collects and treats all of its stormwater on site, and treats its wastewater through a solar-aquatic "living machine" (treating and breaking down waste through a systems of plants, aquatic species, and microorganisms in compact vertical tanks). The bigger challenge is to scale up the organic model to operate at the level of a city and region, and it is this challenge that links the sustainability enterprise most closely to planning.

The growing importance of biomimicry—imitating and learning from nature—in design, policy, and engineering is undeniable, and it is exciting to imagine how future cities and urban environments might be reshaped in ways that are informed and inspired by nature. Buildings and urban built environments have already exhibited biomimical insights. Green building design is perhaps the place where biomimicry is most evident, but there is increasing potential to apply the natural principles and design standards found and tested in nature to cities. Table 4.1 presents Benyus's ten design strategies from nature. Each has obvious and significant appli-

Table 4.1
City Design Based on Principles of Biomimicry

  1. Use waste as a resource.
  2. Diversify and cooperate to fully use the habitat.
  3. Gather and use energy efficiently.
  4. Optimize rather than maximize.
  5. Use materials sparingly.
  6. Don't foul their nests.
  7. Don't draw down resources.
  8. Remain in balance with the biosphere.
  9. Run on information.
 10. Shop locally.

Source: Benyus (1997).

cations to cities. One of the early examples of a building based on biomimicry is the Harare office complex called Eastgate. Designed by Zimbabwean architect Michael Pearce, the complex is inspired by the design of termite colonies and specifically deploys the techniques they use to maintain a constant temperature and humidity. Like a termite mound, Eastgate draws its air in from the base of the building, cools the air by sending it underground, and then circulates this air up and through the structure. There are other examples of sustainable city design and living that find inspiration and guidance from nature, such as the design of the Japanese Shinkansen bullet train, with a nose form based on the kingfisher's beak (Bird 2008). Other possibilities include producing energy in cities through photovoltaics with improved efficiency, designed using plant leaves as a model: improving the efficiency of wind turbine blades by learning from the surface mechanics of humpback whale flippers (which have bumps that greatly improve efficiency); and extracting potable drinking water from humid air by studying the anatomy of insects, which do this with great efficiency. Benyus argues that it makes little sense to ignore the 3.8 billion years of research and development in the natural world from which humans could extract knowledge applicable to their own needs.

Cities are in many ways analogous to living organisms—they require material inputs for survival, produce waste, and have a complex and interconnected metabolism. Yet our city planning and urban management policies often fail to acknowledge this complex metabolism. We treat the inputs and outputs and the resources discretely and individually, not holistically. Our move toward sustainable cities will require an important shift in thinking about cities not as linear resource-extracting machines but as complex metabolic systems with flows and cycles. Ideally, those outputs that have traditionally been viewed as negative, such as solid waste and wastewater, will be reenvisioned as productive inputs to satisfy other urban needs, including the need for food, energy, and clean water. A sustainable urban metabolism drives toward several goals at once: reducing the extent of the material and resource flows required, converting linear flows to circular flows (closing loops), and sourcing and deriving the inputs in the most equitable and least ecologically destructive way possible.

The Metabolism of Cities

Understanding the nature and magnitude of the resource flows required of a city is a first step, and few cities and regions have undertaken it.

The Greater London Authority commissioned such a study, which has set the stage for a number of sustainability plans and initiatives there. *City Limits: A Resource Flow and Ecological Footprint Analysis of Greater London,* completed in 2002, yields a comprehensive picture of the flows and resource demands of this metro region of about eight million (Greater London Authority 2002). Among its key findings: Londoners require almost 50 million tons of materials (including building materials and food) and generate 26 million tons of waste (fig. 4.6). Most of its critical inputs, such as food and energy, are imported and derived from unsustainable sources.

The Greater London Authority has now produced a series of impressive regional strategic plans that seek to address these unsustainable material flows, including an energy strategy that sets ambitious carbon dioxide reduction targets and identifies a variety of strategies to conserve energy and produce renewables (including at least one new zero-energy development in each of the city's thirty-four boroughs). A new regional food strategy calls for more local production and processing (shortening the supply lines) and from more sustainable means.

One of the best examples of a new housing project with a sustainable material flow orientation is BedZED, or Beddington Zero Energy Development, in the London borough of Sutton. BedZED has incorporated explicit utilities for local materials. This innovative green project reflects an effort to tackle unsustainable resource flows and to achieve a more sustainable, circular urban metabolism. More than half of the materials have come from within a thirty-five-mile radius. Wood siding comes from local municipal forests, and bricks are produced by a local brick company (fig. 4.7).

Few urban places have done as much to put the idea into practice as Swedish cities, especially Stockholm. Its various municipal departments and agencies have sought to coordinate their work and to take a comprehensive material and resource flows approach. Stockholm's new urban ecological district, Hammarby Sjöstad, is an extremely powerful example of how a metabolic flows perspective can result in a new approach to urban design and building in a new, dense urban neighborhood. An effort was made to think holistically, to understand the inputs, outputs, and resources that would be required and would result. Figure 4.8 depicts these flows and shows how they were deliberately connected, with substantial energy and conservation benefits. For instance, about a thousand flats in Hammarby Sjöstad are equipped with biogas stoves that utilize biogas extracted from wastewater generated in the community, and biogas also provides fuel for buses that serve the area (fig. 4.9).

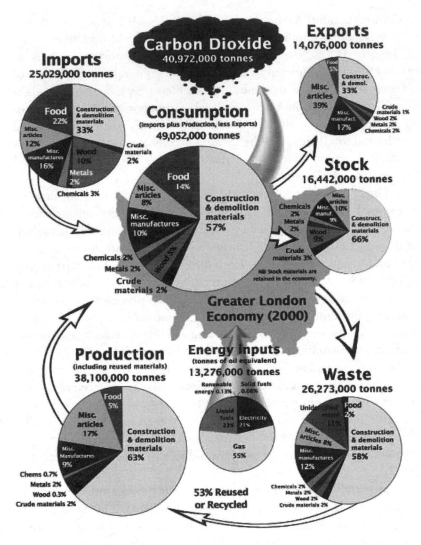

Figure 4.6
London's Metabolism. *Source*: Reproduced by permission of Best Foot Forward
(www.bestfootforward.com).

Figure 4.7
BedZED, London. In designing and building the Beddington Zero Energy Development, or BedZED, in London, emphasis was given to sourcing building materials locally. Brick was sourced from a local brick factory and wood from nearby forests. In the end, more than half the project's building materials were sourced from within a thirty-five-mile radius. *Photo:* Timothy Beatley.

New Urban Infrastructures

Moving cities in a more sustainable direction will also require new ways of conceptualizing traditional urban elements, especially those pertaining to infrastructure. With a long-term decline in global oil supplies in sight and cities facing a raft of new climate impacts and pressures (increased summer temperature highs, drought and water supply issues, elevated air pollution, etc.), resilience has now become a new and important dimension of sustainability. How sustainable a city ultimately is will depend on how adaptive it is. This means developing new ways of providing services, new ways of organizing, new ways of operating, and new kinds of infrastructure. Many cities are already moving in the direction of more distributed systems of infrastructure—toward smaller, decentralized networks of power production that avoid large the large energy losses

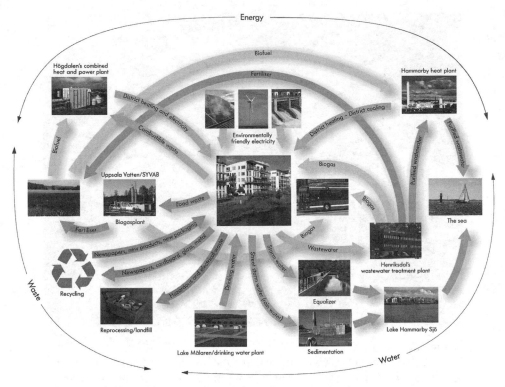

Figure 4.8
Resource Flows in Stockholm's New Urban Ecological District, Hammarby Sjöstad. *Source:* Hammarby Sjöstad; www.hammarbysjostad.se.

associated with long transmission—and, as a result, can cope better with the stresses and pressures of sudden disasters. These networks are systems that can be integrated into neighborhoods and buildings, offering flexibility and control and doing a number of things at once. The city of Sydney, Australia, for instance, released a sustainability plan that calls for a network of "green transformers"—compact facilities that at once produce power through combined heating, cooling, and power technology, collect stormwater and wastewater, extract biogas for energy production, and provide a surface-level park for the neighborhood (City of Sydney 2008).

City leaders and those who plan and design their built environments will need to think much more creatively about water in the years ahead. New forms of urban infrastructure must be designed that collect, treat, and reuse water in novel ways. Chicago architects Sarah Dunn and

Figure 4.9
Hammarby, Stockholm. Hammarby Sjöstad is a relatively dense redevelopment in Stockholm, Sweden, designed from the beginning to take advantage of eco-flows (inputs and outputs) and to show the potential of closed-loop urban systems. Many flats have stoves that burn natural gas extracted from organic household waste collected in the neighborhood. *Photo:* Timothy Beatley.

Martin Felsen of the studio UrbanLab have put forth an interesting new vision for water in that city that profoundly reimagines conventional infrastructure. Dubbed "Growing Water," their concept envisions a network of fifty "ecoboulevards" running from the west of the city to Lake Michigan. This new network of green ribbons would collect stormwater, and would also create a "living machine" to treat wastewater in the city. In turn, the ecoboulevards would represent new green space in the city and would end in the west in larger terminal parks, again representing a rethinking of the very nature of a park. Under this bold proposal the city of Chicago would be "re-engineered as a living system" (UrbanLab n.d.).

Built environments will likely rely much more on on-site, building- and site-integrated systems for power production and water and wastewater handling. The Energy-Plus homes designed by solar architect Rolf Disch in Freiburg, Germany, which produce more energy than they actually need (fig. 4.10), and the new SOM-designed Pearl River Tower in

Figure 4.10
Energy-Plus houses, Freiburg. These Energy-Plus homes, located in the green district of Vauban, Freiburg, Germany, are designed to require a small amount of energy and produce more than they actually need. Residents also have access to good public transit, and an urban environment where walking or riding a bicycle is very easy. *Photo:* Timothy Beatley.

Guangzhou, China, which integrates four vertical-axis turbines into the interior form of the building itself, suggest promising future directions. Increasingly, these new ideas of resilient and sustainable urban infrastructure are finding application in large-scale projects, which are also unusual for holding out ambitious goals and targets. Notable projects in this category include the new ecological cities of Dongtan, near Shanghai, China, and Masdar City, in the United Arab Emirates.

In Dongtan, the vision is explicitly one built on a more circular metabolism, where waste streams are to be harvested, most food is to be produced locally, and the town will produce all of its own power through a combination wind parks, vertical-axis microturbines on buildings, and solar panels. Rice husks will be used as fuel to power an efficient combined heat and power station. Masdar City, planned for an outer district of Abu Dhabi, is being touted as the world's first carbon-neutral city. Its plan incorporates impressive design features directed toward building a dense, walkable city that respects and values the climate in that part of the world. The new infrastructure will include personal rapid transit, a network of small public vehicles (essentially cars) that will take passengers to a specific desired stop. These new, large-scale models of urban sustainability are impressive on many levels, but especially because they represent a positive trend toward more holistic thinking and more integrative design. The planners and designers have thought at once about energy, water, transportation, urban form, and even food production, and how these different sectors and dimensions intersect and might be configured for complementarity.

There is an important new way of seeing infrastructure—indeed, cities overall—in terms of their *resilience*. "Resilience thinking" (to use Walker and Salt's term) is especially helpful in imagining how cities and urban populations might fare in the face of myriad future global pressures and shocks (Walker and Salt 2006). These pressures include global climate change, declining oil supplies, hurricanes and natural disasters of various sorts, economic downturns, and social unrest. To extend the metaphor of a tree, cities need to understand how to bend without breaking, how to adapt and respond to changing circumstances. This means that many of the tenets of sustainability will become redefined in support of the parallel goal of resilience: diversity (social, economic, ecological), redundancy, and decentralized infrastructure.

Houston offers a recent example of the overlapping sustainability and resilience agendas in planning and points the (perhaps unlikely) way in thinking about how cities can be more resilient in the face of changing climate and extreme weather events. With the city still reeling from the impacts of Hurricane Ike, which struck in September 2008 and left thousands of residents without power for weeks, Mayor Bill White appointed a task force to review the resilience of the city's and region's electricity system. The task force's report and recommendations, issued in April 2009, further buttress the shift toward sustainability. Among the key recommendations is the need to move toward more resilient distributed-energy systems such as solar and combined heat and power production, as well as investments in a more intelligent grid (City of Houston 2009).

Glocal Cities

Many challenges remain, however, in implementing the vision of the sustainable city. Western and northern industrialized cities especially are still engines of consumption and draw down a disproportionate amount of the world's raw materials and resources. Both as a matter of fairness and for long-term global sustainability, we need new political and economic mechanisms that provide both accountability for the distant impacts of local urban consumption and new ways of fostering and supporting more ecologically restorative supply lines. The view of cities as complex sets of metabolic flows should help guide us in dealing with those situations (especially in the shorter term) where some degree of reliance on resources and energy from other regions of the world still occurs. Understanding that food transported to large American cities, despite great efforts to promote local and regional production, will still occur suggests that efforts be made to mitigate or compensate for the energy consumed and the carbon emitted in this process. Perhaps that means contributions to a fund that supports solar and renewable energy projects in these regions and countries or carbon sequestration projects.

Some have argued for the *glocal* city—one profoundly interested in and connected with the rest of world culturally and informationally but which understands that with historical and present patterns of consumption come new responsibilities, including the need to reduce unnecessary and opulent consumption, the need to help cities in the developing world address their resource management challenges and poverty, and ideally skip over the unsustainable periods of fossil-fuel dependence and industrialization. New regimes for fair trade are needed as well, such as mechanisms for harnessing urban consumers increasingly bothered by the deleterious effects of their largely uninformed purchasing decisions.

Perhaps this view of cities suggests the need to forge new sustainable (and equitable) relationships between and among regions in the world, and where cities strive for new sustainable relationships with their (international transboundary) hinterlands, through mechanisms such as sustainable sourcing agreements, region-to-region trade agreements, and urban procurement systems based on green certification standards. Embracing a metabolic view of cities and metropolitan areas takes us in some interesting and potentially very useful directions.

The Challenges Ahead

There are challenges that remain today, of course, in utilizing the sustainability framework in planning. Some have argued that the literal meaning of sustainability in current conditions is inappropriate and uninspiring: why would we want to sustain the present conditions of global society, the high rates of poverty, the profound inequities in access to resources, the depleted fisheries, and the degraded and badly functioning ecosystems? In this regard, it is not sustainability but restoration that is needed. Most who advocate for sustainability as a concept plead the matter as semantics, but the limitation remains. Others argue that the current meanings and expressions of sustainability must be more deeply moving and inspiring. Beth Meyer of the University of Virginia argues strongly that beauty must be taken into account in any design or future sustainability agenda (Meyer 2008).

A variety of more pedestrian challenges will need tackling, of course. Overcoming the limitations that keep disciplines apart is one challenge, if we are to forge more holistic urban approaches and understand infrastructure in a more multifunctional way. Economic incentive structures throughout society need to be modified, both to eliminate perverse disincentives to sustainability (e.g., utility rate structures that lower prices as greater quantities are consumed) and to put into place positive, encouraging incentives (e.g., density bonuses for green rooftops, property tax systems that take into account the positive value of a site or location made green by planting new trees or reducing the extent of impervious surface).

The beauty of sustainability is in the eye of the beholder. The debate continues over how much of our sustainable community or city should be made highly visible, versus the proposition that renewable energy and other sustainable technologies should be so thoroughly integrated that they in essence become invisible. The San Diego affordable green project Solara demonstrates the potential conflict: the city of Poway (in which the project lies) insisted that the PV panels (the development's signature features) not be visible from the streets or sidewalks. City officials even required the panels to be readjusted after the project was finished because a few of the solar panels peaked out in spots. Contrary to this point of view are others (myself included) who find much that is beautiful here: the blue-gray luminance, to be sure, but also the commitment to the future and to tackling tough environmental problems that they represent.

One of the most significant challenges to sustainability in my mind also represents one of the greatest opportunities. There is a risk that, given the model of a sustainable city or community, one simply assumes the task is to assemble, perhaps in slightly different ways, a future vision from a set of common tools or ideas. One of the main critiques of sustainability may be the one sometimes leveled at new urbanism: despite the desire to be different, many of the communities look and feel alike. The challenge (and opportunity) in sustainability is to build in a profound and large way on the unique qualities of a place—unique histories, unique and special ecologies and nature, special social relationships and communities. This does not mean rejecting the most promising sustainability ideas and technologies just because they are being used in other places but understanding that the unique context of place (and the need to nurture a sense of place and commitment to place) is important to consider as well.

In this way, the new agenda of urban sustainability does seem to be placing, in the model projects put forth and touted, an emphasis on a kind of tabula rasa approach. New cities like Masdar generate great excitement at international planning conferences, but the greater challenge will be retrofitting existing cities and urban areas, retooling and reconfiguring our present cities to be equally as resource efficient and sustainable. Masdar trumpets the incorporation of traditional design features—the walled city with narrow, shaded streets that builds on the traditions of Middle Eastern city form—and this is good. Sustainability, even promulgated through very modern technological ideas, should be equally applicable to our existing urban fabric.

Reaching the broader public and convincing it of the need for personal action remains a challenge, though the general public has shown an uptick in its understanding of the most important sustainability issues. Serious efforts to infiltrate mainstream media and popular culture with the message of sustainability have not occurred in the United States, though there are lessons and examples from other parts of the world. One of the greatest challenges to sustainability will be to keep it on the front burner of individual and collective attention. It is a bit discouraging that more than thirty-five years after Callenbach's *Ecotopia* was published, we are not much closer to broadly realizing the vision he provocatively sketched out.

On the positive side, few concepts have been so quickly embraced by virtually every sector in society. Every university, it seems, has a campus sustainability initiative, and new sustainability curricula are appearing in many universities. Businesses today aspire to be green and sustainable, and sustainability is increasingly a framework and an organizing concept for city, state, and national government initiatives. There is now even friendly competition among cities to see which can be the greenest and most sustainable. Sustainability has been adopted by almost every major global development institution, from the UN to the World Bank, as an important goal and set of operating principles. Sustainability also clearly responds to the times in which we live, in which global environmental problems are soaring. Business as usual is no longer an acceptable option as climate change, biodiversity loss, water and resource limits, and global poverty argue for a profoundly different approach to the future.

Sustainability has emerged as a powerful and important concept for the profession of planning, and for the practice of planning around the world. As the discussion in this chapter shows, sustainability has become a major stated goal in community plans and an organizing concept for planning as a profession and process (e.g., Berke and Manta-Conroy 2000). This is perhaps not surprising, in light of the field's long-standing priorities in the areas of environmental protection and conservation, social equity, and economic development. And new concerns about climate change and the role of cities and community design have further elevated the importance of the environmental planning agenda. Sustainability weaves together these important strands of planning values and thinking and appeals to the visionary, aspirational, and forward-looking dimensions of planning. The idea of sustainability, malleable to accommodate evolving perspectives, has created a space in which different stakeholders in the planning process are able to come together and develop a practical future vision (different from the status quo) that creatively combines vibrant, livable communities with a lighter footprint on the planet and a deeper connection to place and people.

Notes

1. The people of the Six Nations, known commonly as the Iroquois, believed that every decision should take into account and show respect for the next seven generations.

2. The precautionary principle holds that if an action of decision or project is likely to cause significant harm or damage, there is an obligation to err on the side of action, to anticipate and prevent damage, and to thoroughly identify the range of alternatives available that will achieve desired goals without damage. See O'Brien (2000).

References

American Forests. 2001. *Urban Ecosystem Analysis Atlanta Metro Area*. August. Washington, DC: American Forests.

Beatley, Timothy. 2000. *Green Urbanism*. Washington, DC: Island Press.

Benyus, Janine M. 1997. *Biomimicry: Innovation Inspired by Nature*. New York: Harper Perennial.

Berke, Philip, and Maria Manta-Conroy. 2000. Are We Planning for Sustainable Development? An Evaluation of 30 Comprehensive Plans." *Journal of the American Planning Association* 66 (1): 21–33.

Bird, Winifred. 2008. Natural by Design. *Japan Times*, August 24.

Callenbach, Ernest. 1975. *Ecotopia*. New York: Bantam Books.

City of Boulder. 2007. City of Boulder Social Sustainability Strategic Plan. May. www.bouldercolorado.gov/files/final_sss_plan_060608.pdf.

City of Copenhagen. 2007. *Eco-Metropole: Our Vision for Copenhagen 2015*. Copenhagen, Denmark.

City of Houston. 2009. *Mayor's Task Force Report: Electric Service Reliability in the Houston Region*, April 21.

City of New York. 2008. *PlaNYC: A Greener, Greater New York*. New York.

City of Sydney. 2008. *Sustainable Sydney 2030*. http://www.sydney2030.com.au.

Edwards, Andrés R. 2005. *The Sustainability Revolution: Portrait of a Paradigm Shift*. Gabriola Island, BC: New Society Publishers.

Ehrlich, Paul R. 1968. *The Population Bomb*. New York: Ballantine Books.

Girardet, Herbert. 2008. *Cities People Planet: Urban Development and Climate Change*. New York: Wiley.

Greater London Authority. 2002. *City Limits: A Resource Flow and Ecological Footprint Analysis of Greater London*. Prepared by Best Foot Forward Ltd., London.

IUCN. 1980. *World Conservation Strategy: Living Resource Conservation for Sustainable Development*. Geneva: IUCN.

Lindenmayer, David B., and Jeffy F. Franklin. 2002. *Conserving Forest Biodiversity: A Comprehensive Multiscaled Approach*. Washington, DC: Island Press.

McDonough, William. 2002. Buildings Like Trees, Cities like Forests. http://www.mcdonough.com/writings/buildings_like_trees.htm.

McDonough, William, and Michael Braungart. 2002. *Cradle to Cradle: Remaking the Way We Make Things*. New York: North Point Press.

Meadows, Donella H., Jorgen Randers, and Dennis Meadows. 1993. *Beyond the Limits: Confronting Global Collapse, Envisioning a Sustainable Future*. Post Mills, VT: Chelsea Green Publishers.

Meadows, Donella H., Jorgen Randers, and Dennis Meadows. 2004. *Limits to Growth: The 30-Year Update*. Post Mills, VT: Chelsea Green Publishers.

Meadows, Donella H, Jorgen Randers, Dennis Meadows, and William W. Behrens. 1974. *The Limits to Growth: A Report for the Club of Rome's Project on the Predicament of Mankind*. New York: Universe Books.

Meyer, Elizabeth. 2008. Sustaining Beauty: The Performance of Appearance: A Manifesto in Three Parts. *Journal of Landscape Architecture* (Spring):6–24.

Newman, Peter, and Isabella Jennings. 2008. *Cities as Sustainable Ecosystems: Principles and Practices*. Washington, DC: Island Press.

Newman, Peter, and Jeff Kenworthy. 1999. *Cities and Sustainability*. Washington, DC: Island Press.

O'Brien, Mary, 2000. *Making Better Environmental Decisions: An Alternative to Risk Assessment*. Cambridge, MA: MIT Press.

Pinchot, Gifford. 1908. *The Conservation of Natural Resources*. Farmers Bulletin 327. US Department of Agriculture, Washington, DC: US Government Printing Office.

Platt, Rutherford H., Rowan A. Rowntree, and Pamela C. Muick, eds. 1994. *The Ecological City: Preserving and Restoring Urban Biodiversity*. Amherst: University of Massachusetts Press.

Register, Richard. 1987. *EcoCity Berkeley: Building Cities for a Healthy Future*. Berkeley, CA: North Atlantic Books.

Register, Richard. 2006. *EcoCities: Rebuilding Cities in Balance with Nature*. Gabriola Island, BC: New Society Publishers.

Soleri, Paolo. 2006. *Arcology: The City in the Image of Man*. Mayer, AZ: Cosanti Press.

UrbanLab. n.d. Growing Water. http://www.urbanlab.com/urban/growingwater.html.

Wackernagel, Mathis, and William Rees. 1998. *Our Ecological Footprint: Reducing Human Impact on the Earth*. Gabriola Island, BC: New Society Publishers.

Walker, Brian, and David Salt. 2006. *Resilience Thinking: Sustaining Ecosystems and People in a Changing World*. Washington, DC: Island Press.

Wilson, E. O. 1993. Biophilia and the Conservation Ethic. In *Biophilia: The Human Bond with Other Species*, ed. Stephen Kellert and E. O. Wilson. Cambridge, MA: Harvard University Press.

Wilson, E. O. 1984. *Biophilia*. Cambridge, MA: Harvard University Press.

World Commission on Environment and Development. 1987. *Our Common Future*. Oxford: Oxford University Press.

II
Ideas about Territoriality

5

Regional Development Planning

Michael B. Teitz

The genealogy of ideas in regional planning is long and tortuous, its exploration taking us on a twisting path.[1] Yet its origins are firmly planted in the ideas of the eighteenth-century Enlightenment in Europe and North America, that astonishing period when thinkers, inspired by the scientific advances of earlier scholars, dared to consider the proposition that human societies could be redesigned for the better on the basis of reason. That is our starting point. Although regional planning is often conflated with city planning, as in the names of many academic departments and in the standard histories of the field (the distinction being primarily one of scale), the intellectual origins of urban planning are not the same as those of regionalism and regional planning. At a time when one very significant form of regional planning, namely, regional development, has diminished, while others, such as metropolitan planning, are resurgent, pursuit of that difference may help us understand what is happening now.[2]

This chapter comprises seven parts. Following the introduction, the concept of region is explored, especially the idea of region in relation to planning. The next four sections take ideas, and to some extent practice, in regional development planning through four eras: (1) the utopian era, from the mid-nineteenth century up to 1930; (2) the heroic era, from 1930 to 1945; (3) the development era, from 1945 to 1985; and (4) the global era, from 1985 on. I conclude with some reflections about the future.

In conventional expositions, regional planning is often divided into two forms, the first dealing with planning for metropolitan areas that go beyond city boundaries and the second addressing planning for regions defined on other bases—in recent history, mainly for purposes of economic and social development. Since another chapter in this book covers metropolitan regions, this chapter takes a larger view of the evolution of ideas in regional planning, together with attention to regional planning for development, which was theorized early in the development of the field but rose to prominence in policy and action only during the Great Depression and after World War II.

The Concept of Region in Relation to Regional Planning

The concept of region, understood historically, involves two kinds of perception—one holistic and to a degree organic, the other classificatory and instrumental. Both can be traced far back intellectually. Early geographers looking at the world saw physical divisions, such as plains, deserts, or river basins, but they also recognized social, political, economic, and cultural divisions in the forms of occupancy of the land by specific human groups. Herodotus in *The Histories* speaks of places as geographic entities, such as Africa, and as the homelands of peoples differentiated linguistically and ethnically (Herodotus 1998). His rich descriptions and their blending of people and places, of history and geography, powerfully evoke the interaction of people, place, and homeland.

The modern intellectual form of the idea that complex and longlasting regional entities might be created by the interaction of human and natural action emerged in the late nineteenth and early twentieth centuries. French and German geographers identified regions in which stable patterns of agriculture, settlement, and land use reflected a long-term balance between the human and the natural. Scholars such as Paul Vidal de la Blache (1922) in France and Friedrich Ratzel (1882) in Germany created new fields of regional and cultural geography to study these unique regions—*paysage* in France, *Landschaften* in Germany. This is not surprising, given the modest degree to which the nation-state penetrated French life, and the multiple small states in Germany (Robb 2007). Meanwhile, anthropologists, studying indigenous peoples in colonial territories, saw similar patterns in the balance of their mode of life in relation to the natural worlds they inhabited. This idea was also present in socialist and anarchist thought in the late nineteenth century, especially in the ideas of Pierre Joseph Proudhon ([1863] 1959), Elisée Reclus (1905–1908), and Peter Kropotkin ([1899] 1974).[3] Patrick Geddes's ([1915] 1972) conception of regional planning advanced it further. For these thinkers, the region was a real and organic entity in its own right, expressing human life, culture, and therefore community.

The second idea of region sees it as an analytic and instrumental concept providing spatial structure for a scientific view of the world. Regions are appropriate spatial entities, either for the study of some phenomenon or for the attainment of some objective. This meaning of region takes a functional or instrumental view appropriate for identifying, classifying, and understanding phenomena. This does not mean that the object identified as a region is unreal; but whether a physiographic area of the Earth, a realm with a particular climate or natural fauna, a metropolitan labor market, or a political sphere of influence, it is defined by the phenomenon and is used to explain or to influence it. Indeed, a region may be constructed as a complex of industries and populations, as was the intent of Marxist theorists in the Soviet Union. This view of region, formalized and subordinated to the phenomena of interest, is familiar in the intellectual landscape of planning, from regional land-use and transportation plans to plans for habitat preservation and sustainability, though the latter also reflect a more organic view of region.

Many observers of regional theory have noted that the concept is slippery—that it loses its coherence when subject to close examination. Certainly, instances exist in which the meanings described above overlap. Nonetheless, the distinction between an organic perception of region and a classificatory and instrumental view is fundamental to understanding how the regional idea relates to planning, embodying an antinomy between community and instrumental rationality. Conventionally, planning has been seen as grounded in Enlightenment ideas—that there are universals in society as well as nature, that human beings are essentially the same everywhere, that reason may be applied fruitfully to human affairs, and that it is possible to remake human society for the better (Berlin 1980). Such a rational, scientific attitude is the foundation of problem solving, as in the early efforts to cope with the problems of the industrial city. For the region, it implies an analytic rather than a holistic view.

Yet, as Isaiah Berlin (1976, 1980) has noted, Enlightenment thinkers were challenged from the outset by another view, emanating partly from religious tradition but stemming intellectually most strongly from a historicist tradition traceable to Giambattista Vico ([1744] 1968). That Counter-Enlightenment saw human societies as unique and noncomparable, embodying truths not accessible to rational-scientific modes of thought. This path generated the darker messages of Johann Georg

Hamann (1999) and Johan Gottfried Herder (1969), attacking rationalism and emphasizing group identity (including, ultimately, nationalism), as well as the emergence of the Romantic movement, also opposing rationalism and deeply influencing landscape design in planning.

However, for the idea of region and for planning, the legacy of the Counter-Enlightenment is most clearly expressed in the desire for and notion of community, that elusive entity that pervades planners' thought (Teitz 1985). From the conflict between *Gemeinschaft* and *Gesellschaft* in nineteenth-century Vienna, expressed in the ideas of Camillo Sitte and Otto Wagner, to Jane Jacobs and the freeway battles of twentieth-century New York, the conflict between the rationalizing demands for efficiency in the evolving capitalist city and the human needs and rootedness of local populations—the tension between rationality and community—has never disappeared, though at times one or the other has been ascendant. For the history of ideas in regional planning, it constitutes an inescapable leitmotif.

Utopian Regionalism, 1850–1930

The idea of regional planning, as it emerged in the second half of the nineteenth century, was intellectually rooted in utopian streams of thought, albeit often inspired by the Jeffersonian and utopian elements in the formation of the United States, as well as distrust of government. In contrast, urban planning was intensely practical. Social reformers such as Edwin Chadwick and Robert Snow in public health, Lawrence Veiller in housing, or Jane Addams in social welfare built the foundations for the field by making things happen. Although some utopian thinkers, such as Robert Owen and, later, Ebenezer Howard, attempted to make their ideas reality, others, notably Charles Fourier and the socialists and anarchists who followed, went little beyond writing and advocacy.[4] For early regional planning, the story is fundamentally one of ideas.

The history of those ideas has been extensively studied, notably by John Friedmann, Clyde Weaver, and Peter Hall (Friedmann and Weaver 1979; Weaver 1981, 1984; Friedmann 1987; Hall 2002). Friedmann and Weaver identify four strands of thought over this early period: utopianism, anarchism, regional geography, and sociology. However, with the exception of the regional geographers, the writers in all of them fall under the general rubric of utopian, with the distinction that the anarchist/socialist stream is overtly political, while the others are much less so.[5]

The utopian strand of thought, as identified by Weaver (1984), flows from Robert Owen and Charles Fourier in the early nineteenth century, through Edward Bellamy, and on to Ebenezer Howard and the Garden City movement in the early twentieth century. This utopian strand might best be characterized as the root of planning for metropolitan regions, responding to the congestion, poverty, and ill health prevalent in the cities created during the Industrial Revolution. It parallels efforts to ameliorate conditions within the cities by the reformers and progressives, and also leads to the American advocates of urban dispersal, notably Mary Simkhovitch and Florence Kelley, who popularized the idea in the 1905 *Exhibit on Congestion of Population.*

The anarchist/socialist strand of regional thought is a primary origin for the idea of regional planning beyond the city. The anarchists' search for the transformation of social and economic relations through decentralization of the social economy and regional federalism is seen by Weaver (1984, 39) and Hall (2002, 150) as central to the evolution of regionalism. Weaver grounds this development squarely in industrialization, the consolidation of the nation-state, and national markets, which together with the growing power of the bourgeois class led to centralization of production and the creation of national core-periphery structures that dislocated traditional relationships and identities. Facing these onrushing developments, socialist and anarchist thinkers from Pierre Joseph Proudhon onward sought solutions in restructuring production, both socially and spatially.

Proudhon ([1863] 1959) sought a response to the monopolistic tendencies of industrialization in the ideas of mutualism and federation. Producers associations, joined in freely contracted arrangements both vertical in production and horizontal in geographic space, as fundamental social units, would constitute the new "social republic," constantly shifting in contractual relations and joined in federated relationships from the workplace to the continental level. Government, in the coercive sense, would cease to exist.

These ideas, the foundation of anarchism, would be taken up and given form for regional planning by three successor figures: Elisée Reclus, Peter Kropotkin, and, in an attenuated form, Jean Charles-Brun. Commentators differ on the significance of each of these thinkers and their relative importance to planning in comparison with Ebenezer Howard and the metropolitan stream of ideas discussed above. Nonetheless, taken together, they account for key components in regional planning thought.

Reclus (1905–1908), a geographer, attempted to substantiate anarchist ideas empirically by demonstrating historically both the just nature of small-scale, collectivist societies and their close and beneficial relationship with the physical environment. Kropotkin ([1899] 1974) also advocated mutual aid, viewing cooperation as the most critical factor in species' evolution. His major contribution was to argue for decentralized production for local markets, laying out the case for a new form of decentralized production that would combine industry and agriculture, and, with new technology, would enable the formation of self-sufficient regions. The final thinker in this triumvirate, Jean Charles-Brun (1911), forms a bridge to the third strand of thought in nineteenth-century regional planning ideas, namely, the French regionalist school of geographers discussed above. However, his major contribution was his advocacy for "regionalism" as a movement. French regionalism of the late nineteenth and early twentieth centuries responded both to the strong centralist tendency of the French state and the loss of the historical economic base and identity of French provincial areas. As such, it was very different from the anarchism of Kropotkin or Reclus—far less revolutionary in its political and social demands, and seeking an accommodation with state power that would preserve and enhance regional autonomy and diversity. Simultaneously patriotic for France and advocating for economic and educational development, this regionalism worked within the system.

Weaver identifies a fourth strand of thought in regional planning ideas he calls "sociology" (Weaver 1984, 46ff.), grounding it in August Comte (Kremer-Marietti 1972) and Frédéric Le Play ([1877–1889] 1982), leading to Patrick Geddes. Comte, the founder of sociology and positivism, the scientific study of society, influenced Le Play, an influential engineer and sociologist. Le Play saw the family and its integration with the environment, mediated through technology, as critical to improving the condition of the poor, which he had extensively documented through surveys. This empirical grounding, together with the formulation of the idea of *famille, travail, lieu*, translates into the familiar, if inverted, "place-work-folk" of Patrick Geddes ([1915] 1972). Le Play may also be counted as a seminal thinker about the idea of development itself, originating the ideas later driving regional development planning (Thornton 2005).

Far ahead of his time, Patrick Geddes recognized an ecological imperative for human life and perceived the regional city (for which he coined the term "conurbation"), thereby contributing critically to both the metropolitan and the developmental streams of regional planning. His advocacy of "survey before plan" and his novel ideas for the sensitive reconstruction of historic cities, shown in his work in India, were also seminal. However, Geddes's most influential contribution to regional development planning ideas came through his identification of the river basin as a powerful organizing concept for planning. His use of the river basin as an organizing regional principle had an immediate and long-lasting significance. The idea of the "valley section," Geddes's vision of a landscape in balance with nature, is clearly grounded in his knowledge of biology, together with the fledgling science of ecology. Geddes used the idea in an ambitious way, to account for the distribution of human activity, both urban and rural, positing hierarchies of natural forms, human occupancy, and settlement types that could form a region for human mutual cooperation (Welter 2002, 61). As with Kropotkin, that possibility would come about through technological means, especially electricity, ushering in a "neotechnic" era.[6] Although Geddes's ideas were surely utopian, at the same time, they were the first that would be directly translated into regional development planning in action.

The final phase of the regional planning utopian era saw the adoption of Geddes's ideas in the United States. Peter Hall (2002, 155) frames the transition primarily in terms of Lewis Mumford's intellectual partnership with Geddes and the formation of the Regional Planning Association of America (RPAA), which actively promoted the idea of regional planning throughout the 1920s. Hall's account, however, does not fully describe other influences at work at the time, notably the role of political scientists, such as Charles E. Merriam, and sociologists, such as Howard W. Odum. They were part of a larger transformation of the American university system that saw the introduction of new ideas and techniques for social science research in economics, sociology, political science, and geography. These ideas and capabilities, directed toward regional development, would be called on during the next era of regional planning.

Heroic Regionalism, 1930–1945

Since Achilles, heroes have not been noted for ideas; instead, they act. For the history of regional planning, the Great Depression, the New Deal, and World War II were times for action. Nonetheless, that action often saw the fulfillment of ideas that had long been germinating. Most commentators identify the main surge of regional planning activity with President Roosevelt's New Deal. Roosevelt, no ideologue and intensely pragmatic, was willing to experiment and try radical new ideas in an attempt to counter the unprecedented economic disaster of the Great Depression. Faced with financial collapse, massive unemployment, declining industrial production, and rural immiseration, he mobilized new people for government service on a scale never before seen. Among them were thinkers and researchers, such as Charles E. Merriam and Wesley C. Mitchell, and Rexford Tugwell, an agricultural economist, together with planners, such as Charles Delano, who had been influential both in Chicago and in New York.

The atmosphere of Roosevelt's "Brain Trust" was sympathetic to planning, and national and regional planning entered the agenda. Eleanor Roosevelt campaigned for the formation of rural settlements that would disperse the unemployed, providing some ability to raise food in addition to any employment that might be possible. Delano, Tugwell, and Stuart Chase gave form to the Public Works Bill of 1933 that provided funding for new towns through the Resettlement Administration. Clarence Stein of the RPAA group aided this effort. Nonetheless, as Hall (2002, 171) notes, in general they were too socialist and utopian to have much impact on practice, though their ideas were widespread.

The foremost concrete regional planning achievement of the New Deal was the adoption of Geddes's ideas in the formation of the Tennessee Valley Authority (TVA) and the implementation of its program of dam building for electrification, navigation, and flood control. The TVA began with a very broad mandate—flood control, electrification, resettlement, town building, education, and agricultural development—which remained unfulfilled, largely because of deep political divisions. The gulf between the holistic vision of a plan that would enhance the life of all the region's inhabitants and the demands of economic expediency and war turned out to be unbridgeable. Today, the TVA is largely an electric power utility. Yet in the longer view, the lives of the people of the Tennessee Valley were substantially changed, mostly for the better, even though, as Hall (2002, 177) notes, much of the power was siphoned off for plutonium production in World War II. Formerly the poorest agricultural region of the United States, the valley no longer holds that title. Although parts are still very poor, as a whole, the Tennessee Valley is very much in the American mainstream. Yet the largest impact of the TVA, ironically, may have been in the realm of ideas. The concept of successful river basin planning was to capture the imagination of a new generation of planners on a much larger scale, giving rise to countless copies after 1950.

Other manifestations of the impulse to plan during the New Deal took form both nationally and regionally. Nationally, a series of planning organizations began with the U.S. National Planning Board (NPB) in 1934, succeeded by the U.S. National Resources Board and the U.S. National Resources Committee (NRC), 1935–1943. The doctrine on which these efforts were grounded was essentially that of the RPAA and the Southern Regionalists, namely, "a planned approach to regional reconstruction, based on attaining a new equilibrium or regional balance . . . [through] industrial decentralization, new town building, power and highway construction, and educational and political reform" (Weaver 1984, 66).

The NPB and NRC set to work to prepare for this effort. Bringing together scholars and researchers, mainly in social science disciplines, they produced *Regional Factors in National Planning* (National Resources Committee 1935), a study overseen by a political scientist, John M. Gaus, and influenced by Howard Odum. The staff of the NPB and NRC attempted to define criteria for planning regions in the United States (Weaver 1984, 68), eventually falling back on river basins and associated commissions. In the course of their efforts they produced, in Hall's words, "a prodigious multiplication of paper" (Hall 2002, 173). In fact, there may have been much more than that, but not in the form that we usually expect from planning. Despite Hall's conclusion that for all the effort, "it is hard work to find anything out there on the ground," they produced a generation of people who could think in terms of planning for development, and who would play important roles in theory and practice after the war ended. In the meantime, during the war itself, all attention was focused on mobilization and the associated planning needs. Regional planning would be postponed for the duration.

Regional Development Planning: Doctrine, Application, and Critique, 1945–1985

The Idea of Development
World War II had many results, but few more important than the rapid acceleration of the process of dismantling European and U.S. colonial empires, while the Russian empire expanded, as did the American, though transformed in its mode of influence. With that collapse, and out of the devastation of the war and fear of a recurrence of the Great Depression, there emerged a new international organization, the United Nations, and new institutions, such as the World Bank and the International

Monetary Fund, which reconstructed the world's financial system under the 1944 Bretton Woods agreement. Although these organizations were oriented toward the interests of what would come to be known as the developed countries, the break between the Soviet bloc and the West meant competition for influence among the new nations of the world. Development became a powerful motivating idea, not only in the industrialized countries that had wrestled with it during the Great Depression but now also in the nonindustrialized nations of Africa, the Middle East, and Asia. For regional planning, these changes reflected the transformation of the idea of development from a biological conception of societal evolution to an instrumental one—changing the trajectory of a nation or a society in order to realize specific economic, social, or political objectives. With these changes came a mix of old and new ideas, first as received development doctrine, and second in the form of intense critiques.

The Emergence of Standard Development Theory and Doctrine
In the competition for development ideas, countries such as India and China, which followed a more socialist path, took their cue from the industrial development of the Soviet Union.[6] That meant intensive capital investment in heavy industry, transportation, and electric power, along with dam construction. For other, newly decolonizing, countries, the primary model for development was derived from a mixture of Keynesian macroeconomics and conventional microeconomic theory. Robert Solow's (1957) neoclassical extension of the Harrod-Domar macroeconomic model showed economic growth flowing from increasing capital and labor, the central problem being to ensure the appropriate rate of growth for each. The more accessible work of W. Arthur Lewis (1955) and Walt Whitman Rostow (1960) was also very influential. Lewis argued that development must necessarily imply inequality of income, both to motivate effort and to generate savings for capital investment. Rostow's model of growth codified and historicized the process in five stages, from traditional society, to transitional, to take-off, to drive to maturity, to high mass consumption. Capital investment was the key to growth, either from savings from rising trade and productivity or from external investment. The latter, especially, might come from international sources, creating infrastructure that would in turn improve productivity. The great virtue of the model was that it seemed to promise a path for countries still dominated by subsistence agriculture, even though their reality was often more powerfully affected by colonial, plantation agri-

culture. The fundamental unit of analysis was the country, and national policy was supercedent.[7]

These approaches dominated Western thinking and investment in development in the postwar years. Challenging them, however, were perceptions of regional and spatial polarization or spatial unevenness in development. Gunnar Myrdal (1957) argued that development could be a virtuous circle of "cumulative causation," but he also recognized that development could be uneven. From initial, favorable locations it might "spread" beneficially, yet also cause a "backwash" effect, draining capital and people from regions with less competitive power and creating problems both of equity and of politics. Albert Hirschman (1958) similarly described "trickle-down" and "polarization" effects. The question, of course, was which form of effect would dominate. Myrdal suggested that regional backwardness and stagnation could last for a very long time, if not indefinitely, while Hirschman inclined to the view that the trickle-down process would ultimately dominate. In some ways, these two positions, with their implications for balanced or unbalanced growth, would establish the line between the standard, evolving development doctrine, generally favored by economists, and the critical development doctrine expounded by almost everyone else at one time or another.

If novelty and political importance focused attention on developing countries, the issue of lagging regions in advanced countries had not disappeared. In those countries, particularly the United States, Britain, and France, the first wave of reconstruction and prosperity after World War II gave way to concerns about regions that did not seem to be participating in the postwar economic growth. Why growth did or did not occur in specific places had long been studied by geographers, but in the postwar environment scholars began to apply new analytic ideas and techniques to the issue of spatial development. Walter Isard's (1956) integration of location theory with neoclassical economics was matched by the effusion of papers from a new breed of analytic geographers working with William Garrison at the University of Washington. The regional implications of these ideas were not long in coming. Douglass North (1956) entered into a famous debate with Charles Tiebout (1956) over the role of exports in regional growth. North's assertion that exports drove growth in the historical process of industrial development also resonated with policymakers in international organizations and in developing countries, offering a shortcut through the stages of growth (Friedmann and Weaver 1979, 99). Debates about import and export substitution became an early form of critique of development ideas.

At about the same time, John Friedmann made a key shift from the idea of the territorial or river basin region to the functional, city-based region as the appropriate foundation for development policy, arguing that the urban system constituted the real structure within which economic development occurred. He reworked this idea over the next two decades, reshaping development theory and moving to a more critical view of regional development as a process driven by innovation clusters in core regions at the points of highest interaction and spreading to linked regions that were dependent (Friedmann 1972; Friedmann and Weaver 1979). This view connected directly with the idea of growth poles that originated with François Perroux (1955) and was initially more sectoral than spatial, but was rendered in regional terms by Jacques Boudeville (1961) (Meardon 2001). In light of the later evolution of development theory, this was a critical shift, since it set up the debate between area development and the idea of concentrating development efforts on a few key centers (Friedmann and Weaver 1979, 128–129; Weaver 1984, 82).

By 1975, looking back on a decade of work, Friedmann could write, with some satisfaction, "There are few major countries that have not adopted some form of regional planning" (Friedman 1975, 801). He reviewed advances in theory and research, citing the field research of geographers such as Edward Soja (1968) and Peter Gould (1970) on modernization, together with many comparative country studies, notably by Lloyd Rodwin (1970a). Even so, he concluded, "Despite this wealth of information, it cannot be claimed that we really know whether and in what sense regional policy and planning may be said to work. There can be little doubt, however, that such planning corresponds to a variety of perceived national needs" (Friedmann 1975, 802). Yet even before Friedmann wrote, Rodwin (1970b) was expressing reservations, and major new intellectual and ideological challenges were in progress.

Critical Responses to the Standard Theory
Until the mid-1960s, debates and critiques of standard development theory took place largely within the framework of neoclassical economics and social science. Especially strong were the debates over rural-urban migration and efforts to control the growth of dominant cities, especially in socialist countries. Within planning, this was reflected in the theory of growth poles—whether they could jump-start development in lagging regions, or whether they were simply bad investments that would delay national economic growth. Even Friedmann's call for a shift from territo-

rial to functional bases for development planning still occurred within that larger paradigm, though he was beginning to challenge it.

From the 1960s onward, however, in both national and regional development planning, a new ideological note was struck. In the larger realm of international and national economic development, the process of decolonization exploded, with national movements for independence, growing resistance to racial discrimination and inequality, and the rise of new ideological positions. The radical critique of colonialism by Fanon (1963) heralded a new militancy in national liberation movements from Algeria to Iran to South Africa. It was at this time that the term "Third World" came into wide usage, designating those countries that were neither in the Western bloc nor in the socialist realm, and implying that the decolonizing countries could follow a separate path. With these developments came new streams of thought on regional planning and development.

One of the difficulties in tracing regional planning ideas during this period is the multiplication of strands of thought. Historically, Euro-American regional planning had focused either on the metropolitan region or on the development of economically lagging industrial, agri-cultural, or resource regions. Now this distinction was overlaid with the question of developed (First World) versus undeveloped (Third World) areas, and in addition, critiques from very different ideological posi-tions.[8] The most striking illustration of this can be seen in the 1960s and 1970s with the resurgence of Marxist thought. In the social sciences and related disciplines, notably in geography, sociology, and planning, and even to some extent in economics, the received doctrines came under fierce attack.

The critics' ideas were heavily influenced by Marxism, supplemented by anticolonialism and antiracism. Underdevelopment and dependency theory, seen by Weaver as "the first truly *political* economic model to gain currency since the Second World War" (Weaver 1984, 113), envis-aged underdeveloped countries as essentially exploited and trapped by their political and trading relations with industrialized countries. Concern for indigenous peoples and the poor, both in the shantytowns of the rapidly growing cities and in the agricultural areas, led to formulations that saw standard development and trade liberalization efforts, especially by the World Bank and the IMF, as essentially favoring the wealthy nations, in particular the United States.

By the 1970s, although it was clear that the first UN Development Decade had not met its promises, what might replace the standard model was not clear. For Latin America, dependency theory (Quijano 1968; Sunkel 1969; Frank 1967) offered a prescription that called for lessening economic ties with the United States, both through import substitution and through endogenous development, but policies based on these models did not succeed. As the 1980s approached, no development model seemed viable. Much the same could be said for regional development. Charles Gore, attempting to demolish the foundations of regional development planning, cited Ross and Cohen as saying, "Regional planning has become a necessity in most countries. But nobody seems to know quite what it is, and no nation seems to know how to do it" (Gore 1984, 236).

A similar upheaval occurred in the Euro-American realm of regional analysis. Marxian critiques of planning by writers such as Manuel Castells (1977) and David Harvey (1973) were complemented by many critiques during the 1980s directed toward regional planning, mostly focused on theoretical inadequacies and problems of inequality in European and American regions. Charles Gore (1984) produced the single most coherent attack on regional planning from any point of view, arguing that it was entirely subordinate to state objectives pursued in the interest of groups that control the state. In the end, though, he proposed no alternative. On the other hand, Ann Markusen (1987a), also writing from a Marxian perspective, saw regions and regionalism as an integral part of the development of the United States. Paying relatively little attention to regional planning per se, Markusen illuminated the role of regions and regionalism in American history and politics, basing her analysis on political power and interest, within a rich conception of the idea of region as a spatial realm in which such interests interlock and sustain each other.

Regional Planning in a Globalizing World, 1985–2000

The collapse of the Soviet Union in the 1980s accelerated profound changes in the world economy and the development process. By 1979, Friedmann had presciently identified transnational enterprise as a key feature of development, along with China, though his interpretation of China's path to development turned out to be wrong (Friedmann 1979, 164–169). With the prospect of the United States as the world superpower, accompanied by a political and ideological shift to the right, neoliberal trade and development policies came to dominance. For development, this implied inward investment and export-led growth as the dominant paradigms (Stiglitz 2003). The 1986 Uruguay Round of trade negotiations, which continued until 1994, and the formation of the World Trade Organization (WTO) introduced unprecedented trade and financial liberalization and deregulation, which in practice favored the United States and other developed countries over poor countries, but also encouraged new flows of capital and investment. The model was that of the so-called Asian Tigers—Korea, Malaysia, Singapore, and Thailand—which had experienced very rapid growth through export-led development, linking their cheap labor with multinational companies and markets in the United States.

In the event, the drive toward globalization realized huge economic growth at the world scale while greatly widening the gap between rich and poor, both within and between countries. The most successful countries, exemplified by China, both encouraged inward investment and resisted U.S. and European demands for fully open trade—demands that never mentioned removal of the domestic subsidies and tariffs on sectors, such as agriculture, in the rich countries, which might have made a real difference. Smaller and weaker countries suffered repeated financial crises as capital flooded in and out, with IMF requirements exposing them to unemployment and economic distress. This pattern was most prevalent in Latin America, but it also extended to Korea, Thailand, Malaysia, and Indonesia, which suffered severe recessions or depressions (Stiglitz 2003, 214).

A second major shift in the 1980s was the recognition that new technology in information and communications was profoundly affecting productivity and patterns of consumer demand, with implications for development. Silicon Valley had been identified early as a region of extraordinary economic power (Saxenian 1994). But although the recognition of Silicon Valley spawned dozens of efforts to imitate it, those efforts were grounded in a shift from the region to the sector or industry as the principal driver of development. Paradoxically, even as the most influential regional transformation in decades took place, the underlying theory shifted back to the export base, combined with technological innovation.

Three important streams of ideas in regional development and planning remained influential into the twenty-first century: (1) the shift from a regional to a sectoral focus for development, with economic development as the goal; (2) the rise of supranational regionalism and its infranational consequences, together with the reemergence of ethnic regionalism as a powerful force; and (3) the environment as a key factor in development.

The Sectoral and Institutional Turn

The rise of radical ideas in planning was accompanied during the early 1980s by a new argument that turned on the question of production. Neo-Marxian scholars looked at the changing world, identifying a fundamental shift from mass production (called "Fordist" production in the terminology of the time) to a "post-Fordist" form of production that seemed to be grounded in smaller-scale firms, dense networks of interactions among them, and geographically bounded areas. The work of Michael J. Piore and Charles F. Sabel (1984), describing production systems in Bologna, stimulated in the United States a major stream of writing, especially by Allen J. Scott and Michael Storper (Scott and Storper 1986; Storper 1991; Storper and Scott 1992). They, with many others in geography, sought to construct theoretical frameworks and empirical foundations for understanding the industrial transformation that was occurring. While still focused on space and region, the insights of this group were fundamentally about industrial organization, institutional structure, networks, and their political manifestations.

The perception that what came to be called "high technology" was a key driver for development led to a search for dynamic sectors and reshaped ideas about what they were and how they worked. In the process, the idea of regional planning diminished. Saxenian's (1994) influential book, *Regional Advantage,* presented an articulate view of how the high-tech sector in Silicon Valley worked, and how innovation could occur in a networked environment, drawing in part on Piore and Sabel. It was foreshadowed and followed by a wealth of research that attempted to define and characterize high technology itself, and to show how it embodied political forces (Markusen 1987b; Glasmeier 1991). Bishwapriya Sanyal and his co-authors sought to extend this understanding to developing countries (Schön, Sanyal, and Mitchell 1998). Since it was evident that high-technology centers could not be everywhere, scholars and practitioners drew on ideas from many sources, as far back as Alfred Marshall in the 1890s, and Edgar M. Hoover (1937), to identify clusters of firms and sectors that could form viable bases for development (Porter 1998, 2000; Bergman, Fesser, and Sweeney 1996; Hill and Brennan 2000). The rediscovery of geography by economists, notably Paul Krugman (1991), added theoretical and methodological rigor, and stressed the role of increasing returns to scale in the process of development, though offering few practical suggestions.

This surge of research and ideas was accompanied by a shift in thinking about regional development. For developing countries, this period saw a shift in policy by the World Bank and other institutions that reflected a new conventional understanding that development required much stronger institutional foundations in governance and the development of human capital, all within the larger driving power of inward investment. Development policy was framed in these terms, whether for the rapidly growing cities or for rural areas. For lagging regions in wealthy countries, the aim was to bring inward investment. Marketing as a prime economic development strategy saw a resurgence, courting multinational firms in both high- and low-technology sectors. Geographers such as Philip Cooke (1995) and Michael Keating (2003) identified a "new regionalism" (only one among several that have been put forward in the past two decades) that saw the region as a locus for development policy that would be grounded in the attraction of new investment capital. Through the process, endogenous innovation and capital formation could begin to occur, bringing such regions onto a path of growth. Despite much criticism, this synthesis remains the dominant strategy for regional and local economic development (Lovering 1999).

Supranational and Infranational Regionalism

Even as regional planning, as understood in the decades after World War II, declined, regionalism certainly did not. A vibrant, largely supranational version was part of the neoliberal, trade-based agenda for development. As globalization and international trade grew, questions emerged of how it would be managed, both for the major players and for those countries suffering from its consequences. As issues with the WTO's "whole world" conception emerged, larger players and their multinational corporate counterparts sought to solidify their positions through the creation of supranational, regional trade agreements, of which the North American Free Trade Agreement (NAFTA) was the exemplar, followed by Mercado Común del Sur, or the Common Market of the South (MERCOSUR), and the Free Trade Area of the Americas (FTAA).

Reflecting this tendency, scholars have identified yet another "new regionalism" to describe this process (Preusse 2004; Breslin et al. 2001). Arguing from the perspective of economics and political science, scholars in this realm saw economic integration at a world scale to be inherently desirable in promoting growth, but nonetheless as generating problems of inequity and environmental degradation, which slow the process. To capture the benefits, it becomes beneficial for some smaller sets of countries to conclude agreements among themselves. Negotiating bargaining power among them remains a problem.

Of course, earlier thinkers on the topic of customs unions, notably Jacob Viner (1950), considered these issues, but from a regional perspective, the case of the European Union provides a rich source of insight. Perhaps uniquely in history, the formation of the EU, which began explicitly as a customs union, has resulted in explicit and very powerful regional policies—in effect, regional planning at a continental scale. The provision of funds for lagging regions in member states might seem a cynical maneuver to ensure the adherence of states to the EU and to attract new members, but over time it has been much more. Substantial resources—some 348 billion euros over 2007–2013—have been budgeted for the Structural Funds, the Cohesion Fund, the European Solidarity Fund, and the European Investment Bank, seeking to "reduce structural disparities between EU regions, and promote real equal opportunities for all."[9] For example, regional policy in Ireland was widely regarded as very effective. Apparently regional projects now also vie for honors. In February 2008, the EU website reported:

The "RegioStars" prize-giving ceremony took place yesterday evening in Brussels, as part of the "Regions for Economic Change" conference. The most innovative and economically effective projects were rewarded, completed using European funds awarded to regions in Europe. . . . Their projects will serve as examples for the other regions of Europe.[10]

It's enough to make a confirmed regionalist misty-eyed. Nonetheless, this is regional policy and planning for integration on a scale not seen since the early development of the United States.

Less edifying is the reemergence in the past two decades of regional and ethnicity-based conflicts. Whether violent struggles for independence, as in Darfur, Kosovo, Sri Lanka, and East Timor, or infranational ethnic conflicts, as in Burundi and numerous other African states, these regional tragedies seem endless. In a minor key, they appear in European movements in the Basque region, Catalonia, Wales, and Scotland, among others. In Africa, much of the problem has been attributed to colonial and postcolonial failures; other observers point to the end of the cold war, inequality in trading power, and the growing global pressure on resources in the absence of any prospect for improvement in the lives of indigenous peoples (Rothchild 1997).

How this phenomenon might translate into positive results in the absence of some effective larger framework, such as the EU in Europe, is not self-evident. In the European context, it suggests the formation of what amounts to city-states with surrounding rural tributary areas. Singapore has demonstrated such a possibility. For Africa, the prospect is not good; the states formed after the breakup of colonial empires are fiercely protective of their independence but often failing as civil societies. Considered in the light of the continuing growth of large cities, with their potential for violence, the likelihood is that it will take many years before stability and growth are achieved, but it is only such growth that holds out a possibility of coexistence of ethnic groups.

The Environment as a Regionalizing Factor

A third global force in the past two decades has been the growing awareness of the environment, especially in relation to climate change. Environmental consciousness had been a key element in Patrick Geddes's ideas, partly as a result of his training in biology and ecology. In part, the idea of a natural order within which planning should take place persisted into the second quarter of the twentieth century, as people like Benton MacKaye carried forward the conservation ethic of Geddes and John Muir. However, the modern form of environmentalism in the United States became widespread only in the 1970s, especially through the work of Luna Leopold, Rachel Carson, and other activists who succeeded in passing major environmental legislation. In itself, that legislation was not specifically regional in focus, using more general forms of regulation, as in the Endangered Species Act or the National Environmental Policy Act. Nonetheless, environmental conservation began to manifest itself in very specific regional forms, such as air and water quality management districts or habitat conservation plans, both of which involved urban areas and their peripheries, as well as larger geographic areas.

In the 1990s and the first decade of the twenty-first century, growing awareness of the impending consequences of global climate change, together with pressure on energy and other resources, meant that regional environmental concerns took on new urgency. Battles over habitat loss in the Arctic or rain forest destruction in the tropics are fought out in specific geographic spaces that rarely coincide with national boundaries. Even more daunting, efforts to address carbon dioxide production and distribution require spatial frameworks that are worldwide in scale, even as they also imply changes in behavior down to the level of the individual or household. Perhaps it is no accident that in this period, geographers have turned away from the idea of region to the concept of scale as a central theoretical concern (Smith 1995). Some of this work is theory without much real grounding, but one cannot help but be struck that such a shift should have occurred at precisely the time when the old categories do not seem to be sufficient. Yet it is interesting to note that when climate policy is applied to transportation at the metropolitan scale, it does include a distinct regional component that also ties to land use.

Conclusion: The Prospect for Regional Planning

In the second decade of the twenty-first century, the prospect for regional planning is mixed. At the urban metropolitan scale, a resurgence of regional policy and planning is occurring as it becomes evident that the governance structures of the past, with their fragmentation of key responsibilities, are inadequate for the emergent problems. For development planning, in both high- and low-income countries, the region has faded as an organizing concept.

In developing countries, especially those that are experiencing rapid growth, national governments and international aid organizations look toward sectoral solutions, broadly defined. Within the logic of international trade and market-based development, they seek to attract inward investment in growing industrial sectors, together with human capital enhancement through education and better decisions and coordination through institutional change, either within government in the traditional sense or through extragovernmental organizations. For some countries, notably China, the strategy is working beyond the dreams of anyone in development planning a few decades ago. They struggle with the adverse regional consequences of these policies, but broadly speaking, the regional approach is in retreat because it provides little or no leverage within the strategy. Even in many of the poorest countries, it is doubtful that the storm of ethnic conflict and violence will cause changes in their basic development strategy. For the most part, in a neoliberal, global trading regime, their elites simply see no alternative to hanging on and extracting such capital as they can export to safer places.

In the developed countries, the story takes a different form, for which the changing curriculum in planning schools provides a good illustration. From the 1960s on, many programs adopted regional development and planning as one of their main areas of concentration. (Metropolitan regional planning had largely faded out.) By the 1990s, regional development concentrations had morphed into local and regional economic development planning, often tied closely to community development. A similar process can be seen in practice. In the United States, local economic development planning expanded even as the federal government retreated from regional development and urban policy. Cities needed to do something to deal with the dramatic changes occurring in the economic system, and they had nothing else. Inevitably, this meant a sectoral approach, whether in industry or labor. Over time, the search for viable sectors has moved beyond technology to the creative class (Florida 2002) and the arts (Markusen and Johnson 2006), but at heart it is the same. At the same time, as we have noted, the role of regions and regional identity still seems significant for development policy in the EU.

Regional development planning ideas, both in theory and in doctrine for practice, appear to be at low ebb. However, regional planning has proved to be a resilient idea, and it should not simply be written off as part of a discarded past. There has been a resurgence of interest in regionalism at the metropolitan and megapolitan levels. The continuing dilemma of how to bring the poorest nations (and the lagging regions in the richest) out of poverty is still with us, manifesting in failed initiatives and regional ethnic turmoil. Ultimately, even as the world is globalized, the desire of people to identify with place is unlikely to disappear. Humans have always been a migrating species, but everywhere they stopped, they settled down. That urge is far too deeply rooted in human evolution to vanish in our time.

Notes

1. This essay was originally prepared for the Seminar on Ideas in Planning, Department of Urban Studies and Planning, the Massachusetts Institute of Technology, March 17, 2008. The author is indebted to John Friedmann, Ann Markusen, John Herbert, Solly Angel, Elisa Barbour, and Bettina Johnson for their insights and personal communications on this topic and for perceptive editorial suggestions.

2. Although no comprehensive history of regional planning takes the story up to the present, one cannot study its history without acknowledging a huge debt to John Friedmann, Clyde Weaver, and Peter Hall. Their joint and individual analyses are a foundation for scholarship on this subject up through the 1980s (Friedmann and Weaver 1979; Weaver 1981, 1984; Friedmann 1987; Hall 2002).

3. Marx did not pay much attention to the regional question, in the sense described here. Although his Hegelian, historicist, and holistic approach might have led him in this direction, he used class and historic phases as key elements of theory. His followers in the Soviet Union, however, believed they were building new socialist regions as industrial complexes (Kolosovskiy 1961).

4. The followers of Fourier did attempt to create new communities.

5. This characterization differs from Weaver (1984, 33) who defines utopian planning more stringently as requiring belief in class cooperation, faith in rationality, and avoidance of politics. Given subsequent history, it is hard to see how

socialists were any less utopian in thought even where they attempted to put their ideas into practice.

6. Peter Hall (2002, 88), for example, sees Howard as the key figure in the development of modern planning as a whole, while giving the anarchists a lesser but important intellectual role, principally in the development of regional planning. Clyde Weaver (1984) clearly gives primacy in regional planning to the French thinkers and Kropotkin, and through them to Patrick Geddes ([1915] 1972).

7. Friedmann (1979, 91–92) places the first mention of regional planning in this context in a UN report from 1951.

8. The problem of nomenclature for distinguishing groups of countries, from rich-poor, to advanced-backward, to developed-undeveloped-underdeveloped-less developed, to First World-Third World, to, most recently, North-South, continues to bedevil discourse in this area. How to characterize countries or regions without seeming to disparage them is a formidable task that is only made more difficult by the characterizations' implicit ideological meanings.

9. See http://europa.eu/scadplus/leg/en/s24000.htm.

10. See http://ec.europa.eu/regional_policy/index_en.htm.

References

Bergman, Edward, Edward Feser, and Stuart Sweeney. 1996. *Targeting North Carolina Manufacturing: Understanding the State's Economy through Industrial Cluster Analysis.* 2 vols. University of North Carolina Institute for Economic Development, Chapel Hill. Raleigh: North Carolina Alliance for Competitive Technologies.

Berlin, Isaiah. 1976. *Vico and Herder: Two Studies in the History of Ideas.* London: Hogarth Press.

Berlin, Isaiah. 1980. *Against the Current: Essays in the History of Ideas.* New York: Viking Press.

Boudeville, Jaques. 1961. *Les espaces économiques.* Paris: PUF.

Breslin, Shaun, Christopher Hughes, Nicola Phillips, and Ben Rosamond. 2001. *Regionalism in the Global Political Economy: Theories and Cases.* London: Routledge.

Castells, Manuel. 1977. *The Urban Question: A Marxist Approach,* trans. Alan Sheridan. London: Edward Arnold.

Charles-Brun, Jean. 1911. *La régionalisme.* Paris: Bloud et Cie.

Cooke, Philip. 1995. *The Rise of the Rustbelt.* London: UCL Press.

Fanon, Frantz. 1963. *The Wretched of the Earth,* trans. Constance Farrington. New York: Grove Press.

Florida, Richard. 2002. *The Rise of the Creative Class: And How It's Transforming Work, Leisure, and Everyday Life.* New York: Basic Books.

Frank, Andre G. 1967. *Capitalism and Underdevelopment in Latin America.* New York: Monthly Review Press.

Friedmann, John. 1972 *A General Theory of Polarized Development.* New York: Ford Foundation, Urban and Regional Advisory Program, Chile.

Friedmann, John. 1975. Regional Development Planning: The Progress of a Decade. In *Regional Policy: Readings in Theory and Applications,* ed. John Friedmann and William Alonso. Cambridge: MIT Press.

Friedmann, John. 1987. *Planning in the Public Domain: From Knowledge to Action.* Princeton, NJ: Princeton University Press.

Friedmann, John, and Clyde Weaver. 1979. *Territory and Function: The Evolution of Regional Planning.* Berkeley: University of California Press.

Geddes, Patrick. (1915) 1972. *Cities in Evolution: An Introduction to the Town Planning Movement and to the Study of Civics.* London: Williams & Norgate.

Glasmeier, Amy. 1991. *The High-Tech Potential: Economic Development in Rural America.* New Brunswick, NJ: Center for Urban Policy Research, Rutgers University.

Gore, Charles. 1984. *Regions in Question: Space, Development Theory and Regional Policy.* London: Methuen.

Gould, Peter R. 1970. Tanzania1920–1963: The Spatial Impress of the Modernization Process. *World Politics* 22 (2): 149–170.

Hall, Peter. 2002. *Cities of Tomorrow: An Intellectual History of Urban Planning and Design in the Twentieth Century.* 3rd ed. Oxford: Blackwell.

Hamann, Johann Georg. 1999. *Sämtliche Werken.* Edited by Josef Nadler. Wuppertal: Brockhaus.

Harvey, David. 1973. *Social Justice and the City.* London: Edward Arnold.

Herder, J. G. 1969. *J. G. Herder on Social and Political Culture.* Edited and with an introduction by F. M. Barnard. Cambridge: Cambridge University Press.

Herodotus. 1998. *The Histories.* Trans. Robin Waterfield. Oxford: Oxford University Press.

Hill, Edward, and John Brennan. 2000. A Methodology for Identifying the Drivers of Industrial Clusters: The foundation of regional competitive advantage. *Economic Development Quarterly* 14 (1): 65–96.

Hirschman, Albert O. 1958. *The Strategy of Economic Development.* New Haven, CT: Yale University Press.

Hoover, Edgar M. 1937. *Location Theory and the Shoe and Leather Industries.* Cambridge, MA: Harvard University Press.

Isard, Walter. 1956. *Location and Space Economy.* Cambridge, MA: MIT Press.

Keating, Michael. 2003. The Invention of Regions: Political Restructuring and Territorial Government in Western Europe. In *State/Space: A Reader,* ed. Neil Brenner, Bob Jessup, Martin Jones, and Gordon MacLeod. Oxford: Blackwell.

Kolosovskiy, N. N. 1961. The Territorial-Production Combination (Complex) in Soviet Economic Geography. *Journal of Regional Science* 3 (1): 1–25.

Kremer-Marietti, Angèle. 1972. *Auguste Comte, la science sociale*. Paris: Gallimard.

Kropotkin, Peter. (1899) 1974. *Fields, Factories and Workshops*. London: Hutchison.

Krugman, Paul. 1992. *Geography and Trade*. Cambridge, MA: MIT Press.

Lewis, W. Arthur. 1955. *Theory of Economic Growth*. London: Allen & Unwin.

Le Play, Frédéric. (1877–1879) 1982. *La réforme sociale*. In *Frédéric Le Play on Family, Work, and Social Change*, ed. Catherine Bodard Silver. Chicago: University of Chicago Press.

Lovering, John. 1999. Theory Led by Policy: The Inadequacies of the "New Regionalism" (Illustrated from the Case of Wales). *International Journal of Urban and Regional Research* 23 (2): 379–395.

Markusen, Ann. 1987a. *Regions: The Economics and Politics of Territory*. Totowa, NJ: Rowan & Littlefield.

Markusen, Ann. 1987b. *High Tech America: The What, How, Where and Why of the Sunrise Industries*. London: Unwin Hyman.

Markusen, Ann, and Amanda Johnson. 2006. *Artists' Centers: Evolution and Impact on Careers, Neighborhoods, and Economics*. Minneapolis: Hubert Humphrey Institute of Public Affairs, University of Minnesota.

Meardon, Stephen J. 2001. Modeling Agglomeration and Dispersion in City and Country: Gunnar Myrdal, François Perroux, and the New Economic Geography. *American Journal of Economics and Sociology* 60 (1): 25–57.

Myrdal, Gunnar. 1957. *Economic Theory and the Underdeveloped Regions*. London: Duckworth.

National Resources Committee. 1935. *Regional Factors in National Planning and Development*. Washington, DC: Natural Resources Committee.

North, Douglass C. 1956. Exports and Regional Growth: A Reply to Tiebout. *Journal of Political Economy* 64 (2): 165.

Perroux, François. 1955. Note sur la notion de "pole de croissance." *Economie Appliquée* 7: 307–320.

Porter, Michael E. 1998. Clusters and the New Economics of Competition. *Harvard Business Review*, November–December.

Porter, Michael E. 2000. Location, Competition and Economic Development: Local Clusters in a Global Economy. *Economic Development Quarterly* 14 (1): 15–34.

Preusse, Heinz G. 2004. *The New American Regionalism*. Northampton, MA: Edward Elgar.

Proudhon, Pierre-Joseph. (1863). 1959. *Du principe fédératif*. In *Œuvres complètes de P.-J. Proudhon*. Paris: Librairie Marcel Rivieres.

Quijano, Anibal. 1968. Dependencia, cambio social, y urbanizacion. *Revista Mexicana de Sociologia* 30: 526–620.

Ratzel, Friedrich. 1882. *Anthropogeographie*. Stuttgart: J. Engelhorn.

Reclus, Elisée. 1905–1908. *L'homme et la terre*. Paris: Librairie Universelle.

Robb, Graham. 2007. *The Discovery of France: A Historical Geography from the Revolution to the First World War*. New York: Norton.

Rodwin, Lloyd. 1970a. *Nations and Cities: A Comparison of Strategies for Urban Growth*. Boston: Houghton Mifflin.

Rodwin, Lloyd. 1970b. Regional Development Planning and Regional Planning in Less Developed Countries: A Retrospective View of the Literature and Experience. *International Regional Science Review* 3 (2): 113–131.

Rothchild, Donald. 1997. *Managing Ethnic Conflict in Africa: Pressures and Incentives for Cooperation*. Washington, DC: Brookings Institution Press.

Rostow, Walt Whitman. 1960. *The Stages of Economic Growth: A Non-Communist Manifesto*. Cambridge: Cambridge University Press.

Saxenian, AnnaLee. 1994. *Regional Advantage: Culture and Competition in Silicon Valley and Route 128*. Cambridge, MA: Harvard University Press.

Schön, Donald, Bishwapriya Sanyal, and William Mitchell, eds. 1998. *High Technology and Low-Income Communities: Prospects for the Positive Use of Advanced Information Technology*. Cambridge, MA: MIT Press.

Scott, Allen J., and Michael Storper, eds. 1986. *Production, Work, Territory: The Geographical Anatomy of Industrial Capitalism*. London: Allen & Unwin.

Smith, Neil. 1995. Remaking Scale: Competition and Cooperation in Prenational and Postnational Europe. In *Competitive European Peripheries*, ed. H. Eskelinen and F. Snickars, 59–74. Berlin: Springer.

Soja, Edward W. 1968. *The Geography of Modernization in Kenya*. New York: Syracuse University Press.

Solow, Robert M. 1957. Technical Change and the Aggregate Production Function. *Review of Economics and Statistics* 39 (3): 312–320.

Stiglitz, Joseph E. 2003. *The Roaring Nineties: A New History of the World's Most Prosperous Decade*. New York: Norton.

Storper, Michael. 1991. *Industrialization, Economic Development and the Regional Question in the Third World: From Import Substitution to Flexible Production*. London: Pion.

Storper, Michael, and Allen J. Scott, eds. 1992. *Pathways to Industrialization and Regional Development*. London: Routledge.

Sunkel, Osvaldo. 1969. National Development Policy and External Dependence in Latin America. *Journal of Development Studies* 6 (1): 23–48.

Teitz, Michael B. 1985. Rationality in Planning and the Search for Community. In *Rationality in Planning*, ed. Michael Breheny and Andrew Hooper. London: Pion.

Thornton, Arland. 2005. Frederick Le Play, the Developmental Paradigm, Reading History Sideways, and Family Myths. Working paper, Population Studies Center, University of Michigan, Ann Arbor.

Tiebout, Charles. 1956. Exports and Regional Economic Growth. *Journal of Political Economy* 64 (2): 160–164.

Vico, Giambattista. (1744) 1968. *The New Science*. Ithaca, NY: Cornell University Press.

Vidal de la Blache, Paul. 1922. *Principes de géographie humaine* (*Principles of Human Geography*). Paris: Colin.

Viner, Jacob. 1950. *The Customs Union Issue*. New York: Carnegie Endowment for International Peace.

Weaver, Clyde. 1981. Development Theory and the Regional Question: A Critique of Spatial Planning and Its Detractors. In *Development from Above or Below? The Dialectics of Regional Planning in Developing Countries*, ed. Walter B. Stöhr and D. R. Fraser Taylor. New York: Wiley.

Weaver, Clyde. 1984. *Regional Development and the Local Community: Planning, Politics and the Social Context*. New York: Wiley.

Welter, Volker M. 2002. *Biopolis: Patrick Geddes and the City of Life*. Cambridge, MA: MIT Press.

6

Metropolitanism: How Metropolitan Planning Has Been Shaped by and Reflected in the Plans of the Regional Plan Association

Robert D. Yaro

This chapter examines the origins and development of the idea of metropolitanism and the reality of metropolitan planning in the United States. It describes how powerful intellectual and political traditions have impeded the growth and effectiveness of metropolitanism and how these have been overcome to produce the robust planning initiatives now under way in many areas of the country. Metropolitanism has been both shaped by and reflected in the work of the Regional Plan Association (RPA), the nation's oldest independent metropolitan planning, research, and advocacy organization, and its ad hoc predecessor group, the Committee on the Regional Plan of New York and Its Environs. In particular, this chapter examines how the concept of metropolitanism has been manifested in the RPA's three landmark regional plans, completed in 1929, 1968, and 1996. It also explores how metropolitan planning practice and theory have been shaped by these plans, and where metropolitan planning is now heading.

Defining Metropolitanism

Metropolitanism describes the way that the vast majority of Americans live their lives. The Brookings Institution's Metropolitan Policy Program has described metropolitanism as

not only where but also in some sense how Americans live—and it does this in a way that the city-suburb dichotomy does not. People work in one municipality, live in another, go to church or the doctor's office or the movies in yet another, and all these different places are somehow interdependent. Newspaper city desks have been replaced by the staffs of metro sections. Labor and housing markets are area-wide. Morning traffic reports describe pileups and traffic jams that stretch across a metropolitan area. Opera companies and baseball teams pull people from throughout a region. Air or water pollution affects an entire region, because pollutants, carbon monoxide, and runoff recognize no city or suburban or county boundaries. The way people talk about where they live reflects a subconscious recognition of metropolitan realities. Strangers on airplanes say to each other, "I'm from the Washington [or Houston or Los Angeles or Chicago or Detroit] area." They know that where they live makes sense only in relation to other places nearby, and to the big city in the middle. Metropolitanism is a way of talking and thinking about all these connections. (Katz and Bradley 1999)

Metropolitanism is a school of planning thought that promotes urban development in a continuum from the central city to its periphery by diffusing and promoting density and growth within a defined regional boundary. It promotes this targeted growth by encouraging development in the centers of metropolitan areas. It has been opposed since its early stages by proponents of "regionalism," a view that promotes the dispersed development of satellite cities in a region. The regionalist movement started with Scottish geographer Patrick Geddes and his American followers, including Lewis Mumford, Benton MacKaye, and other early twentieth-century advocates of regional planning in the United States. The regionalist outlook is also closely associated with the British and American Garden Cities movement, which began with Ebenezer Howard's 1902 book, *Garden Cities of To-morrow*. This gave rise to Britain's Garden Cities movement and was succeeded by the development of several generations of new communities in the United States, beginning with the World War I–era Emergency Fleet Corporation's housing developments, designed by Clarence Stein and others.

Over time, what has come to be known as metropolitanism has changed its emphasis and has moved from promoting development from the center of the metropolitan area outward to promoting growth in a series of centers within the region and protecting environmental systems within the growth boundaries of urban and suburban development.

Metropolitanism is now being promoted by the Brookings Institution, the RPA, and many other civic, business, and public sector planning, research, and advocacy groups as a movement to empower metropolitan regions to take charge of their futures and organize themselves to improve their quality of life, economic prospects, mobility systems, housing markets, sustainability, and other aspects of metropolitan life.

Metropolitan planning is a mechanism being used by a growing number of metropolitan regions to systematically address these concerns. Many metropolitan regions are also creating regional plans and action strategies to address climate change, including steps to mitigate the production of greenhouse gases that cause global climate change and to temper the impacts of changes that are already under way.

Since the early twentieth century, thinking about regions in terms of their metropolitan structure has taken hold and succeeded because of its enormous potential to increase the economic, environmental, and equitable development of a geographic area. At the beginning of the twenty-first century, metropolitanism has gained ground. reflecting the increased densities and size of human settlements and the fact that 80 percent of the U.S. population now lives in metropolitan areas. It has also been promoted as a result of the growing awareness of decision makers and opinion leaders that many of the fundamental problems facing densely populated areas can only be addressed at the metropolitan scale and in the long-range planning cycles encompassed by metropolitan plans.

The impetus to create new metropolitan plans has been especially strong on the West Coast since the mid-1990s. Beginning with Portland's Metro 2040 Plan, completed in 1995, virtually every large metropolitan region between Seattle to San Diego has created a new metropolitan plan. New plans developed in California have become known as "blueprint plans," following the completion of the Southern California Compass Blueprint Plan for the six-county Los Angeles region by the Southern California Association of Governments in 2005. These plans are now being used to advance California's clean air and carbon-reduction goals.

Portland's landmark plan was also the first in the nation to use a process of extensive civic engagement, now called "regional visioning." Portland was followed by Salt Lake City, Utah, where the visioning process was led by Envision Utah, a nonprofit organization with strong leadership from Governor Mike Levitt, key business leaders, and the influential Church of Latter Day Saints. Since these landmark metropolitan plans for Portland and Salt Lake City were completed, a score of other major U.S. metropolitan areas, including Chicago, Atlanta, Boston, Austin, and Phoenix, have used similar regional visioning processes to develop new metropolitan plans. In most cases these regions used simulation techniques to build public support for more compact, transit-oriented development patterns. It is clear that the Portland, Salt Lake City, and other visioning plans have had important long-term influences on metropolitan development patterns and public attitudes.

The tradition that led to these plans had its origin in the 1929 Regional Plan of New York and Its Environs. It took hold there as a means to handle the complex issues resulting from the industrial nature of the New York area, including congestion and pollution at the center of the metropolis. The RPA was incorporated in 1929 to promote implementation of the monumental plan, which had been completed that same year by its predecessor group, the ad hoc Committee on the Regional Plan of New York and Its Environs. The RPA is an independent, not-for-profit organization that has completed two additional comprehensive plans, in 1968 and 1996. While the RPA is not a business group, it does have strong connections to the region's business and civic leadership. This relationship helps shape the RPA's research, planning, and advocacy work. By engaging the business and civic leaders in the New York–New Jersey–Connecticut Metropolitan Area, the work of the RPA and its regional plans has been rooted in a deep commitment to the participation of its major stakeholders. It is important to note that the business and civic leaders of the region are usually the same persons and organizations and that their philanthropic interests help guide the RPA's plans. The RPA's regional plans are long-range, regionwide strategic plans for the thirty-one-county New York–New Jersey–Connecticut Metropolitan Region, the nation's largest metropolitan region; the plans are built around the RPA's goal of promoting the livability, economic vitality, and sustainable development of the region. All three plans have covered a wide range of issues and concerns, including transportation and mobility, urban form, economic structure, environmental and open space protection, housing, social equity and workforce skills, and education concerns.

In many ways, for nearly a century the RPA has both influenced and mirrored the thinking of metropolitan planners and theorists in New York, across the United States, and around the world. As the nation's largest urban region, New York has always been in the vanguard of urban and metropolitan development and planning. This is because urban problems emerge in New York early and at a scale that requires metropolitan-scale solutions. It is also influenced by the availability of financial resources. With a $1.2 trillion metropolitan economy, the New York region has the financial means and philanthropic values needed to support the RPA's work. And in many cases, the innovations that have emerged in the RPA's plans and actions in New York have inspired similar thinking and similar actions in large metropolitan regions in both the United States and Europe.

Forces Impeding Metropolitanism and Metropolitan Planning

Since the 1920 Census, a majority of U.S. residents have resided in urban areas. Today, more than eight out of ten U.S. residents live in metropolitan areas, and more than half the population lives in the largest twenty-five metropolitan areas. Despite these shifts, however, most of the nation's political power and control of the national policy agenda has continued to reside with the states and in rural regions and the suburban portion of metropolitan regions. This is a product of several strong traditions and biases:

• *Anti-urbanism*   Throughout its history, the United States has had a strong anti-urban bias, undercutting the political power of metropolitan regions. This anti-urban bias also reflects persistent nativist and anti-immigrant prejudices that work against urban and metropolitan regions, which until recently received the vast majority of immigrants.

• *Federalism*   The U.S. Constitution established a federal republic, relegating all powers not specifically reserved for the federal government to the states, including most of the powers shaping urban and metropolitan form, such as land-use planning and regulatory powers, taxation, and other responsibilities. Powerful state agencies drive policies and investments in most states, and despite forty years of "one man, one vote" redistricting in state legislatures, rural interests remain overrepresented in many state legislatures.

• *Entrenched localism*   In much of the country there is also a strong tradition of localism and home rule, and distrust of distant (including metropolitan) public authorities. Most responsibility for land-use regulation, housing, and other concerns has been devolved by the states to the municipal, not the metropolitan, level. Consequently, most metropolitan governance and planning organizations have only modest powers or are dominated by municipal interests.

• *The city-suburb divide*   Most metropolitan regions remain sharply divided between their urban and suburban components, a situation that undercuts the ability of metropolitan agencies to speak with a united voice.

• *Antimetropolitan bias*   Even in the planning profession there was an early and persistent antimetropolitan bias by regional planners, who saw metropolitan growth and development as a threat to natural resources and "indigenous" (at the time meaning native-born, white Anglo-Saxon) communities and culture. In the early years of the twentieth century, two schools of thought promulgated different ideas about planning: metropolitanism and regionalism. The regionalist view promoted Garden Cities—systems of differentiated and lower density enclaves—whereas the metropolitanists promoted growth continuously over the metropolitan landscape. In this respect, regionalists accused metropolitanists of encouraging development against environmental resources and landscapes. Unfortunately, the regionalists' vision took the form of sprawl and has burdened society with an unsustainable development pattern based on suburbs.

In sum, the problem with the idea of metropolitanism is that it runs counter to a number of powerful, deeply engrained ideas and the structure of American political institutions. Despite this, the idea still persists, in part because there is no clear alternative to managing large urban systems outside a metropolitan framework. The reality of life in the twenty-first century is that the vast majority of Americans live in metropolitan places knit together by very strong transportation, economic, environmental, and other systems. Metropolitanism has been successful despite all the obstacles to its implementation because of its clear appeal to the nature of our interdependent and regional problems and, most important, the potential solutions this perspective enables.

From an Agrarian to a Metropolitan Nation

Since the founding of the Republic more than two centuries ago, there has been a tension between two conflicting visions of America, one agrarian and the other urban. Two of the founding fathers, Thomas Jefferson and Alexander Hamilton, became vociferous advocates for these divergent views. Jefferson believed that America should remain a democratic, largely egalitarian nation of landowning yeoman farmers, living in an agrarian landscape punctuated by small market towns. Hamilton, on the other hand, believed that America's future lay in its transformation into an urban nation with a strong industrial economy. The U.S. Constitution reflected their alternative viewpoints in the historic compromise whereby Hamilton agreed to relocate the national capital from New York to Washington in return for concessions from Jefferson to permit the creation of a strong banking system and a strong, centralized currency. This compromise laid the foundation for the nation's transformation from a largely agrarian to a largely urban nation in the nineteenth and early twentieth centuries, a process that continues today. Hamilton also promoted this transformation through his personal efforts to establish the Bank of New York in 1784 and his investment in the creation of Paterson, New Jersey, the nation's first planned industrial city.

Although the rural and small town ideal retains a strong hold on the national psyche, America has long been a metropolitan nation. Metropolitan regions—agglomerations of urban and suburban centers with shared landscapes, economies, transportation and environmental infrastructure systems, and housing and employment markets—are the engines of the national economy, a focal point for its culture and communication systems and the proving ground for tens of millions of immigrants who have been brought into the mainstream of national life.

National, state, and local plans, policies, and investments rarely reflect this reality, however. The U.S. federal system puts states—not metropolitan regions—in command of most important economic development and transportation issues. And strong home rule traditions and entrenched municipal and county governments in most of the country jealously guard their land-use planning and regulatory powers. These two powerful forces leave metropolitan planning agencies and organizations in most areas without strong powers or a base of public support.

Origins of Metropolitanism and Metropolitan Planning

By the turn of the twentieth century, following decades of urbanization, rapid industrialization, and multiple waves of immigration, a number of large metropolitan regions emerged in the Northeast and Midwest. Foremost among these were New York, Chicago, Boston, and Philadelphia. All these cities engaged in extensive annexation programs through which suburban communities were incorporated into the fast-growing center cities. A number of political forces enabled late nineteenth-century annexation efforts to succeed in these places. Among them was the desire of urban elites of Northern European extraction to draw in fast-growing (and predominantly WASP) suburban areas in order to maintain political control despite rapid immigration from Southern and Eastern Europe. At the same time, suburban areas wanted access to metropolitan water and sewer, transportation, and other systems that were controlled by center cities. These forces combined to build the necessary political support for large-scale annexation in northeastern and midwestern cities in the late nineteenth and early twentieth centuries. Later in the twentieth century, the impetus for annexation was reduced by the accession to power in urban centers by Irish, Italian, and Jewish political groups and by the creation in Boston, New York, and other regions of metropolitan-scale public authorities that could provide large-scale infrastructure systems to suburban as well as urban communities.

Metropolitan thinking was clearly behind the creation of these institutions. In 1895, for example, the Commonwealth of Massachusetts created the Metropolitan Parks District, followed by the Metropolitan Water and Sewer Districts, to meet the regional infrastructure needs of dozens of municipalities in the Boston metropolitan area. In 1897, Boston built the nation's first subway, followed by New York and other cities. Then in 1898, Greater New York was established, which consolidated the cities of New York and Brooklyn, five counties, and dozens of smaller municipalities under a unified general-purpose metropolitan government. Of note, Greater New York's boundaries were permanently fixed by state legislation and have never been modified to reflect the growth of the metropolis since 1898.

During this same period, Frederick Law Olmsted, George Kessler, and other prominent landscape architects promoted the creation of metropolitan park systems in regions across the country. In an 1870 address to the American Social Science Association titled "Public Parks and the Enlargement of Towns," Olmsted reflected on the economic, hygienic, and social benefits of Central Park after its first twelve years of use:

It must be remembered, also, that the Park is not planned for such use as is now made of it, but with regard to the future use, when it will be in the center of a population of two millions hemmed in by water at a short distance on all sides. . . . The question of the relative value of what is called off-hand common sense, and of special, deliberate, business-like study, must be settled, in the case of the Central Park, by a comparison of benefit with cost. During the last four years over thirty million visits have been made to the Park by actual count, and many have passed uncounted. . . . As to the effect on public health, there is no question that it is already great. . . . The Park, moreover, has had a very marked effect in making the city attractive to visitors, and in thus increasing its trade, and causing many who have made fortunes elsewhere to take up their residence and become tax-payers in it. (Olmsted 1973, 169–173)

On the West Coast, cities such as San Francisco and Los Angeles created metropolitan water supply systems, diverting rivers and building aqueducts that stretched for hundreds of miles. At the same time, private railroad companies built metropolitan-scale commuter rail networks in more than a dozen of the nation's largest metropolitan regions.

Chicago became a hotbed of metropolitan thought and action during this period. Until the consolidation of Greater New York in 1898 it vied with New York to become the nation's largest city. Metropolitanism was at the heart of planning efforts for both cities. Chicago's rapid growth and competitive impulses led to the 1893 Columbian Exposition and later to the creation of Chicago's signature lakefront park system. When pollution from the Chicago River threatened the city's Lake Michigan water supply, Chicago simply reversed the flow of the river to dump its sewage into the Mississippi River system. And when flooding along the low-lying river and lakefront undercut the development potential of the city's downtown business and retail Loop area, Chicago simply elevated the city.

This can-do approach to urban development—a clear function of the business community's influence and engagement in civic matters—led to the creation of the nation's first comprehensive city plan, Daniel Burnham and Edward Bennett's 1909 Plan of Chicago. Although Burnham correctly received public acclaim for the plan, two other business and civic leaders, Charles Dyer Norton and Frederic Delano, deserve much of the credit for envisioning the plan, building the civic leadership and political resolve necessary to create and implement it and raising the funds to hire Burnham to write the plan in the first place.

Metropolitan Planning Comes to New York

Following his business and planning success in Chicago, and after a brief stint as secretary to President William Howard Taft in Washington, Norton moved to New York in 1911 to become vice president of J.P. Morgan's First National Bank of New York. He was followed shortly after by Delano. At the time, New York was growing at a prodigious rate, having already expanded well beyond the rigid boundaries of the consolidated city established only a generation earlier.

New York was also becoming overwhelmed by rapid population growth and congestion, and related and recurring epidemics and crime. Waves of immigration from Southern and Eastern Europe had created vast slums in districts across the city and led to widespread questions about the region's ability to bring these groups into the economic and social mainstream. The new phenomenon of mass automobile ownership was creating unprecedented congestion on the region's roads. Shipping, warehousing, and manufacturing throughout Manhattan threatened to overwhelm the city's already crowded streets and residential and business districts at the same time that the city was becoming a national and even global center of finance, industry, and communications. Finally, the telephone and long-distance power transmission threatened to transform communications and industrial production. But these trends also provided new opportunities to transform the city and its surrounding metropolitan region in positive ways, through the planned deconcentration of population and industry to the region's suburbs and outer reaches. In this context, the regionalists and metropolitanists competed with each other for the solution to the pressing problem of urban congestion.

In London, similar trends had by the early twentieth century led to the creation of metropolitan police forces, schools, and water and sewer systems and an extensive network of social housing estates built by the London County Council. Raymond Unwin was championing Letchworth and Welwyn Garden Cities and Hampstead garden suburb as prototypes of what was envisioned as a metropolitan network of Garden Cities and suburbs designed around Ebenezer Howard's vision of planned deconcentration of the London metropolitan region. Howard's identification of the most salient issue facing society—urban concentration and density—and his proposal to overcome this problem with a series of magnet cities were articulated as follows:

Each city may be regarded as a magnet, each person as a needle; and so viewed, it is at once seen that nothing short of the discovery of a method for constructing magnets of yet greater power than our cities possess can be effective for re-distributing the population in a spontaneous and healthy manner. (Howard [1902], 1965, 44–45)

Charles Dyer Norton became convinced that the scale of New York's problems required a comprehensive plan similar to his Plan of Chicago. But the sheer size and complexity of the New York region, he believed, would require a plan that was *regional* in scale, covering the whole twenty-two-county, three-state *metropolitan* region. Just as he had in Chicago, he convened an ad hoc group of business and civic leaders to advance the concept. In 1922, Norton brought Raymond Unwin to New York to consult on the idea of creating a regional plan. That same year Norton and Delano organized a group of regional planning advocates into the Committee on the Regional Plan of New York and Its Environs and secured a major grant from the Russell Sage Foundation to fund development of the plan. As in Chicago, Norton felt that the leadership of the planning effort needed to come from the business and civic sectors, since the problems they were addressing were too important to be left to the politicians and since regional concerns cut across political boundaries. As in Chicago, the plan would require a visionary planner who could organize the large professional team that would be needed to develop the plan. Norton hired an English disciple of Unwin, Thomas Adams, to lead the creation of the regional plan. As Peter Hall has suggested, it was important that Adams worked well with Norton's vision since he was a "businessman's planner," and also important that he disagreed with other Americans, such as Lewis Mumford, who were promoting a Garden Cities approach to urban problems (Hall 2002). In the context of the uniquely American antimetropolitan ideas mentioned earlier, Adams's work on New York's regional plan provided the groundwork for the early development of metropolitanism, in reaction to both the urban problems agreed on by most commentators and the proposed solutions of intellectuals such as Howard.

The initiation of the regional plan was part of a broader intellectual and political movement in the 1920s to create order out of chaos in the development of the New York metropolitan region. This sense of crisis undoubtedly gave a strong boost to metropolitanism and helped it overcome the issues that were impeding development and growth. In 1921, the Port Authority of New York (now the Port Authority of New York and New Jersey) was established through an interstate compact between the states of New York and New Jersey to rationalize interstate freight and related port facilities. Also in New York, in 1923 a group of visionary sociologists, architects, housing advocates, and regional planners established the Regional Planning Association of America (RPAA), a loose-knit, ad hoc group that would convene from time to time to debate regional planning concerns for New York and the nation. RPAA's economist, Stuart Chase, summarized the group's thinking about regional planning:

The regional planning of communities would wipe out uneconomic national marketing, wipe out city congestion and terminal wastes, balance the power load, take the bulk of coal of the railroads, eliminate the duplication of milk and other deliveries, short circuit such uneconomic practices as hauling Pacific apples to New York customers by encouraging local orchards, develop local forest areas and check the haulage of western timber to eastern mills, locate cotton mills near cotton fields, show factories near hide producing areas, steel mills within striking distance of ore beds, food manufacturing plants in small giant power units, near farming belts. Gone the necessity for the skyscraper, the subway and the lonely countryside! (Chase 1925, 146)

Among the group's members were journalist and philosopher Lewis Mumford, architects Clarence Stein and Henry Wright, theorist Clarence Perry, housing expert Catherine Bauer, real estate executive and investor Alexander Bing, and forester and regional planner Benton MacKaye. Although Perry and other RPAA members served as staff members or consultants to the Regional Plan of New York and Adams consulted on the RPAA's plans for a model "New Town for the Motor Age" at Radburn, New Jersey, a growing schism developed between the "regionalists" of the RPAA and the "metropolitanists" of the RPA. The regionalists pursued planning based on the principle of autonomous cities spaced across the landscape, while metropolitanists looked pragmatically at diffusing and creating density and growth within a region's boundary.

In 1925, Lewis Mumford edited the *Regional Plan* issue of *Survey Graphic*, creating a manifesto for the RPAA and including several essays highly critical of the expansion and densification of New York, which Mumford termed the "Dinosaur City" (Mumford 1925). Mumford's essay was the first in a long list of books and essays on the impending collapse of New York, publications that seem to emerge each time the city enters an economic downturn and that espouse antimetropolitan views.

Then, in 1928, MacKaye published *The New Exploration*, a book on regional planning that called for containing the "metropolitan invasion" and organizing regions around their natural resource systems. MacKaye believed that networks of greenways and "townless highways" (limited access highways) could be established as "levees" against the metropolitan "flood" (i.e., the expansion of metropolitan areas into the suburbs). MacKaye sought these tools to control metropolitan growth, which he believed threatened to inundate the rural and primeval places surrounding every large metropolitan area and destroy the network of small towns and villages that remained the repository of what he termed "indigenous" values and culture, which MacKaye saw as the bedrock of American civilization.

In 1931, the RPA released *Building the City*, the final and summary volume of the Regional Plan of New York and Its Environs. This set the stage for an important exchange of essays by Adams and Mumford in the June and July 1932 issues of the *New Republic* magazine highlighting the philosophical and pragmatic differences between the RPAA regionalists and the RPA metropolitanists. In a nutshell, Mumford argued that the RPA's plan provided cover for the capitalist forces of metropolitan expansion and densification, while Adams argued that the RPAA's intellectuals and dilettantes were living in a fantasy world in their belief that metropolitan growth and densification could be prevented or accommodated entirely in a network of greenbelt towns surrounding the urban core of the region. According to Peter Hall,

Mumford condemned the [RPA] plan in almost every last particular. Its spatial frame, wide as it might seem, was too narrow; it accepted growth as inevitable, ignoring the potential of planning to influence it; it failed to consider alternatives; it continued to allow overbuilding of central areas; it condemned the last remaining piece of open space near to Manhattan, the Hackensack Meadows of New Jersey, to be built over; it dismissed garden cities as utopian, it condoned the filling-in of suburban areas; through its rejection of the principle of public housing, it condemned the poor to live in poor housing; it favored yet more subsidy for the commuter lines into Manhattan, thus helping create more of the very congestion it condemned; its highway and rapid-transit proposals were an alternative to a community-building project, not a means toward it. . . . Despite appearances to the contrary, it really meant a drift to yet more centralization. (Hall 2002, 167)

Adams's concern was rooted in practical considerations and the acknowledgment that the region was fixed and that only incremental, marginal change was possible. He summarized his disagreement with Mumford from a pragmatic point of view, criticizing Mumford as utopian:

This is the main point on which Mr. Mumford and I . . . differ—that is whether we stand still and talk ideals or move forward and get as much realization of our ideals as possible in a necessarily imperfect society, capable only of imperfect solutions to its problems. (quoted in Hall 2002,167)

In the 1930s, the RPA went on to advocate for its proposals for bridges, tunnels, parkways, parks, and housing developments. These visions were largely realized through the advocacy of the RPA's second chairman, Frederic Delano, who was the uncle of the New York governor and later U.S. president, Franklin Delano Roosevelt. In 1932, Delano was asked by President Roosevelt to chair the National Planning Board (later renamed the National Resources Planning Board). This agency coordinated plans for Depression-era public works and promoted the creation of state and regional planning agencies to develop public works plans and strategies, and to develop plans that mirrored those prepared by the RPA in other regions.

Many of the large infrastructure and city-building projects envisioned by the Regional Plan, and funded by the New Deal's public works programs, were built by Robert Moses, New York's "master builder." Moses led a series of public agencies and authorities under the auspices of New York City and New York State, which oversaw the largest expansion of public works in the region's history. Under Moses' leadership, dozens of the RPA's extensive public works proposals were built over a thirty-year period beginning in the early 1930s, including the Triboro, Whitestone, Throgs Neck, and Verrazano bridges, the Midtown and Brooklyn-Battery tunnels, and the Long Island and Hudson Valley park and parkway systems. Moses built many of these major public works projects with funding provided by Roosevelt's New Deal.

Under Delano's leadership, metropolitan areas across the country were required to develop regional plans in order to qualify for federally funded public works projects, providing a powerful incentive for metropolitan-scale regional planning. And unlike in the earlier period of annexation, metropolitan cooperation for infrastructure development did not require wholesale restructuring of metropolitan governance systems. Instead, state and regional authorities, many inspired by Robert Moses' example, were established to build large-scale projects. In New York, the Port Authority also built the RPA's proposed trans-Hudson roadway bridges and tunnels and carried out the RPA's proposals to relocate the seaports from Manhattan's Hudson River waterfront to New Jersey and build the region's airports. Among the RPA's major infrastructure proposals, only the railroad projects did not proceed—a result of a lack of cooperation on the part of private railroad companies, the absence of public funding for this purpose, and the disinterest of Robert Moses, Austin Tobin, and other public officials.

By 1940, and the early years of World War II, the RPA's major infrastructure projects had largely been completed. After the war, the RPA began to focus on a new set of issues facing New York and metropolitan America: the emerging challenges of suburban sprawl, the move of employment and housing to the suburbs, the loss of open space, and the changing nature of the nation's economy. In the 1950s the RPA collaborated with the Harvard School of Public Administration to conduct the Metropolitan Region Study, which examined these emerging trends in both the New York region and nationwide. The resulting multivolume report laid bare the essentials of the economic history of the New York region, showing how its industries grew out of one another and emphasizing the part that labor and housing played in this process by making available workers for these industries. The early crucial role of the port and the later crucial role of "clustering," which enabled firms to share facilities and workforces, were also analyzed. The study also discussed the region's advantages and disadvantages for different kinds of businesses and industry, and the interrelation between the jobs in the region and the people who lived in it. It traced the movement of jobs geographically in and out of the region as a whole, and also outward within the region, relating this outward movement to such developments as the thinning out of population in inner-city areas and the continuing boom in suburban areas. The problems besetting the multitude of local governments in the region were analyzed, as was the crisis of commuting and rapid transit services. Finally, the study projected the metropolis into 1985, picturing it as the sum of all the infinitely complex forces of its history that would come to bear if they were not altered in their future operation by governmental actions of unprecedented magnitude.

The Second Regional Plan

This analysis set the stage for the RPA's Second Regional Plan, completed in 1969. The RPA expanded its planning region from twenty-two to thirty-one counties, to incorporate the rural and wilderness areas surrounding the metropolis. In part this reflected the RPA's adoption of the regionalist views of Benton MacKaye and others concerning the need for regional plans to address the needs of these areas as well as the urbanized areas of the region. MacKaye's and Mumford's regionalist and landscape ideas were incorporated into the more metropolitanist ideas of the RPA more as a result of the need to coordinate growth in the new centers that had emerged since the first plan and concern over natural resources management in the expanded boundaries of the region. To a great extent, in the late 1960s and early 1970s the old disagreement between the RPAA and the RPA was overcome, beginning with the RPA's adoption of a more holistic view of planning that included planning for other centers within the metropolitan area and having a more proactive stance on natural resources preservation. The Second Regional Plan was built around several key components that shaped subsequent thinking about the New York metropolitan region and metropolitan planning. Among them were the following:

• *Spread city*   The RPA anticipated that then emerging patterns of urban sprawl (which the RPA called "spread city") would threaten the success of both cities and suburbs, and concluded that bold steps would be needed to rein in sprawl in New York and across the country. The plan helped inspire the subsequent growth management and smart growth movements.

• *Regional centers*   The Second Regional Plan reconceptualized the region as a polycentric region and identified a dozen regional centers that could become major mixed use employment centers as the region continued to decentralize. All of these centers would be connected by a revitalized regional rail system, operated by a new Metropolitan Transportation Authority (MTA) that would assume control of the failing commuter rail system from bankrupt private railroads. The plan inspired subsequent plans for Tokyo, Paris, and other cities that reconceptualized these places as polycentric regions.

• *The race for open space*   The plan authors coined the term "open space" and initiated an ambitious strategy to create federal, state, regional, municipal, and private parks and preserves designed to prevent sprawl and protect critical recreational and scenic landscapes. The plan promoted the creation of state open space acquisition programs in all three states in the region, which resulted in the creation of a million-acre open space system in the New York metropolitan region by 1990. It also promoted the creation of the Gateway National Recreation Area (the nation's first urban national park), the Delaware Water Gap National Recreation Area, Fire Island National Seashore, Minnewaska State Park, and other important parks and preserves. Finally, the RPA's Open Space program inspired the nationwide land trust and open space preservation movement across the country.

• *Urban design Manhattan*   The plan promoted the creation of new, dense urban forms built around an "accessibility tree"—essentially, vertical transit systems that situated important mixed use, high-density urban nodes on top of major transit hubs. The concept inspired the World Trade Center, Citicorp Center, and other major urban development projects in Manhattan and elsewhere and presaged the national transit-oriented development movement.

In the 1970s and 1980s the RPA led local planning efforts in Stamford and Bridgeport, Connecticut; White Plains, downtown Brooklyn, and Jamaica, New York; and Jersey City, Newark, and New Brunswick, New Jersey, to create strong regional centers in these places. It also led advocacy efforts to provide funds to the newly established MTA and New Jersey Transit (NJ Transit) to rebuild the region's deteriorated subway and commuter rail networks. And the RPA continued its advocacy for land preservation and parks in such places as the New Jersey Pinelands and New Jersey Highlands, Sterling Forest in the Hudson Valley, and other threatened open spaces.

Third Regional Plan

By the late 1980s, the New York region had undergone a profound transformation. The city itself was reeling from national trends of disinvestment in cities, middle-class flight, and suburban sprawl. New York

City faced widespread housing abandonment in the Bronx and Brooklyn, rising crime rates, and failing schools. The city experienced the first population decline since the American Revolution as major employers fled to the suburbs and other parts of the country. Newark, Bridgeport, and other urban centers experienced similar declines, even as open space disappeared in a new era of very low-density suburban sprawl. A new wave of immigration threatened to create large new ghettos in New York and other cities, and highway congestion worsened as the region stopped building new highways.

In response to these threats, in 1990 the RPA initiated its Third Regional Plan, with a sharpened focus on all of these issues. A core principle used in developing the plan was that all of its key recommendations had to have been either already implemented and evaluated in other regions or demonstrated in the New York region. With this principle in mind, the RPA staff investigated and documented urban innovations in transportation, environmental protection, urban design, growth management, and other issues in London, Paris, Tokyo, Shanghai, Toronto, Portland, San Francisco, and other cities. The RPA's plan then proposed ways in which these models could be adapted and replicated in the New York region.

The regional rail concepts being implemented in Tokyo and Paris, for example, became the subject of exchange visits involving key transportation agency officials and opinion leaders. These concepts were then adapted to form the RPA's Regional Express proposal in the Third Regional Plan. They are now being implemented through three "megaprojects"—the Second Avenue Subway, Access to the Region's Core (ARC), and East Side Access projects—representing the largest transit expansion program in New York since the 1930s. Two of these projects, East Side Access and the Second Avenue Subway, are now under construction. New Jersey governor Chris Christie terminated his state's participation in the third, the ARC rail tunnel under the Hudson, late in 2010 because of concerns over cost overruns. Governor Christie's decision underscores the difficulty of sustaining political will in support of large public works projects over the over the long time frame needed for their completion.

Where innovations had not already been demonstrated in other places, the RPA led demonstrations of innovative planning concepts in the New York region. On Long Island, for example, the RPA helped develop plans for the Long Island Central Pine Barrens Commission, a regional land-use regulatory commission created and managed through a bottom-up process. The commission's management plan, prepared by the RPA, incorporated the nation's first regional transfer of development rights system. In another demonstration project, the RPA led efforts in New Jersey to reform the state's brownfield reclamation law and to apply this law in Union County, which had the state's largest concentration of brownfields. RPA staff then worked with municipal and state officials and developers to walk several model reclamation projects through the new state regulatory process.

This approach illustrates the RPA's pragmatic tradition, stretching back to Charles Dyer Norton, Thomas Adams, and Frederic Delano. While the association often promotes visionary ideas, the organization's credibility rests on its ability to pursue the implementation of these ideas within the political realities of the region. The RPA is staffed by professional planners, architects, and engineers and is governed by a board of directors composed of business, civic, and intellectual leaders of the region that provides guidance on priorities for research planning and advocacy of the organization.

In some cases, however, the concepts included in the RPA's plans do not achieve immediate political acceptance. In these cases the RPA staff waits until political opportunities present themselves, which may be years or even decades later. Overall, the vast majority of the RPA's key recommendations in its three regional plans have been adopted over the years as a result of the logic of the proposals themselves, the credibility of the organization, and the effectiveness and persistence of its advocacy efforts.

The implementation of the Third Regional Plan demonstrates how the concept of metropolitanism has been retailored to address both the new challenges facing metropolitan regions in the twenty-first century (e.g., climate change, brownfield remediation, the back-to-the-inner-city movement) and chronic metropolitan concerns (e.g., congestion, natural resource protection, public health) in new ways.

Similar to the earlier RPA planning efforts, the plan was overseen by a committee. An extensive process of public consultation and civic engagement was initiated as the plan was being developed, including annual regional assemblies and area-wide forums to vet draft plan recommendations. Each of the demonstration projects noted above also was overseen by an advisory committee to develop the concepts. In this way, hundreds of stakeholders, opinion leaders, and agency officials were engaged in working out the key components of the plan.

The RPA pioneered extensive public participation in its Second Regional Plan in the 1960s, using, for example, televised "town meet-

ings" to test and build public support for the plan's key recommendations. The extensive civic engagement process utilized in preparing the
Third Regional Plan built on these examples. While the association did
not employ such innovations as regional visioning and electronic town
meetings in preparing the plan, it has used these techniques in implementing the plan.

The plan was organized around the "three E's"—strategies to improve
the region's economy, environment, and social equity. This was probably
the first time that the concept of the three E's was incorporated in the
regional planning process. These ideas emanated from the experience
gained by the RPA in more than seventy years of work that illuminated
the interrelatedness of different activities of society. This was galvanized
in the late 1990s as a "triple-bottom-line" focus on the three E's as a
reflection of the interdisciplinary and multisectoral nature of the late
twentieth-century metropolis. It is interesting to note that regional planning has moved beyond solely infrastructure planning and is involved in
more social and economic planning as a result of its attention to the three
E's framework for regional planning and the recognition that a skilled
workforce and more equitable access to employment are as important
to the region's success as are more traditional regional planning concerns,
such as infrastructure and urban form.

The plan was completed in 1996. Its final report, titled *A Region at
Risk*, presented proposals for $75 billion in new investments in trans-
portation and environmental infrastructure. The plan was organized
around five major campaigns:

• *Greensward* A "metropolitan greensward" consisting of a dozen new
"regional reserves"—large protected landscapes encompassing entire
watersheds and natural resources systems—was a key geographic
proposal.

• *Mobility* Integration and expansion of the region's separate commuter rail and subway networks with the creation of several Regional
Express, or Rx Rail, lines, loosely modeled after Paris's RER system,
was a prominent transit proposal. This is a good example of how
ideas from other countries are borrowed as they prove successful in
advancing regional well-being. When planning is based on best
practices, the outcomes can be readily ascertained and experimentation
and trial-and-error approaches avoided. As noted earlier, the regional rail
projects proposed in the plan are already approved and under
construction.

• *Centers*   The Third Regional Plan expanded on the Second Regional Plan's concept of regional centers by calling for the creation of a new network of suburban centers, linked to each other through a modernized regional rail network.

• *Workforce*   The plan's major proposals called for reforms and investments in urban K–12 education systems, English language training, and lifelong learning systems to address the education needs of the region's growing populations of immigrants and minorities and prepare them for jobs in the modern workforce and civic engagement.

• *Governance*   The creation of a new regional infrastructure bank and reforms to existing public authorities, as well as tax and other reforms, were among the plan's major governance proposals. A proposed "Tri-State Infrastructure Bank" would administer a long-range capital program for the region's transportation and environmental investment needs. This capital program would finance new systems as well as maintenance of existing capital assets. The RPA's recommendation was adapted from successful models in other states and from proposals to create a national infrastructure bank.

The role of the RPA as an independent, not-for-profit organization is purely advisory. But as a result of the extensive civic engagement process and demonstration projects utilized in developing the plan and the RPA's extensive advocacy efforts, most of the plan's key transportation, urban development, and open space protection recommendations have already been completed, or are under construction, or are under serious consideration by implementing authorities. In every case, the RPA staff has worked closely with elected and appointed officials, editorial boards, and other opinion leaders to build support for the plan's recommendations.

Most of these advocacy efforts have involved building coalitions of civic and business groups, many of them convened, staffed, chaired, or coordinated by the RPA. This model of metropolitanism differs from earlier models in bridging the earlier technical and top-down planning approaches and a more bottom-up and participatory public process that ensures all concerns are included in plan formulations. From the initial set of plan formulations, only the most appropriate ideas with committed political support are pursued further. The RPA's advocacy efforts have also involved intense civic engagement in the form of public forums or charrettes to bring together stakeholders, public officials, and concerned citizens to discuss the initiatives. On a few occasions the RPA and its coalition partners have also engaged in paid advertising, focus groups, Internet-based advocacy campaigns, and other efforts to build public support for its recommendations.

In an early success, in 1995 and 1996, as the Third Regional Plan was being completed, the RPA convinced newly elected New York governor George Pataki and his administration to adopt the plan's regional rail concept. Pataki immediately adopted the plan's proposal to connect the Long Island Railroad to Grand Central Terminal on Manhattan's East Side through the unused 63rd Street tunnel. Following an advocacy campaign by the RPA in 1997–1998, the Pataki administration and the MTA also adopted the RPA's proposal to build the second Rx link, the Second Avenue Subway, running the full length of Manhattan. A third megaproject endorsed by the plan as part of its Rx system, the two new ARC tunnels connecting NJ Transit to Manhattan, was adopted by the state of New Jersey and the Port Authority in 2003.

The open space and centers programs of the Third Regional Plan have had similar successes. As the plan was being developed, the RPA participated in efforts to create the Central Pine Barrens Commission on Long Island to protect a 100,000-acre preserve identified as one of the regional reserves in the plan. Legislation to create this bottom-up regional commission was adopted by the New York state legislature in 1996, following years of controversy and litigation over development in the Pine Barrens. This effort inspired similar efforts in New York City's upstate water supply watersheds in the late 1990s and in the New Jersey Highlands and Long Island Sound reserves since 2003.

The RPA's centers campaign has achieved similar success. The RPA has led master planning, rezoning, and redevelopment planning efforts in several centers, including Stamford and Bridgeport, Connecticut; Downtown Brooklyn and the Nassau Hub, New York; and Newark and the Somerset Regional Center, New Jersey. Local communities are willing to work with RPA because of its recognition in the region and its ability to connect local communities with regional resources and a professional staff that can provide technical assistance funded by philanthropic sources. The RPA has cooperated with NJ Transit in its successful Transit Village program, through which master plans and redevelopment plans have been developed for more than a dozen centers served by NJ Transit's commuter rail services. The RPA has also initiated efforts to transform Manhattan's Far West Side into a third Manhattan business district. The area was rezoned for this purpose in 2005, and plans are under way to expand and transform Pennsylvania Station into a new Moynihan Station (named after Senator Daniel Patrick Moynihan, an early supporter of the plan). The transformed Moynihan Station will provide additional transportation capacity and spur redevelopment efforts. All of this is being supported by an RPA-convened coalition—the Friends of Moynihan Station—and was abetted by the RPA's efforts to prevent the controversial proposal to build a new football stadium on the West Side Waterfront.[1]

Despite its success in promoting action on the key recommendations of the Third Plan's mobility, centers, and greensward campaigns, the RPA has had less success with its workforce and governance campaigns. The RPA has led several reverse-commute demonstration projects and has promoted transit links on the Metro-North Railroad and Long Island Rail Road that promote reverse commutes from New York City to suburban employment centers. Mayors Michael Bloomberg in New York City and Cory Booker in Newark have strongly encouraged efforts to transform urban school systems in those cities, although the RPA has not played an active role in those efforts. And although the region has invested $75 billion in transit investments since the Third Regional Plan was completed in 1996 (much of it as a result of advocacy efforts by the Empire State Transportation Alliance, which was convened and is staffed and co-chaired by the RPA), the region has not adopted the infrastructure bank or other finance reforms recommended in the Third Regional Plan.

Toward a New Era of Metropolitan Planning

When the RPA initiated its Third Regional Plan in 1990, virtually no large metropolitan region in the United States had completed a strategic regional plan of this type in decades. The predominance of other interests—national, state, and local—since World War II detracted from the ability of regional planning to move forward. By the mid-1990s, however, a number of regions, including Portland, Chicago, Atlanta, and Seattle, had initiated similar efforts, in part inspired by the RPA's experience with the Third Regional Plan. Renewed public interest and support for regional planning owes in part to the growing recognition of the limitations of purely local or statewide planning points of view that account for political boundaries but not for economic, environmental, and social dimensions of activities that are more metropolitan in reach. To a great extent, the regional movement that has emerged since the 1990s is a result of a long overdue recognition of the reality of metropolitan America, especially as climate change, sprawl, and economic development achieve higher priority as issues of regional scale. Beginning with the Portland 2040 planning effort in the mid-1990s, a number of regions, including Salt Lake City, Los Angeles, Phoenix, Sacramento, and San Diego, have undertaken regional "visioning" and planning initiatives, all involving extensive public participation in scenario-based planning efforts.

These efforts have been supported and in many cases funded by the expanded metropolitan planning requirements of the Intermodal Surface Transportation Efficiency Act of 1991. ISTEA and its successors, TEA-21 and SAFETEA-LU, have all strengthened the regional planning requirements for receipt of federal transportation funds and have promoted the current generation of metropolitan plans. The Obama administration has proposed a further expansion of these programs and a broadening of their purview to include metropolitan housing, regional equity, environmental, and climate concerns, in addition to transportation concerns. The administration's $200 million Sustainable Communities Initiative is providing regional planning grants to metropolitan areas for the first time in a generation. Metropolitan planning is nevertheless not a response to federal inducements. On the contrary: it is a bottom-up approach undertaken by civic leaders in different communities that aims to guide sustainable growth through pragmatic plans that encompass a broad set of issues. In many cases, metropolitan planning organizations (MPOs), charged by the federal government with transportation planning for metropolitan regions with more than 50,000 people, have initiated their own regional funding efforts in parallel with the civic initiated ones, giving them control of billions of dollars in new transit investments, further strengthening these organizations.

A Look to the Future: Will the United States Become a Metro Nation?

Despite strong efforts by the Republican-dominated House of Representatives to limit the authority of the U.S. Environmental Protection Agency (EPA) to regulate greenhouse gas emissions, concerns over climate change are again inducing a new wave of metropolitanism in the United States centered on climate concerns as well as equity and social issues. As a result of the U.S. Supreme Court's 2007 decision to classify carbon dioxide as a "classified air pollutant," or CAP, the EPA is expected to issue new regulations requiring that MPOs coordinate clean air and transportation plans to achieve greenhouse gas reduction and climate protection goals, as well as transportation and air quality goals.

Most climate experts and regional planners believe that carbon reductions cannot be achieved without significant changes in settlement patterns and transportation systems designed to reduce automobile and truck use. Almost inevitably this will require that MPOs initiate stronger land-use planning efforts to achieve CO_2 reductions, further strengthening the role of metropolitan planning institutions. Growing public support for climate protection could also build a new base of support for metropolitan-scale climate initiatives and more effective metropolitan planning designed to achieve this goal. A major challenge for metropolitan planning has always been building this public support, and the challenges ahead will require that new coalitions and alliances be forged among diverse stakeholders to create viable and robust plans that are implementable with broad public support.

The idea of metropolitanism has been around for nearly a century. It has influenced the construction of essential infrastructure projects and guided metropolitan development patterns. Metropolitanism has had many lives and seems to come back in different forms; every generation over the past century has faced the need to understand its problems from a regional point of view. Today, the Brookings Institution's Metropolitan Policy Program is advancing an ambitious and well-funded campaign designed to promote federal, state, and metropolitan policies and investments oriented to the needs of the nation's metropolitan areas. The RPA, through its America 2050 program, is promoting a national infrastructure investment plan that will provide an additional impetus to metropolitan areas to meet their infrastructure needs. Both of these efforts have the potential to bolster local initiatives to create more effective metropolitan planning and governance.

Despite multiple successes, metropolitan initiatives will inevitably conflict with the values and institutions described at the beginning of this chapter as impediments to metropolitanism and more effective metropolitan planning. The prerogatives and powers of state and municipal governments won't go away, and much of the nation retains a strong anti-urban, antimetropolitan bias, particularly as the debate over illegal immigration intensifies. But there is reason to believe that despite these impediments, America may finally start acting in its own self-interest as a "metro nation" and empower a new generation of more effective metropolitan planning.

Note

1. Some critics, notably Hunter College planning professor Tom Angotti in his book, *New York for Sale* (Angotti 2008), have been critical of the RPA's position on other large urban development projects, such as the vast Atlantic Yards redevelopment project in Brooklyn. The RPA declined to oppose this project when a number of other civic groups did. Angotti argues this was because real estate interests dominated the RPA's board of directors. But at the time, only a few of the sixty board members had ties to the real estate industry. In fact, unlike most other major civic groups in New York, the RPA board represents not just real estate interests but a broad range of business, civic, and academic institutions. Further, the association's policies and actions are largely driven by the staff, not the board.

What really drove the RPA's position on the Yards was the staff's belief that this strategic location, near downtown Brooklyn, with its high concentration of subway and commuter rail lines, was an appropriate place for high-density residential and commercial development. In addition, the RPA had just completed a contentious but successful campaign to oppose the Bloomberg administration's proposal for a football stadium on Manhattan's West Side. The RPA staff and board also felt that the RPA could not be "against everything" and would have to choose its battles carefully. Nor did they relish the thought of another confrontation with City Hall on the heels of the West Side stadium fight, in light of the mayor's strong support for both the stadium and the Atlantic Yards project.

The RPA's leadership also felt that the Yards project was a "done deal" because of the strong support from both the mayor and the governor. And unlike the stadium project, there was no chance of overturning the Yards project in the legislature. For all these reasons, the RPA made the decision to focus on improving the project's site plan and public spaces, reducing its visual impact on adjoining communities, and improving the developer's payment to the MTA for the purchase of air rights over the Atlantic Terminal station area. The project subsequently received all of its necessary permits, despite opposition from several civic and community groups.

References

Angotti, Tom. 2008. *New York for Sale*. Cambridge, MA: MIT Press.

Chase, Stuart. 1925. Coals to Newcastle. *Survey* 54: 143–146.

Hall, Peter. 2002. *Cities of Tomorrow*. Oxford: Blackwell.

Howard, Ebenezer. (1902) 1965. *Garden Cities of To-morrow*. Cambridge, MA: MIT Press.

Katz, Bruce, and Jennifer Bradley. 1999. Divided We Sprawl. *The Atlantic Monthly Online Digital Edition*, December 1999. http://www.theatlantic.com/past/docs/issues/99dec/9912katz.htm.

MacKaye, Benton. 1928. *The New Exploration: A Philosophy of Regional Planning*. New York: Harcourt, Brace.

Mumford, Lewis. 1925. The Fourth Migration. *The Survey: Graphic* 54:130–133.

Olmsted, Frederick Law, Sr. 1973. *Forty Years of Landscape Architecture: Central Park*. Cambridge, MA: MIT Press.

7

Territorial Competitiveness: Lineages, Practices, Ideologies

Neil Brenner and David Wachsmuth

Since the 1980s, the notion of *territorial competitiveness* has become one of the foundations of mainstream, "entrepreneurial" approaches to local economic development (Harvey 1989a). This concept is premised on the assumption that subnational territories—cities and metropolitan regions, in particular—must compete with one another for economic survival by attracting transnationally mobile capital investment. Concomitantly, the invocation of territorial competitiveness is generally accompanied by the assertion that various types of national, regional, or local institutional transformation and policy reorientation are required in order to enhance locationally specific socioeconomic assets. Such assumptions—and, more generally, a widespread sense of panic among policymakers and urban planners regarding the perceived "threats" of worldwide interlocality competition—have figured crucially in the proliferation of a broad array of policies oriented toward promoting urban territorial competitiveness during the last three decades. Such policies have appeared in diverse forms (neoliberal, centrist, and social democratic), at various spatial scales (from the Organisation for Economic Co-operation and Development [OECD] and the World Bank to metropolitan regions, municipalities, and even neighborhoods), and under a range of labels (industrial districts, clustering, science parks, technopoles, human capital, global cities, creative cities, and so forth). But they have all generally entailed an abandonment of earlier concerns with sociospatial redistribution and "balanced" urbanization and a concerted emphasis on enhancing the "attractiveness" of a local economy for external capital investment, positioning a city strategically within supranational circuits of capital, bolstering local socioeconomic assets, and downsizing large-scale public agencies. In this sense, the rise of territorial competitiveness as a concept has been intertwined with a major reorientation of urban governance regimes across the world economy. This chapter explores the lineages of territorial competitiveness discourses within and beyond the field of urban planning, their intellectual basis, and their implications for public policies oriented toward promoting local economic development.

We argue that, despite its contemporary pervasiveness, the concept of territorial competitiveness is premised on flawed intellectual assumptions and serves primarily as a means of ideological mystification in the sphere of local policy development. Rather than offering a basis for viable local economic development, it obfuscates the restructuring processes that are under way within and among contemporary cities, and thus contributes to the formulation of ineffective, wasteful, and socially polarizing policies. Our somewhat gloomy conclusion is that, because so many localities within the global interurban system have adopted policies oriented toward the promotion of territorial competitiveness, significant strategic disadvantages accrue to those localities that attempt to opt out of such policies, or to adopt alternatives to them. Thus, in the absence of comprehensive global or supranational regulatory reform, escape routes from this "competitiveness trap" presently appear circumscribed.

Our analysis is focused primarily on North American and Western European developments during the last thirty years. It is important to note, however, that the concept of territorial competitiveness has been mobilized as a key element of local economic policy and urban planning discourse in cities, regions, and states throughout the world economy (Fougner 2006). More systematic analysis of territorial competitiveness policies in cities of the global South awaits further research and debate. We hope that the critical orientation elaborated here might provide a useful reference point for such discussions.

"Compete or Die"

Since the early 1980s, one of the foundations of mainstream approaches to local economic development planning in North America and Western Europe has been the notion of an intensified global competition among cities for external capital investment and for localized competitive advantages. In this view, global economic restructuring is a ferociously competitive struggle not merely between capitalist firms but between *economic territories*, generally cities or city regions. According to one of the contributions to a volume titled *European Cities in Competition*, "In the present context of internationalization, the historical competition between cities has acquired a special importance. Every large European city tries to find the right mode to compete with others in an increasingly competitive framework. That competition is played out at two levels: the global and the European" (Sánchez 1996, 463). Analogous assumptions regarding the intensification of interurban competition in Europe underpin a special issue of the journal *Urban Studies* devoted to the theme of competitive cities (see, e.g., Begg 1999; Gordon 1999). Countless additional examples of such arguments can be found throughout the recent academic literature on urban development.

These visions of intensified interlocality competition have also been pervasive in local policy and urban planning discourse, beginning in the United States during the 1970s and soon thereafter diffusing to Western Europe, East Asia, and beyond. References to the "threat," "problem," or "challenge" of interurban competition abound in policy reports, press releases, and glossy brochures published by municipal governments, planning offices, and urban economic development agencies throughout the world. Various models of the changing global and supranational urban hierarchies, often influenced by politically neutered versions of world city theory, have come to figure prominently in such documents, enabling local boosterists and political entrepreneurs proudly to advertise their own city's ranking while representing as dramatically as possible the ways in which other closely ranked cities are poised to threaten local competitive advantages. Although the structure of world urban hierarchies remains a matter of continued debate among academic urbanists (Taylor and Hoyler 2000), most city marketing agencies have developed homegrown "benchmarking" techniques for representing their own city's ranking within the hierarchy in the most favorable light possible. Indeed, the assumption that cities compete against one another has become so naturalized among local policymakers that most discussions of the issue accept such competition as a fact and turn immediately to the problem of local economic development strategy.

The notion of interlocality competition has played an essential role in what Harvey (1989a) has famously labeled "entrepreneurial" urban policies, which entail the mobilization of local political institutions to enhance the territorially embedded competitive advantages of cities and city regions in relation to supranational or global spaces of perceived economic competition. As a result of their intensive focus on the need to bolster place-specific socioeconomic assets, such strategies of local economic development have also been characterized as urban locational policies (Brenner 2004). Crucially, then, there is a direct link between the visions of worldwide interlocality competition surveyed above and the increasingly widespread emphasis in policy and planning circles on localized forms of territorial competitiveness: policies oriented toward the latter goal are generally justified as strategic responses to the former state of affairs.

Commenting on the European situation in the 1990s, Dutch urbanists Van den Berg and Braun (1999, 987) assert this connection quite explicitly by declaring that "cities and towns are waking up to the fact [*sic*] that an entrepreneurial and anticipatory policy is called for to cope with urban and regional competition." Most academic commentators on entrepreneurial cities have likewise tended to accept uncritically these "declarations of economic war" among local policymakers and boosterists, taking for granted that they represent a relatively transparent reflection of a transformed geoeconomic situation and that territorial competitiveness represents a coherent, justifiable concern in such a context. As Bristow (2005, 285) explains, "Competitiveness is portrayed as the means by which regional economies are externally validated in an era of globalisation, such that there can be no principled objection to policies and strategies deemed to be competitiveness-enhancing, whatever their indirect consequences." In short, urban commentators, planners, and policymakers alike appear to have convinced themselves that interlocality competition has become an ineluctable fact of life in an age of "globalization" to which localities have no choice but to adjust or else risk incurring serious economic disadvantages. Both in theory and in practice, contemporary discourses of interlocality competition and territorial competitiveness suggest a grim categorical imperative: "*compete or die*" (Eisenschitz and Gough 1998, 762).

Geoeconomic Contexts of Territorial Competitiveness Policy

Policy responses to this new categorical imperative—whether under the rubric of urban entrepreneurialism, or urban locational policy, or territorial competitiveness—must be contextualized in relation to at least four fundamental geoeconomic transformations of the last three decades (here we draw extensively on the argument of Leitner and Sheppard 1998, 286–293): (1) processes of deindustrialization and reindustrialization, (2) the information and communications revolution, (3) the rise of flexible forms of industrial organization, and (4) the globalization of finance capital.

Deindustrialization and Reindustrialization

The post-1970s round of deindustrialization and reindustrialization has generated a dramatic decline in older industrial regions and equally dramatic growth within sunrise regions specialized, in particular, in producer and financial services, high-technology industries, and other advanced forms of revitalized craft production (Storper and Scott 1989). Confronted with these global sectoral shifts, urban and regional planners have explored new ways of influencing the sectoral composition of their territories—whether through the phasing out, subsidization, or modernization of traditional mass production industries, through the nurturing or direct financing of economic development in high-tech or producer and financial service sectors, through the mobilization of property, venture capital, and new infrastructural investments to develop entirely new sectoral specializations within a region, or through some combination of these strategies. These policy responses have been closely intertwined with new discourses and practices of competition between particular types of cities—for instance, between cities that are attempting to phase out or modernize traditional industrial sectors, between cities that specialize in similar growth industries, or between cities that are attempting to attract similar types of external capital investment (Krätke 1995, 141).

The Information and Communications Revolution

The information revolution, based primarily on the development of new telecommunications technologies, has dramatically enhanced the capacity of firms to control and coordinate production networks on a global scale (Castells 1996). Meanwhile, the continued deployment of new transportation technologies has caused the cost and time of commodity circulation to decline significantly. Consequently, as Leitner and Sheppard (1998, 288) argue, "locational advantages stemming from accessibility to markets, resources and labour have become less important relative to other site-specific differences between cities (such as labour costs, industrial clusters and local governance systems) in affecting their attractiveness to private investors." These new technological capacities have also enabled firms to shift activities more easily among various possible locations as labor costs, taxes, or political conditions change within particular places. Under these circumstances, local policymakers and urban planners have experienced extensive pressures to construct place-specific locational advantages for firms within their jurisdictions that secure the profitability of existing industries while also serving as magnets for additional external capital investment. Insofar as the competitive advantages of cities and regions are today socially and politically constructed rather than being based on pregiven factor endowments, new regulatory imperatives have arisen on the local and regional scales to coordinate, maintain, and enhance the place-specific preconditions for economic growth (Scott 1998). In most older industrial states, local and regional policymakers have understood these new regulatory dilemmas as a zero-sum competition between locations to attract investment from mobile firms (Cox 1995).

New Forms of Industrial Organization

The erosion of traditional Fordist mass production systems, with their large-scale agglomerations of fixed capital and labor power, has also had important consequences for processes of urban governance. The shift toward flexible forms of industrial organization in recent decades appears to have significantly reduced the costs of fixed investment in any given location for the simple reason that "smaller plants can be built, which take fewer years to pay for" (Leitner and Sheppard 1998, 290). Insofar as fixed investment costs can be paid off swiftly, the mobility of capital is enhanced, for "it now takes fewer years before a production facility is paid for; at which time the firm will reassess the benefits of continuing production in that city" (ibid.). Under these circumstances, local policymakers and planners are confronted with intensified pressures continually to upgrade the infrastructures of transportation, communication, and production within their jurisdictional boundaries in order to anticipate the shifting locational requirements of different fractions of capital.

The Globalization of Finance

Under conditions of sustained economic crisis, capital seeks new outlets to protect itself from devalorization. The massive financialization of capital that has occurred on a world scale since the early 1980s can be viewed as one such strategy to this end (Arrighi 2010). Processes of financialization have changed the conditions for urban and regional governance in significant ways, most crucially by altering the regulatory frameworks through which local and regional governments borrow money to finance and sustain fixed capital investments within their jurisdictions (Leitner and Sheppard 1998, 291–293). The international range of financial institutions, instruments, and mechanisms through which money can be borrowed and lent has massively increased since the 1970s, opening up new financial options for many localities, but also subjecting them more directly to the volatile seas of global financial markets. The bankruptcy of Orange County, California, in 1994 as a result of its speculative investments in futures markets and the near bankruptcy of Jefferson County, Alabama, in 2009 at the hands of J.P. Morgan–designed synthetic derivatives represent two particularly dramatic instance of the major risks to which cities and regions are subjecting themselves in contemporary "casino capitalism" (Strange 1986). Moreover, to the extent that local governments and planning agencies are constrained to repay their loans within a strict time frame, pressures to enhance the capacities and revenues of the local economy or to slash local budgets are also significantly increased (Leitner and Sheppard 1998, 292). In short, as local governments rely ever more extensively on global financial markets to fund economic development projects, they are subjected to a range of new, externally imposed fiscal constraints.

Taken together, these geoeconomic transformations have imposed new pressures on cities and regions throughout the older industrialized world to reactivate economic development within their boundaries. According to Harvey (1989a, 15), the rise of entrepreneurial forms of urban governance—and associated discourses of local territorial competitiveness—required "a radical reconstruction of central to local state relations and the cutting free of local state activities from the welfare state and the Keynesian compromise." Crucially, then, as we argue below, the emergence of territorial competitiveness policy has also been conditioned by a fundamental restructuring of inherited Keynesian state forms and the consolidation of new, post-Keynesian formations of statehood (Brenner 2004).

Contours of Territorial Competitiveness Policy

Within the field of local and regional economic policy, the new emphasis on territorial competitiveness represents a striking discursive and ideological realignment, not only in highly specialized industrial districts and global cities but in traditional manufacturing centers as well. Whereas priorities such as balanced urbanization, territorial redistribution, and sociospatial equalization prevailed across much of the older industrialized and state-socialist world from the 1950s through the mid-1970s (Brenner 2004), the worldwide economic crises of the 1970s seriously destabilized the political coalitions and institutional architectures that had been constructed to promote such agendas. Within territorial competitiveness discourses, cities and city regions are no longer represented as mere transmission belts undergirding national economic regimes or as concentrations of standardized fixed-capital investments and land resources. Instead, they are described as highly flexible, internationalized milieus endowed with place-specific locational assets, innovation networks, and endogenous learning capacities that must be continually upgraded in relation to other "competing" local economies (Storper 1996; Cooke and Morgan 1998). Internal networks of cooperation—both between firms and between major public and private actors—are increasingly viewed as a powerful basis on which to compete more effectively in an uncertain geoeconomic environment (Eisenschitz and Gough 1993).

At any spatial scale, territorial competitiveness policies hinge on the assumption that territorial units, like capitalist firms, compete against one another to maximize profits and economic growth. In this viewpoint, the competitiveness of a given territory flows from its capacity to achieve these goals effectively and durably—whether by attracting inward investment, by lowering investment costs, by increasing productivity, by providing a suitably skilled labor force, by creating an innovative environment, or by means of other strategies intended to enhance the value of economic activities located within its boundaries (Begg 1999). The goal of territorial competitiveness policy, therefore, is to maintain and expand the capacities for profit making and economic growth that are thought to be embedded within, or potentially attracted to, specific political jurisdictions.

For present purposes, it is not necessary to embrace a particular definition of competitiveness, either for firms or for territories. Our main point is simply to observe that, since roughly the early 1980s, national, regional, and urban policymakers and planners across Western Europe, North America, East Asia, and elsewhere have become concerned to enhance various attributes of cities and city regions that are considered to contribute to their competitiveness relative to other global investment locations (Gordon 1999). Given the earlier, Fordist-Keynesian understanding of cities as localized subunits of national economies, this new emphasis on urban territorial competitiveness in relation to supranational circuits of capital represents a striking political, ideological, and scalar realignment (Lovering 1995; Veltz 1997). The proliferation of territorial competitiveness policies during the last two decades is at once an expression and an outcome of this changing conception of how cities and city regions contribute to and function within economic life.

While such policies are frequently justified with reference to the widely disseminated writings of business school gurus such as Porter (1990) and Ohmae (1990), they have been grounded, in practice, on a diverse range of assumptions regarding the sources of competitive advantage within local economies and the role of state institutions in promoting the latter. We shall not attempt here to compare systematically the nationally, regionally, and locally specific types of territorial competitiveness policies that have crystallized during the last three decades, though this would undoubtedly be an illuminating exercise. Instead, we proceed on the mesolevel to specify three axes on which such policies may be located.

• *Forms of territorial competition*   According to Storper and Walker (1989), interfirm competition under capitalism occurs in weak and strong forms. Whereas weak competition is oriented toward the reduction of costs and the redistribution of resources within a given spatial division of labor (static comparative advantages), strong competition is oriented toward the transformation of the conditions of production in order to introduce new technological capacities and a new spatial division of labor (dynamic competitive advantages). Territorial competitiveness policies may likewise be oriented toward weak or strong forms of interfirm competition, depending on the balance of cost-cutting, deregulatory state initiatives and those that attempt to enhance firm productivity and innovative milieus within the jurisdiction in question (Leborgne and Lipietz 1991). Neoliberal or defensive approaches to competitiveness policy attempt to capitalize on weak forms of interfirm competition; they are based on the assumption that lowering the costs of investment within a given territory will attract mobile capital investment and thus enhance its competitiveness. By contrast, social democratic or offensive approaches to competitiveness policy attempt to capitalize on strong forms of interfirm competition; they are based on the assumption that territorial competitiveness hinges on the provision of nonsubstitutable socioeconomic assets such as innovative capacities, collaborative interfirm networks, advanced infrastructural facilities, and skilled labor power. Within any national or local context, the precise balance among neoliberal/defensive and social democratic/offensive approaches to territorial competitiveness policy is an object and outcome of sociopolitical struggles over the form of state intervention into the urban process (Eisenschitz and Gough 1996, 1993).

• *Fields of territorial competition*   Building on Harvey's (1989a) study of urban entrepreneurialism, four distinct fields of territorial competitiveness policy may be delineated according to the particular circuits of capital they target. First, territorial competitiveness policies may attempt to enhance a city's advantages within spatial divisions of labor, generally by establishing or strengthening place-specific conditions for the production of particular types of goods and services. Second, territorial competitiveness policies may attempt to enhance a city's advantages within spatial divisions of consumption, generally by creating or strengthening a localized infrastructure for tourism, leisure, or retirement functions. Third, territorial competitiveness policies may attempt to enhance a city's command and control capacities in the spheres of finance, information processing, and government. Finally, territorial competitiveness policies may target governmental subsidies and investments—spatial divisions of redistribution—to promote local economic development. These policies may be locally mobilized, as when municipalities compete for infrastructure grants from superordinate levels of government, or they may be carried out in a top-down fashion by national state agencies or, in the European context, by the European Commission. While these fields of territorial competition may be distinguished analytically, in practice, most competitiveness policies attempt to enhance a city's position simultaneously within multiple fields.

• *Geographies of territorial competition*   Finally, territorial competitiveness policies entail the delineation of geographic parameters within which the process of economic development is to unfold. There are three key elements here. The first is spaces of competitiveness: the strategic spaces within which place-specific economic capacities are to be mobilized. Central business districts, inner-city enterprise zones, revitalized manufacturing and port areas, and high-technology suburbs are common examples. The second geographic factor is spaces of competition. These are the broader (often global) spaces within which urban economies or their component economic zones are to be positioned as attractive investment locations. The global cities of New York and London are thus understood to be competing within a different global space from, for example, export-processing zones in Manila, Shenzhen, and São Paulo, or manufacturing regions such as Detroit, Manchester, or Dortmund. The final factor is positioning strategies: scale-attuned political initiatives designed to position urban spaces of competitiveness within supranational spaces of competition (Jessop 2002). For instance, some territorial competitiveness policies attempt to transform an urban economy into a key articulation point within a nested hierarchy of regional, national, and supranational economic spaces. Other such policies may attempt to reorganize inherited urban hierarchies—whether vertically, through the promotion of new forms of cooperation among different tiers of state power, or horizontally, through the promotion of transversal alliances among geographically dispersed cities occupying complementary positions in the global division of labor. Therefore, even though all forms of territorial competitiveness policy strive to position cities and regions favorably within supranational circuits of capital, this goal may be pursued through diverse political-geographic strategies.

Territorial competitiveness policies have an inherently speculative character owing to "the inability [of political alliances] to predict exactly which package [of local investments] will succeed and which will not, in a world of considerable economic instability and volatility" (Harvey 1989a, 10–11). Moreover, such policies are often grounded in untenable assumptions and unrealistic predictions regarding the future trajectories of local economic development. Despite these endemic problems, the proliferation of territorial competitiveness policies during the last three decades has engendered a transformation in the character of state intervention in the urban process: the spatially redistributive state forms of the post–World War II period have been largely superseded by a more fragmented, multiscalar constellation of state institutions that explicitly promotes the intensification of uneven spatial development within and beyond their jurisdictional boundaries (Brenner 2004).

Measuring Competition

As territorial competitiveness has become a key orienting principle of urban policy, various state and nongovernmental bodies have directed more attention to measuring it. Fougner (2008) has demonstrated how the "competitiveness indexing" and country benchmarking performed by organizations such as the World Economic Forum have helped discursively normalize the competitiveness concept at the national scale. The quantitative, technocratic methodologies used to construct indices and rank countries are only feasible, though, because of the relative abundance, quality, and uniformity of national statistics. In many cases, the relevant data do not exist for cities and urban regions, while methodological differences in defining cities and metropolitan areas make international comparisons doubly problematic.

It should not be surprising, then, that the last few decades have witnessed a marked increase in efforts to statistically delineate urban regions, to standardize these delineations, and to use them to rank and compare cities with one another. Such initiatives must confront two separate but related questions. First, who is competing? In other words, how is the relevant unit of territorial competition to be defined? Second, what are the stakes and spoils of this competition? In other words, what are the appropriate benchmarks for deciding which territorial units are competing most successfully?

The first question has been by and large answered with reference to the concept of the metropolitan region. This concept was introduced as a statistical measure in the United States around the beginning of the twentieth century but has recently become a major keyword in contemporary discussions among planners and policymakers regarding the prospects of local spaces in the global economy (Scott 2001). During the last several decades, the concept of the metropolitan region (or some variant thereof) is increasingly being adopted throughout the world as the standard urban measurement concept. In the European Union, for example, the pan-EU statistical agency has been collaborating with national governments to standardize the measurement of the "larger urban zone" (LUZ), which is a close proxy for the metropolitan region, so that LUZs are statistically comparable across nations (Carlquist 2006). Similarly, in 2006, the OECD held a conference on standardizing the measurement of metropolitan regions across its member states. A submission to the conference by the Greater London Authority lays out the rationale for doing so:

London, like many cities, requires an international benchmarking standard. It needs to compare itself with other cities for the purpose of identifying best practice for policy. . . . Nor is this need confined to the authorities responsible for London: national and international governments need common standards both to compare the situation of cities and to allocate and implement policy resources. . . . It is our view that having a common standard is more important than having the right standard since in some senses if there is a common standard which represents city-regions in a reasonably consistent way then that itself is the 'right' standard. (Freeman and Cheshire 2006, 2)

There is a tension, however, between the varied spaces of competitiveness that are targeted by contemporary urban policy (from metropolitan regions down to individual neighborhoods) and the pervasive statistical standardization of the metropolitan region as the de facto unit of competitiveness. In many cases, the territorial unit being benchmarked and the territorial unit being targeted by competitiveness policies are completely different. For example, the recent Toronto Board of Trade (2009) competitiveness report compares the Toronto metropolitan region with a host of others, even though the Toronto metropolitan region encompasses four different regional governments (in whole or in part) and fully twenty-four different municipal governments. Which government or government agency is expected to act on the report's findings? Moreover, most metropolitan areas are simply commuting zones. Even assuming the possibility of policy coordination across the relevant state agencies, a commuting zone is only likely to be a sensible unit of analysis for specific types of policies (notably labor market interventions).

The metropolitan region, for better or for worse, has become the primary way to define the city as a globally competitive unit. But what are these metropolitan regions competing at? Historically, efforts at quantifying national competitiveness have focused on macroeconomic indicators such as gross domestic product, terms of trade, and productivity. But beginning in 1979, with the publication of the *Report on the Competitiveness of European Industry,* and gaining widespread acceptance in the writings of Porter (1990), academic and governmental bodies began attempting to quantify national competitiveness directly. Each of the two major annual competitiveness reports currently published—*The Global Competitiveness Report* and *The World Competitiveness Yearbook*—constructs multidimensional indices to measure, respectively, "the set of factors, policies and institutions that determine the level of productivity of a country" and "the ability of nations to create and maintain an environment which sustains the competitiveness of enterprises" (Fougner 2008, 313). The substantial difference between these two formulations already demonstrates that "competitiveness," unlike GDP or terms of trade, is an ambiguous term; the challenge is not only to measure it but also to elaborate a definition that is precise enough to enable such measurement.

Urban competitiveness benchmarks began to be produced somewhat after national ones, particularly since the early 1990s. Although the discursive terrain of urban competitiveness benchmarking is still in formation, the two most influential concepts for such discussions have been "global cities" and "creative cities." The former notion is loosely derived from the pioneering work of Friedmann (e.g., Friedmann and Wolff 1982) on hierarchies of world cities within the new international division of labor, and Sassen (2001) on the concentration of financial and producer services functions in specific urban regions. However, most benchmarking strategies that invoke such concepts bracket the strongly critical thrust of Friedmann's and Sassen's interventions, which emphasize the socially polarizing consequences of financialization and labor market dualization within metropolitan regions. Instead, those who invoke the global cities concept for benchmarking purposes generally adopt an affirmative, boosterist approach to cities' efforts to position themselves strategically as financial centers within the global division of labor. Florida (2002), who popularized the idea of creative cities, has focused much more unapologetically on competitiveness, benchmarking, and urban policy, and has devoted considerable energies to marketing his own particular formula for local economic development to cities and subnational governments around the world (Peck 2005). Florida argues that a new "creative class" is the linchpin of modern economic success and that cities must compete to attract these highly mobile creative professionals through supply-side policies to attract technology, talent, and tolerance. Despite the dubious methodology, Florida has become quite successful in selling municipal governments on his Creativity Index (Peck 2005).

Both approaches to urban benchmarking suggest specific, privileged domains of global urban competition. In this respect they differ from the general national competitiveness rankings discussed above (although the Creativity Index, as an example, in practice is nearly as broad as either of the two major national indices). But the underlying arbitrariness of competitiveness benchmarking makes it a common tool for boards of trade, place-promoting agencies, local chambers of commerce, local economic development corporations, and other urban development interests to justify policies that supposedly enhance competitiveness. There are usually two different messages, each aimed at a different target. One is the purported need to promote competitiveness and is aimed primarily at local government; the other is the city's purported success at promoting competitiveness and is aimed primarily at mobile capital. The local "competitiveness reports" that are produced by such organizations tend to follow national ones in comparing cities across a broad range of indicators (see, e.g., Europe Economics 2008; Toronto Board of Trade 2009). As long as governmental and nongovernmental organizations remain committed to the idea of urban regions as the key competitive territorial units in the global economy, we should expect initiatives to increase quantitative measurement and comparison of these regions to continue.

Decoding Territorial Competitiveness

The premise of competitiveness benchmarking is that it clarifies the process by which cities and city regions compete. But the very concept of territorial competitiveness is a cipher: it masks as much as it reveals about urban governance and interlocality interaction in the contemporary age (Budd 1998; Bristow 2005). Consequently, like other popular catchphrases in the contemporary globalization debates—such as the "hypermobility" of capital, the "weakening" of the state, and the "deterritorialization" of social space—the notion of territorial competition must be systematically decoded.

As a number of commentators have indicated, the notion of territorial competitiveness rests on an untenable analogy between capitalist firms and urban territories (Leitner and Sheppard 1998, 301). According to Krugman's now famous polemic against popular U.S. economists such as Reich and Thurow, competitiveness becomes a "dangerous obsession" when applied to any organizational entities other than capitalist firms. It is logically incoherent, in Krugman's view, to apply the concept of competitiveness to national territories because they "have no well-defined bottom line": "countries . . . do not go out of business" and thus cannot be understood appropriately as wealth-creating machines (Krugman 1994, 31). Insofar as firms must define their "bottom line" straightforwardly in terms of profits, Krugman argues, they are the only organizations to which the attribute of competitiveness can be defensibly ascribed. On this basis, Krugman concludes that the notion of territorial competitiveness should be eradicated both from social scientific investigation and from political debate, for it contributes to vacuous analyses and wasteful policies.

Given the problematic, amorphous character of the notion of competitiveness when applied to territorial units rather than firms (see also Begg 1999; Budd 1998; Bristow 2005), what explains the proliferation of local strategies for achieving this elusive but almost universally endorsed goal during the last three decades? Why, in short, has the "dangerous obsession" of local territorial competitiveness become such a popular indulgence among policymakers and other local boosterists? Unfortunately, Krugman's critique brackets this question by attributing such policies to the supposed intellectual sloppiness and incompetence of their proponents. Yet as Dicken (1998, 88) cautions,

Whether Krugman is right or wrong in his analysis, there seems little likelihood of policy-makers actually heeding his warnings and refraining from both the rhetoric and the reality of competitive policy measures. As long as the concept of national [or local] competitiveness remains in currency then no single state [or municipality] is likely to opt out.

Critiques by Krugman and others notwithstanding, it would be seriously misleading to dismiss the intense policy concern with something called "competitiveness" as a mere conceptual fallacy or ideological fantasy. Rather, we suggest that the rise of territorial competitiveness policies represents a more general realignment of contemporary state institutions toward various forms of transnational economic competition, signaling the formation of what some authors have termed "competition states" (Cerny 1990; Jessop 2002). Although neoliberalism is a particularly significant manifestation of this multiscalar, productivist reorientation of state power, it is only one among many political forms in which such competition states have been consolidated.

But here emerges a second major problem with the concept of territorial competitiveness. It attributes to cities agentic properties and posits their competitive interaction as unified territorial collectivities, but the political-institutional conditions under which localities might become agentic and adopt competitive orientations toward other localities are generally presumed rather than interrogated. As Harvey (1989a, 5) notes, the reification of cities as "active agents" must be avoided insofar as capitalist urbanization is "a spatially grounded social process in which a wide range of different actors with quite different objectives and agendas interact through a particular configuration of interlocking spatial practices." Cities are localized social structures in which any number of highly antagonistic spatial practices—including class relations, accumulation strategies, and diverse political-ideological projects—arise and are reproduced (Cox 1995). Accordingly, as Budd (1998, 670) explains, "To propose cities or regions competing with each other presupposes a unity of purpose between the constituent economic and social interests and that city governance has an autonomy and freedom of manoeuvre."

The point, however, is not to deny that the different actors located within cities may, under certain conditions, organize collectively to promote common interests and agendas but rather to emphasize that such collective mobilizations cannot be abstractly presupposed. As Cox and Mair (1991, 198) explain,

If people interpret localised social structures in explicitly territorial terms, come to view their interests and identities as "local", and then act upon that view by mobilising locally defined organisations to further their interests in a manner that would not be possible were they to act separately, then it seems eminently reasonable to talk about "locality as agent."

The local territorial alliances that result from such mobilizations have played an important role in the historical geography of capitalist urbanization. For instance, urban growth machines—coalitions of land-based elites oriented toward a maximization of local property values—have long played a shaping role in U.S. urban development and represent what is perhaps the paradigmatic example of such alliances (Logan and Molotch 1987). Other forms of local territorial alliances, based upon diverse regimes of public-private collaboration, cross-class coalitions and place-based attachments, have likewise emerged throughout the historical geography of capitalist urbanization in other national contexts (Harvey 1989b; Markusen 1987; Stone and Sanders 1987).

According to Harvey's (1982, 419–420) classic analysis of the issue in *The Limits to Capital*, the essential basis for the formation of local territorial alliances is the fact that

a portion of the total social capital has to be rendered immobile in order to give the remaining capital greater flexibility of movement. The value of capital, once it is locked into immobile physical and social infrastructures, has to be defended if it is not to be devalued.

Therefore, territorial alliances to promote economic growth within a particular city or city region are generally anchored within those factions of capital and labor whose resources and interests are most closely tied to large-scale immobile infrastructures and investments within the city, such as real estate, fixed-capital outlays, utilities, and infrastructural facilities. Harvey's (1982, 420) explanation of this fundamental and recurrent tendency toward a "regionalization of class and factional struggle" under capitalism is worth quoting at length:

Some factions of capital are more committed to immobile investment than others. Land and property owners, developers and builders, the local state and those who hold the mortgage debt have everything to gain from forging a local alliance to protect and promote local interests and to ward off the threat of localized, place-specific devaluation. Production capital which cannot easily move may support the alliance and be tempted to buy local labour peace and skills through compromises over wages and work conditions—thereby gaining the benefits of co-operation from labour and a rising effective demand for wage goods in local markets. Factions of labour that have, through struggle or historical accident, managed to create islands of privilege within a sea of exploitation may also rally to the cause of the alliance. Furthermore, if a local compromise between capital and labour is helpful to local accumulation, then the bourgeoisie as a whole may support it. The basis is laid for the rise of a territorially based alliance between various factions of capital, the local state and even whole classes, in defense of social reproduction processes (both accumulation and the reproduction of labour power) within a particular territory. The basis for the alliance rests, it must be stressed, on the need to make a certain portion of capital immobile in order to give the remainder freedom to move.

The resultant territorial alliances are grounded in formal and informal partnerships among diverse local institutions and actors, including chambers of commerce, trade unions, local planning authorities, the city government itself and, above all, different factions of capital and labor (Cheshire and Gordon 1996; Stone and Sanders 1987). As Harvey (1989b, 148) elsewhere notes, the overarching objective of such territorial alliances is "to preserve or enhance achieved models of production and consumption, dominant technological mixes and patterns of social relations, profit and wage levels, the qualities of labor power and entrepreneurial-managerial skills, social and physical infrastructures, and the cultural qualities of living and working" (see also Harvey 1989b, 148–155). To accomplish these wide-ranging goals, territorial alliances generally mobilize scale-specific accumulation strategies in which certain locally rooted locational assets are selected and actively promoted (Jessop 1998).

We thus arrive at the following result: cities and city regions can be said to engage in interlocality competition only to the extent that *territorial alliances* are formed—whether at local or supralocal scales—with the explicit goal of promoting a specific locality as a unit within such competition. In the absence of such alliances, it is logically incoherent to speak of the city as an agent, and in the absence of an entire *urban system* permeated by such alliances, it is logically incoherent to speak of interlocality competition. Interlocality or territorial competition is therefore better understood as a horizontal relationship between growth- and investment-oriented territorial alliances rather than as a vertical relationship between immobile places and mobile flows of capital, or, with reference to conventional notions of capital versus communities, flows versus places or the global versus the local. It is a shorthand term, in this view, for describing the *macrogeographic field of strategic interaction* among competing, locally or regionally based territorial alliances.

From this perspective, territorial competitiveness policies cannot be explained simply as a localized response to the supposed constraints imposed by enhanced interlocality competition; they must be seen, first and foremost, as basic animators of that competition that simultaneously naturalize it and make it appear inevitable. And as the number of territorial alliances engaged in such competitive interactions expands, powerful incentives to adopt competitiveness-oriented urban policies, and thus to join the competitive fray, are imposed on those localities that had previously attempted to opt out (Leitner and Sheppard 1998). Nonetheless, the role of territorial competitiveness policies as a generative force within interlocality competition cannot be grasped adequately if they are interpreted only as a reaction to externally imposed pressures. The shift toward territorial competitiveness policies is best conceived not merely as a transition undergone by individual cities but as a *relational* transformation of a large-scale urban hierarchy owing to the intensified competitive interaction of multiple local territorial alliances within it.

Regulatory Failures of Territorial Competitiveness Policy

Territorial competitiveness policies are now pervasive in cities and city regions across the world economy, but their apparent omnipresence tells us little regarding their effectiveness in practice. In fact, despite the claims made on behalf of such policies by their advocates, there is little empirical evidence that they actually serve the purposes to which they are put. Rather, the bulk of critical social science analysis of such policies suggests that their main effects are regressive and dysfunctional, whether in economic, administrative, or political terms (Leitner and Sheppard 1998; Cheshire and Gordon 1996; Bristow 2005).

As we have discussed, the perception of intensified interlocality competition enhances competitive pressures on subnational administrative units to offer favorable terms to potential investors. As territorial competitiveness policies have subsequently been diffused, the potential disadvantages of a failure or refusal to introduce them have escalated (Leitner and Sheppard 1998). Despite this, there is currently little evidence that territorial competitiveness policies generate positive-sum, supply-side gains for local economies, for instance by upgrading locally embedded industrial capacities. More frequently, such initiatives have entailed public subsidies to private firms, leading to a zero-sum redistribution of capital investment among competing locations (Cheshire and Gordon 1996). In this manner, territorial competitiveness policies may induce inefficient allocations of public resources as taxpayer revenues are channeled toward the promotion of private accumulation rather than toward the general conditions of production or social expenditures. Hence, as Cheshire and Gordon (1995, 122) conclude, "much territorial competition [among cities] is pure waste."

Additionally, the proliferation of territorial competitiveness policies has encouraged "the search for short-term gains at the expense of more important longer-term investments in the health of cities and the well-being of their residents" (Leitner and Sheppard 1998, 305). Even though some cities have managed to acquire short-term competitive advantages through the early adoption of territorial competitiveness policies, such advantages have generally eroded as analogous policies have diffused among similarly positioned cities within wider spatial divisions of labor. In this sense, while territorial competitiveness policies have helped unleash short-term bursts of economic growth within some cities and regions, they have proven far less effective in sustaining that growth over the medium or long term (Peck and Tickell 1994).

A further problem concerns the limited geographic reach of territorial competitiveness policies, which generally entail the targeting of strategic, globally connected urban regions, or specific locations therein, as the engines of national economic dynamism. Such policies are premised on the assumption that enhanced urban territorial competitiveness will benefit the broader regional and national space economies in which cities are embedded. In practice, however, territorial competitiveness policies have contributed to the establishment of technologically advanced, globally connected urban enclaves that generate only limited spillover effects for their surrounding territories. This tendency toward "glocal enclavization" is articulated at a local scale, as advanced infrastructural hubs and high-technology production centers are delinked from adjoining neighborhoods, and at supralocal scales, as globally competitive agglomerations are delinked from older industrial regions and other marginalized spaces within the same national territory (Graham and Marvin 2001). The resultant intensification of sociospatial polarization may undermine macroeconomic stability; it may also breed divisive, disruptive political conflicts.

Particularly in their defensive, neoliberal forms, territorial competitiveness policies have encouraged a race to the bottom in social service provision as national, regional, and municipal governments attempt to reduce the costs of capital investment in their territorial jurisdictions. This process of regulatory undercutting is dysfunctional on a number of levels: it aggravates rather than alleviates municipal fiscal and regulatory problems, it worsens life chances for significant segments of local and national populations, and it exacerbates entrenched inequalities within national urban hierarchies (Eisenschitz and Gough 1998).

The aforementioned regulatory problems may assume more moderate forms in conjunction with offensive, social democratic forms of territorial competitiveness policy. Nonetheless, offensive forms of territorial competitiveness policy are likewise prone to significant crisis tendencies. First, like defensive approaches to territorial competitiveness policy, offensive approaches "operate . . . as a strategy for strengthening some territories vis-à-vis other territories and other nations" (Leborgne and Lipietz 1991, 47); they thus intensify uneven development beyond the territorial zones in which they are deployed. The macroeconomic instability that subsequently ensues may undermine the very localized socioeconomic assets on which offensive territorial competitiveness policies depend (Leborgne and Lipietz 1991). Second, even more so than defensive forms of territorial competitiveness policy, offensive approaches to urban economic development suffer from serious problems of politicization. Their effectiveness hinges upon being confined to locally delineated areas; yet the apparent successes of such strategies at a local scale generate intense distributional pressures as other localities and regions within the same national territory strive to replicate the "recipe" or to reap some of its financial benefits (Eisenschitz and Gough 1996).

The proliferation of place-specific strategies of territorial competitiveness exacerbates coordination problems within and among national, regional, and local state institutions. First, because territorial competitiveness policies enhance the geographic differentiation of state regulatory activities without embedding subnational competitive strategies within an encompassing national policy framework, they undermine the organizational coherence and functional integration of state institutions. Second, this lack of supranational or national regulatory coordination in the field of urban policy may exacerbate the economic crisis tendencies discussed above: it enhances the likelihood that identical or analogous growth strategies may be replicated serially across wider urban systems, thus accelerating the diffusion of zero-sum forms of interlocality competition (Amin and Malmberg 1994).

Finally, the proliferation of territorial competitiveness policies has generated new conflicts regarding democratic accountability and political legitimation. Many of the new, highly fragmented institutional forms established to implement territorial competitiveness policies are dominated by nonelected government bureaucrats, technical experts, property developers, and corporate elites who are not accountable to the populations most directly affected by their activities (Swyngedouw, Moulaert, and Rodriguez 2002). While this lack of political accountability may enable regulatory agencies to implement such policies more efficiently, it systematically undermines their ability to address broader social needs and to maintain territorial cohesion. It may also generate serious legitimation deficits if oppositional social forces are able to politicize the negative socioeconomic consequences of territorial competitiveness policies or their undemocratic character.

These considerations paint a much gloomier picture of territorial competitiveness discourse and practice than that found in the mainstream literature on local economic development or, for that matter, that advanced by territorial alliances mobilized around specific projects to promote locational policies within cities or city-regions. Our analysis suggests that territorial competitiveness is, at core, an ideological keyword that facilitates regressive institutional and political shifts, undermines the localized preconditions for economic development, destabilizes the organizational infrastructure for urban and regional governance, and contributes to the erosion of inherited relays of democratic accountability. To be sure, we do not mean to suggest that either the ideology or the practice of territorial competitiveness is in itself the cause of the developments sketched above, which are obviously intertwined with a complex ensemble of geoeconomic and geopolitical transformations and institutional contestations. Our goal, rather, has been to expose some of the problematic intellectual assumptions that underpin this concept, to outline some of the problematic uses to which it has been put, and to underscore its essentially political-ideological character.

Beyond the Competitiveness Trap?

Paradoxically, despite the massively dysfunctional consequences outlined above, the widespread adoption of policies oriented toward local territorial competitiveness imposes powerful constraints on any subnational governance institutions that attempt to forge alternative policy orientations. Insofar as national states, regions, and cities that try to opt out from competitiveness policies or other entrepreneurial strategies may accrue serious economic disadvantages in terms of lost investment, jobs, and tax revenues, the "incentive . . . to try to gain at the expense of other states [and cities]" remains powerful (Dicken 1998, 88). As Harvey (1989a, 10) analogously notes of entrepreneurial urban policies (invoking Marx's famous description of intercapitalist competition as an "external coercive power" over individual capitalists):

Indeed to the degree that inter-urban competition becomes more potent, it will almost certainly operate as an "external coercive power" over individual cities to bring them closer into line with the discipline and logic of capitalist development.

These arguments point toward the urgent question: can an alternative discourse and practice of local economic development be elaborated? Can localities escape from the "competitiveness trap" to which they have apparently been consigned over three decades of worldwide geoeconomic and geopolitical restructuring?

At the present time, it remains to be seen whether the dysfunctional and regressive consequences of territorial competitiveness policy will provide openings for more progressive, radical democratic approaches to local and regional economic development—LeRoy (2007) has outlined a list of regulatory reforms that, in the U.S. context, would seriously curtail the dynamic of interlocality competition—or whether, by contrast, competitiveness-oriented agendas will be entrenched still further in the underlying institutional structures of urban and regional governance. Should this latter outcome occur, we have every reason to anticipate the crystallization of still leaner and meaner urban geographies in which cities engage aggressively in mutually destructive place-marketing policies, in which transnational capital is permitted to opt out from supporting local social reproduction, and in which the power of urban citizens to influence the basic conditions of their everyday lives is increasingly undermined. As we contemplate this grim scenario, Harvey's analysis of urban entrepreneurialism is once again remarkably prescient. As he explains (1989a, 16),

The problem is to devise a geopolitical strategy of inter-urban linkage that mitigates inter-urban competition and shifts political horizons away from the locality and into a more generalisable challenge to capitalist uneven development. . . . [A] critical perspective on urban entrepreneurialism indicates not only its negative impacts but its potentiality for transformation into a progressive urban corporatism, armed with a keen geopolitical sense of how to build alliances and linkages across space in such a way as to mitigate if not challenge the hegemonic dynamic of capitalist accumulation to dominate the historical geography of social life.

How, when, and where such a geopolitical strategy might be adopted, and what slogan might be most appropriate to its aspirations—the "right to the city" may provide one salient possibility (Marcuse 2009; Lefebvre 1996)—are questions that remain to be fought out in cities, city regions, and at all other spatial scales of governance.

References

Amin, A., and A. Malmberg. 1994. Competing Structural and Institutional Influences on the Geography of Production in Europe. In *Post-Fordism: A Reader*, ed. A. Amin, 227–248. Cambridge, MA: Blackwell.

Arrighi, G. 2010. *The Long Twentieth Century*, 2nd ed. London: Verso.

Begg, I. 1999. Cities and Competitiveness. *Urban Studies* 36 (5/6): 795–810.

Brenner, N. 2004. *New State Spaces: Urban Governance and the Rescaling of Statehood*. Oxford: Oxford University Press.

Bristow, G. 2005. Everyone's a "Winner": Problematizing the Discourse of Regional Competitiveness. *Journal of Economic Geography* 5 (3): 285–304.

Budd, L. 1998. Territorial Competition and Globalisation: Scylla and Charybdis of European Cities. *Urban Studies* 35 (4): 663–685.

Carlquist, T. 2006. Revision of the Larger Urban Zones in the Urban Audit Data Collection. Paper presented at the conference, "Defining and Measuring Metropolitan Regions," Paris, November 27.

Castells, M. 1996. *The Rise of the Network Society*. Cambridge, MA: Blackwell.

Cerny, P. 1990. *The Changing Architecture of Politics*. London: Sage.

Cheshire, P., and I. Gordon, eds. 1995. *Territorial Competition in an Integrating Europe*. Aldershot, UK: Avebury.

Cheshire, P., and I. Gordon. 1996. Territorial Competition and the Predictability of Collective (In)Action. *International Journal of Urban and Regional Research* 20 (3): 383–399.

Cooke, P., and K. Morgan. 1998. *The Associational Economy*. New York: Oxford University Press.

Cox, K. 1995. Globalisation, Competition and the Politics of Local Economic Development. *Urban Studies* 32 (2): 213–224.

Cox, K., and A. Mair. 1991. From Localised Social Structures to Localities as Agents. *Environment & Planning A* 23 (2): 197–214.

Dicken, P. 1998. *Global Shift*. 3rd ed. New York: Guilford Press.

Eisenschitz, A., and J. Gough. 1993. *The Politics of Local Economic Development*. New York: Macmillan.

Eisenschitz, A., and J. Gough. 1996. The Contradictions of Neo-Keynesian Local Economic Strategy. *Review of International Political Economy* 3 (3): 434–458.

Eisenschitz, A., and J. Gough. 1998. Theorizing the State in Local Economic Governance. *Regional Studies* 32 (8): 759–768.

Europe Economics. 2008. *The Competitiveness of London*. Policy report to the London Chamber of Commerce and Industry. April 2008. London: Europe Economics.

Florida, R. 2002. *The Rise of the Creative Class*. New York: Basic Books.

Fougner, Tore. 2006. The State, International Competitiveness and Neoliberal Globalization. *Review of International Studies* 32:165–185.

Fougner, T. 2008. Neoliberal Governance of States: The Role of Competitiveness Indexing and Country Benchmarking. *Millennium—Journal of International Studies* 37 (2): 303–326.

Freeman, A., and P. Cheshire. 2006. Defining and Measuring Metropolitan Regions. Paper presented at the conference, "Defining and Measuring Metropolitan Regions." Paris, November 27.

Friedmann, J., and G. Wolff. 1982. World City Formation: An Agenda for Research and Action. *International Journal of Urban and Regional Research* 6:309–344.

Gordon, I. 1999. Internationalization and Urban Competition. *Urban Studies* (Edinburgh, Scotland) 36:5–6, 1001–1016.

Graham, S., and S. Marvin. 2001. *Splintering Urbanism*. New York: Routledge.

Harvey, D. 1982. *The Limits to Capital*. Chicago: University of Chicago Press.

Harvey, D. 1989a. From Managerialism to Entrepreneurialism: The Transformation in Urban Governance in Late Capitalism. *Geografiska Annaler, B*, 71 (1): 3–18.

Harvey, D. 1989b. *The Urban Experience*. Baltimore, MD: Johns Hopkins University Press.

Jessop, B. 1998. The Narrative of Enterprise and the Enterprise of Narrative: Place-marketing and the Entrepreneurial City. In *The Entrepreneurial City*, ed. T. Hall and P. Hubbard, 77–102. London: Wiley.

Jessop, B. 2002. *The Future of the Capitalist State*. Cambridge: Polity Press.

Krätke, S. 1995. *Stadt, Raum, Ökonomie*. Basel: Birkhäuser Verlag.

Krugman, P. 1994. Competitiveness: A Dangerous Obsession. *Foreign Affairs* (March–April):28–44.

Leborgne, D., and A. Lipietz. 1991. Two Social Strategies in the Production of New Industrial Spaces. In *Industrial Change and Regional Development*, ed. G. Benko and M. Dunford, 27–49. London: Belhaven.

Lefebvre, H. 1996. Right to the City. In *Writings on Cities*. Trans. E. Kofman and E. Lebas, 61–181. Malden, MA: Blackwell.

Leitner, H., and E. Sheppard. 1998. Economic Uncertainty, Inter-urban Competition and the Efficacy of Entrepreneurialism. In *The Entrepreneurial City*, ed. T. Hall and P. Hubbard, 285–308. Chichester: Wiley.

LeRoy, G. 2007. Nine Concrete Ways to Curtail the Economic War among the States. In *Reining in the Competition for Capital*, ed. A. Markusen. Kalamazoo, MI: Upjohn Institute.

Logan, J., and H. Molotch. 1987. *Urban Fortunes*. Berkeley: University of California Press.

Lovering, J. 1995. Creating Discourses Rather Than Jobs. In *Managing Cities*, ed. Patsy Healey et al., 109–126. London: Wiley.

Marcuse, P. 2009. From Critical Urban Theory to the Right to the City. *City* 13 (2–3): 185–197.

Markusen, A. 1987. *Regions*. Totawa, NJ: Rowman & Littlefield.

Ohmae, K. 1990. *The End of the Nation State*. New York: Free Press.

Peck, J. 2005. Struggling with the Creative Class. *International Journal of Urban and Regional Research* 29 (4): 740–770.

Peck, J., and A. Tickell. 1994. Searching for a New Institutional Fix. In *Post-Fordism: A Reader*, ed. A. Amin, 280–315. Cambridge, MA: Blackwell.

Porter, M. 1990. *The Competitive Advantage of Nations*. London: Macmillan.

Sánchez, J.-E. 1996. Barcelona: The Olympic City. In *European Cities in Competition*, ed. C. Jensen-Butler, A. Shachar, and J. van Weesep. Surrey, UK: Avebury.

Sassen, S. 2001. *The Global City*. 2nd ed. Princeton, NJ: Princeton University Press.

Scott, A. J. 1998. *Regions and the World Economy*. London: Oxford University Press.

Scott, A. J., ed. 2001. *Global City-Regions*. Oxford: Oxford University Press.

Stone, C., and H. T. Sanders, eds. 1987. *The Politics of Urban Development*. Lawrence: University Press of Kansas.

Storper, M. 1996. *The Regional World*. New York: Guilford.

Storper, M., and A. J. Scott. 1989. The Geographical Foundations and Social Regulation of Flexible Production Complexes. In *The Power of Geography*, ed. J. Wolch and M. Dear, 19–40. Boston: Unwin Hyman.

Storper, M., and R. Walker. 1989. *The Capitalist Imperative*. Cambridge, MA: Blackwell.

Strange, S. 1986. *Casino Capitalism*. Oxford: Basil Blackwell.

Swyngedouw, E., F. Moulaert, and A. Rodriguez. 2002. Neoliberal Urbanization in Europe. *Antipode* 34 (3): 542–577.

Taylor, P. J., and M. Hoyler. 2000. The Spatial Order of European Cities under Conditions of Contemporary Globalization. *Tijdschrift voor Economische en Sociale Geografie* 91 (2): 176–189.

Toronto Board of Trade. 2009. *Toronto as a Global City*. Policy report. March 2009. Toronto: Toronto Board of Trade.

Van den Berg, L., and E. Braun. 1999. Urban Competitiveness, Marketing and the Need for Organising Capacity. *Urban Studies* (Edinburgh, Scotland) 36 (5/6): 987–999.

Veltz, P. 1997. The Dynamics of Production Systems, Territories and Cities. In *Cities, Enterprises and Society on the Eve of the 21st Century*, ed. F. Moulaert and A. J. Scott, 78–96. London: Pinter.

III

Ideas about Governance

8

Urban Development

Mohammad A. Qadeer

Development in the Urban Context

This chapter is essentially a historical survey of ideas about urban development as they evolved in the twentieth century, particularly after World War II. Which ideas about urban development guided city planners and developers at various times in both the First World and the Third World? How do concepts and models of urban development travel between the two worlds? Where do the ideas come from, and how do they evolve over time? These questions are probed in this chapter.

Urban development is the process of organized growth and restructuring of human settlements. It occurs in two ways. First, at the level of a project, new or renewed activities are developed on specific sites. The site-specific scale is the domain of planning regulations, environmental impact assessments, and so forth. Second, at the city or regional level, the spatial structure is realigned through both area-wide policies and programs and the cumulative effects of site-specific developments. The city or regional scale is the province of what has been variously called general, comprehensive, community, or master planning. Such an area-wide plan has been called the "constitution for development" (City of Los Angeles 2007).

Although development at both site and area levels is visibly apparent in the form of buildings, utilities, facilities, and services, these physical expressions reflect a community's socioeconomic goals. For example, in zoning bylaws development is typically defined as "the construction of a new building or other structure on a lot, the relocation of existing building on another lot or the use of a tract of land for new uses" (City of New York, City Planning Commission 2007). Yet land improvements and changes in physical environment invariably are meant to serve human activities and purposes. Therefore, the broader meaning of development in the urban context extends beyond the processes of construction and building to the functions and purposes served by these activities.

Accordingly, in this chapter I focus on the broader scale of urban development, namely, the ideas and models that have framed the development of human settlements in general and cities in particular. The development control exercised at the scale of a site, through zoning and other regulations, is not our concern. However, the area-wide objectives and policies, which these tools help implement, are of interest.

With a majority of the world's population living in cities and towns, societal development depends on the efficiency and equity of urban systems. The provisions of infrastructure, housing, businesses and industries, transport and community services have become an integral part of ideas about development (World Bank 2000). Thus, urban development is nested in national development.

Ideas about urban development arise in tandem with models of development. They grow out of the same ideological soil. How have ideas of urban development evolved? To answer this question, we must track the successive phases through which ideas about urban development have developed.

Mapping Ideas about Urban Development

Ideas about and visions of urban development arrive in successive waves; they do not show a linear, evolutionary pattern. Yet there is a parade of such ideas marching to the tunes of the times. Table 8.1 lists visions of how cities can be made more livable, efficient, orderly, or beautiful as a whole or in parts. These images and notions arose in successive periods in response to the urban challenges of the respective times. Furthermore, the political narratives of each period have shaped these ideas.

A few points about table 8.1 need to be clarified. First, the periods are best understood as links in a chain and not as discrete spans of time. Second, the ideas listed for each period do not necessarily terminate with the period but continue to be in force in some form in succeeding periods. Third, the origins of most ideas cannot be pinned to a point in time; therefore, they have been assigned to the period in which they gained currency. With these caveats, table 8.1 can be read as a map of the evolution of urban development ideas.

Three Phases of the Urban Development Discourse

Modern ideas about urban development can be organized in three historical periods, each representing a distinct paradigm. Each also corresponds to a distinct phase of political ideology in Western, largely
Anglo-Saxon, societies.

The first phase lasted from the early twentieth century to the end of
World War II. It laid the foundations of modern urban planning and
forged the idea that a city is a collective entity that must be developed
in orderly and efficient ways under public guidance. The second phase
began in the 1950s and lasted until the mid-1970s. It witnessed the
expansion of the public role in urban development and the transformation of the concept of urban development from concerns with the orderliness, efficiency, or beauty of the physical space to the realization of public
welfare and social justice as the goals of development. The third phase,
beginning in the mid-1970s and continuing to the present, reflects the
conservative spirit of the Reagan-Thatcher era, which reduced the role
of the state, on the one hand, and expanded the agenda of urban development by adding environmental and energy conservation to the goals
of urban development on the other. What forces shaped these phases and
what their seminal ideas were are discussed below.

Table 8.1 presents both the practical ideas and overarching visions
that arose in different phases. It also differentiates between the ideas
guiding urban development in the First World (largely Anglo-Saxon) and
those prevailing in the Third World (largely English-oriented countries),
pointing out their interdependence. With this introduction, let us turn to
an examination of each of the three phases.

Phase 1: The Emergence of Modern Urban Perspectives

The First World
In the First World, modern ideas about urban development arose in
response to epidemics, poverty, and crowding of the industrial city. Public
health measures such as urban water and sewerage systems, fire and
building codes, and rudimentary zoning controls on the use of land laid
the basis of the City Functional ideas. Paralleling these ideas were notions
of the City Beautiful and the Garden City, which married the qualities
of convenience and beauty with amenity and orderliness to form the
goals of urban development (Hall 1988). Nor should we forget Le

Table 8.1
Urban Development Ideas and Strategies

Years	First World	Third World
Phase 1		
Pre–World War II	Public health and sanitation.	Native town and colonial city
	Beauty and amenity	Sanitation
	Convenience and functions	Defense and army bases
	Garden City	Monumental city
	Radiant City of towers	
	Zoning and building regulations	
Phase 2		
1945–1959	Public housing and postwar reconstruction	National five-year plans and housing programs
	Garden suburbs	Displaced persons resettlement
	Green belts	Satellite townships
	National highways programs and urban road networks	Master plans
	Urban renewal and slum clearance	Rural development
	New towns	Land development schemes and urban core housing
	Regional economics	
	Segregation of land uses	
	Shopping malls	
	Downtown rebuilding	
1960–1975	City is people	Thesis of overurbanization
	Comprehensive plans and policies	Dualistic cities: formal vs. informal
	Advocacy planning and citizen participation	Secondary cities strategy
	Urban rehabilitation and conservation	Squatters upgrading
	Exploding metropolis and suburbanization	Water supply and sewerage schemes
	City containment and regional planning	New capitals
	Community planning	Urban development and investment plans

Table 8.1
(continued)

Years	First World	Third World
	Neighborhood improvement	Land titles and regularization
	Urban land-use and transportation models	
	Environmental standards	
	Wedges of open space corridors of development	
	Central city and satellite centers urban form	
Phase 3		
1976–1990	Energy-efficient development	Slum improvement
	Communicative planning	Sites and services
	Growth management	Self-help
	Historic preservation	Urban action plans
	Enterprise zones	Growth centers
	Local economic development	Intermediate cities strategy
	Housing conservation	National urban strategies
	Gentrification	Urban infrastructure programs
	Waterfront revival	Urban management
	Coastal zone management	Enabling approach
	Public-private partnership for development	Megacities
	Regulatory reforms	National conservation strategies
	Equity planning	National housing strategies
	Sprawl and compact development	Urban reforms
	Women and planning	Privatization of services
1991–2010	Smart growth	Sustainable cities
	New Urbanism	
	Sustainable development	Free trade and foreign investment
	Global cities	Housing finance
	Globalization	Urban governance

Corbusier's vision of clearing away the "dying" industrial city and building the Radiant City (1933) of high rises set in a park of open spaces
laced with highways (Hodge 1998; Hall 1988).

Yet the pre–World War II period laid the foundations for modern
notions of urban development that continue to affect urban planning
to this day. It also institutionalized urban planning as a public activity.
How did these ideas spread into the Third World? Let us turn to this
question.

The Third World

In the Third World, the pre–World War II period was an era of colonialism. Of course, the recorded history of many Third World countries
(India, China, Egypt, Iraq) goes back to ancient times, and so do their
ideas about cities (Auboyer 1962, 117–127). Those ideas are not entirely
extinct. They still exert some influence through the long-honed traditions
of community building. Being primarily concerned with the modern, even
contemporary times, I will skip to the twentieth century.

The first half of the twentieth century was a period of colonialism.
The indigenous city in Asia or North Africa was organized in caste, clan,
or occupational guild's quarters, with the geometrically laid fort-palace
occupying a high ground near a river. Its crowded bazaars and narrow
residential streets converged on the main temple or mosque, which
formed the focal point.

Colonial rulers grafted European notions of sanitation, racial superi-
ority, and space onto this indigenous city plan. The result was what has
been called a colonial city of dualistic urban structure in which the space
outside the indigenous city—a separate district of low-density bungalow
estates, arcaded markets, offices, and parks aligned along wide roads—
was developed for the colonial establishment (King 1990; Abu-Lughod
1980). In capitals and other large cities, army bases, called cantonments,
were built in the European idiom as the third component of the colonial
city. Undoubtedly, these ideas were largely meant to serve colonial interests and were limited to the "European" sections of the Third World
cities.

The colonial city was the conduit for the dissemination of Western
ideas of urban development, capitalist economy, and class segregation
(King 1990). Some of the then new technologies and ideologies of urban
development were introduced in colonial cities at almost the same time
as in European cities. For example, Karachi had a tramway linking the
commercial center with the port in 1885. Bombay (now Mumbai) had

building legislation to regulate construction activity in 1850 and the Town Improvement Trust to plan development schemes at the same time. Lagos had a town improvement ordinance in 1863. Even "the father of town planning," Patrick Geddes, spent years in India promoting his approach of "conservative surgery" for indigenous cities, starting in 1914. The point is that some urban planning ideas and practices that had just emerged in Europe found their way into colonial cities without any time lag.

All in all, in the First World, the prewar period provided some examples of regulated urban development and witnessed the formulation of urban planning ideals. In the Third World, this period split the pre-industrial city into modern and traditional towns, resulting in varying visions of development. Yet the modern idioms of urban development, though not attainable for a majority of urban residents, were tantalizingly visible in selected parts of the colonial city. Coming out of this period, two themes laid the foundation of modern urban development. Public investments and collective action produced the framework for urban development, and an orderly and balanced development became the model of urban growth.

Phase 2: The Social Production of Urban Discourses

The First World
The second phase began after World War II and lasted until the mid-1970s. In this period, urban planning evolved from an architecture- and engineering-based practice to a social sciences–driven policy discipline.[1] Economics, geography, politics, and sociology transformed ways of thinking about cities. These disciplines introduced an empirical and humanistic outlook in which lived experiences were given more weight than grandiose ideas of imagined urban order. Instead of sweeping visions such as City Beautiful or Broadacre City (Frank Lloyd Wright), urban development came to be a strategy of promoting affordable housing, improving transit facilities, or integrating racial ghettos.

The ideology of public welfare came to characterize urban development. The state assumed the responsibilities of providing for the basic needs, including housing and social services, of the poor who had fallen on hard times. In the United States, the Housing Act of 1949 set out the goal of "a decent home and a suitable living environment for every American family." The political imperatives of the postwar reconstruction, the cold war, and the necessity of forging a capitalist alternative for a caring society and building the infrastructure of an affluent society were the factors that gave rise to this ideology of welfarism.

Table 8.1 lists the major urban development programs of this second phase. It was a prolific period for ideas about urban development and planning. They ranged from strategies of financing homeownership and involving citizens in urban planning to programs of New Town and regional highway development. An illustrative example is the maturing and expansion of the mortgage insurance and the secondary mortgage markets, which revolutionized the housing industry and laid the groundwork for the suburbanization of cities. Similarly, the public housing program, initially meant for war veterans in the United States, was extended to the poor and welfare recipients in the 1950s. In the UK, council housing became a mark of the welfare state that was built by the Labour Party in the postwar period. These socioeconomic measures sparked an urban explosion in Europe and North America.

The ideas of phase 2 can be subsumed under three policy themes: (1) modernizing old cities, (2) urban expansion and the containment of metropolises, and (3) the democratization of the urban development process.

Modernizing Old Cities

The postwar cities of Europe and North America were congested and dotted with slums, particularly in their centers. The urban renewal programs (1954 in the United States and 1955 in the UK) were the bold innovations of the times meant to redevelop slums and renew central business districts to bring old cities into contemporary times. Large sections of the central city were cleared and sold to commercial developers for building multistory office and apartment buildings. The emerging city image was Corbusian in spirit (Hall 1988, 226).

The story of urban renewal is not reassuring. It was a social disaster, uprooting a large number of the poor, particularly blacks, from physically blighted but socially vibrant communities. Many poor residents of downtowns experienced the highways and urban renewal programs as "the federal bulldozer" (Anderson 1964). Civil protests, most notably the riots of 1964–1967 in the United States, sparked a veritable revolution in ideas about urban development.

Urban renewal was revised to promote the conservation and rehabilitation of neighborhoods and housing. The Model Cities program (1965) of President Johnson highlights the changing perspective of urban development. The program aimed at eliminating urban poverty through upgrading whole neighborhoods by conserving and increasing housing, improving businesses, and providing health, welfare, and educational services, along with the simultaneous improvement of major local institutions. All this was to be achieved not by commands from city hall but with the involvement of residents. It combined social policy initiatives with physical development. The program did not fulfill its promise, but from the perspective of urban development ideas, it was very important. It underlined the change in the conception of urban development, which began to be viewed as both a matter of physical restructuring and a strategy of socioeconomic advancement.

The shedding of public programs in the late 1970s led to public-private partnerships for infrastructural projects and community development (discussed further in the next chapter). The privatization thrust of the 1980s transformed such initiatives into the process of gentrification of neighborhoods. The time was propitious for Jane Jacobs's idea of a livable neighborhood and vibrant street as the building blocks of a city (Jacobs 1962). Take care of the neighborhood and the city will be taken care of, Jacobs suggested. This was the bottom-up view of urban development that came out of the reactions to the broad-sweep urban renewal.

Urban Expansion and the Containment of the Metropolis

Population growth as well as people's desire to own homes and live in green settings promoted the development of suburbs and the sprawling of cities far out into the countryside, forging a new idiom of urban development. With its wide roads for cars, commercial activities packaged into climate-controlled malls, and detached and semidetached homes lining the meandering streets in parklike settings, segregated from workplaces and stores, the suburb became the template of urban development. These new realities brought to the fore the challenges of orderly growth and containment of metropolises.

In the First World, a host of ideas about the development of the urban periphery were formulated in phase 2 (see table 8.1). Britain pioneered the planting of New Towns around London as countermagnets to the exploding metropolis. The United States experimented with private New Towns to drain away sprawl, as in Reston, Virginia; Columbia, Maryland; and Irvine Ranch, California, but such efforts were too few to make any difference. Still, the idiom of the self-contained New Town on the metropolitan periphery was another urban development idea that found expression in this period.

A vision of a regional city organized as corridors of development laid along a spine of highways and rail lines, alternating with wedges of open spaces, gained currency in late 1960s and early 1970s. Regional plans were prepared for Washington, D.C., Baltimore, Copenhagen, Ottawa, and other metropolitan areas. Similarly, as Gary Hack points out in chapter 2, the idea of a greenbelt surrounding a metropolis to contain it was tried in London, Ottawa, and Toronto, among many other places.[2] Yet in the United States, these visions were preempted by the Interstate Highway program of the mid-1950s, which crisscrossed and connected cities, opening them up for expansion and forging the model of a motorized city, à la Los Angeles.

Democratization of the Urban Development Process

One outcome of the popular agitation against urban renewal was a reexamination of the processes of decision making and urban development. Elites and professionals were discredited and citizens were invested with the right to participate in decisions about local development. Paul Davidoff's seminal article from 1965 offered "advocacy planning" as an alternative model for urban decision making (Davidoff 1965). It realigned the processes of production of urban development ideas and community decision making by promoting the practice of citizen participation. Britain followed with its own government-mandated public participation based on the principle enunciated in the Skeffington Report that it "matters to all of us [members of the public] that we should know that we can influence the shape of our communities" (quoted in Rydin 2000, 185).

The urban discourse started laying more emphasis on the processes of development, downgrading discussions of future end-states and big plans. In the planning discourse, the process and not (so much) the substance came to the forefront of urban theorizing. This theme has deeply engaged planning academics, who have spun out different theorizations of citizen-driven planning processes, such as transactive planning (Friedmann 1973), communicative planning (Innes 1995), and collaborative planning (Healey 1997), discussed in chapters 12 and 13 of this book.

Urban development evolved from an exercise in physical planning to a strategy for raising the quality of life. Community building through social policies, housing stock management, public transport, recreation opportunities, and welfare services became the favored idea of urban development. Social planning and local economic development revised the strategic image of the city. This was a critical transformation in the concept of a city.

Environmental protection and energy conservation emerged on the social agenda in the early 1970s. Environmental impact assessments of urban projects began to be incorporated into the planning processes of selected cities and regions. Similarly, the concept of energy-efficient development excited some interest. These were ideas of environmental protection and energy conservation applied to urban development. They were the harbingers of the sustainable cities idea that came in the 1990s.

Phase 2 in the Third World

The aftermath of World War II ushered in revolutionary times across the Third World. One by one the colonial empires folded and independent national-states emerged all across Asia, Africa, and Latin America. The independence of India and Pakistan (1947) was the hinge in history that marked the beginning of the era of independent nation-states in the Third World. For most of the countries, independence came with the colonial legacy of poverty, illiteracy, and economic delay. Yet independence fired people's expectations of a good life. These conditions set the stage for the process of urban development and inspired ideas for dealing with it.

As mentioned above, Third World cities had been divided in two distinct parts, traditional-indigenous and modern-colonial. After independence, these two parts came to mark differences in social class and sectoral affiliation of the residents. The modern sections of a city are planned (formally laid out) and equipped with some basic services, whereas the indigenous parts largely grow incrementally, almost house by house and street by street, severely lacking infrastructure. The development ideas for the two segments of the city come from different sources, though in practice they influence each other. Modern developments are based on adaptations of Western ideas. The indigenous city grows on the basis of an amalgam of historical practices, religious and cultural norms, and economic and technical imperatives of contemporary times.

In phase 2, the dual city fragments further into components of varying levels of modernity, legitimacy and traditions. I am here hinting at the emergence of the informal sector—particularly in the shape of squatter colonies—on the one hand and planned suburbs of modern provenance on the other. Between the two lie what I have called the new indigenous communities (NICs), namely, the lower-middle-class housing estates, formally laid out according to local standards and with clear land titles but unapproved by development authorities (Qadeer 1983, 181–184). The scope of NICs can be observed from the fact that in Delhi, 1,300 out of 2,000 developed housing colonies were unauthorized, though they had multistory buildings. The point is that a multiplicity of urban forms has emerged in the Third World.

Table 8.1 lists a host of urban development ideas that swept through the Third World in the period 1950–1975. The proliferation of urban ideas in the Third World is a direct result of the production of development ideas by international institutions. From the UN, World Bank, USAID, and others, periodic waves of development ideas arise and sweep through Third World countries. The diffusion of these ideas has had a major impact on the discourse of urban development in the Third World. They carry an aura of authority and power, as they come packaged with international aid. In one sense, the process of production of development ideas is more organized and focused for the Third World than for the First World, as the international agencies have taken on the role of think tanks for the Third World.

Space limitations do not allow me to discuss all the ideas circulating in the Third World during phase 2 and listed in table 8.1, but I have created two clusters for purposes of discussion, emphasizing (1) housing as the driving force of urban development and (2) runaway urbanization. They are examined below.

Housing as the Driving Force of Urban Development

In newly independent countries, people flock to cities in search of security and opportunity. Apart from the rural to urban migration, many countries had to host refugees displaced by redrawn political boundaries. Squatter colonies sprang up in many cities. Thus, resettlement of displaced persons and in-migrants and housing of the emerging middle classes became pressing issues. Early organized efforts of urban development consisted of building housing estates and new settlements. These efforts were followed by planning and building suburbs, satellite towns, and new capitals such as Chandigarh, Brasília, and Islamabad during the 1950s and early 1960s, as well as housing colonies for the poor and shelterless. Urban development was viewed through the lens of land development and house-building projects.

By the 1970s, urban development in the Third World had become a self-generating process driven by the market and people's informal initiatives. The organized body of knowledge, planning concepts, and international ideas largely affected the formal segment of the city. Yet even these imported ideas were modified by local practices, both organized and unorganized. For example, although land uses were meant to be segregated in planned suburbs, as soon as those were built, schools, offices, and clinics began appearing in the bungalows of residential areas.

By the 1960s, planned suburban communities for the middle and upper classes had become the hallmark of modern development. In the unplanned sphere, squatters organized by land dealers and land grabbers were expanding the city incrementally.

Third World cities' squatter settlements have become a major challenge of urban development. They have received a lot of attention from Western scholars, city planners, and policy advisers. The division of the Third World city into formal and informal sectors has inspired a range of ideas about the dual nature of such cities. Initially identified by Latin American scholars, the concept of duality was extended to cities by Geertz (1963), Abrams (1964), and the International Labour Organization (1972). Yet the reality of the Third World city is more complicated than the duality model suggests. It is a community segmented physically, socially, and culturally.

Squatter upgrading or regulated squatting became the favored solution in the 1980s and continues to be the primary means for accommodating rural migrants in the Third World city. Dubbed the "enabling approach," regulated squatting also appealed to the advocates of market solutions to urban problems who came to prominence in the 1980s and 1990s. It reduced the public's responsibility for housing poor migrants.

Controlling and Channeling Urban Growth

Another prominent theme in the second phase was the rapid growth in size and density of Third World cities. Population accretion in Third World cities prompted First World concerns about the "exploding metropolis." By the 1970s, major cities in the Third World were bypassing the historically big cities of Europe and the United States both in size and in rate of growth. How to contain them was the concern.

The ideas put forth for controlling urban growth largely recapitulated the strategies tried in the First World. Creating self-contained peripheral communities or satellite townships that could function as "reception areas" for in-migrants was a popular idea. New Bombay and Korangi township (Karachi) are two examples of this kind of development. On a large regional (provincial) scale, the idea of strengthening secondary cities (second- or third-tier cities) through industrial and infrastructural development gained currency in the late 1970s. By phase 3—the1980s and 1990s—these ideas had merged into the concept of the national urban strategy, which swept through the Third World under the auspices of the UNDP and the World Bank.

Master Plans

Following the Soviet practice of Five Year Plans for national development, many Third World countries included "housing and urban development" as a sector in their national plans. Thus, the Third World countries started having national plans for housing and urban development in the 1950s, moving ahead of the First World on this score. For example, India has had ten five-year plans, starting in 1951, each with a sizable component of housing and urban development programs. In its Third Five Year Plan (1961–1966), urbanization was linked to the process of economic development.

One of the components of these national urban development programs was the preparation of master plans to guide the orderly development of individual cities. Local planners seized on the master plan idea as a tool for controlling and guiding city growth. It appealed to Third World planners as an instrument of planned development and public control.

The master plan generally has been an ineffective tool, however. It has largely taken the form of a blueprint for projected land uses, densities, facilities, institutions, and circulation for both the existing and yet-to-be-developed sections of a city. It outlines the paths of growth of the city and sometimes projects land requirements. All in all, a conventional master plan has proved to be a static picture of the future development of a city, one whose primary use has been to identify areas of future land development. It has seldom included any systematic strategies or policies to implement its vision. Yet its identification of land for future development came in handy for private developers of housing estates.

How widespread this physical planning view of urban development has been is indicated by the fact that in India, by 1995, 879 master plans for cities had been approved and another 319 were in various stages of preparation (Bhargava 2001, 169). India was not alone in adopting master plans; other countries of the Third World, such as Nigeria (Braimah 1993), have followed a similar path.

Before I conclude the discussion of the second historical phase of urban development ideas, it is important to review briefly the role of international agencies in the formulation of concepts and policies in the Third World. Urban development was not on the agenda of aid agencies until the late 1960s, except for funding some advisory missions and occasional water and sewerage projects.[3] The World Bank started funding urban projects in 1972. It viewed urban development as a task of building institutional capacity and financing projects of infrastructure and "sites and services." Between 1972 and 1981, the World Bank funded sixty-two projects at a cost of $4.6 billion (World Bank 1983, table 1, pp. 11–12). Urban development became a matter of project and program development for infrastructure and land development.

Phase 3: Constructing the Narrative of the Postindustrial City, 1975–2010

By the early 1970s, the conceptual ground of urban development had begun to shift again. The oil crisis of 1973 and the end of the Vietnam War in 1975 marked the beginning of a new era in world affairs. In the First World, these events precipitated the fiscal crisis of the state; in the Third World, they triggered a debt crisis. Left-liberal ideologies came to be questioned, and ideologies of the right began to gain ground.

From 1969 to 1993, Republicans continuously occupied the U.S. White House except for the brief interlude of Jimmy Carter's presidency (1977–1981). President Reagan in the United States (1981–1989) and Prime Minister Thatcher in Britain (1979–1990) sought to dismantle the welfare state and vigorously championed the free market, deregulation, and privatization. The discourse of urban development could not have remained unaffected.

During phase 3 of ideas about urban development, the emphasis gradually shifted toward a combination of market-oriented and environment-sensitive narratives. The outcomes of the programs of the1960s—such as public housing, urban renewal, metropolitan containment, and master plans—fell short of their promises. Both the Right and the Left criticized urban approaches. From the right, critics pointed to the multitude of interests operating in urban settings and the need for incremental and marginal balancing of their competing demands. Such a complex phenomenon cannot be adequately managed through governmental commands and plans, they maintained; the market and political bargaining do the job better (Altshuler 1965; Banfield 1970). Market-based modes of development, they argued, are not only efficient, they also give people choice and liberty.

The left-liberal criticism ran the gamut from the charge of elite domination to Marxist analysis of urban problems. Marxist scholars maintained that the urban crisis was embedded in the structure of the capitalist city. The pursuit of profit necessitates the intervention of the state to remedy the difficulties of commodity production and to ensure the reproduction of the labor force through housing and other measures of public welfare (Harvey 1973; Massey and Megan 1982; Dear and Scott 1981).[4]

Given such wide-ranging critiques of ideas and practices from the 1960s, new narratives about urban development arose to meet the challenges of the postindustrial cities, particularly in the First World. Most characteristically, the era increasingly tilted toward market-based solutions of urban problems, even as a second wave of environmental and energy conservation ideas and practices swept the urban development discourse. As table 8.1 suggests, these two idea tracks have been interwoven in the urban narratives of phase 3, and have coalesced around three themes.

The First World City: Managing Urban Development

In the period 1975–2010, urban development came to be conceived of in terms of sectors and projects. Comprehensive visions for the whole city gave way to segmental plans for improving smaller neighborhoods, the local economy, or waterfronts. "No more big plans" was the catchphrase of the late 1970s. This phase offered nothing comparable to the comprehensive visions of Garden Cities or New Towns; instead, this emerging sector-driven approach can be described as urban managerialism.

Urban managerialism redefined physical development and spatial organization in urban development. Managers view physical space as the "motherboard" on which social and economic activities are imprinted. In phase 3, the conceptual struggle has been to find the right balance between physical planning and policy approaches to urban development.

Market-Driven Instruments of Urban Development

The ideological shift toward market-based approaches generated a series of notions about and models for the management of urban development. By the late 1970s, concern over the cost of development in the city had given rise to efforts to streamline regulations and reduce the regulatory burden on private developers. Enterprise zones, where regulations and taxes were light, became a popular strategy to attract investment and build a city's economic base (Hall 1988, 355–357). Public-private partnerships for developing derelict areas and megaprojects gained currency in the 1970s and 1980s, epitomized by London's Docklands and New York's Battery Park City (Fainstein 1994).

Perhaps the most innovative of the market-based instruments for guiding urban development of the 1970s was the transfer of development rights (TDR). This mechanism, developed in the United States, severed the development potential from the physical land and treated it as a commodity. The British struggled for decades to wrest the development rights of private lands into public hands, and American policymakers turned such rights into a marketable commodity. Overall, on both sides of the Atlantic, market-driven concepts of urban development have been ascendant.

Sustainable Cities

The rise of environmental consciousness and the internationally recognized need to balance the right to development with the responsibilities to conserve the environment led to a number of ideas about sustainable urban development. These ideas came in two distinct waves. The first occurred around the time of the UN Conference on the Human Environment (1972) and resulted in the institutionalization of the practice of environmental impact assessments for major urban projects. In the United States, the impact assessment gained acceptance slowly, but projected fiscal impacts and the service demands of development were combined to construct growth management strategies. An urban development proposal could be assessed not only for its conformity with zoning and planning regulations but also in terms of the demands it would place on a community's capacity to service it both technologically and financially. Thus, a proposal's impacts on the capital budget of a jurisdiction and cost-revenue balance became the yardsticks of viable development.

A second wave of environmentalism, launched in the 1980s, focused on energy conservation, smart growth, compact development, and green cities, and coalesced in the 1990s in the broad notion of sustainable development (an idea that is evaluated by Timothy Beatley in chapter 4). As a result, the sustainable use of environmental and energy resources has been woven into narratives about and the execution of urban development.

Sustainable development as a concept incorporates the fundamental idea of urban planning: the compact development and containment of cities, discussed in detail by Gary Hack in chapter 2. As Robert Fishman makes clear in chapter 3, the neotraditional town planning that was transformed into the New Urbanism movement during the 1990s and 2000s aimed at containing sprawl and designing communities with reduced reliance on the car by mixing land uses, building compact neighborhoods, and preserving land and greenfields (Duany 2003). New Urbanism revived Jane Jacobs's ideas about the design of neighborhoods and structuring the city. It is urban development from the ground up rather than from the top down. It also brought the urban development discourse to the project scale.

Overall, phase 3 in the First World is characterized by the transformation of the urban development discourse from the structural to functional, from the physical to the socioeconomic, and in scale from the comprehensive to the project size. Of course, elements of this discourse can be traced back to phase 2, but they matured in phase 3. There are many common threads linking ideas from one period to the next. For example, the idea of a compact city or multifunctional neighborhood surfaced in the 1950s; however, by the 1980s it was being reinterpreted as an outcome of economic and social measures rather than primarily as a matter of physical layout. The ends have not been drastically revised but the means have changed.

The Discourse of Third World Urban Development in Phase 3

Third World cities have multiple narratives simultaneously affecting their development, formal and informal, international and local. Third World urban narratives often reflect the prevailing viewpoints in the West, yet the informal segments of the Third World city are barely touched by these narratives, and those parts could be home to as much as 55 percent (India) or 96 percent (Sierra Leone) of the urban population.

The World Bank was in the business of funding urban infrastructural projects by the early 1970s. Its financial clout gave it a preeminent position among the international agencies for policy-making purposes. In 1978, UN-HABITAT, the UN Human Settlements Programme, was established as an agency of the UN. The international agencies linked with the bilateral aid organizations, as well as Western universities and research institutions, formed a web of idea production for Third World urban development. The scale of international involvement in the Third World's urban development can be judged from the fact that between 1980 and 1991, the World Bank and its affiliates loaned $1.156 billion on concessional (low-interest or grants) terms and $5.675 billion (in 1985 constant dollars) on nonconcessional (at market interest rates) terms (Satterthwaite 1993, table 1, p. 4).

The political and economic elites of the Third World are frequently inspired by images of Western "prestigious" cities. It is not uncommon for Third World leaders to proclaim they intend to make their city the Paris or London of the East. They visualize urban development as a matter of building skyscrapers, flyovers and highways, and shopping malls. The Dubai or Shanghai syndrome of walled estates and glass towers is a vivid expression of this narrative. It continues to inspire the elites of many cities in the Third World.[5]

These multiple narratives have spawned a variety of ideas and policies for urban development in the Third World. As can be observed from table 8.1, many of these ideas have a Western ring to them. For example, ideas about such matters as national conservation strategies, intermediate cities, urban economic development, and mixed use neighborhoods reflect the corresponding Western notions. The reflection of Western concepts and models in Third World ideas is an indication of the Third World's intellectual dependency, but it is also an acknowledgment that urban problems have universal dimensions. A global discourse seems to have emerged in the realm of urban development. The ideas circulating in the Third World in this period can be summed up in the following five themes.

Aided Self-Help for Housing the Poor

The burgeoning problem of squatters and slums continued to draw much of the conceptual energy in the early 1970s (Turner 1967). For a while, the strategy of producing "sites and services" to provide housing opportunities for low-income households was at the forefront of the urban narrative. Similarly, the upgrading of existing squatter and slum settlements by providing services and security of tenure commanded much attention. These models were based on mobilizing private savings and self-help to induce poor people to provide for their own shelter needs while the government organized the basic provision of land and infrastructure. This approach was presented as the rational solution to the shelter needs of the poor in the Third World cities, and is discussed in detail by Peter Ward in chapter 11.

These ideas swept through the Third World in the 1970s, but by the mid-1980s they had begun to disappear from the urban discourse. International interest shifted to other topics. For example, the World Bank loaned, on concessional as well as nonconcessional terms, current $1.25 billion for the site-and-service provisions as well as for upgrading projects in the period 1972–1981 (World Bank 1983, 15), but in the subsequent period of 1980–1989 it loaned only $0.57 billion in 1985 dollars.

Some criticized the site-and-service strategy for producing slums, but at the same time, the self-help approach stimulated many community initiatives for improving living conditions. The usual processes of land invasions and informal subdivision have continued to coexist alongside the organized community development efforts of low-income populations (Badshah 1996).

Despite the focus on squatter settlements and slums, both forms of developments have continued to expand in Third World cities. The slum population in South Asian cities is growing at almost the same rate as the total urban population—2.2 percent and 2.89 percent per year, respectively. In sub-Saharan African cities, the slum population is growing at almost double the rate of urban growth.

Action Plans for Cities

In the 1970s, ideas about citywide plans began to change. The British model of the Urban Structure Plan (1965) had an impact on master planning exercises in the Third World. It was also in line with the emerging American approach of conceiving of comprehensive plans as policy documents rather than as detailed blueprints for the development of an area.

In the Third World, the Ford Foundation showcased these ideas in Kolkata (Calcutta) by supporting the Basic Development Plan for the Calcutta Metropolitan Region (1966). It was a social, economic, and physical development strategy offering sectoral investment programs and policies for public action. Madras (1978), Manila (1982), Karachi (1976), and Lahore (1981), among other large cities, followed Calcutta's urban action planning for the development of housing, transportation, community services, and land uses, with the assistance of the World Bank, the UNDP, or British or U.S. aid agencies.

These exercises forged a new idiom of comprehensive planning by visualizing city planning as a matter of setting infrastructural, transport, waste disposal, and land-use goals and developing investment criteria, as well as proposing organizational arrangements for their realization. This new approach reconceived cities as socioeconomic systems and webs of institutions—very much a First World idea. It is not a surprise that international management consulting firms are now engaged in preparing urban development plans.

Market-Oriented Urban Policies

Many of the phase 3 ideas privileged the market for guiding urban development in the Third World. Led by the World Bank's "enabling approach," the international institutions packaged their policy prescriptions to rely on market forces and community initiatives for the provision of services and shelter within the framework of public policies that streamlined regulations, promoted popular participation, and targeted public investments to ensure efficiency and equity (UN-HABITAT 1996, 337–338). The enabling approach pulled together ideas that had grown incrementally in the implementation of urban projects in the 1980s. The World Bank's strategy conditioned project finance on a triad of affordability, cost recovery, and replication, and such ideas underscored a shift in the urban paradigm. Urban development could now be seen as the process of unleashing and directing private resources, with the public sector acting as the stimulator, regulator, and backstop.

Despite such new strategies, the urban crisis in the Third World has been unremitting. Even with public investment in such domains as water, sewerage, electricity, and squatter upgrading during the 1980s, most national and city authorities failed to provide adequate shelter and infrastructure for their growing populations.

Megacities

By the 1990s, the megacities of the Third World had outgrown the big Western cities. In 1950, New York was the only megacity of more than 10 million population. By 1985, there were nine megacities, with Calcutta, Mumbai, Mexico City, and São Paulo joining the parade. By 2005 there were twenty-five megacities, most the Third World. This gigantism of Third World cities gave rise to concern over the spatial concentration of the national population, followed by policy ideas about how to cap city growth and redistribute population. Also, planners from outside the Third World became interested in the internal structure of Third World megacities.

The concern with megacities led to an interest in the national spatial distribution of economic activities and population, which in turn spawned a round of proposals for national urban and settlement strategies in a number of countries. Professor Harry Richardson, for example, advised Pakistan, Egypt, Thailand, Kenya, Peru, and Indonesia in the 1990s on behalf of the World Bank and USAID as those countries prepared their national urban strategies. Like most such studies, the Western-proposed strategies made assumptions about the capacities of local and national governments that were not borne out by realities.

Similarly, the idea of countermagnets to draw activities and populations away from big cities found expression in an "intermediate cities" strategy that gained some traction in the literature and among policy advisers. All in all, megacities evoked some interest on the part of planners but no policy measures that could rationalize their growth.

In the 2000s, the process of globalization almost silenced the megacities discourse. Global market forces limited the scope of policy making for the national spatial economy and thereby diminished the possibilities of affecting the growth and size of cities. No one has found ways of restraining the growth of megacities except to note that they begin to decentralize as they grow big.

Urban Development from Below

Spurred by local protest movements against rapid transit, slum redevelopment, or environmental improvement projects that uproot long-established residents and businesses, a set of ideas about community-oriented, low-cost approaches to urban development has emerged as a new urban development paradigm in the Third World. International and national NGOs and local community organizations have contributed many elements of this alternative narrative. Curitiba, Brazil, has demonstrated that transportation, waste disposal, and infrastructure can be improved effectively through low-cost technologies and community-based initiatives. The paradigm has many elements, including bus rapid transport, community sanitation, and waste disposal projects (as in Orangi Town, Karachi); the use of local materials for house construction; working with land dealers to develop low-cost residential and building lots; and promoting small businesses and environmentally friendly technologies. It is a project-driven approach in which citywide development comes from cumulative improvements of the elements of an urban system (Hasan 1999; Badshah 1996). Typically, local groups initiate small projects to address one or another problem, and with their success, the effort is extended to other issues. Even if this approach falls short of a systematized and comprehensive model, the emergence of an alternative and functional paradigm is worthy of note. Some of these ideas, such as the Curitiba model, have floated up to the First World.

Interpretations and Conclusions

The ideas of development in urban planning have traced a spiraling path over the past six decades. They have evolved from an almost one-dimensional focus on physical development to multidimensional conceptions of urban change. They have evolved from simple to complex notions, from structural to functional descriptions, and from design to policies. The conclusions posed here arise from the foregoing analysis of the three phases of the ideas and models that have characterized the development of human settlements of the recent past.

In the evolution of ideas, probably the most striking change is in the conception of city structure. A city has come to be regarded as a socioeconomic system in which physical space is a critical but not defining factor. This view of the city has transformed the practice of urban planning. Yet the adage that the more things change, the more they remain the same also has some resonance in the discourse of urban development.

Urban development continues to be conceived of in terms of land uses, transportation, infrastructure, housing, community services, and environment, though the notions of how these elements are organized have been substantially revised. For example, housing for the poor is an enduring interest in urban planning, but its realization has become a matter of land policy, service strategy, mortgage finance, and community organization, rather than just a question of building public housing. The objectives of urban development have expanded in scope yet have changed relatively little, whereas the instruments for realizing such objectives have evolved considerably.

This chapter has proceeded on two parallel tracks, examining development ideas in the First World and the Third World in the same time periods. In the First World, urban development ideas emphasized postwar public welfare ideals with a focus on public housing, urban renewal, capital works, comprehensive plans, and zoning regulation. The reaction to these ideas, however, shifted the focus to processes of decision making, social planning, and policy discourses. By the mid-1970s (phase 3), right-leaning ideologies were driving planning, resulting in market-based instruments that emphasized urban management strategies with environmental sensitivity. A host of innovative ideas, such as New Urbanism, smart growth, and local economic development, came to the fore in this period. Yet these were not citywide, comprehensive visions but segmental concepts addressing specific urban problems.

Ideas about urban development in the Third World have tended to follow multiple tracks and do not show a tidy evolution. The fragmented structure of Third World cities precludes the emergence of a cohesive discourse about urban development. Yet beginning with their colonial heritage, Third World cities were subject to Western ideas of planning and development. After independence, Third World countries came under the influence of international agencies for aid and advice, so development ideas continued to be largely produced abroad.

Periodically, international agencies unleashed a wave of ideas and policies that swept through Third World cities. Before one wave could work its way through with lessons learned, a new wave would arise to swamp it. In one decade, sites and services and land titling dominated urban narratives; the next decade offered institution building, local governance, and privatization as the solutions to urban problems. These periodic waves have preempted the process of national learning from experiences and the systematization of local knowledge.

The roots of urban narratives lie in notions of public welfare, collective goods, and social interdependencies. The shift toward market-based approaches, interestingly, is often justified on instrumental grounds—that human welfare will be better served by relying on market measures than on public initiatives and interventions. Advocates of this theory do not dispute the goals of public welfare; they simply envision realizing them in more "efficient" terms. This is the thrust of the new conservative ideology first articulated in the Thatcher-Reagan era.

Urban development ideas will likely go through another cycle. Their evolution has not been and is not likely to be linear. A majority of the world's population is already living in cities, most of it in the Third World. Third World cities have yet to figure out how to provide basic infrastructure and services for all, not to speak of jobs and housing for the exploding youth populations. Vast swaths of Third World rural regions are also reaching thresholds of urban densities requiring urban services and municipal governments (Qadeer 2004). Paralleling the urban challenges of the Third World are the problems of stubborn "poverty amid affluence" and deteriorating as well as inadequate infrastructure in First World cities. Global warming is another force that requires immediate response. Together, these factors may bring about a global revival of public investments in urban development, sparking another shift in narratives.

Notes

1. After graduating with a degree in sociology, when I enrolled for Ekistics (Doxiadis's version of urban planning) studies in Greece in 1960, social scientists were still viewed as interlopers in the planning profession. I was not sure until I came to the United States for doctoral studies in 1964 that I would have a future in urban planning. By the time I started teaching planning in 1970, architects and engineers had dwindled to a small minority among the young planners.

2. Incidentally, this idea has been revived recently under the rubric of smart growth.

3. The international aid agencies initially looked on urban development and housing as a consumption sector and not worthy of investment financing. In the 1950s and 1960s, they largely focused on advice more than on financial aid. USAID sent Charles Abrams, for example, on fourteen housing advisory missions in the late 1950s and 1960s. C. Doxiadis was funded by the Ford Foundation to spread his gospel of Ekistics and Dynapolis, a linearly expanding city whose "heart has room to grow," in Pakistan, Ghana, Iraq, Lebanon, and other countries. Under the Colombo Plan, Britain funded experts' services for advising Commonwealth countries on town planning and housing.

4. The Marxist position outlined here is drawn from what Hall calls his "inadequate summary" (Hall 1988, 336).

5. The current race in Kuala Lumpur, Dubai, and Shanghai to build the tallest building is a manifestation of this viewpoint, as are the frequent announcements to beautify cities by building fountains and installing illuminations.

References

Abrams, Charles. 1964. *Man's Struggle for Shelter in an Urbanizing World*. Cambridge, MA: MIT Press.

Abu-Lughod, Janet. 1980. *Rabat*. Princeton, NJ: Princeton University Press.

Altshuler, Alan. 1965. *The City Planning Process*. Ithaca, NY: Cornell University Press.

Anderson, Martin. 1964. *The Federal Bulldozer: A Critical Analysis of Urban Renewal, 1949–62*. Cambridge, MA: MIT Press.

Auboyer, Jeannine. 1962. *Daily Life in Ancient India*. London: Phoenix Press.

Badshah, Akhtar A. 1996. *Our Urban Future*. London: Zed Books.

Banfield, Edward C. 1970. *The Unheavenly City: The Nature and Future of Our Urban Crisis*. Boston: Little, Brown.

Bhargava, Gopal. 2001. *Development of India's Urban, Rural and Regional Planning in 21st Century*. New Delhi: Gyan Publishing House.

Braimah, Aaron Aruna. 1993. Urban Planning and development. In *Urban Development in Nigeria*, ed. Robert W. Taylor. Aldershot, UK: Ashgate.

City of Los Angeles. 2007. Los Angeles General Plan Elements. http://cityplanning.lacity.org/complan/gen_plan/Generalplan.htm.

City of New York, City Planning Commission. 2007. Zoning Resolution. www.nyc.gov.html/dcp/pdf/zone/art01c02/pdf.

Davidoff, Paul. 1965. Advocacy and Pluralism in Planning. *Journal of the American Institute of Planners* 31 (November): 331–338.

Dear, Michael, and Allen Scott, eds. 1981. *Urbanization and Urban Planning in Capitalist Society*. London: Methuen.

Duany, Andres. 2003. *The New Civic Art: Elements of Town Planning*. New York: Rizzoli.

Fainstein, Susan S. 1994. *The City Builders*. Cambridge: Blackwell.

Friedmann, John. 1973. *Retracking America*. New York: Anchor Books.

Geertz, Clifford. 1963. *Peddlers and Princes: Social Development and Economic Change in Two Indonesian Towns*. Chicago: University of Chicago Press.

Hall, Peter. 1988. *Cities of Tomorrow*. Oxford: Basil Blackwell.

Hasan, Arif. 1999. *Understanding Karachi*. Karachi: City Press.

Harvey, David. 1973. *Social Justice and the City*. London: Edward Arnold.

Healey, Patsy. 1997. *Collaborative Planning*. Vancouver: University of British Columbia Press.

Hodge, Gerald. 1998. *Planning Canadian Communities*. Toronto: ITP Nelson.

Innes, Judith. 1995. Planning Theory's Emerging Paradigm: Communicative Action and Interactive Practice. *Journal of Planning Education and Research* 14 (3): 183–190.

International Labour Organization (ILO). 1972. *Employment, Incomes and Equality: A Strategy for Increasing Productive Employment in Kenya*. Geneva: ILO.

Jacobs, Jane. 1962. *The Death and Life of Great American cities*. London: Jonathan Cape.

King, Anthony D. 1990. *Urbanism, Colonialism and the World Economy*. London: Routledge.

Massey, Doreen, and Megan, R. 1982. *The Anatomy of Job Loss: The How, Where and Why of Employment Decline*. London: Methuen.

Qadeer, Mohammad A. 1983. *Urban Development in the Third World: New York*. Frederick: Praeger.

Qadeer, Mohammad A. 2004. Urbanization by Implosion. *Habitat International* 28.

Rydin, Yvonne. 2000. *Urban and Environmental Planning in the UK*. London: Palgrave Macmillan.

Satterthwaite, David. 1993. Financial and Other Assistance Provided to and among Developing Countries for Human Settlements. London: International Institute for Environment and Development. Prepared for UNCHS (Habitat). Manuscript.

Turner, John. 1967. Barriers and Channels for Housing Development in Modernizing Countries. *Journal of the American Institute of Planners* 33:167–181.

UN-HABITAT. 1996. *An Urbanizing World: Global Report on Human Settlement, 1996*. Oxford: Oxford University Press.

World Bank. 1983. *Lending for Urban Development 1972–82*. Washington, DC: World Bank.

World Bank. 2000. *Entering the 21st Century: World Development Report 1999/2000*. Oxford: Oxford University Press.

9

Public-Private Engagement: Promise and Practice

Lynne B. Sagalyn

Government officials, policy analysts, practitioners, and academics from diverse contexts across the globe have enthusiastically endorsed the promise of public-private (PP) engagement to solve pressing problems of public policy. The endorsement often is a rallying cry for a change in policy or reform of a prevailing policy regime, as is evident in typical PP slogans such as "partnerships for progress," "a new framework for infrastructure," "a tool for economic modernization," "helping to address the urban environmental crisis," and "meeting the investment challenge." Not infrequently, the actual meaning of the PP label is ambiguous, its use a rhetorical tactic to expand the political appeal of the policy strategy. The PP rubric can mean different things: informal collaboration, formal organizational alliance, and contractual business venturing, if not an exactly equal sharing of risks and rewards as commonly connoted by *partnership*. Whichever institutional format prevails in practice, the thrust of the PP approach shifts the focus from the conventional adversarial relationship between sectors to addressing and solving problems based on mutually reinforcing relationships fostered by an alignment of interests.

In theory and practice, the idea of a public-private partnership (PPP) blurs distinctions between roles and actions traditionally considered properly public and those traditionally considered private. Loosening these fixed distinctions has generated creative solutions to vexing urban problems, yet as the PP strategy reaches into ever more areas of public goods and services, policymakers and analysts are increasingly uneasy about the loss of traditional public sector values, which seem to get jettisoned en route to mutual benefit through close collaboration. Planners, in turn, worry about the connection—or lack thereof—of PPPs to the world of planning and its established principles, codified methods, and regulatory tools. Blurring the conventional PP distinction challenges the values of public agency. And the loss of that distinction raises core questions of policy: What are the rules of engagement under the new PP paradigm? Who sets them, and to what effect, in economic, political, and planning realms? These vexing governance questions continue to challenge experts after more than three decades of PPPs.

In this chapter I argue that a troublesome gap exists between the promise and the practice of PPPs. The PP paradigm invokes a formidable list of public benefits: collaborative advantage, resourcefulness, fiscal pragmatism, risk sharing, market-based efficiency, productivity enhancement, and innovation in the design and management of public services. On the performance side, however, evidence of the strategy's effectiveness is not extensive, and the evidence that does exist suggests a mixed track record (Daniels and Trebilcock 1996, Boarse 2000, Public Citizen 2003, HM Treasury 2003, Flinders 2005, Siemiatycki 2006; Koppenjan 2005; Murray 2006; Cambridge Systematics 2006; U.S. Department of Transportation, Federal Highway Administration [USFHWA] 2007a, 2007b).[1] Moreover, the thin body of evidence does little to counterbalance the pressing issue of PPP governance, which is a nagging concern on the administrative side of the policy scorecard. While this policy concern is hardly unique to the PP model, the political rhetoric and elevated expectations of performance from cooperative (as opposed to adversarial) sector relationships shine a spotlight on the accountability issue and amplify the political risks of adopting the PP model as a governance reform tool.

Over the course of several decades of practice, public administrators working with expert consultants have put in place new procedures governing particular pieces of the PP process. As a distinct field of planning practice, PPP is more established today than when I began researching this activity in the mid-1980s. Yet the selective processes and procedures still fall short of benchmark best practices of public governance. The shortfall is most obvious in the realm of financial and managerial accountability. Left unmanaged, it exposes governments to political risks above and beyond the technical and financial risks of a project. In other words, the lack of strong governance controls and procedures ups the ante of the PP approach, unnecessarily raising the hurdle for policy success.

My earlier writings on city building (Sagalyn 1990, 2001) addressed this accountability factor. The political context for PPPs in the United States today, however, is substantively different because the contemporary targets of the PP approach—airports, turnpikes, bridges and tunnels, municipal infrastructure, and environmental projects—directly touch the day-to-day lives of far more people in comparison to complex urban redevelopment projects. For that reason alone, these newer PP initiatives are more visible and their projected costs and benefits are more understandable to all constituencies: citizens at large, civic groups, interest groups, elected officials, and the policy community. Moreover, by materially increasing access to specialized information and expanded opportunity for civic engagement, the Internet has fundamentally reshaped the channels through which we press for accountability from elected officials and has dramatically accelerated the timing of an expected response.

To make my argument, I first describe the forces giving rise to the PP strategy and its ever-widening range of practice. In this section I also discuss the challenges of complexity that adhere to PP projects and how they activate the issues of governance. PP arrangements are legally difficult to design and negotiate, and ambitious policy objectives pursued by elected officials graft onto the PP strategy, adding further complexity. Moreover, the status of government as a partner imposes particularly complex demands on contracting. These conditions largely define the PP exercise and impose a particular prerequisite for success: Public players need institutional and political skills as well as technical knowledge to effectively administer in this field. While the PP strategy holds the promise of greater productivity by harnessing market forces and breaking down formal and established distinctions between public and private spheres of activity, this hoped-for gain in efficiency is vulnerable to policy mandates and regulatory constraints layered onto PP projects. To ensure political success, rules of engagement are needed to provide a best practices road map for this valuable urban strategy, and these rules are discussed in the second section of the chapter. Governance protocols, capacity building, and comparative research on performance form the basis for my conclusion that theoreticians and practitioners of the PP strategy need to address an agenda for building PP policy performance.

Public-Private Partnerships in Practice

Public officials around the globe have adopted the idea of PPPs in response to three powerfully motivating situations: in the United States, as a real estate strategy to redevelop declining downtowns, transform waterfronts, and revitalize inner-city neighborhoods (an approach that in the UK is typically called "regeneration"); in developing countries, as a fiscal solution to the increasing demands for infrastructure and urban services arising from rapid urbanization; and in Canada, the UK, and Western European countries, as a means of devolving responsibilities from central to subnational levels of government. The growing policy preference for PP arrangements marks a broad global convergence of economic forces and changing political paradigms. For the public sector, PP symbolizes the search for greater efficiency of urban service delivery and resourceful mobilization of private capital as governments around the world face increasing fiscal constraints from limited (or cash-starved) budgets and ongoing heightened voter sensitivity to taxes. For the private sector, PPPs represent a potential cornucopia of investment opportunity in existing and emerging urban markets across the globe.

Based on the logic of pragmatism, PPP advocates make compelling arguments for bridging public and private sectors through alliance, collaboration, and partnership. They cast these arrangements as innovative and resourceful ways of dealing with the intensifying demands of urbanization or critical needs for economic development. Citing a combination of economic and institutional forces, infrastructure policy specialists in particular emphasize the core role PPPs can play in meeting the pressing need for new large-scale investments and the equally urgent need to refurbish existing systems. For national governments and international donor organizations anxious to enhance productivity and stimulate economic growth, PPPs represent an efficient means to expand the scope of their development investments and simultaneously tap advanced technological expertise.

The worldwide momentum for PP solutions has emerged from a broad and diverse coalition that sees the strategy as a governance reform tool as much as a pragmatic fiscal imperative. Complex urban problems and a better quality of urban services, these policy reformers argue, are no longer singularly solvable by traditional forms of state intervention. Multifaceted approaches are required, including new institutional arrangements that devolve power from the national center to local entities of government and reinvent local models of governments by engaging the private market to deliver urban services in cooperation or competition with public agencies (Osborne and Gaebler 1993; Moore and Pierre 1998; Engberg 2002). International funding organizations such as the World Bank, the Asian Development Bank, the Japan Bank for International Cooperation, and the Inter-American Development Bank have entered the PPP advocacy tent seeking to promote and expand the development of needed infrastructure around the world (USFHWA 2007a).

And relatively recently, the European Union accepted the PPP as a "complementary implementation tool," linking PPP use to its initiatives for economic development and competitiveness (European Commission [EC] 2003, 2004; Newman and Verpraet 1999; Elander 2002; Grimsey and Lewis 2004). In so doing, the European Commission was building on the experience of a number of Organisation for Economic Co-operation and Development countries that have well-established programs. The UK's Private Finance Initiative (PFI), begun in 1992, is the best known, but other countries with significant PP projects include Finland, Germany, Greece, Italy, the Netherlands, Portugal, and Spain (International Monetary Fund 2004). In the United States, the Department of Transportation through its surface transportation administration aims to expedite urban transportation projects by encouraging state and local transportation agencies to consider the "selective use" of PP approaches and has put out substantive materials to support that position (USFHWA 2007b, 4–2). The extensive scope of PPPs in transportation activity in the continental United States is evident in figure 9.1. Some leading politicians have adopted PPPs as part of their ruling party's wider "modernization" agenda, as did Labour Party's Tony Blair when he became prime minister of the UK in 1997 (Flinders 2005).

Opportunity and Experimentation

Beyond the search for increased efficiency in the delivery of urban services and the fiscal pressure to mobilize substitute private capital for infrastructure investments, the momentum for PP arrangements represents a response to heightened awareness among private market professionals—developers, construction management firms, and infrastructure consortia and their investment bankers, lawyers, and specialized consultants—of new economic opportunities within urban markets around the globe. This is a relatively new phenomenon, with two distinct but mutually reinforcing forces. After decades of public sector incentives aimed at attracting private investment capital into urban neighborhoods and commercial districts, changing demographic patterns in the United States are pulling private equity investments into previously capital-starved urban markets, newly labeled "emerging markets." Globally, rapid population and the prospect of economic opportunity that has historically drawn people to cities will, demographic experts project, produce a twenty-first-century "urban gigantism" as the developing world spawns cities with populations between one and five million that rapidly grow in unprecedented numbers (Montgomery 2007).

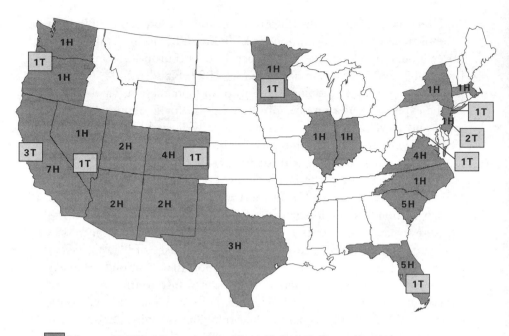

Figure 9.1
Major Surface Transportation PPPs in the Continental United States since 1991.
Source: USFHWA (2007b).

The global convergence of practice reflects a particular political pliability inherent in the PP strategy. In some countries, the PPP has been an experimental innovation (the Netherlands, Spain, Finland); in others, an ideological force (the UK, Canada, Australia); and in still others, a variant on a history of mixed enterprise (the United States, France, Singapore). Government officials have applied the PP model to an ever-broadening set of urban service needs, though some services, like prisons, remain controversial (Grimsey and Lewis 2004; Verkuil 2007). In the realm of urban service infrastructure, PP projects take in wastewater and sewage treatment works, power plants, pipelines, telecommunications infrastructure, public-use motorways, toll roads, toll bridges, tunnels, road upgrading and maintenance, railways, subways, light-rail systems, airport facilities, harbors, affordable housing, student housing, school buildings, government offices, fire and police stations, hospitals and other health service facilities, social housing, prisons and secure training centers, parking stations, and museums, among other projects for recreation and tourism (see table 9.1 for a list of illustrative PP projects). In the realm of urban redevelopment, what began with initiatives for downtown development now includes waterfront transformation, historic preservation, brownfield development, neighborhood commercial center revitalization, community development lending, and military base conversions. Whether for urban redevelopment/regeneration, transportation and environmental infrastructure, or economic development, the PP model and its many variants has become the policy of choice for municipal government in the United States and an increasing number of governments in Europe and Asia. Between 1985 and 2004, for example, more than $2 billion of worldwide PP infrastructure projects had been planned and funded, with 53 percent of them completed by year end 2004 (USFHWA 2007a, 2–2).

The open character, flexible format, and customization of project-specific business terms and conditions for the PP sharing of risks and responsibilities makes the PP model highly adaptable (Sagalyn 2006, 2007). The precise mechanisms of ownership and finance and the specific obligations for production and delivery of urban goods and services can be rearranged to produce different allocations of public and private responsibility, which is what government officials in the UK, North American, Europe, and Asia have been experimenting with for the past three decades. Their experimentation has produced a broad range of institutional formats, as described in table 9.2. Pure *privatization*—in which government disengages totally through transfer of ownership to a private firm, which takes over assets and assumes responsibility for service delivery—differs from the many formats for *contracting out*, which in turn differ legally and financially from the *joint venture*. Formats for contracting out are forms of procurement, and they typically circumscribe the nature of the PP relationship to what is specified in the contract. In contrast, the joint venture or development agreement PPP commonly used for regeneration and economic development projects, for example, typically involve a mutual commitment to the venture greater than what is transmitted in the development agreement. In practice, these agreements implicitly cover what cannot be anticipated—a mutual commitment to deal with unexpected project-threatening crises if and when they occur, which may mean renegotiating the agreement if necessary to ensure successful execution of the project (Frieden and Sagalyn 1989;

Table 9.1
Illustrative Sample of Public-Private Projects in North America

Type of Project	PP Format*	Date Begun**
Development		
Abbotsford Hospital (BC)	BDFOM	1987
Battery Park City (Manhattan, New York City)	DDA	1969
Beverly Hills and Montage Gardens (CA)	DDA	2000
California Plaza (Los Angeles)	DDA	1981
CityPlace (West Palm Beach, FL)	DDA	2002
Downtown Silver Spring (MD)	DDA	1999
Excelsior and Grand (St. Louis Park, Minneapolis, MN)	DDA	2001
Rowes Wharf (Boston)	DDA	1985
Southside Works (Pittsburgh, PA)	DDA	2000
Yerba Buena Center (San Francisco, CA)	DDA	1980
Redevelopment		
42nd Street/Times Square (Manhattan, New York City)	DDA	1980
Atlantic City Outlets—The Walk (NJ)	DDA	2002
Belmar (Lakewood, CO)	DDA	2002
Burnham Hotel at Reliance Building (Chicago)	DDA	1998
Fruitvale Village (Oakland, CA)	DDA	2002
James F. Oyster School/Henry Adams House (Washington, D.C.)	DDA	1999
Horton Plaza (San Diego, CA)	DDA	1977
Union Station (Washington, D.C.)	DDA	1985
Transportation		
Alliance Airport (TX)	DDA	1989
California State Route 91 HOV Lane	BTO	1995
Charleswood Bridge (Winnipeg, ON)	DBFO	1993
Chicago Skyway Lease (IL)	Concession	2004
Dulles Greenway (VA)	DBFO	1988
E-470 Tollway (CO)	DBO	1985
JFK Airport Terminal 4 (New York City)	DDA	1995
Highway 407 (ON)	DBO	1993
Hudson-Bergen Light Rail (NJ)	BOT/DBOM	1994
Indiana Toll Road Lease	Concession	2005
Las Vegas Monorail (NV)	BOT/DBOM	1993
Pocahontas Parkway Route 895 (VA)	DBFO	2004
Pearson International Airport Terminal 3 (Toronto, ON)	DBFO	1986

Table 9.1
(continued)

Type of Project	PP Format*	Date Begun**
Prince Edward Island Bridge (PEI)	DBFOT	1985
Richmond-Airport-Vancouver Line (BC)	DBFO	2001
Route 28 (VA)	DBT	2002
South Bay Expressway Route 125 (CA)	DTO franchise	1991
State Highway 30 (Texas)	DBFO concession	2006
Water and Sewer Infrastructure		
Atlanta Water Service (GA)	O&M contract	1998
Franklin Waste Water Treatment Plant (OH)	DBFOT	1995
Phoenix Water Treatment Facility (AZ)	DBO	2000

Notes: *DDA, Disposition and development agreement. See table 9.2 for other initialisms.
**Date project begun generally means the start date of public sector planning. In select instances where that date is not available from online information, the date begun represents the date the private vendor was selected.

Bovaird 2004; Sagalyn 2001). Beyond the particulars of specific institutional formats, all PP arrangements share an important common attribute: the negotiated allocation of risk, responsibility, and control between public and private partners. This is the core of the PP business relationship, in theory and practice, so much so that it even shapes the potential for partnership (van Ham and Koppenjan 2002).

The variations in arrangements for contracting out represent a veritable alphabet soup of initialisms (see "project delivery approaches" in fig. 9.2). From these, government officials can choose among diverse alternatives to the traditional public sector procurement model, which many experts identify as bureaucratically inefficient and costly. These alternatives bundle the legal and contractual dimensions of delivering urban goods and services—ownership, finance, construction, operation, and maintenance—in different ways, or what I call "positional combinations." These combinations are graphically portrayed in figure 9.3 as a continuum—100 percent public to 100 percent private—of role combinations for providing urban services, redeveloping cities and neighborhoods, and fostering economic development.

Table 9.2
Formats for Public-private Project Implementation

Type of PP Model	Initialism	Public Interface
Privatization		Asset sale
Sale-leaseback		Asset sale and contracting
Concession/franchise		Licensed service agreement
Outsourcing/contracting		Generalized procurement
Service provision contracts		Service procurement
Design and construct	D&C	
Design-build-operate	DBO	
Design-build-finance-operate	DBFO	
Design-construct-manage-finance	DCMF	
Design-build-finance-operate-manage	DBFOM	
Operate and maintain	O&M	
Operate, maintain, and manage	OM&M	
Build-own-operate	BOO	
Build-own-operate-maintain	BOOM	
Build-own-operate-remove	BOOR	
Rehabilitate-own-operate	ROO	

Notes:
Outsourcing or contracting out   Arrangement in which the public sector maintains ownership or policy control (e.g., rate setting) of a function but contracts with a private operator to discharge that function through some type of procurement process over a contractually defined period of time.
Procurement process   Arrangement in which the public sector decides on a mix of rights and responsibilities—risk allocation, operation, financing, maintenance, performance—of a service over a contractually defined period of time.
Franchise   Arrangement in which a private firm is granted a license to operate or provide services in a particular territory for a contractually defined period of time.
Concession   Legal arrangement in which a private firm is granted land or property for a particular purpose (to provide water and electricity) for a contractually defined period of time in return for services, after which the infrastructure is returned to the public entity.
Business Improvement District   Business-initiated territorial arrangement within a city in which all property owners or businesses are subject to additional tax assessments that are used to fund services and improvements within the district and to pay for the administrative costs of the BID operations (Briffault 2000, 368).

Table 9.2
(continued)

Type of PP Model	Initialism	Public Interface
Capital provision contracts		Service procurement and capital asset
Build-transfer-operate	BTO	
Build-operate-transfer	BOT	
Build-lease-transfer	BLT	
Build-lease-transfer-maintain	BLTM	
Build-own-operate-transfer	BOOT	
Build-own-operate-train-transfer	BOOTT	
Design-operate-transfer	DOT	
Lease-renovate-operate-transfer	LROT	
Rehabilitate-operate-transfer	ROT	
Business improvement district	BID	Special taxation and co-decision making
Community development bank	CDB	Co-capitalized lending venture
Redevelopment partnership		Project-specific joint decision making
Joint venture agreement	JV	Co-investment "mixed enterprise"

Community development bank   Lending venture jointly capitalized by government and private sector funds and designed to leverage private capital for loans, guarantees, venture capital, grants, and technical assistance to small businesses in disadvantaged neighborhoods. The Los Angeles Community Development Bank, for example, created by the U.S. government in 1995, was capitalized with $435 million from the U.S. Department of Housing and Urban Development and $210 million from regional commercial banks (Rubin and Stankiewicz 2002).

Redevelopment partnership   A project-based arrangement that typically involves co-investment by the public sector. The public investment may involve all manner of direct or indirect financial assistance as well as regulatory relief, bureaucratic expediting, and related forms of project assistance. The public entity (or entities) may or may not be a co-owner of the project in the legal sense, notwithstanding profit-sharing arrangements.

Joint venture   Arrangement in which private and public entities jointly undertake the development (and perhaps operation and maintenance) of a facility that will provide services.

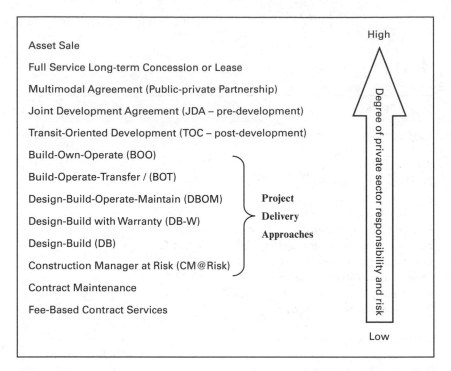

Figure 9.2
Project Delivery Approaches. *Source:* USFHWA (2007b).

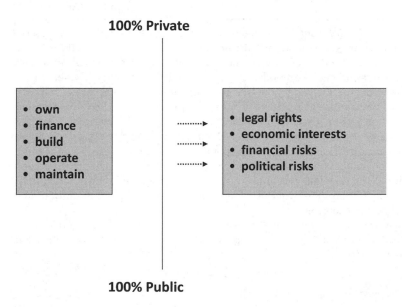

Figure 9.3
PP Positional Continuum.

For infrastructure projects, the delivery approaches are differentiated by three core elements: the services bundled (the degree of private control over service delivery and the extent of policy control retained by the public entity), the financial commitment of the private sector (investment risk), and the ability and willingness of the public sector to share financial risk (public risk taking). Whichever format public officials choose, service delivery is redirected from unidirectional agency to PP co-production and decision making, and it is this institutional move that challenges the structure and values of public sector agencies (Engberg 2002). Politically, the emphasis shifts as well: "What matters is what works," said Britain's former prime minister Tony Blair in an often quoted phrase (*Financial Times* 1998, cited in Newman and Verpraet 1999, 489).[2] In short, adoption of the PP strategy signifies political regime reform.

Making generalizations about contracting out is tenuous because substantial variations in procurement laws and procedures exist worldwide (and within federalist government systems such as the United States). Yet more than the involvement of private enterprise per se, *bundling* is what distinguishes PP infrastructure contracting arrangements. Bundling ties together traditionally discrete procurement processes of design, financing, construction, operations, and maintenance. By vertically integrating some or all of these functions, bundling creates the potential for greater economic efficiency because private companies have a financial motivation to think in ways that might generate greater productivity and cost efficiencies *over time*, that is, for the duration of their service contract (Daniels and Trebilcock 1996). Bundling also can open up to competition a set of economic activities previously excluded from that process (Grimsey and Lewis 2004).

Implementation Challenges

In theory, the market-based logic of PPP promises to deliver design and management innovations as well as economic efficiencies. In practice, the institutional architectures needed to execute these multiple objectives remain complex. The list of hurdles to implementation can be daunting. Case studies of partnerships show that the processes and procedures necessary to select private concessionaires, service providers, or real estate developers willing and able to operate in the public interest pose a challenge to existing public expertise. Moreover, the contract arrangements and joint venture agreements necessary to implement these projects are exceedingly difficult to design and negotiate. Accordingly, public players must be skilled politically to deal with multiple constituencies in both public and private realms, as well as technically versed in the details of what it takes to deliver the infrastructure service or redevelopment/ regeneration project.

The details of specific project conditions and the ambitions of public objectives matter a lot as well. Political cultures vary and shape the institutional context of contracting. Rate-setting constraints on cost recovery or profits, extraordinary programmatic public benefits, or other policy mandates can create potential losses in economic efficiency and reduce private investment value (Daniels and Trebilcock 1996). Low levels of competition resulting from a field of bidders narrowed by the high level of performance or technical expertise or regulatory constraints required of the public request for proposals (RFP) process create complex economic problems for PP projects. Bidders are likely to add on risk premiums to cover a range of possible situations: a requirement for a contractual price guarantee, potential contract penalties for delays, and apprehension about capricious government action. When PP projects are carried out by numerous independent public agencies and proliferate in number, fragmentation of policy coordination can present another policy problem (Flinders 2005). Alternatively, when driven by a central government, as in the case of airport privatization in Australia, the process might "quarantine" adjacent commercial development from the scrutiny of state and local planning processes (Freestone, Williams, and Bowden 2006). And, as nearly all reviewers of case-based experience point out, PPPs cloud accountability.

Government detachment is the linguistic myth of privatization. That is the policy reality quite evident in case analyses of PP projects, not surprisingly. The reallocation of roles inherent in the PP paradigm creates complex combinations of legal rights, economic interests, and financial risks, and these complicate (and compromise) the theoretical promise of the PP approach. It is not unusual for PP arrangements to create contingent liabilities for public entities; after all, implementing complex redevelopment or infrastructure projects carries enormous financial risks. These risks include shortfalls in projected usage, downward shifts in market demand, cost overruns, entitlement failures, costly program changes due to development requirements, premature loss of assets or termination of leases, publicly sponsored competition, and lower-than-anticipated residual values for assets. Since government actions create assets with private sector value and embed economic rights—long-term fee-based revenue streams, special development incentives, and opportunities to capture value from adjacent real estate development—

PP arrangements readily beget political exposure in the potential giveaway of "too much," even if officials follow best practices of public administration.

Researchers who have examined PPPs in detail, for example, offer persuasive evidence that contracting out may involve government-backed financing, regulatory restrictions, and ongoing subsidy, or implicate other public policy concerns that involve ongoing monitoring of governance. Daniels and Trebilcock (1996) reviewed three high-profile Canadian infrastructure projects: Highway 407 toll roadway in the northern region of the Greater Toronto area, the Prince Edward Island Fixed Link Bridge across Northumberland Strait, and the redevelopment of Pearson International Airport (in two phases, Terminal 3 followed by Terminals 1 and 2). Despite the depiction of economic benefits to the government from private sector efficiency and risk bearing, they found that each project included some significant role for government in project financing or long-term subvention. The decision to develop the project through a PPP did not eliminate sensitive public policy concerns, right-of-way and eminent domain issues, and monopoly pricing concerns, among others. Rather, the need to respond to these policy concerns created tension with the need to provide credible assurances to the developer/operator that "the franchise value of the undertaking would not be debased ex post by direct government action" (ibid., 388).

Like many investments taken on by government, PPPs confront a well-established list of political hazards. First, of course, there is the failure to form a partnership, as well as the failure to complete a project, both of which are haunting probabilities for any government official. Van Ham and Koppenjan (2002) analyzed formation risk in some detail in their analysis of nine transport projects in the Netherlands. They found that success was not a given but was most likely when the decision-making process required the active engagement of the partners.

Complexity is a second factor (Sagalyn 2007). Whether driven by fiscal pragmatism or regime reform, the PP strategy is demanding in terms of policy ambition as well as financial feasibility. For both redevelopment (regeneration) and infrastructure projects, the product is also complicated in its technical specification. With infrastructure bundling, for instance, bidding private partners often form consortia ("virtual corporations") because "the functions involved are highly specialized and entail deployment of quite different bodies of complementary expertise and resources" beyond the capabilities of individual firms unless a firm is vertically integrated (Daniels and Trebilcock 1996, 390). For redevelopment projects, state and local government entities regularly collaborate to facilitate funding, marshal powerful financial incentives, or expedite entitlement approvals (Sagalyn 2001). The whole gets fashioned into a project-specific organizational network governed by the business terms and conditions of the contracting arrangement, concession or franchise agreement, long-term ground lease, or disposition and development agreement.

Managing relations is a third factor. Each side of the relationship is typically populated with multiple players, public and private entities themselves often representing infrasector collaborations. Public officials responsible for managing negotiations for a PP project face a high hurdle in securing agreement among government players to not one but a series of interlocking agreements detailing each participant's rights and obligations in implementing the PP project.

PP projects are threatened by a number of other generic political risks, including stakeholder resistance and active citizen or community opposition, contract mispricing, overgenerous economic incentives, and interference from political officials that could beget favoritism and corruption. All of these situations can generate litigation (and certainly project delays) and can result in project failure even if the project wins its judicial challenges. Because PPPs represent a paradigm shift, political risks specific to the PP strategy—most notably, financial failure reverting to public takeover or buyout—are potential liabilities capable of inducing political backlash and pushback. This is where the processes and procedures aligned with traditional norms of governance and designed to address specific PP issues, identified in table 9.3, can help shield the PP strategy from premature abandonment.

Table 9.3
Governance Norms

Norms	PP Issues
Accountability	Procedural fairness
Ban on conflicts of interest	Transparency
Administrative and judicial appeal	Confidentiality/proprietary rights
Disclosure	Confidentiality agreements
Rights protection	Information imbalances
Stakeholder participation	Normative regime change
	Devolution/policy fragmentation
	Centralization
Social equity	Social equity

Toward Rules of Engagement

The theory and rhetoric behind the PP movement have set up high performance hurdles for these projects. Advocates promoted the strategy as a multidimensional tool: a means of providing more cost-efficient delivery of urban services, stimulating innovations in technology and the design of complex physical infrastructure projects, shifting the very substantial risks of public capital investment to private ownership, reducing the bureaucratic snags to getting projects through the approvals system, and expediting the time it takes to implement large-scale public initiatives in city building, regeneration, or economic development. This set of arguments for PPPs represents a fully loaded promise of reform for urban governance at a time when direct government action needs both a new cloak of political optimism and a deep source of capital funding.

The limited evidence on performance from detailed case studies of ambitious and complex PPP projects, mostly for physical infrastructure, however, consistently reveals that results have been considerably less than the theoretical and rhetorical claims. For example, on risk transfer and cost efficiencies, performance results so far present a weak story line. For the majority of case studies discussed in published research, academics found that government ended up sharing significant financial risks, either in the form of a long-term public subvention (in Canada, the Prince Edward Island Fixed Link/Confederation Bridge and the Richmond-Airport-Vancouver Line; in the UK, the National Air Traffic Services and the Devonport Dockyard; in the United States, the Tacoma Narrows Bridge project) or takeover (in the UK, the Channel Tunnel Rail Link; in Hungary, the M1-M5 Motorway; in the United States, the Camino Columbia project in Texas), government-backed financing for the entire project (in Canada, Highway 407), or government payment of compensation for contract cancellation (in Canada, the Redevelopment of Pearson Airport Terminals 1 and 2).

We have learned from individual case studies that the actual benefits of contracting do not flow automatically from the bundling format of PP infrastructure projects. The story is not much different for PP redevelopment (regeneration) projects, which, by comparison, are technically less specified and programmatically more fluid during the early stages of developer selection and design and development. In each, public sector players are put in the position of having to acquire or rapidly develop sophisticated institutional skills and the political acumen necessary to execute agenda setting, contract negotiation, and policy oversight of complex PP projects. These are public sector responsibilities that no government official can formally delegate to the private sector and expect to keep governing. This mandate for policy governance means coping with the demands for transparency, the dilemma of confidentiality, and the politics of consultation with a wide range of stakeholders. Based on their study of the Asian experience with PPP infrastructure projects, Kumaraswamy and Morris (2002) found the primacy of political skills to be essential.

In this arena, where the line between public and private blurs, how do we define the proper role of each sector? Or, in the absence of clear norms, how do we define the appropriate scope of action, the reasonable level of financial and hands-on engagement with the private sector? How should we think about "rules of engagement" for PP arrangements when public officials have no clear blueprint for operating in this blurred sphere (fig. 9.4)?

We are not starting with a blank slate. Public officials can draw on administrative protocols from several widely used governance frameworks. These include regulatory schemes set up by statute and administered through formalized processes and specialized institutions (e.g.,

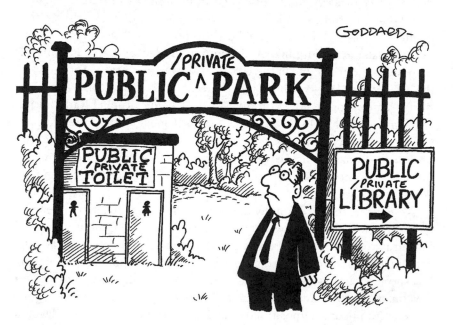

Figure 9.4
Public/Private Park. *Source:* © Clive Goddard, www.CartoonStock.com.

regulatory schemes for land-use and environmental control), programmatic rules and procedures attached to sources of funding from other levels of governments or granting foundations (e.g., block grant funding or economic development programs), and informal norms of consultation established overtime through trust and influence (e.g., vetting among powerful interests and community groups). Norms of best practice in public administration have emerged over the decades from a mix of political traditions, notions of procedural fairness, and open dialogue; from policy controversy that often engages the media to emphasize what is missing in open debate and less than transparent decision making; and from the appealing but vexing concept of the public interest. However vague the concept may seem, "public interest" reflects an underlying public-private distinction: We do not expect the profit-oriented private players to act, without incentives, in the public interest, but we do expect public officials to act beyond their own self-interests.

A full discussion of what it would take to craft rules of engagement for PP ventures is beyond the scope of this chapter. A list of commonly accepted norms of best public practice, however, would include accountability, procedural fairness (including provision for administrative and judicial appeal of decisions flowing from government powers), a ban on conflicts of interest, transparency and standards of disclosure, rights protection for citizens and property owners, stakeholder participation, and, in certain realms, social equity to mediate market-driven outcomes.

The introduction of market-driven benchmarks in the PP process challenges established policy norms and is bound to trigger political controversy. The public sector with profit ambitions? Public profit for what use? In 2005, the first privatization of a toll road in the United States, the city of Chicago, for example, sold a ninety-nine-year operating lease for the Chicago Skyway to private interests for $1.83 billion. Shortly thereafter, the state of Indiana sold a seventy-five-year concession for the 157-mile East-West Toll Road for $3.85 billion. In assessing the monetary impact of these transactions, where is the greater public interest? In proceeds used to close a budget gap and set up reserves, with only a small portion set aside for a neighborhood improvement fund (as did the city of Chicago), or in the 100 percent targeting of proceeds to fund specific transportation projects in toll road counties around the state for broad public benefit (as did the state of Indiana)?

Risk sharing, which is at the core of PP arrangements, places a heavy emphasis on confidentiality, particularly when the business terms and conditions of an agreement are being negotiated. Hammering out the details of complex agreements requires meeting behind closed doors. The issues raised by closed-door negotiations for redevelopment deals remain unchanged since I first wrote about the accountability dilemma (Sagalyn 1990). For infrastructure projects the accountability dilemma embedded in confidential partnership agreements poses a distinct and intellectually challenging problem involving proprietary rights. Ghere (2001, 444), for example, asks us to consider what such ownership could mean in the case of a large-scale municipal water operation or state corrections facility:

First, partnerships may involve the sale of existing capital facilities (such as a water treatment plant) or provide for the private partner to finance and own a new facility. Second, a fee-for-service partnership might convey a fee-based revenue stream to the private firm. In such an arrangement, the private partner could be viewed as "owning" a customer base and, indeed, may exercise rate-setting authority. Third, control over operations—including assumption of a public-employee workforce—could also constitute a form of asset creation. And fourth, it is conceivable that, in certain cases (for example, with park systems, toll roads, or corrections), partnerships could arrange for real estate transactions accruing to the private firm.

Operating for profit under market conditions, a private vendor understandably wants to protect its competitive position. Acting rationally, it will condition its engagement in bidding and negotiation on some type of confidentiality agreement restricting the sharing of proprietary technical, business, financial, or legal information. While this restriction may not cover the full period of the long-term agreement, bidders will aim for as long a period as possible, but will certainly insist on specified durations related to project-sensitive phases, including planning and contract negotiation.

This was the case with Vancouver's RAV project, where, Siemiatycki (2006) explains, the "confidentiality screen" may have kept the city manager from sharing information about the vendor consortium's controversial cut-and-cover construction method with the Vancouver City Council "even if there were parts of the plan that could be to the detriment of constituents" because that information was part of the proprietary bid. "The level of secrecy required to maintain the integrity of the private-public-partnership delivery model," he wrote, "calls into question whether the RAV-project governance structure threatened the fiduciary responsibility for the civil service or provided the necessary accountability to the elected officials who were responsible for deciding whether to approve the project" (ibid., 148).[3] Strict confidentiality agreements can also shield the full costs of these projects and make difficult, if not impossible, the task of evaluating the actual efficiency gains from privatization contracts.

But as with other aspects of PP implementation, procedural variations in practice shape governance implications (see Briffault 2001). Confidentiality need not be total. Public officials can establish clear standards for what information must be kept confidential (Siemiatycki 2006, 2007). Confidentiality need not be coterminous with the contractual term. If the scope and timing of confidentiality are subject to limits, greater transparency can be built into the PP process. For example, under the procedures established by the state of Texas in 2003 authorizing PPPs through Comprehensive Development Agreements (CDAs), information submitted by bidders remains confidential until a final contract is signed with the winning bidder. More to the point, the state's Department of Transportation can provide modest compensation (up to $1 million) to losing bidders for use of intellectual property included in the proposal (Durbin Associates 2005, cited in Ortiz and Buxbaum 2007, 19).

Over the course of several decades, government officials and their consultants have development formalized processes and procedures for selecting private developers and operating vendors, reviewing and evaluating responses to RFPs, documenting deals, and conducting public hearings. Some officials have produced management audits, even financial audits, of PP projects. Still, the procedures of PP transactions are specialized, and they are less likely to be as familiar or as readily understood or as transparent as conventional procedures for public vetting. Moreover, because they engage the private sector in the provision of public goods and services, these PP ventures generate particularly complex economic issues for which we have few precedents of best practice. The confidentiality issue is a case in point. The tension between confidentiality and transparency in large-scale infrastructure projects is not limited to PP projects, nor is it likely to be resolved by reverting to the traditional model of project delivery. And the same can be said for the broader set of policy issues surrounding the PP strategy.

Toward an Agenda for Policy Performance

In the United States, Europe, and Asia, experience with PP initiatives has brought to the fore common issues of governance, independent of performance results. PPPs represent a political challenge to the structure and values of public sector agency. They involve difficult issues of contracting compared to the traditional model of public procurement. And because the agreement (implicit if not explicit) involves risk sharing, they place a heavy emphasis on confidentiality, which heightens the role of disclosure and legislative oversight. Because the policy strategy leverages private capital, PPPs are biased toward market-based investments and only secondarily, if at all, address social equity concerns.

On the other hand, the strong case for PPPs has gathered widespread support because of a number of conceptually compelling arguments that are unlikely to fade away, especially in fiscally pressed environments, likely to predominate in the near future. PPPs have stimulated accelerating application to urban infrastructure and planning projects across the globe. Case-based results have selectively demonstrated modest efficiencies and innovation. Through their capacity to ensure the provision of urban services and stimulate economic productivity through private investment, PPPs have become a powerful and essential instrument in the tool kit of policymakers. Their biggest promise lies in the future, as public and private players work through the kinks of complex risk-sharing agreements and policy analysts mine the experiences for insights to improve efficiencies in practice.

How stakeholders respond to the governance issues of PPPs will inevitably depend on both the cultural traditions and the policy context of country-specific PP initiatives. But the mandates central to the agenda for policy performance of PPPs are universal: governance protocols, capacity building for public officials, and comparative research on outcomes.

Notes

1. I can offer several (less than satisfying) explanations for this state of affairs. First, a PP project takes a long time to execute before data can be marshaled for evaluation, and the full implications of performance may not be understood for many years after a project's completion. Second, in the absence of a statutory or administrative mandate or a political decision to repurchase a concession or provide a subsidy, government stakeholders do not have strong self-motivation to undertake ex-post evaluations that might reveal disappointing results or embarrassing and costly construction overruns. Third, the information needed to assess the performance of a PPP more often than not is confidential. Fourth, because each project has a nearly unique set of complexities, general lessons are hard to come by (Sagalyn 1990, 2007), especially from experiences in emerging market economies.

2. Until 1992, when new regulations superseded the Private Finance Initiative, British governments operated under rigid rules inhibiting the involvement of private sector capital in the financing of public sector projects (Flinders 2005, 220).

3. The literature presents other anecdotal examples of failed accountability. For example, Rosenau (1999) cites the situation in which Corrections Corporation of America (CCA) was reported to have "explicitly misinformed" city and state officials about the security risk of inmates housed in a Youngstown, Ohio–based private prison. Instead of "promptly notifying" officials when five murderers escaped, CCA attempted to cover it up. "If the same event happened in a public prison," she asks, "would accountability dynamics have been different?" She cites accountability problems in policy-level partnerships in the electric service sector as well, and instances of failed government responsibility that are not hard to come by. In short, no sector is a priori more accountable or immune to lapses. "Hard evidence is absent," she notes, and "both sides make convincing cases" (ibid., 20).

References

Boarse, J. P. 2000. Beyond Government? The Appeal of Public-Private Partnerships. *Canadian Public Administration* 43 (1): 75–92.

Bovaird, T. 2004. Public-Private Partnerships: From Contested Concepts to Prevalent Practice. *International Review of Administrative Sciences* 70 (2): 199–215.

Briffault, R. 2001. Public Oversight of Public/Private Partnerships. *Fordham Urban Law Journal* 28:1357.

Cambridge Systematics, Inc. 2006. Background Paper No. 1: National Perspective: Uses of Tolling and Related Issues. *Washington State Comprehensive Tolling Study, Final Report,* vol. 2 (September): 20.

Daniels, R. J., and M. J. Trebilcock. 1996. Private Provision of Public Infrastructure: An Organizational Analysis of the Next Privatization Frontier. *University of Toronto Law Journal* 46 (3): 375–426.

Durbin Associates. 2005. A Study of Innovations in the Funding and Delivery of Transportation Infrastructure Using Tolls. Final Report of the Pennsylvania House of Representatives Select Committee on Toll Roads. November; http://www.pahouse.com/yourturnpike/documents/FINAL%20.PDF.

Elander, I. 2002. Partnerships and Urban Governance. *International Social Science Journal* 54 (2): 191–204.

Engberg, L. A. 2002. Reviews: Public-Private partnerships. Theory and Practice in International Perspective. *Public Administration* 80 (3): 601–614.

European Commission. 2003. Directorate-General Regional Policy. *Guidelines for Successful Public-Private Partnerships.* March. Brussels: European Commission, Directorate-General Regional Policy. http://europa.eu.int/comm/regional-policy/sources/docgener/guides/PPPguide.htm.

European Commission. 2004. Directorate-General Regional Policy. *Resource Book on PPP Case Studies*. June. Brussels: European Commission, Directorate-General Regional Policy. http://europa.eu.int/comm/regional-policy/sources/doc-gener/guides/PPPguide.htm.

Financial Times. 1998. Perplexed by Blair's *je ne sais quoi*. June 15, 17.

Flinders, M. 2005. The Politics of Public-Private Partnerships. *British Journal of Politics and International Relations* 7 (2): 215–239.

Freestone, R., P. Williams, and A. Bowden. 2006. Fly Buy Cities: Some Planning Aspects of Airport Privatization in Australia. *Urban Policy and Research* 24 (4): 491–508.

Frieden, B. J., and L. Sagalyn. 1989. *Downtown, Inc: How American Rebuilds Cities*. Cambridge, MA: MIT Press.

Ghere, R. K. 2001. Probing the Strategic Intricacies of Public-Private Partnership: The Patent as a Comparative Reference. *Public Administration Review* 61 (4): 441–451.

Grimsey, D., and M. K. Lewis. 2004. *Public Private Partnerships: The Worldwide Revolution in Infrastructure Provision and Project Finance*. Cheltenham, UK: Edward Elgar.

HM Treasury. 2003. *PFI: Meeting the Investment Challenge*. London: The Stationery Office.

International Monetary Fund. 2004. Public-Private Partnerships. Report prepared by the Fiscal Affairs Department, in consultation with other departments, the World Bank, and the Inter-American Development Bank. March 12. http://www.imf.org/external/np/fad/2004/pifp/eng/031204.htm.

Koppenjan, J. F.M. 2005. The Formation of Public-Private Partnerships: Lessons from Nine Transport Infrastructure Projects in the Netherlands. *Public Administration* 83 (1): 135–157.

Kumaraswamy, M. M., and D. A. Morris. 2002. Build-Operate-Transfer-Type Procurement in Asian Megaprojects. *Journal of Construction Engineering and Management* 128 (2): 93–102.

Montgomery, M. R. 2007. Estimating and Forecasting City Growth in the Developing World. Presentation to the Stony Brook University and Population Council, June 6.

Moore, C., and J. Pierre. 1998. Partnership or Privatization? The Political Economy of Local Economic Restructuring. *Policy and Politics* 16 (3): 169–173.

Murray, S. 2006. Value for Money? Cautionary Lessons about P3s from British Columbia. June. Canadian Centre for Policy Alternatives—BC office, Ottawa.

Newman, P., and G. Verpraet. 1999. The Impacts of Partnerships on Urban Governance: Conclusions from Recent European Research. *Regional Studies* 33 (5): 487–491.

Osborne, D., and T. Gaebler. 1993. *Reinventing Government: How Entrepreneurial Spirit Is Transforming the Public Sector*. New York: Plume, Penguin Group.

Ortiz, I. N., and J. N. Buxbaum. 2007. *Protecting the Public Interest: The Role of Long-Term Concession Agreements for Providing Transportation Infrastructure*. USC Keston Institute for Public Finance and Infrastructure Policy, Research Paper 07-02. June. Los Angeles: University of Southern California, Keston Institute.

Public Citizen. 2003. Water Privitization Fiascos: Broken Promises and Social Turmoil. March. www.wateractivist.gov.

Rosenau, P. V. 1999. Introduction: The Strengths and Weaknesses of Public-Private Policy Partnerships. *American Behavioral Scientist* 43 (1): 10–34.

Rubin, J. S., and G. M. Stankiewicz. 2002. The Los Angeles Community Development Bank: The Possible Pitfalls of Public-Private Partnerships. *Journal of Urban Affairs* 23 (2): 133–153.

Sagalyn, L. B. 1990. Explaining the Improbable: Local Redevelopment in the Wake of Federal Cutbacks. *Journal of the American Planning Association* 56 (4): 429–441.

Sagalyn, L. B. 2001. *Times Square Roulette: Remaking the City Icon*. Cambridge, MA: MIT Press.

Sagalyn, L. B. 2006. Meshing Public & Private Roles in the Development Process. In *Real Estate Development: Principles and Process*, rev. ed., ed. M. Miles, G. Berens, and M. A. Weiss. Washington, DC: Urban Land Institute.

Sagalyn, L. B. 2007. Public/Private Development: Lessons from History, Research, and Practice. *Journal of the American Planning Association. American Planning Association* 73 (1): 7–22.

Siemiatycki, M. 2006. Implications of Private-Public Partnerships on the Development of Urban Public Transit Infrastructure: The Case of Vancouver, Canada. *Journal of Planning Education and Research* 26:137–151.

Siemiatycki, M. 2007. What's the Secret? *Journal of the American Planning Association* 73 (4): 388–403.

U.S. Department of Transportation, Federal Highway Administration. 2007a. Case Studies of Transportation Public-Private Partnerships around the World. Final Report, Work Order 05–002. Prepared for the Office of Policy and Governmental Affairs by AECOM Consult Team. July 7. www.fhwa.dot.gov.

U.S. Department of Transportation, Federal Highway Administration. 2007b. Case Studies of Transportation Public-Private Partnerships in the United States. Final Report ,Work Order 05–002. Prepared for the Office of Policy and Governmental Affairs by AECOM Consult Team. July 7.

van Ham, H., and J. Koppenjan. 2002. Building Public-Private Partnerships: Assessing and Managing Risks in Port Development. *Public Management Review* 4 (1): 593–616.

Verkuil, P. R. 2007. *Outsourcing Sovereignty: Why Privatization of Government Functions Threatens Democracy and What We Can Do About It*. New York: Cambridge University Press.

10
Good Governance: The Inflation of an Idea

Merilee Grindle

Good governance is a good idea. We would all be better off, and citizens of many developing countries would be much better off, if public life were conducted through fair, judicious, transparent, accountable, participatory, responsive, well-managed, and efficient institutions. For the millions of people throughout the world who live in conditions of public insecurity and instability, corruption, abuse of law, public service failure, poverty, and inequality, good governance is a mighty beacon of what ought to be.

Because of this intuitive appeal, good governance has rapidly become a major ingredient in analyses of what's missing in countries struggling for economic and political development. Researchers have adopted the concept as a way of exploring institutional failure and constraints on growth. Putting governance right has become a major aspect of development assistance. Advocates have linked the advancement of a variety of issues to improved governance. By the 2000s, a significant portion of the development agenda was related to good governance; international development agencies created departments of governance, employed a small army of governance advisers and researchers, included governance components in their assistance packages, and increased funding for good governance initiatives.

Intuitively and in research, good governance is a seductive idea: who, after all, can reasonably defend bad governance? Nevertheless, the popularity of the idea has far outpaced its capacity to deliver. In its brief life, it has also muddied the waters of thinking about the development process, confounding causes and consequences, ends and means, necessity and desirability. The trajectory of this idea—an introduction that provides new energy to research and practice, mounting popularity as it is adopted by a host of academics and practitioners, and inflation as it becomes increasingly essential to end goals in development—is not uncommon in the field of development. Indeed, the field can be credited with much faddism of the magic bullet variety, overly in thrall to ideas that promise to deal effectively with a host of constraints on prosperity and equity. Community development, basic needs, participation, sustainability, appropriate technology, and a host of other ideas—the history of development thinking is littered with elastic concepts that grow in inclusiveness as they become popular. None of them is necessarily a bad idea, and some are probably very good ideas, but all have fallen short of the inflated expectations of their proponents.

These ideas grow through a common trajectory: an idea with normative appeal is adopted broadly by researchers, organizations, and causes as an umbrella for the particular issues that each holds dear. The concept often resolves an immediate problem—how to explain what is being researched, done, or advocated in a concise, attractive, and intuitive way. Linking one's work to the concept can serve as a basis for establishing a research reputation, engaging an organization in a common mission, building a coalition for change, or attracting funds for further work. While those sheltering under the conceptual umbrella often have a good understanding of the underlying complexity of the issues they deal with, communicating about them is simplified. And, with time and usage, a normative idea can become conflated with the notion of development itself, a kind of ideological cure-all for complex and difficult problems of history, society, politics, and economics. If only there were "good governance," or "participation," or "sustainability," many come to believe, these problems could be dealt with effectively, and development, however defined, could be achieved. This trajectory is not inevitable; for whatever reasons, however, some ideas prove especially attractive to researchers, organizations, and advocates, and expanding use and inflated expectations are common results.

With time, also, the expansion of a normative concept to legitimize action on multiple fronts leads to disappointment: it does not "deliver" development. Having failed to meet high expectations, or having unearthed knowledge of new constraints, such concepts are often devalued as the field moves on to new ideas that promise to deliver. This is a possible future for the concept of good governance. But throwing away ideas that fall short of expectations is rarely warranted, and good governance is a useful concept. It calls needed attention to the institutional underpinnings of effective economic and political management. Yet this laudable idea has become conflated with the capacity to generate growth, alleviate poverty, and bring effective democracy to peoples in poor countries. Rather than discarding it because it has grown all-encompassing and essential to any notion of development, scholars and practitioners should instead seek a reasonable understanding of what efforts to introduce good governance can deliver—and what they cannot. Scholars and practitioners should also assume more realistic expectations about how much good governance can be expected in poor countries struggling with a plethora of demands on their capacities to pursue change. In this chapter, I explore how and why the concept of good governance emerged and grew too large, and then suggest ways in which academics and practitioners can become more sensitive to the limitations of fads and to curb the tendency to idea inflation.[1]

Good Governance: The New Kid in Development Discourse

Governance is widely understood, when used with regard to government or the public sector, to refer to the institutional underpinnings of public authority and decision making. In this way, governance encompasses the institutions, systems, "rules of the game," and other factors that determine how political and economic interactions are structured and how decisions are made and resources allocated (World Bank 2007, i; United Nations Development Programme [UNDP] 1997, 12; Department for International Development [London] [DFID] 2001, 9; Hyden, Court, and Mease 2004; Kaufmann 2003, 5).[2] Clearly implicit in the general concept is the notion that good governance is a positive feature of political systems and that bad governance is a problem countries need to overcome.

Good governance most generally refers to a list of admirable characteristics of how government ought to be carried out—"Sweden or Denmark on a good day, perhaps," as Matt Andrews (2008) has written. Indeed, much of the concept's popularity can be linked to the positive images it embodies. For the World Bank, for example, attractive characteristics of good governance are accountability and transparency, efficiency in how the public sector works, rule of law, and ordered interactions in politics (World Bank 2007, 1). The United Nations Development Programme (UNDP), which has taken a strong interest in the promotion of good governance, singles out characteristics such as participation, transparency, accountability, effectiveness, and equity as most important (UNDP 1997, 12). Hyden, Court, and Mease (2004) refer to dimensions of good governance—participation, fairness, decency, efficiency, accountability, and transparency—that are equally evocative.

Good governance at times is also used to refer to normative concerns about what government should do—reduce poverty, or maintain macroeconomic stability, or provide basic services. The UK's Department for International Development (DFID), for example, a recognized leader in focusing attention on governance issues in the international donor community, identifies a series of "capabilities," most of which are expectations about what governments should do—ensure voice, promote macroeconomic stability, facilitate growth that is poverty reducing, advocate for policies that positively affect the poor, ensure the universal provision of basic services, ensure personal and national security, and pursue accountable government (DFID 2001, 9). Elsewhere, "goods" such as property rights, education, and health care are included as indicators of good governance. Kaufmann (2003, 5) includes both how and what features, such as accountability, political stability, effectiveness; rule of law; and control of corruption. Thus, in the bundle of good things that have come to be understood as good governance, qualities of institutions are often combined with expectations about the promotion of particular kinds of policies.

Despite some differences in the definition, the idea of good governance has also resonated across a wide political spectrum and accommodated to multiple interpretations. For those on the political right, good governance has meant order, rule of law, and the institutional conditions for free markets to flourish. For those on the political left, good governance incorporates notions of equity and fairness, protection for the poor, for minorities, and for women, and a positive role for the state. For many others found along the continuum from right to left, the concept is attractive for its concern with order, decency, justice, and accountability.

The emergence and popularity of the idea of good governance can be credited to more than its attractive characteristics and admirable policy goals, however. Indeed, by the late 1980s, a confluence of intellectual and experiential trends had given increased visibility to this idea.[3] Particularly in the fields of economics and political science, and echoed in practitioner and advocacy communities, the concept was a useful way to acknowledge the important role of the state in development. It took on greater life as a solution to a practical dilemma faced by development practitioners: how to frame political interactions in a way that appeared to be apolitical. It also grew in influence as the result of research practices that privileged large samples of countries over in-depth analysis of individual cases, suggesting a link between methodology and understanding. And the good governance concept became even more popular when advocates of various causes found it a useful umbrella under which to present and justify their particular concerns. The idea of good governance thus proved useful—and flourished from the late 1980s well into the 2000s and beyond.

Origins: Rehabilitating the State

The idea of good governance owes much to the intellectual resurrection of the state as a positive player in economic and political development. The state, of course, had long been at the center of development practice; from mercantilism in sixteenth-century Europe to import substitution in the mid-twentieth century in late-developing countries, the state was a leading actor in investment decisions and an advocate of policies to spur growth. Similarly, the academic literature of the 1950s to the 1970s recognized the important role of states in the development process. Economists argued that in poor countries, the state needed to provide investments that would stimulate economic development, and political scientists found that centralized states were important for nation building and political modernization.[4]

Despite this long history, and also because of it, by the mid-1970s, academic researchers had begun to raise a series of questions about state-led growth and state-dominated political societies. Their concerns mirrored an increased awareness of the potential for states to fail in their developmental responsibilities. By the early 1980s, questioning the positive contributions of the state to development had turned into a profound critique of theory and practice and had generated a watershed of anti-statist research and commentary in the development literature.[5] With increasing regularity, the virtues of free markets were found to be far superior to the vices of statism, and highly centralized states were held to account for quashing local communities and the associational life that is essential to democracy and limited government. Development practitioners, led by international development agencies, followed suit, with advice and aid focused on reducing the role of the state in development and, somewhat later, advocating for a strengthened civil society.

In practice and in theory, this strong anti-statist perspective was relatively short-lived, even though skepticism about the state continued to characterize research and practice. As the 1980s gave way to the 1990s, specialists in development economics became more interested in the role of institutions in the life of market economies as a result of both experience and theory-building initiatives (see Killick 1989). In practice, the fall of the Soviet Union, followed by a very rapid transition to a market economy in Russia—chaotically and with devastating consequences for the vast majority of the population—underscored the role of institutions such as property rights, contract law, and regulatory rules for a properly functioning market (Goldman 2003). These important institutions, in turn, were creations of the state; an effective state, then, was rehabilitated as an important condition for effective markets.

On the more academic front, Douglass North published his widely read work, *Institutions, Institutional Change and Economic Performance,* in 1990. This work, along with an increasing interest in the "new institutional economics," focused new attention on the long-term evolution of the "rules of the game" and how they shape development trajectories (see, e.g., Williamson 1991). Simultaneously, a lively literature on the East Asian "tigers" generated two important findings: the state had assumed an extremely important role in the emergence of some of them— underlining the positive role that states could play in development—and their vibrant economies did not rely on similar kinds of state action, suggesting that countries could pursue distinct strategies with regard to the role of the state in their development (Amsden 1989; Wade 1990). Increasingly, researchers claimed that it was not the size of the state that mattered. More important was its quality, and quality was a function of state institutions and their credibility.[6]

Discussions of politics demonstrated the same intertwining of theory and practice. Transitions to democracy in the 1980s and early 1990s, particularly in Latin America and Eastern Europe, encouraged political scientists to pay more attention to the institutional infrastructure characterizing different kinds of regimes (Huntington 1991; O'Donnell, Schmitter, and Whitehead 1986; Lipjhart and Waisman 1996). Practice thus stimulated advances in theory. Similarly, efforts to explain the lack of development in a number of African countries, along with increasing concern about autocratic and brutal governments, focused research attention on the role of institutions in political development (Rothchild and Chazan 1988; Chabal 1986; Wunsch and Olowu 1990). At the same time, researchers found steady work in the analysis of constitutional structures, electoral and party systems, political corruption, and the management of the state. At the level of theory, the notion of state autonomy and its limitations was the subject of considerable intellectual interest. This trend took on an identity as a movement for bringing the state back in, as an influential book argued (Evans, Rueschemeyer, and Skocpol 1985).

Beginning in the mid-1980s and accelerating during the 1990s, then, academic literature and development discourse more generally flourished with discussions of the role of institutions in development and the positive contributions that states must make if market economies and democracies are to work effectively. By 1991, the bellwether *World Development Report* included a chapter titled "Rethinking the State"; in 1997, the annual volume was subtitled *The State in a Changing World* (World Bank 1991, 1997).[7] This indicated in very important ways that the state, although often creating impediments to development, had been rehabilitated; to the extent that the state embodied institutions or set the rules of the game for economic and political life, its activities were central to the development process. Not surprisingly, those states that managed these tasks well were credited with good governance.

Popularity: Providing a Fig Leaf

The popularity of the idea of good governance owes something to the fig leaf. As interest in institutions and the role of the state increased throughout the decade of the 1990s, it was not long before multilateral and bilateral development agencies began actively discussing a characteristic emblematic of any notion of bad governance—corruption. Indeed, the World Bank declared that corruption was "the single greatest obstacle to economic and social development" (quoted in Brinkerhoff and Goldsmith 2005, 209). And, stimulated in part by researchers at the World Bank, exploring the causes of corruption became a major focus of development economists.[8] Similarly, issues such as accountability and transparency, which in many contexts implied a relationship between the governors and the governed, emerged as potent weapons in the battle against corruption. As many countries installed more democratic regimes, the role of citizens, elections, and civic organizations in forcing governments to be good gained prominence (see, e.g., Putnam 1993).

This discussion was an opportunity for researchers to investigate new issues and constraints on development, to delve into a world of ambiguity and attempt to bring clarity to the actions and interactions of institutions, politicians, public officials, decision making, leadership, and resource allocation. It called attention to the way citizens and states interacted. The consequences of this new interest were evident across the social sciences. For some economists, for example, the ways in which markets operated differently in different countries could be understood as artifacts of distinct institutions and the incentives they embodied. In political science and history, market-like rational actor models of the decision making of politicians were questioned by those arguing for institutions and path dependence in the diverse historical trajectories of countries (Steinmo, Thelen, and Longstreth 1992; Pierson 2004). In economics and other fields, new institutionalism focused attention on the behavioral incentives embedded in different kinds of rules of the game. The management sciences adopted the "new public management" that encouraged institutional engineering for more effective management of public affairs.[9] For students of African development in particular, the issue of leadership failure became prominent. Regime transition, democratization, democratic consolidation—all became topics of renewed interest.

If, as specialists argued, domestic factors are central explanations for development successes and failures, and if states and the rules of the game can be shown to be important to economic and political development, and if issues such as corruption and leadership failure are critical constraints on development, and if the legitimate realm of state authority implies some necessary contract with civil society, then development requires active engagement in the practice of government and in the contract between governors and governors. Intervention—to create new institutions, to modify long-existing ones, to build systems that are immune to corruption, to bring citizen voice to decision making—takes theory and practice to the center of governments, where politics sets the themes and boundaries of what can occur.

While generating a range of intriguing questions for researchers, this formulation created a significant dilemma for practitioners in international development agencies. Work to create, strengthen, or alter institutions and to acknowledge a role for civil society implied becoming more actively engaged in the inner workings of government. Such activities meant doing much more than designing and advising on appropriate policies. It meant advocating action against corruption in public affairs, encouraging the development of organizations to monitor government actions and political activities, increasing the relevance of citizen voice in political decision making, speaking out against leadership failures, and other activities that made notions of purely technical advising and assistance difficult to sustain. Could such international organizations be effectively engaged with the state and civil society in these ways without "being political?" Would they be running afoul of ideas such as national sovereignty? Their charters, after all, committed them to significant restraint in political matters.

The concept of good governance proved an important fig leaf for resolving this dilemma. It allowed international agencies to discuss and become more engaged in politics. As suggested by Hewitt de Alcántara (1998), governance was a hygienic way of dealing with political institutions and interactions—like corruption, accountability, and leadership—that came to be seen as impediments to development and to the effective use of development assistance. The concept of good governance provided a technical approach to this delicate issue, a way of avoiding direct reference to political interactions. It was a concept that helped them escape "an intellectual and practical dead-end into which they had earlier been pushed by their extreme reliance on free-market ideals" (ibid., 106).[10]

Certainly, the discussion of good governance captured great interest among the international development organizations; they have all undertaken or supported research on the issue and they each have major publications that demonstrate the importance of the concept to development. Between 2002 and 2007, for example, the World Bank loaned $22.7 billion for projects related to public sector governance and rule of law, while the UNDP spent $5.18 billion on democratic governance initiatives between 2004 and 2007 (World Bank 2007; UNDP 2008.12). While some of this funding was no doubt a relabeling of programs and projects of long duration, new initiatives that might have seemed overly political in the past could be instituted under the rubric of good governance.

Popularity: Providing a Capacious Umbrella

The role of large-N studies of the sources of growth and development was also important in increasing the value and popularity of the concept of good governance among researchers and practitioners. As the concept generated interest in the scholarly literature, researchers increasingly asked, "What is the relationship between good governance and development?" Beginning in the 1990s, and accelerating in the 2000s, researchers used sophisticated econometrics to measure and assess how various conditions of governance affected development. They studied how corruption limited growth, how independent central banks contributed to macroeconomic stability, how property rights stimulated growth, and how parliamentary institutions were more conducive to political stability than presidential ones. These and a variety of other studies pointed in a consistent direction—to significant relationships between good governance and important goals such as growth, poverty reduction, aid effectiveness, efficient bureaucracies, and higher foreign and private investment (World Bank n.d.).

Some studies utilized econometric analysis to address cause-and-effect relationships also. Daniel Kaufman and other researchers, for example, demonstrated that the relationship between development and governance was more than correlational; good governance was shown to be a cause of development (Kaufmann and Kraay 2002). As concluded by the World Bank in a review of forty studies, there was "overwhelming evidence that good governance is crucial for successful development, as measured by high per capita income. Per capita income is a strong predictor of poverty rates, infant mortality and illiteracy, suggesting that good governance improves the well-being of the poor" (World Bank 1999, 1). Increasingly, then, the idea of good governance became a way not only to assess the role of the state in development and invade safely the minefield of domestic politics, it became a defining quality for development and a necessary condition for it. The normative ingredients of the definition of good governance were shown empirically to be not only conducive to development but also necessary to it.[11] That definitions differed, and that considerable controversy surrounded how to measure good governance, did not constrain commitment to its essential nature for development.

In a similar way, the idea of good governance was useful as an umbrella concept to describe a wide variety of good things. Thus, for example, the human rights community claimed, with considerable force and reason, that countries with good governance respected human rights. Environmentalists argued that good governance meant effective stewardship of the environment and sustainability of development practices. Empowerment of women, community management of forests, selective affirmative action, land-use planning, legal aid for the poor, anticorruption measures, and a variety of other conditions came to be associated with good governance. Once a belief had been generated that good governance was essential to development—even a precondition for it—then it was certainly advantageous for advocates to have their cause listed among the characteristics of good governance. To the extent that international development agencies, foundations, and others were increasing funding for good governance activities, the attraction of being part of the good governance movement grew.

Thus, the concept of good governance proved expansive enough to embrace many causes. Each of these causes is no doubt good and worthy of support and commitment. Yet by identifying good governance as a precondition to development, each of these good causes became transformed into a necessary component of initiatives to stimulate growth and political stability. Getting developed became more and more onerous as increasing numbers of preconditions were tacked on to the agenda. This is a dangerous situation. The danger is not the advocacy or the good things that various groups advocate. The danger is overloading the development agenda, inflating what "must be done" beyond the capacities of most countries, and making good governance a precondition (rather than a result or ancillary process) for development to occur.

Research, Practice, and Advocacy: Creating an Elastic Agenda

Thus, the good governance agenda expanded. Some years ago, I reviewed annual *World Development Reports* from 1997 (the year in which the publication fully recognized the "rehabilitation" of the state as a positive contributor to development) to 2002 in an effort to understand how governance was being used in a publication that often sets the tone and agenda for much applied development thinking and action. The results are instructive of the process of idea inflation (Grindle 2004). From 45 different issues identified with the concept in 1997, by 2002, the *WDR* suggested 116 ways that developing countries needed to attend to characteristics of good governance. The concept was used to refer to specific policies, laws, institutions, and strategies for development. The list of things that needed to be in place for good governance was on a roll.

Research, development practice, and advocacy thus combined to create a strong consensus on the importance of good governance. As an elastic concept, and as an intuitively attractive one, it was difficult to resist. In academic research, we have statistical proof that good governance is critical to development. In development practice, we have mountains of evidence of bad practice and weak institutions constraining the potential for development. In advocacy, we have a multitude of organizations—international and domestic—demanding that "their" issues— whether it is the environment, human rights, fair trade, gender equity, or other good—be included on the development agenda. Each of these sources makes good arguments about the centrality of good governance and shows logically why countries need it. In each of these ways, the concept has become more essential to development. Nevertheless, given the expansion and the popularity of the idea, it is useful to pose some critical questions about the role of good governance in development, challenging researchers, practitioners, and advocates to step back and assess its promise realistically and historically.

Expecting Too Much by Explaining Too Much?

Good ideas have a tendency to be credited with more importance in the development process than they may actually have. They may even come to be treated as causal in development, thus setting an agenda specifying what countries must accomplish before they can develop that may not be reasonable or historically valid. The role of ideas in development may even reveal a tendency to think of developing countries as a blank slate for experiments with solutions to complex and historically embedded constraints. These dynamics contribute to long agendas and muddy thinking. In the end, advocates of good governance who conflate good governance and development are suggesting that "the way to develop is to become developed" (Andrews 2008, 9). If we return to the research and practice related to good governance, we can see the ways in which conceptual inflation leads to muddy thinking, the evolution of possibly inappropriate models, and the practical implications of a long and elastic agenda.

Muddy Thinking about Development

Large-N cross-country analyses have most consistently shown that good governance is an essential ingredient in development; as we have seen, some research shows it as prior to and causal of development. Such studies are undertaken in a search for regularities, for patterns that hold across countries and that illuminate the importance of particular variables in these patterns. In governance research, for example, researchers can assess the "bang for the buck" that institutions such as secure property rights or an autonomous central bank contribute to economic growth across a variety of countries, or the role of competitive elections in political stability cross-nationally.

Inevitably, because patterns are rarely universal except at the most banal level, some countries may exhibit good performance on the dependent variable—economic growth, say—but not score well on the independent variable—property rights, say, or low corruption—even while most countries conform to a predicted relationship. Characteristically, researchers disregard these outliers and focus on the explanatory value of the cases that fit the regression line. Important insights and questions can be generated by looking at the outliers, however, not simply in terms of explaining why these particular cases are outliers but also in terms of raising some questions about the relationships being studied (Osborne and Overbay 2004). In-depth research on particular country experiences, then, can illuminate conditions, relationships, and processes that are obscured by large-N studies.

For example, with any of a variety of reasonable measures of good governance, China and Vietnam are likely to score low.[12] Yet these countries have amassed extremely impressive records for consistently high growth rates and poverty reduction, in the case of China over the course of three decades. They are also very large countries—China the largest in the world—whose performance probably ought not be overlooked in terms of what it suggests about the importance of good governance. If this and other countries can develop in significant ways without at the same time demonstrating clear good governance, shouldn't researchers consider such cases as important to a theoretical relationship between governance and development?

A similar kind of caution comes with a consideration of Bangladesh, a country sometimes credited with having virtually no government at all and which ranks among the lowest fourteen countries on the Transparency International Corruption Perception Index. Nevertheless, this country has recently chalked up several consecutive years of growth rates in excess of 5 percent a year, a longer history of significant growth than at any other time since the country gained independence (World Bank n.d.). Peru, Panama, Tanzania, Algeria, and India might also emerge as outliers whose performance is unexpected, given a hypothesized relationship between various dimensions of governance and growth—none of them is exemplary on standard indicators of governance. Similarly, advanced industrial countries often grew significantly before they had anything approaching good governance (Chang 2002).

The relationship between democracy and good governance is also complex in practice. Many Latin American countries, for example, have democratic institutions yet show high rates of corruption, low levels of transparency, and poor performance on other dimensions of good governance. Some East Asian countries have demonstrated that it is possible to have relatively good governance with very little democracy.

Neither is good governance consistently associated with good public performance. By most measures of governance, for example, the United States scores high. Its macroeconomy is relatively well managed, government action is for the most part fairly transparent, and its government is accountable to its citizens. Yet the response to Hurricane Katrina in 2005 was not only a profound failure of leadership at local, state, and national levels, it was also clearly a massive failure of governance. The systems put in place to protect citizens didn't work, the institutions that were supposed to allocate authority and responsibility among different levels of government didn't function, and the organizations set up to deal with emergencies were simply not up to the task. The fact that these systems, institutions, and organizations failed the poor, racial minorities, and the marginalized simply underscores the failure of governance in a political system reputed to have met the challenge of good governance. In contrast, in terms of being able to cope with unanticipated demands on it, the Pakistani government responded quickly and relatively effectively to the massive earthquake, also in 2005, despite overall low rankings in terms of governance. These outliers suggest that when researchers conflate good governance with the capacity to grow, the existence of democracy, or the actual capacity of government to perform consistently well, they are probably oversimplifying very complex relationships.

Here, my point is not that the econometrics were mistaken, the formulas misspecified, or the concepts poorly operationalized and measured (although this might be the case). I am rather suggesting that the outliers can force us to ask, "Just how important is the relationship?" Or, "Under what conditions does this relationship hold and when does it not?" If a country like China can grow consistently for three decades with demonstrably poor governance—and certainly nothing like political democracy—it seems useful to assess whether the relationship between growth and good governance is as consistent as is often stated. When the United States can exhibit a massive failure of governance, it suggests that the idea may be more slippery than imagined. Where outliers are large, important countries, more attention rather than less should be paid to what their experience has to say about the overall pattern discovered in the research. In a critique of the literature linking growth and governance, Kurtz and Schrank (2007) indicate the consequences of muddy thinking by concluding that "the oft-asserted connection between growth and governance lies on exceedingly shaky empirical pilings."

Models and Their Replication

As a result of research and practice indicating that good governance is critical to development, institutional blueprints for its achievement have become common. There are, then, models and "best practices" for a good parliamentary democracy and effective checks and balances systems. There are blueprints for how to regulate environmental hazards and stock and bond markets; there are blueprints for judicial institutions, tax agencies, and federalism. The list goes on.

If the structure and function of institutions are closely tied to the context within which they emerged and developed, however, the search for institutional blueprints and practices can be misleading. This is the view of a number of researchers who have used in-depth analyses of particular countries or regions to argue that distinct development paths can be credited to unique experiences, particular international contexts, the historical development of relationships between economic and political elites or between elites and masses, or other specific experiences. These researchers argue that broad generalizations about governance overlook how country and regional destinies are shaped by specific international, institutional, policy, and even leadership experiences (Hewko 2002). If this is the case—as the body of literature focusing on path dependence suggests—then institutions may not be easily or successfully transferred from one context to another.

Blueprints and models may also be based on questionable assumptions. For example, in looking closely at the often recommended "Nordic model" of governance, Matt Andrews points out that the governments of Sweden, Denmark, and Norway are organized in distinct ways and involve a series of distinct rules of the game and institutional relationships (Andrews 2008). In this case, it would be appropriate to ask which model of governance is actually implied in the Nordic case.

Similarly, blueprints and best practices overlook the possibility that whether institutions function as anticipated may be subject to timing and context. A good example is the development of an independent central bank in Russia after the fall of the Soviet Union. Few economists would argue with the notion that an independent central bank is important to macroeconomic stability and good governance of the economy, yet in Russia, independence was ceded at a time when the central bank was dominated by an old guard of party apparatchiks who were not particularly interested in modeling the activities of the bank in the way that economic reformers thought necessary (Johnson 1999). It is likely that many a president or minister of finance of a country undergoing a severe economic crisis wishes for less independence of the central bank in order to be able to respond more effectively and rapidly to the crisis. The overall generalization of the importance of independence to good economic management is sound, but it is not necessarily universal or unrelated to specific historical conditions.

A similar distinction can be made in terms of historical sequences of activities. Some researchers, for example, have compared the evolution of civil service systems that were professionalized before the introduction of democracy with those that were introduced in the context of competitive party politics. In the first case, elite civil services were rapidly put in place; in the latter cases, positions in government were long a source of contestation between politicians who wanted to provide jobs for their followers and reformers, who wanted a professionalized civil service. The introduction and evolution of systems can be quite different, depending on their relationship to other major historical transformations.

The Practical Burden of a Long Agenda

The good governance agenda expanded during the decade of the 1990s. Thus, by the early 2000s, it was possible to claim that

Getting good governance calls for improvements that touch virtually all aspects of the public sector—from institutions that set the rules of the game for economic and political interaction, to decision-making structures that determine priorities among public problems and allocate resources to respond to them, to organizations that manage administrative systems and deliver goods and services to citizens, to human resources that staff government bureaucracies, to the interface of officials and citizens in political and bureaucratic arenas. . . . Not surprisingly, advocating good governance raises a host of questions about what needs to be done, when it needs to be done, and how it needs to be done. (Grindle 2004, 525–526)

The problem, of course, is the challenge of fixing a large number of governance deficits, particularly in fragile, weak, or failed states. Any tourist visiting a developing country, let alone an expert in organizational management, legal systems, economic development, infrastructure, or other field, can find plenty of evidence of much that doesn't work well. The deficits in how government works—from the behavior of immigration and customs officials in the airport to the potholed roads in the capital city, to the apparent poverty of citizens, to the paucity of public services, to the lack of infrastructure in rural areas, to the exploitation of women, children, and poor people generally—are usually more than evident. Clearly, much needs to be fixed. But this observation does not go far in suggesting how to go about fixing whatever it is that is in deficit. With so much to do, what determines priorities? With so many demands of things that need to be fixed, where should scarce financial, human, and organizational resources be focused?

At the same time, much is unknown about the timing and sequences involved in "getting fixed." For example, the good governance agenda grew with little attention to the historical experience of countries deemed to have good governance—they didn't always have this, so how did they get better? Priorities, sequences, timing—are all institutions equally important? Are they independent of each other as they develop? How long does it take to develop good governance? Even without good responses to these questions, however, the practical work of "fixing" bad governance has proceeded apace, far outstripping knowledge about how institutions of governance develop over time and the consequences of governance innovations. Within a short period, developing country governments have become laboratories for any number of efforts to generate good governance; many have been overwhelmed by the attention.

Acharya, de Lima, and Moore (2006), using data from 1999 to 2001 and a list of fifty-three bilateral and multilateral development assistance organizations, found that these organizations provided assistance to an average of 107 countries each; recipient countries were dealing with an average of twenty-six donors apiece; forty countries were dealing with thirty or more donors. Further, they discovered that in 80 percent of individual fund transfers between donors and recipients, less than 1 percent of the donor's total aid budget was at stake. They cite Vietnam as a fairly typical example: "In 2002, 25 official bilateral donors, 19 official multilateral donors, and about 350 international NGOs were operating in Vietnam. They collectively accounted for over 8,000 projects, or about one project per 9,000 people" (ibid., 2). Presumably, each project and each transfer of funds implies a series of transaction costs in communications, accounting, paperwork, and other investments of time and energy. While much development assistance is being directed to programs other than governance, the figures themselves suggest the burden on developing country governments that are dealing with a multitude of donors and a long and lengthening agenda. Whatever the cause of such donor overload on individual countries, it may be sapping the very capacity needed to achieve positive results in particular problem areas or sectors.

Weak formal institutions of governance are emblematic of—at times conceptually inseparable from—poor and developing countries. The poorer the country, the likelier it is to have weak or nonexistent institutions for making public decisions, allocating resources, and protecting citizens. Thus, a critical problem of the good governance agenda in practice is the burdens its length places on countries that are in the worst position to respond to them. The elites who dominate such governments are not always interested in improving governance, as this could easily limit their power and access to rents and resources. Even with well-meaning governments convinced of the need to improve governance, the question of where to focus resources and what to do is elusive. The agenda specifies an end goal—good performance defined in various ways as indicated above—but does not indicate how to get there. Should all governance deficits be tackled at once? If not, which ones are most important? Which ones are logically prior to others?

This is particularly true when good governance is considered to be a condition necessary for development to take place. In this line of reasoning, a very great deal needs to be accomplished—with an unspecified timeline—before a country can rest assured that its economy will grow and that its citizens will be treated fairly. Commitment to the good governance agenda as a condition necessary for development means resources and public energies focused on achieving this very difficult goal, and we may well ask whether the resources and energy might better be focused on other aspects of development. The argument is not that good governance isn't important but rather that it might not be essential or necessary for growth and poverty alleviation or democracy. Good governance, in fact, may even be a consequence of development, as Ha Joon Chang (2002) has argued. Again, the example of China in the past thirty years is instructive. In all likelihood, most Chinese citizens would benefit from better governance, but it is clear that economic growth, foreign investment, and poverty reduction have not been contingent on this advance.

Where attention to the good governance agenda has been extensive, some scholars have claimed that much development assistance undercuts the governance capacities of developing countries—the agenda is imposed, the number of reforms thought necessary is overwhelming, the time and attention of public officials are divided among a host of donor activities, and foreign experts take on the task of administering policies, programs, and projects (Bräutigam 2000). Development assistance agencies have to some degree acknowledged this critique by placing more emphasis on ownership and participation by developing country governments and citizens. Nevertheless, in the way these activities work out in practice, the influence of development assistance agencies often remains overwhelming, and ownership and participation can be window dressing for changes initiated and pursued by others. Developing country governments find it difficult to debate the practicality or soundness of ideas that come with promises of funding, or to sort out priorities that donors with significantly more resources to carry out research and analysis are unwilling or unable to do.

As an antidote to the inflation of the governance agenda, several years ago I suggested the idea of "good enough governance" as a way of questioning the length of the agenda and its essentialist message. I indicated that good enough governance means that

not all governance deficits need to be (or can be) tackled at once and that institution and capacity building are products of time; governance achievements can also be reversed. Good enough governance means that interventions thought to contribute to the ends of economic and political development need to be questioned, prioritized, and made relevant to the conditions of individual countries. They need to be assessed in light of historical evidence, sequence, and timing, and they should be selected carefully in terms of their contributions to particular ends such as poverty reduction and democracy. Good enough governance directs attention to considerations of the *minimal* conditions of governance necessary to allow political and economic development to occur. (Grindle 2004, 525)[13]

Skepticism as an Antidote to Idea Inflation?

There is an intimate linkage between theory and practice in development. Throughout the post–World War II history of the social sciences, theories have been adopted and put into practice by development practitioners, and practice has spurred renewed interest in generating theory to advance development and account for the failures of previous applications of theory to practice. Researchers and practitioners will recognize a more general trajectory of parallelism and interaction between what is being discussed by scholars and what is being done in the real world by practitioners. Ideas matter.

Indeed, the role of ideas in the "real world"—and the observation of practice that then generates insights that are adopted in new ideas—is perhaps more dynamic and important in countries struggling with the challenges of development than in already developed countries. In such countries, formal institutions of economic and political governance tend to be less embedded, more fluid and changeable, than they are in already developed countries, so the application and adoption of new ideas, of new ways of doing things, at least at the formal institutional level, face fewer barriers. Moreover, many developing countries have economies and political systems that are prone to crises and instability of various kinds; economic and political crises often open up opportunities for innovation in ways that is much more difficult under business- and politics-as-usual conditions. In important ways, then, developing countries provide laboratories for a succession of new ideas. They also play a role in altering those ideas when their experience does not match expectations or when they resist ideas that are politically impractical.

This is a good reason to be careful of attractive ideas, particularly those that promise a great deal. Skepticism may be particularly useful in such contexts to keep development agendas—like good governance—from become unnecessarily inflated. Indeed, it is useful to keep a few adages in mind in containing idea expansion:

• Development—whether economic or political—is a long-term and complex process; research is far from understanding the timing and the complexity of "getting developed."

• Explorations of historical experience can do much to illuminate issues of timing and complexity.

• When concepts like governance take on strong normative content (good governance), their importance and impact are attractive to researchers, practitioners, and advocates, who in turn may add to the inflation of the concept.

Indeed, the history of the concept of good governance suggests that skepticism is a good intellectual tool for shedding light on why development is such a difficult process and why it is often so elusive. Good governance is important; but, like many other good ideas, it is not a magic bullet.

Notes

1. This paper draws on two earlier publications (see Grindle 2004, 2007).

2. For a discussion of the most often used indicators of governance, see Van de Walle (2006).

3. Good governance is a relatively new concept on the development agenda, although it is tempting to connect late twentieth-century demands for good governance to the "good government" movement of the late nineteenth and early twentieth centuries in the United States, when reformers sought to curtail the influence of party patronage and corruption in public office. It is particularly tempting to do so in comparing the normative tone of the good governance agenda with the moral tone of the earlier good government movement.

4. The work of Raúl Prebisch (1950) and Hans Singer (1991) was centrally important in demonstrating that developing country economies were distinct from those of already developed countries. To overcome inherent trade inequalities, they argued, "peripheral" countries needed activist states. In political science, a series of volumes published under the aegis of the Social Science Research Council's Committee on Comparative Politics was influential in exploring the nation- and state-building activities of developing country governments. See especially Apter (1965).

5. For examples of this work, see Bates (1981), Colander (1984), Krueger (1974), Srinivasan (1985), World Bank (1984), Sandbrook 1986, and Wunsch and Olowu (1990). For a critique of this literature, see Grindle (1991).

6. For a recent discussion of this approach, see Fukuyama (2004).

7. The annual *World Development Reports* are a bellwether of current development thinking in that they explore thematic issues in development and summarize in lay terms much mainstream research on such issues.

8. See especially work by Daniel Kaufmann at the World Bank and Transparency International. The expanded Social Science Citation Index lists 1,003 articles about corruption in the seven years between 2000 and 2007. In the ten years prior to this, 804 articles appeared in scholarly social science journals on this topic.

9. See the discussion of the new public management in Peters (1996).

10. In a parallel way, "civil society" became a hygienic way of discussing issues of citizen mobilization and political participation without seeming "political."

11. For a critique, see Brinkerhoff and Goldsmith (2005).

12. In 2002, China tied with Ethiopia in the Corruption Perception Index of Transparency International. See Brinkerhoff and Goldsmith (2005, 209–210).

13. I first introduced the concept of good enough governance in a paper I prepared for the World Bank in 2002. In the 2004 article, I suggest that a good enough governance agenda would be based on "a more nuanced understanding of the evolution of institutions and government capabilities; being explicit about trade-offs and priorities in a world in which all good things cannot be pursued at once; learning about what's working rather than focusing solely on governance gaps; taking the role of government in poverty alleviation seriously, and grounding action in the contextual realities of each country" (p. 525). For additional discussion, see Grindle (2007).

References

Acharya, Arnab, Ana Teresa Fuzzo de Lima, and Mick Moore. 2006. Proliferation and Fragmentation: Transactions Costs and the Value of Aid. *Journal of Development Studies* 42 (1): 1–21.

Amsden, Alice. 1989. *Asia's Next Giant: South Korea and Late Industrialization.* New York: Oxford University Press.

Andrews, Matt. 2008. Are Swedish Models of Effective Government Suitable in the Development Domain (Or) Do We Need a Theory of Government before We Measure Government Effectiveness? Manuscript, Kennedy School of Government, Cambridge, MA.

Apter, David E. 1965. *Political Modernization.* Chicago: University of Chicago Press.

Bates, Robert H. 1981. *States and Markets in Tropical Africa.* Berkeley: University of California Press.

Bräutigam, Deborah. 2000. *Aid Dependence and Governance.* Stockholm: Almqvist and Wiksell International.

Brinkerhoff, Derick, and Arthur Goldsmith. 2005. Institutional Dualism and International Development: A Revisionist Interpretation of Good Governance. *Administration & Society* 37 (2): 553–566.

Chabal, Patrick, ed. 1986. *Political Domination in Africa.* Cambridge: Cambridge University Press.

Chang, Ha-Joon. 2002. *Kicking Away the Ladder: Development Strategy in Historical Perspective*. London: Anthem Press.

Colander, David C., ed. 1984. *Neoclassical Political Economy: The Analysis of Rent-Seeking and DUP Activities*. Cambridge, MA: Ballinger.

Department for International Development (DFID). 2001. Making Government Work for Poor People: Building State Capacity. Strategy Paper, DFID, London.

Evans, Peter, Dietrich Rueschemeyer, and Theda Skocpol, eds. 1985. *Bringing the State Back In*. New York: Cambridge University Press.

Fukuyama, Francis. 2004. *State-Building and World Order in the 21st Century*. Ithaca, NY: Cornell University Press.

Goldman, Marshall I. 2003. *The Privatization of Russia: Russian Reform Goes Awry*. New York: Routledge.

Grindle, Merilee S. 1991. The New Political Economy: Positive Economics and Negative Politics. In *Politics and Policy Making in Developing Countries: Perspectives on the New Political Economy*, ed. Gerald M. Meier. San Francisco: ICS Press.

Grindle, Merilee S. 2004. Good Enough Governance: Poverty Reduction and Reform in Developing Countries. *Governance: An International Journal of Policy, Administration, and Institutions* 17 (4): 525–548.

Grindle, Merilee S. 2007. Good Enough Governance Revisited. *Development Policy Review* 25 (5): 553–574.

Hewitt de Alcántara, Cynthia. 1998. Uses and Abuses of the Concept of Governance. *International Social Science Journal* 50 (155): 105–113.

Hewko, John. 2002. Foreign Direct Investment: Does the Rule of Law Matter? Working paper, Carnegie Endowment for International Peace, Washington, D.C.

Huntington, Samuel. 1991. *The Third Wave: Democratization in the Late Twentieth Century*. Norman: University of Oklahoma Press.

Hyden, Goran, Julius Court, and Kenneth Mease. 2004. *Making Sense of Governance: Empirical Evidence from Sixteen Countries*. Boulder, CO: Lynne Rienner.

Johnson, Juliet. 1999. Misguided Autonomy: Central Bank Independence in the Russian Transition. In *The Self Restraining State: Power and Accountability in New Democracies*, ed. Andreas Schedler, Larry Diamond, and Marc F. Plattner, 193–311. Boulder, CO: Lynne Rienner.

Kaufmann, Daniel. 2003. *Rethinking Governance: Empirical Lessons Challenge Orthodoxy*. Washington, DC: World Bank.

Kaufmann, Daniel, and Aart Kraay. 2002. Growth without Governance. World Bank Policy Research Working Paper No. 2928. Washington, DC: World Bank.

Killick, Tony. 1989. *A Reaction Too Far: Economic Theory and the Role of the State in Developing Countries*. London: Overseas Development Institute.

Krueger, Anne O. 1974. The Political Economy of the Rent-Seeking Society. *American Economic Review* 64 (3): 291–303.

Kurtz, Marcus J., and Andrew Schrank. 2007. Growth and Governance: Models, Measures, and Mechanisms. *Journal of Politics* 69 (2): 538–554.

Lipjhart, Arend, and Carlos Waisman, eds. 1996. *Institutional Design in New Democracies*. Boulder, CO: Westview Press.

North, Douglass. 1990. *Institutions, Institutional Change and Economic Performance*. London: Cambridge University Press.

O'Donnell, Guillermo, Philippe C. Schmitter, and Laurence Whitehead, eds. 1986. *Transitions from Authoritarian Rule: Comparative Perspectives*. Baltimore, MD: Johns Hopkins University Press.

Osborne, Jason W., and Amy Overbay. 2004. The Power of Outliers (And Why Researchers Should Always Check for Them). *Practical Assessment, Research & Evaluation* 9 (6): 1–12.

Peters, B. Guy. 1996. *The Future of Governing: Four Emerging Models*. Lawrence: University Press of Kansas.

Pierson, Paul. 2004. *Politics in Time: History, Institutions, and Social Analysis*. Princeton, NJ: Princeton University Press.

Prebisch, Raúl. 1950. *The Economic Development of Latin America and Its Principal Problems*. New York: United Nations.

Putnam, Robert. 1993. *Making Democracy Work: Civic Traditions in Modern Italy*. Princeton, NJ: Princeton University Press.

Rothchild, Donald, and Naomi Chazan, eds. 1988. *The Precarious Balance: State and Society in Africa*. Boulder, CO: Westview Press.

Sandbrook, Richard. 1986. The State and Economic Stagnation in Tropical Africa. *World Development* 14 (3): 319–332.

Singer, Hans. 1991. *Growth, Development and Trade: Selected Essays of Hans W. Singer*. Cheltenham, UK: Edward Elgar.

Srinivasan, T. N. 1985. Neoclassical Political Economy: The State and Economic Development. *Politics & Society* 17 (2): 115–162.

Steinmo, Sven, Kathleen Thelen, and Frank Longstreth, eds. 1992. *Structuring Politics: Historical Institutionalism in Comparative Politics*. Cambridge: Cambridge University Press.

United Nations Development Programme (UNDP). 1997. *Governance for Sustainable Human Development*. New York: UNDP.

United Nations Development Programme (UNDP). 2008. *Annual Report 2008: Capacity Development: Empowering People and Institutions*. New York: UNDP, 12.

Van de Walle, Steven. 2006. The State of the World's Bureaucracies. *Journal of Comparative Policy Analysis* 8 (4): 439–450.

Wade, Robert. 1990. *Governing the Market: Economic Theory and the Role of Government in East Asian Industrialization*. Princeton, NJ: Princeton University Press.

Williamson, Oliver. 1991. Economic Institutions: Spontaneous and Intentional Governance. *Journal of Law, Economics and Organization* 7:159–187

World Bank. 1984. *Towards Sustained Development in Sub-Saharan Africa.* Washington, DC: World Bank.

World Bank. 1991. *World Development Report 1991.* Washington, DC: World Bank.

World Bank. 1997. *World Development Report 1997.* Washington, DC: World Bank.

World Bank. 1999. Findings on Governance, Institutions and Development: Empirical Studies of Governance and Development: An Annotated Bibliography. http://www1.worldbank.org/publicsector/findings.htm.

World Bank. 2007. Strengthening World Bank Group Engagement on Governance and Anti-Corruption. March 21.

World Bank. n.d. Good Governance and Its Benefits on Economic Development: An Overview of Current Trends. http://siteresources.worldbank.org/INTWBIG-OVANTCOR/resources/1740479-114911221008.

Wunsch, James S., and Dele Olowu, eds. 1990. *The Failure of the Centralized State: Institutions and Self Governance in Africa.* Boulder, CO: Westview Press.

11

Self-Help Housing Ideas and Practice in the Americas

Peter M. Ward

An important paradigm shift in development planning was under way by the late 1960s, as some researchers began to notice the unintended negative consequences of large-scale, modernized city-building schemes. Lisa Peattie's *The View from the Barrio* (1968), a critique of the Ciudad Guayana experience in Venezuela, led the way.[1] There were others, too, at MIT and elsewhere, who by then had started to advocate for an alternative, bottom-up approach to city building. In architecture, John Turner's graduate classes at MIT introduced students to the nature of urban settlement, and during 1968–1972 he developed the framework for a comparative analysis of "low-income housing systems," which eventually led to major publications (Turner and Fichter 1972; Turner 1976). Turner mentored a number of graduate students who subsequently became the carriers of his ideas not only to their own countries but also to multilateral agencies and nongovernmental organizations. At Harvard, William Doebele's research in Colombia generated a new understanding of informal land development processes. He showed how policymakers could integrate irregular settlements into the land market. In anthropology and sociology, Tony and Liz Leeds, working on Brazil and Peru, were developing a nuanced understanding of squatter settlement typologies. Simultaneously Susan Eckstein at Boston University and Wayne Cornelius at MIT were completing manuscripts based on their doctoral dissertations that examined protests in low-income settlements and offered new insights into the political awareness of the poor.

In retrospect, one can see this groundswell of research was part of a growing disillusionment with the export of the then dominant planning paradigms of state-led modernization. It is paradoxical that the questioning of the orthodoxy came out of the same Cambridge-Boston stable, and in some cases even out of the same research group, that had helped create the orthodox view earlier. At MIT, there was some tension between those who still believed in modernization theory and conventional views of planning and those who were critical and interested in irregular settlements and grassroots development efforts. And while Lloyd Rodwin's impresario skills brought in several people whose ideas were attracting attention at the time, such as John Turner, ultimately the profound differences in approach and philosophy led to their exit.[2]

Even today, almost forty years later as I was on my way to Mexico City and made a stop-over in Boston, I vividly recall my brief encounters with Cornelius, Turner, and Eckstein, and their advice and reflections at the time. They had a major effect on my thinking regarding the importance of self-help housing processes from the bottom up. I also saw the need for a multi- and interdisciplinary approach to understanding self-help. Though I was trained as a geographer, I now draw on the fields of architecture, planning, politics, sociology, urban anthropology, geography, and public policy. Thus, it is no accident that today I teach in two disciplinary programs, sociology and public affairs. Although I did not realize it at the time, the ideas I was introduced to at MIT and Cambridge were to profoundly influence my own subsequent career, and also the professional discourse on self-help settlements. Hence my particular pleasure in contributing to this volume about planning ideas.

In this chapter, I examine how ideas about self-help housing have emerged from different paradigms of development thinking. I also describe how the work of scholars and fellow travelers in other fields has had important complementary (and unwitting) impacts on the evolution of the idea of self-help (Ward 2005). In particular, I address a paradox: while ideas and policies espousing self-help originally evolved in developed societies and were exported with alacrity to developing countries, the relevance and applicability of such ideas for developed societies today are usually ignored. This is yet another reason why writing this chapter on the emergence of self-help housing planning is timely for me personally. After many years of writing about planning, housing, social policy, and governance, my own research has brought me full circle to self-help housing activities, in Latin America as well as in the United States. I am now trying to understand the resurgence of informality and self-help in the United States, which I discuss later in this chapter.

Since the 1950s, the ways in which we view self-help housing and informal self-building have shifted significantly. Until the mid-1960s, both research and policy making were in large part shaped by modernization theory. The Ciudad Guayana project, mentioned earlier, was a prime example of such thinking. But such idealistic thinking had a very limited impact, in part because it failed to engage with the political power brokers in the capital Caracas, and also because it failed to take into account the needs and realities of the poor (Peattie 1987). As a result, modernization theories were criticized by the structuralists, drawing on a number of ideas: Marxian dependency theory, political economy, interdependence, and world systems theory. Ironically, neoliberalism and globalization paradigms emerged a decade later, promoting the downsizing of government and policies to make the market "work" more effectively by improving how urban areas are managed through administrative decentralization and "good governance" (Ward 2005).

There is now a growing concern for sustainability—environmental, fiscal, juridical, and material. If I had to predict the next paradigm shift, this broader concern for sustainability would be a front-runner. I hope that this would lead to a "greening" of self-help practices too. The use of vernacular materials, sustainable sources of energy (solar power and water heating), low-tech and low-energy systems of waste removal and water harvesting, better insulation and weatherization programs, and so on, will help meet the needs of self-help housing users in the future (Ward and Sullivan 2010). In developed nations, such systems are often considered either too expensive or substandard. But as "green housing" initiatives develop and are institutionalized with greater urgency, I hope that these will not become the next generation of ideas to be exported "out there" (to developing countries) but will also be adopted as part of the self-help housing movement in the United States and other developed nations.

First Practice: The Largely Unknown Experiences of 1940s Aided Self-Help

Neither the concept nor the practice of self-help housing is a recent phenomenon. Traditional, vernacular housing in rural areas was mostly self-built by families and kinsmen. In the United States, frontier homesteaders constructed their own homes either in villages or on their farmsteads. Materials came largely from surrounding woodlands, quarries, and mud-pits and were used to construct log cabins, wattle-and-daub structures, cut peat or adobe walls, and roofs made of thatch, wood shingle, or large leaves. These practices continue today in rural and tropical areas (Burnham 1998).

In addition, from the beginning of the twentieth century, "irregular" settlements by migrants were a common feature in rapidly growing urban centers in the United States and Canada. Examples include communities of British immigrants around Canadian cities (1900–1913), southern migrants into northern U.S. cities in the 1920s, dustbowl migrants to Southern California during the 1930s, and rural-urban migrants to industrial centers in the 1940s (Harris 2001). In Nova Scotia, St. Francis Xavier University sponsored a self-help housing project for coal miners in 1938. In U.S. Appalachia around the same time, impoverished miners were supported by the American Friends Service Committee in a self-help housing project called Penn-Craft.

From 1942 to 1975, Canada had a "Build Your Own Home" program that offered financial, legal, and technical assistance to amateur home builders (Schulist and Harris 2002). Before World War II, these self-help areas were outside the economic mainstream, and settlers scrounged materials and used little credit. After 1945, however, owner-built buildings boomed. By 1949, one-third of new homes were owner-initiated, where owners did much of the manual work themselves (Harris 2001). Lenders and building materials suppliers offered credit, advice, and even serviced subdivisions. In suburbs, do-it-yourself was mainstreamed, while in rural areas it remained somewhat informal. Canada's National Council on Self-Help Housing, created in 2002, is one of the agencies in developed countries to accept self-help housing in order to make housing affordable to economically and socially disadvantaged Canadians. In the United States, however, there appears to have been only a grudging acceptance of self-help, and that too only as a means of housing the very poor. In other words, in the United States, self-help is still largely viewed as a temporary expedient or a last resort, not as an important plank in public policy. That is why, during the 1950s and 1960s, the United States preferred low- and lower-middle-income housing production by private developers, who used prefabricated parts to build cookie-cutter homes. This is how suburban communities like Levittown were created.

Hans Harms (1982) describes how recourse to self-help is usually associated with crises in capitalism, when the state is hard-pressed to provide housing for urban workers. He provides examples from mid-nineteenth-century Germany as described by Engels, Puerto Rico's "bootstraps" programs in the 1940s, and even home improvement and conversion programs in London in the 1970s, when first-time homebuyers received subsidies to rehabilitate run-down housing. In the UK during the 1920s and 1930s, so-called "plot-landers" were able to make use of small parcels of land not needed for agriculture to gradually build up "weekend shacks," which were later consolidated into permanent homes (Hardy and Colin Ward 1984). After 1945, homeless people squatted on land in recently vacated military camps. Over the years, various types of "travelers" have also settled on land, often engaging in informal economic activities and building a wide range of dwelling types (Home 2001). Between 1927 and the 1990s, Stockholm had a self-help housing program operating on municipal land, but it too relied heavily on the assembly of prefabricated parts and as a result had limited design flexibility (Schulist and Harris, 2002). Moreover, past and present, do-it–yourself upgrading and home improvements have been commonplace among working and middle-income families in Europe and the United States, and are favored where professional building labor and service providers are expensive.

The Origins of Self-Help in Industrializing Nations

Although the United States was ambivalent at best about supporting self-help housing at home, it played a key role in promoting self-build policies abroad, especially in the newly industrializing nations. Though John Turner and his contemporaries are commonly identified as the principal architects of the self-build policy and its eventual adoption by the World Bank and the United Nations (Turner 1969), the process had begun in the late 1930s, twenty years earlier. In a fascinating historical account, Richard Harris (1998, 1999) documents how Jacob Crane's work at the Housing and Home Finance Agency (HHFA) in Washington, D.C., was, in effect, the beginning of "aided self-help." Indeed, it was Crane who coined the term in 1945. The first major effort was a federally funded project in the city of Ponce in Puerto Rico in 1939. It comprised a site-and-service scheme for the construction of nearly 10,000 owner-built homes by 1960. Crane, who was then assistant director of the U.S. Public Housing Administration, helped create the program in Ponce. Later, between 1947 and 1953, working at the HHFA, he became the linchpin in the promotion of self-help worldwide.

Two interesting features emerge from Harris's analysis. First, even though the United States was not eager to promote self-help at home, it provided federal funding for self-help in Puerto Rico. Moreover, Crane, along with his then boss Raymond Foley, persuaded the federal government to promote self-help as a major element of development policy abroad during the 1950s. Working with national agency heads and other key actors in Peru, Colombia, India, Ghana, the Philippines, and several other nations, the HHFA encouraged these governments to support self-help housing programs. A skillful technocrat, lobbyist, and promoter, Crane was successful in eventually disseminating his ideas to the UN, which sponsored "missions" to developing nations urging government support for self-help. However, Crane had less success with the World Bank, which was then focused on agriculture and large-scale infrastructure provision and did not prioritize housing at that time. Not for another twenty years would urban and housing issues gain traction at the World Bank, with self-help as a central element of housing policies.

The second point to note is that although policy specialists like Charles Abrams and scholars like the anthropologist William Mangin knew of Crane's work and writings, they appear never to acknowledge either his work or the Puerto Rico project, which had been lauded at an international conference held in San Juan in 1960. In Harris's words, "The whispers and silences are deafening" (1998, 167), and it is odd that even Turner and others never acknowledged the real origins of aided self-help. Granted, there was a long time gap between the first round of self-help ideas in the 1940s and 1950s and the second round of similar ideas and their promotion in the late 1960s. Nevertheless, the fact remains that Crane's link with key housing specialists like David Vega Christie in Peru had created an important voice in support of self-help in that country. This also led Eduardo Neira, a Peruvian architect at the Ministry of Public Works, to establish a pilot project with squatters in Arequipa, and it was Neira who had invited John Turner as an adviser to the project. Thus, there are clear links in the intellectual authorship of these ideas, starting with Crane, moving through the U.S. HHFA, to national housing agencies, to the research publications of the 1960s and 1970s, and ultimately to the adoption of self-help policies by international institutions such as the UN and the World Bank. One plausible reason why the real origin of the idea was never properly acknowledged may be that the original idea was associated with heavy-handed U.S. foreign policy during the 1940s and 1950s. This might have generated some resistance to it being incorporated into national housing policies in Peru, Colombia, and elsewhere in Latin America. As in the United States and Western Europe during the 1960s, these countries were constructing large-scale public housing projects and bulldozing for urban renewal—two policies that were then part of conventional wisdom. Perhaps Abrams, Turner, Mangin, and others thought that it was strategically best to "turn the page" on aided self-help *àla (norte) Americana* of the 1940s and 1950s, and start over, offering, in effect, old wine in new bottles

Self-Help Housing as a Response to Rapid Urbanization in Less Developed Countries

By the mid-1960s, a number of creative scholars in sociology, social anthropology, and urbanism had begun to write perceptively about the highly functional and supportive social structures of slums and the destructive effects of urban renewal. For example, in *Family and Kinship in the East End of London*, Young and Willmott (1957) laid bare the social and economic hardships created by "slum" removal programs in Bethnal Green in East London and by relocating families to municipal housing estates in Essex, some twenty miles to the east. Similarly, Herbert Gans's (1962) *Urban Villagers* drew attention to the rich culture of Italian immigrant communities in the West End of Boston that were being destroyed as part of "slum clearance" to make way for new housing and an expanding Massachusetts General Hospital. Jane Jacobs's (1961) *Death and Life of Great American Cities* captured the sentiment exceptionally well, seriously challenging the orthodoxy of slum clearance and social engineering of architects, civil engineers, and urban planners. Jacobs's predictions were proved correct, as design flaws began to emerge. The failure to understand the cultural vibrancy of the slum made urban renewal look worse than the original problem. By the late 1960s, such "great planning disasters" (Hall 1982) were widely recognized, precipitating a crisis of confidence in the planning profession itself (Faber and Seers 1972).

Self-help was a reaction to the inadvertent negative outcomes of urban renewal and the loss of confidence in formal planning mechanisms and architectural orthodoxy at the time. Consequently, arguments for self-help housing prospered, along with support for community architecture, in-situ urban rehabilitation, flexibility, and user control in housing design. If planners, engineers, and architects could not provide solutions that worked for the people, could the people themselves perhaps do better? Especially in Latin America, research had already begun to challenge the prevailing stereotypes of burgeoning "squatter settlements" and "spontaneous self-help settlements" that formed the bulk of new low-income housing stock.

By the early 1970s, sufficient evidence had begun to emerge, largely from British and U.S. architects and sociologists, that the slums were rational responses to poverty (Portes 1972). Moreover, the slum-dwellers were not politically unsophisticated; they could not be duped and manipulated. They were, in fact, engaged in hard negotiations with city and municipal authorities (Leeds 1972). Different formations of such neighborhoods fostered different types of knowledge and varying engagements with politics. Self-help settlements were the crucibles of social learning and political mobilization (Cornelius 1975). They were not immersed in a "culture of poverty," as Oscar Lewis had proposed. Their putative marginality was largely a myth, poverty being structural, born of exploitation, not cultural backwardness or because the poor were steeped in traditional values (Perlman 1976).

Another important turning point in the academic literature was a 1967 review article by the anthropologist William Mangin, published in the *Latin American Research Review* and titled "The Latin American Squatter Settlements: A Problem and a Solution." This article exposed many of the stereotypes about irregular settlements, showing that given a chance, these settlements were upgraded over some fifteen to twenty-five years through self-help, mutual aid, and state-supported interventions.

Turner rooted his advocacy for self-help in such arguments about housing consolidation. In a number of papers, Turner (1967, 1968a, 1969) and Charles Abrams (1964, 1966) argued that self-help was an appropriate response by the urban poor to the incapacity of both governments and the formal housing market to provide housing at an affordable price and on a large scale. Their research and policy advocacy demonstrated that once the poor had acquired land, either by squatting or by some form of informal purchase, people organized and collaborated as a community in a number of ways: leveling streets to make them accessible to public transport; informally hooking up to electricity poles to access electricity for their homes; pressuring local authorities to provide rudimentary services (e.g., water lorries), and so on. At the individual household level, the poor gradually improved their dwellings, replacing provisional shacks with permanent materials. Some areas were less successful in consolidating their homes—for example, residents of homes on steep slopes, in ravines, or on invaded land that was contested by owners—but in general, once established and consolidated, these communities represented an "architecture that worked" (Turner 1968b). Depending on the level of support from local authorities, these areas were gradually incorporated into the formal urban structure. Services were installed, streets were paved, and land titles were transferred to de facto owners.

Homes were improved upon and expanded, both horizontally and vertically into second and third floors (figs. 11.1 and 11.2).

Abrams, Turner, and others argued that supplying housing in this way was better than social housing projects that served only a small number of households. They proposed that governments should harness this "sweat equity" and the initiative to self-build. Governments were also advised to provide technical assistance and at-cost building materials; they should install essential services in stages, starting with electricity and water, later drainage and street paving; and ultimately they should "regularize" land titles to reduce insecurity. Turner (1976) advocated for investment in what he called "elements" of housing—line items rather than fully completed housing units. These were what the people could not provide for themselves, such as primary and secondary water and drainage networks, land title regularization, electricity and street lighting, and so on. He argued that most other aspects of housing consolidation should best be left to the residents themselves, taking into account their varying needs, priorities, and capacities to invest in home construction and improvements.

In his book, *Housing by People: Toward Autonomy in Building Environments,* Turner (1976) eschews what he calls heteronymous systems of housing production that are centrally planned, hierarchical, large scale, and inflexible in design, with one-size-fits-all structures that offer no opportunity for residents to redesign the interior spaces. Turner favored "autonomous systems" that were more efficient, equitable, and able to mobilize more resources. He differentiated between the "supportive shack" and the "oppressive house," and argued that efficiency could be better achieved through self-building, because it produced a variety of products at low prices. Most important, it gave people greater autonomy over their lives, even as it sometimes engaged them with supralocal organizations. Although they were sometimes portrayed as "anarchist architects," Colin Ward and John Turner's arguments were powerful and highly respected.

How Self-Help Housing Became Orthodoxy

From the mid-1960s on, a positive view of self-built housing and support for upgrading of informal settlements were incorporated into various schemes, such as "sites and services," which were planned settlements with basic services installed on lot sites so people could then build their own homes. In tropical Africa, where heavy rainfall required secure roofs

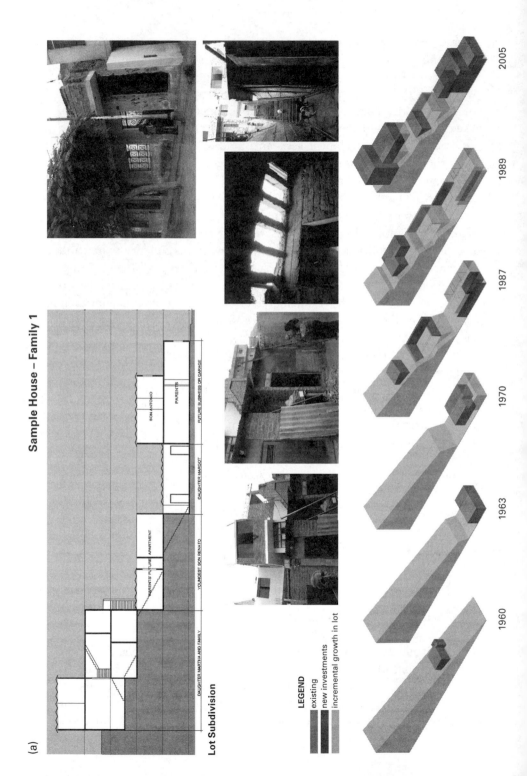

Sample House – Family 1

Lot Subdivision

DAUGHTER MARTHA AND FAMILY

YOUNGEST SON RENATO

PARENTS' FUTURE APARTMENT

DAUGHTER MARGOT

SON ANTONIO

PARENTS

FUTURE BUSINESS OR GARAGE

LEGEND
existing
new investments
incremental growth in lot

(a)

1960   1963   1970   1987   1989   2005

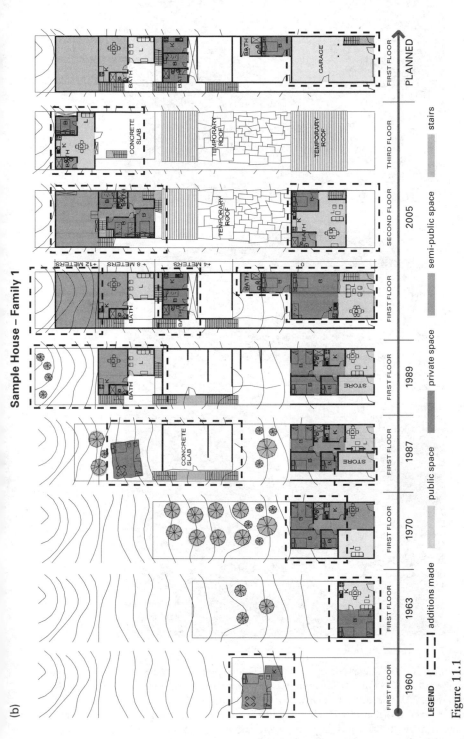

Figure 11.1

(*a*) Plans showing the accretive growth of a self-built home and possible future additions. (*b*) Three-dimensional rendering of home development showing expansions for adult children (*hijo*), workshop (*taller*), etc. *Source*: Rojas Williams 2005; courtesy of Susana M. Rojas Williams.

Figure 11.2
Colonia Isidro Fabela, Mexico City, 1973 and present. *(a)* and *(b)* View toward ring road, 1973. The author rented a room on the third floor of the house in the distance. *(b)* The author in front of that home in 2007. *(c)* Self-build by the author's landlord in 1973, showing use of settlement volcanic rock for walls, industrialized bricks, and preparations for pouring a concrete roof (rear). *Photos*: Peter Ward.

(c)

Figure 11.2
(continued)

for houses, self-help advocates suggested that serviced sites be provided with a secure, sloping roof built on four corner posts. This would allow the self-builders to design and build the remainder of their dwellings. This greater public awareness of the intrinsic benefits of self-help—autonomy, flexibility, "users know best," and sympathy toward local, vernacular traditions—emerged at the same time that formal planning practices were fast losing legitimacy.

Equally important, by the early 1970s bilateral and multilateral agencies, such as USAID and the World Bank, were beginning to take note of self-help housing. Abrams had worked as a technical consultant for USAID. As for the World Bank, with Robert McNamara at the helm a new focus on urbanization emerged, and the bank took a pragmatic approach to housing the urban poor, who by then made up 50 percent

or more of the population of some cities in developing nations. The idea
of aided self-help was attractive to the World Bank (1972). In 1976 the
UN also backed this approach at the first UN Habitat Conference, held
in Vancouver, Canada. This provided a major platform for the propagation of the idea of self-help housing globally. The support of the World
Bank legitimized self-help as an element of good developmental
thinking.

Critiques of Self-Help Housing

Turner's ideas were not without criticism. A number of voices (Harms
1976; Burgess 1982; Ward 1982) began to suggest that Turner's philosophy disregarded true *choice*—resident autonomy and freedom to build—
in favor of what was, in fact, structural *constraint,* namely, poverty and
a lack of effective choice. Critics argued that Turner had glossed over
some of the high social costs of living and raising a family under conditions of high insecurity, without adequate services, and in poor and
hazardous dwelling conditions.

Planners too sometimes balked at Turner's ideas. For example, in the
late 1970s Otto Koenigsberger, a leading and distinguished urban development planner associated with the Development Planning Unit in
London, took issue with me at a public seminar after I had argued for
more public participation in what I saw as a barely incipient planning
process in Mexico City. I had got it totally wrong, he said, because in
Mexico and elsewhere, where so much building is self-help spontaneous
settlements, "it is the people who participate and the planners who are
excluded!" Koenigsberger had a point. In a similar if less adversarial vein,
Baross (1990) described the reverse order by which informality and self-
help provide housing. The orthodox planning of residential areas starts
with site planning and approvals (P), continues with primary infrastructure provision (I), followed by servicing hookups to building sites (S), all
before actual building (B) commences, after which occupation proceeds
(P-I-S-B). In contrast, self-help housing follows a reverse order: people
first occupy land and engage in building, servicing, and then negotiating
for retrospective infrastructure expansion, and eventually are incorporated into the city's master plan (i.e., B-S-I-P).

The most pointed critique of self-help housing was mounted by
Burgess (1982, 1985). An avowed Marxist, Burgess systematically dis-
sected Turner's ideas and argued that self-building focused excessively on
"use value" rather than on "exchange value" of housing. Informal settle-

ments did not function outside capitalism and market relations, he argued, but in another sphere of it (Burgess 1982). Policies to intervene in the informal process only facilitated the penetration of the upper circuit, where capitalism thrived, into the lower circuit of informality and petty capitalism. Burgess also argued that government-supported self-help led to the co-optation of the poor, channeling their demand making in ways that were conducive to more state control. To Burgess, self-help was a mechanism for cheapening the cost of reproduction of labor in two ways: first, by suppressing demand for higher wages, it generated extra profit for employers, and second, by reducing housing costs, it lowered the costs of social reproduction by labor. In essence, self-help did not challenge capitalism but instead helped it to thrive.

Burgess's arguments had considerable veracity, and Turner sought to respond in a more nuanced way (Turner 1982). In the process, both Turner and Burgess made important contributions to the literature, but the fact that neither questioned his own ideology blurred their analyses. Burgess wore his Marxism on his sleeve and dismissed any evidence that self-help policies did not always facilitate the exploitation of the working class. Similarly, Turner's anarchism and humanist zeal romanticized the notions of autonomy and unfettered freedom to build. While there was a real need at the time for Turner's advocacy of self-help and for a fundamental redirection of housing policies, once that redirection had been achieved, Turner should probably have pulled back in his claims, rather than overreaching himself, as in *Housing by People*. Although Turner was relatively muted in contribution to the volume *Self-Help Housing: A Critique* (in Ward 1982), by then the genie was out of the bottle, and self-help housing had become part of mainstream thinking.

In the late 1970s, my own research sought to account for the heterogeneity of housing consolidation within individual settlements. Some dwellings were consolidating modestly, others fast and furiously and were already two or even three stories high, while some had not been consolidated at all. My surveys revealed that surplus household income—cash left over after all living and housing expenses had been paid—was the most significant single determinant of consolidation levels (Ward 1982). That housing consolidation required surplus income was not a surprise, but the study did raise questions regarding "autonomy" and how it affected the rate of self-help housing, and called for a reevaluation of what could realistically be expected of self-help. Two factors seemed likely to reduce the levels of successful self-building. First, declining incomes and reduced spare time meant less cash and less sweat equity

(a)

Figure 11.3
"Wet cores" (sites and services) and self-help additions, Neuquen, Argentina, 2003. *(a)* Slab and single w.c./bathroom, electricity supply and meter. Pre-occupancy. *(b)* Post-occupancy after several years showing self-help extensions to original core. *Photos*: Peter Ward.

(b)

Figure 11.3
(continued)

available for investment; and second, the significant rise in the real costs of building materials after the 1973 oil price hike impacted negatively on housing consolidation.

This became even more of an issue in site-and-service and "wet core-unit" schemes (fig. 11.3), which were fast becoming the poster child of new state-sponsored self-built settlement schemes (World Bank 1972).[3] In reality, these were highly subsidized housing programs that required greater initial as well as ongoing investments, compared to informal settlements that enjoyed greater flexibility since no regular amortization payments for building were required. Moreover, as Burgess had rightly predicted, the formalization of the informal self-help process created additional costs, slowing self-built consolidation. Consequently, formal policies had to be adjusted either by moving the sale of plots one or two income deciles upmarket to the relatively better-off working classes or by reducing the quality of the site-and-service project by lowering plot size and providing fewer services.

Neoliberalism and Self-Help

The 1980s debt crisis and the subsequent policies of fiscal austerity, structural readjustment, and privatization created a new policy environment for the idea of self-help to flourish. Also, the simultaneous democratization of many Latin American nations created a new political environment for the recasting of self-help as an idea conducive to enhanced citizen participation. Bilateral and multilateral institutions utilized the idea of self-help to propagate a range of initiatives, such as new urban management, good governance, and demand-driven investments, which called for reduced social spending, deregulation of business activities, and the celebration of private entrepreneurship by the poor.

These changes had a significant effect. As economic growth slowed, poverty increased, pushing the poor to rely more on household survival strategies. Simultaneously, good governance policies (discussed in greater detail in the previous chapter), which stressed the financial viability of service delivery and full cost recovery, increased the consumption costs of the poor, further reducing their disposable income. As a result, what were once touted as the "resources of poverty"—such as self-help, household consolidation, sharing of space, reciprocity, multiple earning strategies, and so on—could no longer flourish. In fact, by the mid-1990s, a new type of poverty—more deeply entrenched and widespread—had surfaced, making researchers rethink whether the poor enjoyed the "resources of poverty" or suffered from a "poverty of resources" (González de la Rocha 2001).

Recently, public policies have shifted from slum upgrading and site-and-service projects to making housing markets work better for competitive cities. This entails removing the impediments to land and housing supply, regularizing "clouded" land titles to encourage de jure (full) ownership, and providing infrastructure at market price. Also, the past ten years have witnessed government promotion of low-income housing production through the private sector, as in Mexico, which has created massive housing estates in periurban locations but at costs that are affordable only to lower-middle-income groups. Clearly, there is a market for such housing, and some families that would have been self-builders in the past are now opting for these housing types. However, the cookie-cutter designs of these houses offer minimal variation and scope for flexibility and adaptation. In a way, this is a return to the Latin American social interest housing projects of the 1960s, to Levittown in the United States, and to the large housing projects provided by municipal and local governments in Western Europe. Future research will need to ascertain the viability of such large-scale developments, but it seems likely that self-help (DIY) activities will be extremely limited in such physical environments.

The Future of Self-Help Housing

In Latin America, many self-built settlements have gradually consolidated, often forming intermediate rings of growth around large cities. Unlike in U.S. and European cities there is minimal mobility among the original help owners, 80 percent of whom still live on the same lot that they acquired in the 1960s and 1970s. Moreover, over the years these neighborhoods have experienced significant land-use and tenure changes, on-lot population densification, and dwelling subdivisions among the now adult children of former squatters and self-builders. This has created intense physical dilapidation. Such processes require empirical research and rigorous analysis, as well as unconventional thinking about new policies that will assist in situ housing rehabilitation and redesign. This is necessary to meet contemporary user needs and expectations, as well as the refurbishment and retrofitting of infrastructure at both household and community levels. Yet this is a largely unconsidered issue in self-build housing policies because policymakers generally assume that, having been successfully consolidated, these settlements no longer require continuing intervention. This is almost certainly a false assumption: prima facie, these areas, which we call the "innerburbs" (first suburbs), appear to have very real and pressing needs that require new and creative self-help and self-managed solutions as we start thinking about a new generation of housing policy for these older self-help settlements areas (see www.lahn.utexas.org).[4]

Self-Help in the United States: *Colonias* and Informal Homestead Subdivisions

The extensive *colonia*-type settlements along the U.S.-Mexican border and the "informal homestead subdivisions" in the periurban areas of an increasing number of metropolitan centers across the United States are akin to self-help housing in Latin America. Relatively few people are aware of the extent of such informal housing production in the United States (Mukhija and Monkonnen 2006). In 1991, 350,000 low-income residents lived in the *colonias* along the Texas border in what were described as "Third World" housing conditions (Davies and Holz 1992) (fig. 11.4). By the late 1990s the numbers had grown to almost half a million (Office of the Attorney General of Texas 1996; Ward 1999). Similar low-income unincorporated subdivisions outside the border area are now also being noticed (figs. 11.5 and 11.6). Preliminary estimates suggest that as many as three to four million people may be living in these settlements throughout the nation (Ward and Peters 2007). While *colonias* and informal homestead subdivisions differ in a number of respects, both serve low-income households that value home ownership but earn less than the minimum necessary to acquire housing through formal housing financing systems.

In *colonias*, lots varying in size from a quarter acre to one acre are sold off without services by developers, usually under a contract-for-deed arrangement. Residents build or place manufactured homes on these lots. This housing system has flourished along the border because low-income migrants and Mexican Americans have drawn on self-help traditions they learned in Mexico but which can also be used in Texas as an affordable path to home ownership. The average household income in these *colonias* is $600 to $1,000 per month (Ward, Guisti, and de Souza 2004, 39). These are largely Mexican and Mexican-origin households, and residents are often U.S. citizens or legal residents. They make up the new

Figure 11.4
Typical camper in a Texas *colonia* with rudimentary extension. *Photo*: Peter Ward.

(a)

(b)

Figure 11.5
Modular homes in Mike's Colonia, outside Rio Grande City, Starr County, Texas.
(a) Low-cost "modular" home and extension. Note the propane tanks and fenced
lot; both are typical. *(b)* Modular home with obvious evidence of exterior self-
help outside (brick wall and yard). Although not visible, inside, too, sheet rock
and trim installation and other do-it-yourself activities are common. *Photos*:
Peter Ward.

Figure 11.6
Oblique view of an informal homestead subdivision (IFHS), Bastrop County, 15 miles outside of Austin, Texas. *Photo*: Peter Ward.

working poor, who are usually employed in construction, services, and food processing in an adjacent city. The level of poverty is high, and hence home construction in these areas is often quite rudimentary. Since the early 1990s, federal and state legislators have tried to regulate such development. They have tried to provide greater security to home purchasers, extend basic infrastructure to such areas, and offer grants for utility hookups. Most of these policies are designated for economically distressed counties, or *colonia* areas within 150 miles of the border (Ward 1999).

As in Latin America, here too, poor households rely on self-help activities to secure services: water is hooked up to the street network, septic systems are installed and maintained, water is fetched to fill tanks, and mercury lamps are installed to provide street and security floodlights at night. Some nongovernmental organizations have promoted collaborative group efforts to build housing in the border region. Of these, Projecto Azteca in Hidalgo County, Texas, which receives federal and Fannie Mae support, is probably the best known. Many dwellings are manufactured homes, and although there is significant self-building, self-help in these settlements also takes the form of self-management of the housing process.

Many of the same attributes of self-help that have proved so useful in Latin America are now being replicated by low-income households in the United States. Informality, flexibility, and some freedom from regulations make home ownership feasible and affordable, and allows for asset formation in both Latin America and the United States. Research has shown that these informal homestead subdivisions and *colonias* are part of low-wage labor markets in urban centers, such as Laredo and Austin, Texas; Tucson, Arizona; Santa Fe, New Mexico; Greensboro, North Carolina; and Knoxville, Tennessee (Ward and Peters 2007).

As awareness of self-building increases in the United States, policy-makers here can learn by importing some of the insights and best practices from Latin America. This is rarely the case, however. The first step is to acknowledge that self-help exists in our own back yard (Ward 2004). Just as Turner had to counteract the patronizing attitudes of middle-class urban planners and public officials about irregular settlements in Latin America, there is a sense of déjà vu when one hears comments now about *colonia* populations in Texas and other parts of the United States. They are viewed as homes for either undocumented migrants from Mexico or unemployed "welfare" cases, living in environmentally unsound and unsanitary conditions. Consequently, the policy interventions of the 1990s had two objectives. The first was to outlaw the further development of *colonias,* and the second was to provide infrastructure to already settled areas in order to improve health and sanitation conditions (Ward 1999). The problem, however, is that planning ideas are usually predicated on established engineering codes and standards. There is little or no interest in lowering standards, or in moving toward what some scholars call "progressive compliance," whereby poorer communities commit to moving gradually toward meeting codes and standards (Larson 2002). In the future, greater public appreciation of informal homestead subdivisions and those who live in them will be important if these areas are to be upgraded. Knee-jerk reactions and sanctions to regulate and outlaw *colonias* and informal homestead subdivisions are likely to be counterproductive, as they were in Latin America.

Somewhat paradoxically, therefore, while U.S. researchers have been effective in conducting studies of self-help housing in Latin America and in promoting their export to elsewhere as innovative planning ideas, policymakers in the United States have been reluctant to apply those insights to address problems at home. Such an attitude might have been excusable in the 1940s when Crane and others promoted self-help housing in Puerto Rico and elsewhere, but now that so much is known about the strengths of this approach worldwide, the fact that it is disregarded by U.S. policymakers seems nearsighted.

Conclusion

Self-help housing is practiced not only "out there," in less developed countries, it is also a rational response to low-income homesteaders' aspirations to participate in the American Dream. There is much we can do to learn from Latin America, by lateral thinking about policy and self-help activities to benefit the poor in North America. It behooves us to be willing to learn, and not to reinvent the wheel—as scholars or as policy makers. Clearly, there is a need for openness to others' experiences. That is necessary for developing a variety of policy solutions, including self-help, to address the needs of specific groups in the United States.

In reviewing the emergence of self-help as a planning idea, I have explored how and why this idea emerged from the corpus of research and thinking that existed at the time and, more important, how such ideas were shaped by the dominant paradigms of the day. Understanding this connection to dominant paradigms is crucial, not simply because it shapes the way we conduct research, pose questions, and use methodologies but also because it reveals the assumptions and beliefs underlying the theories and methods researchers use, even though not all may be useful. Also, we must consider how far the results generated and the policy positions formulated are likely to gain purchase and be adopted in the policy-making environment. This is not to suggest that researchers should be opportunistic, gauging their findings to fit within the dominant discourse and orthodoxies of the day; quite the opposite. Useful research must test and challenge orthodox ideas and think outside the box, even when one is aware that there may be little chance of these ideas gaining acceptability, at least in the short term. In many respects, this is what John Turner and others did, turning our heads toward the realities of self-help housing and inviting policymakers to rethink their stereotypical views and their misguided policies. By recognizing how ideas flourish and fade within particular social constructions and dominant paradigms of the day, one may more readily accept that ideas evolve and change over time—sometimes by 180 degrees—as this chapter has, I hope, demonstrated.

Notes

1. The invitation to participate in the year-long colloquium series at MIT had particular significance for me, since my early thinking about self-help was influenced by individuals from Boston and Cambridge, Massachusetts. In 1973, as a graduate student of geography from the University of Liverpool, I was en route to Mexico City to begin my doctoral fieldwork on squatter settlements, as they were then called. Earlier that year I had met with the late Tony Leeds, then a professor of anthropology at Boston University, who, with his wife, Liz Leeds, was on sabbatical at Oxford University. Professor Leeds had taken me under his wing, given me access to his personal archives and bibliographic materials, and shared many of his ideas about "squatments," as he called them. It was Tony and Liz who had urged me to make a stopover in Boston to meet several of their colleagues in the Cambridge area at the time—namely, Wayne Cornelius, then in Political Science at MIT; William Doebele at Harvard; John Turner, who together with Lloyd Rodwin and Lisa Peattie formed the "belle epoch" of Architecture and Planning at MIT; and Susan Eckstein, a sociologist who was then an assistant professor at Boston University, where she still teaches. In retrospect, MIT's influence on planning ideas at the time was remarkable. The most known was the project to assist the city of Ciudad Guayana in Venezuela. Led by Lloyd Rodwin and others, this project offered faculty and graduate students an opportunity to engage in policy making and apply conventional planning solutions to a developing country.

2. John Turner was a visiting professor whose star status at the time led to Rodwin's decision to recruit him to MIT on a short-term contract. However, the two had very different perspectives on development and both had large egos, so it is not surprising that they clashed, leading to Turner's return to the UK in the mid-1970s. Another star in the making then was a tenure-track professor, John Friedmann, whose early work on planning theory was disregarded by Rodwin. Friedmann went on to head the planning program at UCLA.

3. "Wet cores" provided a slab and a basic service unit—usually a bathroom/w.c. around which the household could build and extend a dwelling. It ensured a stable foundation and a minimum level of infrastructure, as shown in figures 11.3a and b.

4. These innerburbs in Latin America are the focus of a multi-site collaboration of researchers in eleven Latin American cities working to a common methodology under the umbrella of a University of Texas team. For further details, see www.lahn.utexas.org.

References

Abrams, C. 1964. *Housing in the Modern World: Man's Struggle for Shelter in an Urbanizing World.* Cambridge, MA: MIT Press.

Abrams, C. 1966. *Squatter Settlements, the Problem and the Opportunity.* Washington, DC: Department of Housing and Urban Development.

Baross, P. 1990. Sequencing Land Development: The Price Implication of Legal and Illegal Settlement Growth. In *The Transformation of Land Supply Systems in Third World Cities*, ed. Paul Baross and Jan van der Linden, 57–82. Aldershot, UK: Avebury.

Burgess, Rod. 1982. Self-Help Housing Advocacy: A Curious Form of Radicalism. A Critique of the Work of John F.C. Turner. In Ward, *Self-Help Housing*, 55–97.

Burgess, Rod. 1985. The Limits to State-Aided Self-Help Housing Programmes. *Development and Change* 16:271–312.

Burnham, R. 1998. *Housing Ourselves: Creating Affordable, Sustainable Shelter*. New York: McGraw-Hill.

Cornelius, Wayne. 1975. *Politics and Migrant Poor in Mexico City*. Stanford, CA: Stanford University Press.

Davies, C. S., and R. Holz. 1992. Settlement Evolution of the "*Colonias*" along the US-Mexico Border: The Case of the Lower Rio Grande Valley of Texas. *Habitat International* 16 (4): 119–142.

Faber, M., and D. Seers, eds. 1972. *The Crisis in Planning*. London: Chatto and Windus.

Gans, H. 1962. *The Urban Villagers: Group and Class in the Life of Italian-Americans*. New York: Free Press of Glencoe.

González de la Rocha, Mercedes. 2001. From the Resources of Poverty to the Poverty of Resources? The Erosion of a Survival Model. *Latin American Perspectives* 28 (4): 72–100.

Hall, Peter. 1982. *Great Planning Disasters*. Berkeley: University of California Press.

Harms, H. 1976. Limitations of Self-Help. *Architectural Design*, 46.

Harms, H. 1982. Historical Perspectives on the Practice and Politics of Self-Help Housing. In Ward, *Self-Help Housing*, 17–53.

Hardy, D., and Colin Ward. 1984. *Arcadia for All: The Legacy of a Makeshift Landscape*. London: Mansell.

Harris, Richard. 1998. The Silence of the Experts: "Aided Self-Help Housing," 1939–54. *Habitat International* 22 (2): 165–189.

Harris, Richard. 1999. Slipping through the Cracks: The Origins of Aided Self-Help Housing 1918–1953. *Housing Studies* 14 (3): 281–309.

Harris, Richard. 2001. Irregular Settlement and Government Policy in North America and the Twentieth Century. In *Memoria of a Research Workshop "Irregular Settlement and Self-Help Housing in the United States,"* 13–16, Cambridge, MA, Lincoln Institute of Land Policy, September 21–22.

Home, Robert. 2001. Negotiating Security of Tenure for Peri-Urban Settlement: Traveller Gypsies and the Planning System in the United Kingdom. In *Memoria of a Research Workshop "Irregular Settlement and Self-Help Housing in the United States,"* 1718 Cambridge, MA, Lincoln Institute of Land Policy, September 21–22.

Jacobs, Jane. 1961. *The Death and Life of Great American Cities*. New York: Vintage Press.

Larson, J. 2002. Informality, Illegality and Inequality. *Yale Law & Policy Review* 20:137–182.

Leeds, Elizabeth. 1972. Forms of Squatment Political Organization: The Politics of Control in Brazil. Master's thesis, University of Texas.

Mangin, William. 1967. The Latin American Squatter Settlements: A Problem and a Solution. *Latin American Research Review* 2 (3): 65–98.

Mukhija, V., and P. Monkonnen. 2006. Federal Colonias Policy in California: Too Broad and Too Narrow. *Housing Policy Debate* 17 (4):755–780.

Office of the Attorney general of Texas. 1996. *Forgotten Americans: Life in the Texas Colonias*. Austin, TX. Office of the Attorney General.

Peattie, Lisa. 1968. *The View from the Barrio*. Ann Arbor: University of Michigan Press.

Peattie, Lisa. 1987. *Planning: Rethinking Ciudad Guayana*. Ann Arbor: University of Michigan.

Perlman, Janice E. 1976. *The Myth of Marginality: Urban Poverty and Politics in Rio de Janeiro*. Berkeley: University of California Press.

Portes, Alejandro. 1972. Rationality in the Slums: An Essay in Interpretive Sociology. *Comparative Studies in Society and History* 14 (3).

Rojas Williams, Susana M. 2005. "'Young Town' Growing Up—Four Decades Later: Self-help Housing and Upgrading Lessons from a Squatter Neighborhood in Lima." MCP and SMArchS thesis, Massachusetts Institute of Technology.

Schulist, T., and R. Harris. 2002. "Build Your Own Home": State-Assisted Self-Help Housing in Canada, 1942–75. *Planning Perspectives* 17 (4): 345–372.

Turner, J. F. C. 1969. Uncontrolled Urban Settlements: Problems and Solutions. In *The City in Newly Developed Countries*, ed. G. Breese, 507–534. Englewood Cliffs, NJ: Prentice Hall.

Turner, J. F. C. 1967. Barriers and Channels for Housing Development in Modernizing Countries. *Journal of the American Institute of Planners* 33 (3): 167–180.

Turner, J. F. C. 1968a. Housing Priorities, Settlement Patterns and Urban Development in Modernizing Countries. *Journal of the American Institute of Planners* 34:354–363.

Turner, J. F. C. 1968b. The Squatter Settlement: Architecture That Works. *Architectural Design* 38:355–360.

Turner, J. F. C. 1976. *Housing by People: Towards Autonomy in Building Environments*. London: Marion Boyars.

Turner, J. F. C., 1982. Issues in Self-Help and Self-Managed Housing. In *Self-Help Housing: A Critique*, ed. Peter M. Ward, 99–114. London: Mansell

Turner, J. F. C., and R. Fichter, eds. 1972. *Freedom to Build: Dweller Control of the Housing Process*. New York: Macmillan.

Ward, Peter M., ed. 1982. *Self-Help Housing: A Critique*. London: Mansell.

Ward, Peter M., ed. 1999. *Colonias and Public Policy in Texas and Mexico: Urbanization by Stealth*. Austin: University of Texas Press.

Ward, Peter M., ed. 2004 Informality of Housing Production at the Urban-Rural Interface: The Not-so-Strange Case of Colonias in the US—Texas, the Border and Beyond. In *Urban Informality*, ed. Ananya Roy and Nezar AlSayyad, 243–270. Berkeley: University of California, Center for Middle Eastern Studies.

Ward, Peter M. 2005. The Lack of "Cursive Thinking" with Social theory and Public Policy: Four Decades of Marginality and Rationality in the So-Called "Slum." In *Rethinking Development in Latin America*, ed. Bryan Roberts and Charles Wood, 271–296. Philadelphia: Pennsylvania State University Press.

Ward, Peter, C. Guisti, and F. de Souza. 2004. Colonia Land and Housing Market Performance and the Impact of Lot Title Regularization in Texas. *Urban Studies* 41 (13): 2621–2646.

Ward, Peter, and Paul Peters. 2007. Self-Help Housing and Informal Homesteading in Peri-Urban America: Settlement Identification Using Digital Imagery and GIS. *Habitat International* 31 (2):141–164.

Ward, Peter, and Esther Sullivan. 2010. Sustainable Housing Design and Technology Adoption in *Colonias*, Informal Homestead Subdivisions, and the "Inner-burbs." www.lahn.utexas.org.

World Bank. 1972. *Urbanization (Sector Policy Paper)*. Washington, DC: World Bank.

Young, M., and P. Willmott. 1957. *Family and Kinship in East London*. London: Routledge and Kegan Paul.

IV
Ideas about Professional Reflection

12

Reflective Practice

Raphaël Fischler

A person faces a situation. If the situation is very familiar, little if any learning will take place. If the situation is difficult, one effort follows another until available response resources are exhausted. . . . Any new response accepted for subsequent use becomes *by that fact* incorporated into the organism. That is, learning results. . . .

But further: . . . the whole person is involved in each act—thinking, feeling, impulse, moving, et cetera. . . . We never learn just the one named thing, but always *simultaneously* we are building attitudes, habits, thoughts, et cetera. (Kilpatrick 1935, 610)

The words of William Heard Kilpatrick, professor of education and disciple of John Dewey, encapsulate much of what we understand by reflective practice.[1] Educators have understood for a long time that professional behavior evolves as individuals learn from experience, especially from confrontation with novelty. Although the general idea of reflective practice can be found in writings from as far back as the first decades of the twentieth century, the expression "reflective practice" itself is a fairly new one; it appeared in the scholarly and professional literature only in the 1980s. The emergence of this concept and its diffusion in the field of urban planning were mainly due to the work of a single individual. How this individual built his theory of reflective practice, what sources he drew from, and what following he has had in urban planning are the questions I probe in this chapter. In particular, I explore a paradox: reflective practice has become a very familiar idea among planning scholars and practitioners, but it has not become a significant subject of research in the field; the concept is at once popular and marginal.[2]

The Idea of Reflective Practice in Historical Perspective

Reflective practice is a form of professional activity in which the practitioner assesses her own experience critically and submits it to the scrutiny of others. While believing strongly in her mission, she acknowledges the subjectivity of her assumptions and the limitations of her methods, and she responds to challenges by examining her own ways of thinking and doing. Such a review of ideas and actions can be motivated by the desire to increase one's effectiveness, but it is often prompted by surprise, when established ways of acting are inadequate to deal with new problems (Yanow and Tsoukas 2007). In general, practicing reflectively means learning by doing and learning from doing; at best, it means pushing the boundaries of one's field and questioning one's role in it. Reflective practitioners consciously aim to improve their practice by analyzing their own experience. They improve their professional behavior and ameliorate its effects by sustained inquiry into the causes, meanings, and consequences of their actions.

To understand how professionals learn in action and from action, and to appreciate how they challenge their own assumptions, we must study their practice up close. We need to witness their interactions with clients and superiors and understand their thoughts as they face novel situations that force them to reevaluate what they take for granted. But such detailed accounts of what actually goes on in the mind of a professional planner are rare. Until recently, few people volunteered to articulate their thought process. There is no historical record of the microdynamics of professional planning practice for most of the twentieth century, no archive of first-person narratives or of personal interviews in which practitioners from various generations describe how they reflect in action and on action. It is only in the 1980s that such observations, narratives, and interviews were published in a systematic manner.

True, personal accounts of planning practice did start appearing by the 1930s, as some of the pioneers of the new field of city planning were reaching retirement (e.g., Bassett 1939). Written as autobiographies, these works cover many years of professional and public activities but do not capture either the richness of daily practice or the subtleties of the mental processes unfolding in daily tasks.[3] Sociological studies of city planning in the 1950s and 1960s delved into the details of planning processes—indeed, the planning process was their focus—but they did so with an emphasis on social interactions and on the drama of public decision making, not on individual behavior and cognition (Meyerson and Banfield 1955; Altshuler 1965). The memoirs of planners active in the 1970s, such as *Making City Planning Work*, by Allan Jacobs (1980), and *Making Equity Planning Work*, by Norman Krumholz and John

Forester (1990), offer some detailed narratives that highlight the need for political astuteness and moral backbone to operate effectively in the turbulent world of municipal politics. But only around 1980 did planning scholars begin to record practitioners' stories and reflections. A number of publications from this period showcase planners confronting complex situations, dealing with surprises, and questioning their own assumptions (Baum 1983; Hoch 1994; Forester 1999).

In short, for the first three-quarters of the century of modern planning, there is no evidence of how planners thought in daily practice. We know that some individuals in past decades were innovative, successful professionals, and we can assume that their achievements owed much to reflective practice. Archival material on the work of designers, for example, shows how they grappled with unique situations and responded to the unexpected demands of clients. Also, conference proceedings over the years document how planners responded to criticism from the public and from colleagues. But these professionals would, for the most part, not have identified with the Reflective Practitioner as we define him or her today. As they strove to create a new profession, early city planners did learn from practice, given the novelty of their task, but they were more inclined, for the sake of public legitimacy, to act and speak with authority than with humility. Indeed, they did much to create the image of the expert against which the persona of the Reflective Practitioner is set (Hancock 1967; Moskowitz 2004). The rise of the City Scientific movement and of university education in city planning cultivated a vision of progress based on technological advancement and of professional practice based on the application of scientific knowledge (Ford 1913; Regional Plan of New York and Its Environs [1929] 1974). It is specifically in contrast to this characterization of practice as the application of technical expertise that reflective practice would be defined by the 1980s. Our task now is to explain how the idea and ideal of reflective practice emerged from the critique of modern professionalism.

An important element in the history of reflective practice is the fact that its *theory* was introduced in the field of city planning—and indeed, in many other professional fields—in large measure by one person, Donald A. Schön. Spanning a rich career in consultancy, government, and academia, Schön developed a powerful analysis of how a new product, policy, or plan actually gets designed, what it means to be a professional, and how one learns, individually and collectively. Unable to draft a history of reflective practice as it may have taken place in twentieth-century planning, we can analyze Schön's writings as a "second-best" way to understand the emergence of the idea of reflective practice as a key planning idea.

The Idea of Reflective Practice

To simplify things, one may say that Donald Schön transposed to professional practice what John Dewey said of education. For Dewey, all "learning [occurs] through personal experience" (Dewey [1938] 1997, 21). More precisely, the learning process is driven by "difficulty to be overcome by the exercise of intelligence" (ibid., 79). Learning takes place when one faces unfamiliar situations. In such cases, "we cannot tell just what the consequences of observed conditions will be unless we go over past experiences in our mind, unless we reflect upon them and by seeing what is similar in them to those now present, go on to form a judgment of what may be expected in the present situation" (ibid., 68). What education cultivates in the classroom in a planned way, professional life does in the field in a haphazard fashion: it confronts individuals with puzzling problems that test their ability to observe and decide; it places them in situations that force them, sometimes literally, to stop and think. At those times, the professional-as-learner may reflect on her experience; that is, she may "look back over what has been done so as to extract the net meanings which are the capital stock for intelligent dealing with further experiences" (ibid., 87).

Schön's debt to Dewey is evident (and acknowledged). But Schön's theory of reflective practice is more than a mere elaboration of Dewey's pedagogical doctrine. It is based on four decades of empirical research on the ways in which professionals define problems and design solutions, on the technological and organizational contexts that shape their modes of action, on the meaning of professionalism and the nature of professional knowledge, on the interaction of professionals with clients and colleagues, and, indeed, on the education of professionals.

Schön's first publications appeared at the same time as a number of transformative books that questioned dominant paradigms (Sanyal 1998). Jane Jacobs's *Death and Life of Great American Cities* (Jacobs 1961), Rachel Carson's *Silent Spring* (Carson 1962), and Betty Friedan's *The Feminine Mystique* (Friedan 1963) all critiqued male-dominated technocracy. Strife over civil rights, race riots, and antiwar protests in the 1960s increased the sense of malaise and the need for social and political reforms. In his own writings, however, Schön did not frame the predicament of the 1960s in political terms. He defined the problem of the day as the fast pace of technological change and the instability it created. Schön argued that technological innovation alters the way in which people live in the present and contemplate the future. It provokes anxiety, which in turn makes people cling even more tightly to conventional theories of science and progress. Such theories, much more than specific policies, were the targets of Schön's critique. His goal was not to undo the political status quo but to upset the epistemological status quo (Schön 1986). His aim was not to change specific policies but to alter ways of decision making.

As a graduate student, Schön was inspired by John Dewey's pragmatic theory of inquiry, which was the topic of his dissertation in philosophy at Harvard (Schön 1954). In that work, Schön asks what conditions make for a rational decision-making process. Drawing on Dewey and using examples from everyday life as well as from professional practice (e.g., a driver whose car runs out of gas, a plant manager who is facing work stoppages, a doctor who finds a tumor in a patient), Schön argues that practical decision making—which answers the question, what must be done?—involves problem formulation. A "problematic situation" must be turned into a coherent "problem," a statement of difficulties and possibilities that, through iteration, becomes a plan of action which "would resolve the problematic situation" (ibid., 3). Key elements in this process are the discovery of ends, the design of alternatives, and the use of intuition and metaphors. The professional is no mere technician; his task is to deal with problematic situations that are hard to define objectively and that can sometimes be solved only temporarily, or in a partial rather than comprehensive way.

Schön understood that professional practice in the postmodern era must deal with "situations of [complexity,] uncertainty, instability, uniqueness, and value conflict" (Schön 1983, 49). These situational characteristics make "the patterns of tasks and knowledge [that professionals bring to their work] inherently unstable" (ibid., 15) and render traditional techniques of analysis and decision making inadequate. To train practitioners for such a context, one needs to understand what makes it possible for some individuals to deal successfully with indeterminacy. Their "artful competence" (ibid., 19), as Schön calls it, rests on their ability to reflect *in* action—"thinking what [one is] doing while [one is] doing it" (Schön 1987, xi) —and to reflect *on* action, that is, to examine critically what one did, after the fact. Hence professionals and their educators must appreciate an epistemological shift "from technical rationality to reflection-in-action" (Schön 1983, 21). Schön pursued this goal through four decades of research, teaching, and consulting.

In his first book, *Displacement of Concepts* (Schön 1963), Schön argues that insofar as the new always emerges from the old, innovation requires the transposition of concepts from a familiar situation to a novel one, and their reinterpretation and adaptation. This process of displacement is evident in "sleeping metaphors" (ibid., 79) borrowed from other fields, for example when one speaks of a computer's "memory." Such metaphors can help us define phenomena that we want to control, mentally and functionally. For example, a planner may speak of a "slum" as a "cancer" that needs to be taken out before it spreads to healthy urban tissue. Metaphors enable us to see things in useful (though not always beneficial) ways, as things that are familiar problems. They allow for the "selective inattention [that is] essential to action" and for "the openness to disturbing novelty [that is] essential for discovery" (ibid., 97; see also Schön 1978). For Schön, discovery "is always a social process" (Schön 1963, 99). It requires a dialogue with real or imagined critics. The need to frame puzzling situations by "selective inattention," the emotional investment professionals make in their tasks and environments, and the dialogue (social or internal) that is necessary to make sense of a problematic situation—all these are insights that Schön inherited from Dewey and developed further in his work.

Schön's next book, *Technology and Change* (1967), focuses on the social impacts of technological change. It introduces another idea that earned Schön notoriety, the notion of an assumed "stable state." People delude themselves, Schön claims, when they believe that their identity and the practices, occupations and institutions that underlie their identity are stable; they fool themselves when they assume that historical change leaves value systems unaffected. But Schön does not really analyze this general "self-deception" (Schön 1967, xiii). His critique at this point is more modest and at the same time more relevant to planning in that it questions the "rational view of invention as an orderly, plannable process" (ibid., xviii). Schön argues that innovation has an element of "nonrationality," in the sense that it does not consist in the rational application of scientific means to established objectives. Rather, it involves "a complex process in which goals are discovered, determined and modified along the way" rather than given from the start and in which "leaps of decision" are made without adequate evidence. It is a process without end because a proposed solution typically "responds to the problems of earlier efforts and creates new problems requiring solution." "Invention is full of unanticipated twists and turns," Schön notes. "It is," he adds, "a juggling of variables in response to problems and opportunities discovered along the way" (ibid., 8–41 passim).

Planning for innovation must acknowledge the role of nonrationality and uncertainty in decision making. Good planning to foster change does not impose a set design from the top; it calls for openness to change and to the initiatives of all stakeholders. It requires that team members have the freedom to address individual feelings and interpersonal relations, to challenge preconceived ideas about mandates and methods, to confront taboos, and to define ends as well as means. This requires, in turn, that all stakeholders trust each other's ability to make good decisions with imperfect information, to exercise discretion without arbitrariness, to tolerate experimentation, and to share responsibility for success and failure. Making good decisions in the face of uncertainty requires an attitude that Schön, together with Chris Argyris, would later define as the behavioral model of the Reflective Practitioner, which they labeled Model II behavior.

In his next book, *Beyond the Stable State* (1971), Schön proposes that in an era of fast-paced innovation, "Individuals must somehow confront and negotiate, in their own persons, the transformations which used to be handled by generational change." They must "become adept at learning" and their institutions must become "'learning systems', that is to say, systems capable of bringing about their own continuing transformation" (Schön 1971, 27, 30). To do so, organizations must recognize not only their explicit but also their implicit theories of action, and their members must learn to recognize both their "espoused theories" and their "theories-in-use." Espoused theory is theory a professional uses to justify her actions when asked to do so; theory-in-use is theory that guides her actions in reality and that is revealed by them. In learning organizations, planners can work as designers of multidisciplinary networks, as negotiators, brokers, or facilitators, as managers of a dialogical process through which problems are defined and solved.

Thus, in 1971 Schön emerges as a critic of dominant planning practice, particularly its pretense of mastery and control. In a situation characterized by the loss of the stable state, he argues, the conventional (rational/experimental) model of decision making can neither represent the reality of planning nor even serve as a normative model of planning. Since planners cannot aspire to the same rigor as scientists working in a lab, public problems cannot be addressed through controlled experiments. Schön warns planners that it is impossible to know a situation fully, to understand all its causes and consequences, to test alternative responses in a rigorous manner, to generate standard solutions to problems.[4]

Having dismissed the dominant planning model, Schön closes *Beyond the Stable State* by asking what a proper model might be. He considers the alternatives—the imposition of a given view by authority, ideological commitment to a specific approach, nihilism and inaction, and systems analysis—but rejects them all as either unacceptable or inadequate. Only an existentialist approach, he claims, can be valid. What matters most is experience "in the here-and-now," experience of the particular situation at hand, in all its uniqueness. This means that the professional must give up the illusion of control and must see herself as a "learning agent." She must be able to listen. She must be able to "tolerate the anxieties of confrontation" with messy realities and conflicting viewpoints. She must, in the end, adopt "an ethic for existential knowing" which is "a code for public learning" (Schön 1971, 232, 236). Under this code, the professional must resolve important dilemmas of practice: the dilemma between the desire for security and the acknowledgment of uncertainty, the dilemma between the necessity of conviction and the recognition that beliefs are subjective, the dilemma between the need for reasoned action and the knowledge that decision making requires leaps of faith.

Schön elaborated these ideas with Chris Argyris, a social psychologist and organizational theorist at Harvard (Argyris and Schön 1974). In *Theory in Practice*, Argyris and Schön formalized the concept of theory-in-action (or theory-in-use) and developed the ideas of single-loop and double-loop learning (first proposed by W. R. Ashby). Their aim was to help professionals "become competent in taking action and simultaneously reflecting on this action to learn from it" (ibid., 4). To acquire this competence, practitioners must become conscious of the theories-in-use that guide their actions, that is, the generally subconscious, informal reasons they have for doing what they do. For example, a planner may define his mandate officially as the application of zoning regulations in the public interest; but his actions may reveal that what truly motivates him is to participate in the design of real-estate development projects.

From confrontation with a puzzling or difficult situation one can learn better ways of performing one's tasks. But one can also learn to reframe one's tasks and to revise both the descriptive and normative schemes through which one understands reality. In the first case, single-loop learning helps one be technically more efficient; in the second case, double-loop learning helps one redefine the ideas, perspectives, and norms that one brings to the performance of one's tasks. The planner in charge of zoning, for example, may learn to process an application faster. That is single-loop learning. He may also learn to change his priorities when negotiating with an architect over a given project, caring more about the quality of their exchange in the long run than about the number of changes he is able to impose. That is double-loop learning.

There is much resistance to changing one's theories-in-use. Only when professional effectiveness is compromised and single-loop learning fails is one generally willing to question one's practice in a fundamental manner. Practitioners who suppress feedback, internal and external, will stick to their theories-in-use even if this makes them even more dysfunctional. To Argyris and Schön, this is an example of Model I theories-in-use, the dominant model among professionals. Practitioners who adopt double-loop learning in their conversation with the situation and with others work under Model II theories-in-use. The "governing variables" (Argyris and Schön 1974, 15) of Model I and Model II are very different. In Model I, control is of the essence. Practitioners presume that they are dealing with win/lose situations, that Model I is the modus operandi of others, that an objective, unemotional stance is a condition of effectiveness, and that testing assumptions openly is too risky. Under Model II, dialogue is primordial. Here, key principles are: maximizing the validity and transparency of information, including information on values and objectives; maximizing the possibility of making free and informed choices; and maximizing responsibility for choices made.[5]

The Reflective Practitioner, published in 1983, is to a large extent a summation and elaboration of ideas that Schön had put forward earlier.[6] Applying his ideas now to diverse fields of practice, such as architecture, city planning, management, and psychotherapy, Schön relies on five case studies—among them the classic chapter titled "Some of What a Planner Knows" (Schön 1982) (in which a planner interacts with a developer on the basis of a Model I theory-in-use)—to sharpen his own understanding of reflective practice.[7] His starting point is that excellence in professional practice requires artistry as well as science and that much professional knowledge lies beyond the conscious thoughts of practitioners, let alone their formal theories (Schmidt 2000). In developing his argument, he comes back to key ideas from previous books: the crisis of legitimacy of the professions and of their technocratic ambitions; the importance of framing in the definition of problems and tasks; the nature of reflective practice as "a [metaphorically] reflective conversation with a unique and uncertain situation" (Schön 1983, 130) and as "a literally reflective conversation" with the client (ibid., 295); the unity of thinking and doing in knowing-in-action and in reflecting-in-action; the ability to learn from experience by surfacing and questioning theories-in-use; the distinction between Model I and Model II theories-in-use; the difference between single-loop and double-loop learning. Once again, Schön emphasizes the possibility of social learning from the exposure of organizational dilemmas and conflicts and the consequent reevaluation of routines, principles, and values, and he urges professionals to recognize uncertainty and error, to welcome challenges, to acknowledge their values and feelings, and to understand their roles as advocates and facilitators. In a masterful synthesis of the "demystification of professional expertise" (ibid., 345), Schön argues most convincingly that professional legitimacy lies in one's ability and willingness to reflect-in-action.

The Widespread Diffusion but Limited Impact of Schön's Ideas

Although planning academics cite Schön's writings—in particular *The Reflective Practitioner*—quite frequently, most pay lip service to his ideas, usually mentioning that the purpose of their theoretical and pedagogical work "is to help young planners to become, as Donald Schön has taught us, reflective practitioners" (Friedmann 1995, 157). (The clear exceptions are John Forester [1985, 1987, 1991, 1999], who worked with Schön, and Howell Baum [1990, 1995, 1997a, 1997b].) This state of affairs is borne out by a review of scholarly articles in the field of urban studies and planning that appeared in the twenty-five years following the publication of *The Reflective Practitioner* and in which the work of Donald Schön is cited. Of the 253 journal articles found to have one or more references to Schön's writings, very few represent an attempt to apply Schön's theory in novel ways, to test his propositions as hypotheses, to expand on his ideas, or otherwise to engage his work in a direct manner. Virtually no title (or abstract) clearly indicates a debt to Schön or a disagreement with him (for an exception, see Filor 1994). And even when a title refers to reflective practice, the authors do not necessarily mention Schön and his work (e.g., Balducci and Bertolini 2007). This is in contrast to fields such as education, social work, or management, where authors explicitly address Schön's ideas and express that engagement in the title of their articles (e.g., Hart 1990; Kullman 1998; Weshah 2007).[8] In planning, Schön's name is mentioned often but his ideas are debated rarely.

The idea of reflective practice did gain real currency in one particular subfield of city planning, planning education. Here, Schön's strong and clear propositions (Schön 1970, 1985, 1987; Schön and Nutt 1974) make his work a nearly unavoidable reference. The relative weight of practical instruction—as opposed to theoretical teaching—and the manner of imparting it—by means of case studies, role-playing, studio projects, internships, and the like—remain key issues in any discussion of professional education, in planning as in other fields. Respect for Schön's work among planning educators was expressed through the institution, in 1999, of the Don Schön Award for Excellence in Learning from Practice by the Association of Collegiate Schools of Planning (ASCP). The award recognizes student papers, theses, or reports for "excellence in the writer's personal and/or professional learning from practice and in the analysis of that learning" (ACSP 2011). From the entries submitted for the award (which I have read as member of the selection committee), one can see that the meaning of reflection-in-action and reflection-on-action is not altogether clear among students and among the professors who support their submissions. Most submitted essays present accounts of practical work done in a practicum or action research. Very few, however, really document reflective practice among their authors—an ability to learn from the research or consulting experience—or among the subjects whose actions they describe. In contrast to the helping professions, management, and other fields, planning has not seen a sustained "reflective turn" in the study of professional practice and education (Schön 1991).

The paucity of a serious debate on Schön's theory of reflective practice in planning may be due to problems inherent in that theory. First, it is a rather complex theory with areas of vagueness. For example, the ideas of "knowing-in-action," "theory-in-action," and "reflection-in-action" are not easy to grasp intuitively or analyze empirically, nor are they easy to distinguish one from the other. Like other such notions created to explain human behavior (e.g., Pierre Bourdieu's *habitus*), "theory-in-use" suffers from a lack of clear definition. Theories-in-use are assumed (rather than known) to exist, and their actual contents remain somewhat obscure.

Second, the theory of reflective practice is very much a theory of individual behavior, in which larger economic and political factors receive little attention. Schön did address policy issues in the book he co-authored with Martin Rein (Schön and Rein 1994). *Frame Reflection* brought together Schön's work on reflective practice with Rein's work on policy making to show how policy controversies could be resolved when participants reflectively explored their own problem definitions. But even this book has been faulted for "play[ing] down the role of power in intractable conflicts" (Gray 1996, 577; see also Gilroy 1993; Smith 1999).

Third, Schön's work is an inquiry into organizational behavior and organizational learning. Yet planning researchers in the past two decades have shown little interest in studying organizations in the same way, preferring instead to focus attention on group processes that transcend the boundaries of established organizations and, in fact, challenge such boundaries (e.g., Innes 1992).

Finally, the limited dialogue between planning scholars and Schön may also be due to Schön's dislike of traditional planning research. He did not write for an academic audience and he did not feel the need to situate his contribution in the existing planning literature. He displayed little appreciation for contemporary planning theory except for the work of scholars such as John Forester and Howell Baum, who write about practitioners with empathy (Schön 1994). Schön had little patience with the "high-level interpretation" that is fashionable in scholarly publishing and with the jargon-filled writing that passes for good prose in academia. In contrast to such theoretical posturing, he preferred "the practical good sense and wisdom" that thoughtful practitioners display (ibid., 131, 136).

However modest the engagement of planning academics with Schön's ideas, it seems to be even more modest, ironically, among practicing planners. Reflective practice is a reality, and it has been documented (e.g., Forester, Fischler, and Shmueli 2001). But there is little evidence that the theory of reflective practice has significantly influenced what planners do. In contrast to such concepts as "sustainable development," "new urbanism," "smart growth," "citizen participation," or "democratic governance," the notion of reflective practice is not the stuff of official plans or public policies. There is no movement, no state law, not even a press release that indicates a collective commitment to reflective practice by practicing planners. In the marketplace of ideas that inform practice, qualities of urban form (usually expressed in terms such as sustainable, green, or otherwise smart development) and of democratic decision making (conveyed by terms such as governance, participation, or inclusion) have acquired more importance than qualities of professional comportment.

No survey has been conducted to examine how many planning professionals see themselves as reflective practitioners, what they believe the adjective "reflective" actually means, whether they assess their own practice according to that standard, or how the present might compare with the past in those respects. The website of the American Planning Association provides limited and rather imperfect evidence on these issues. A search of the site yields few mentions of the term "reflective" (in the sense that interests us here) and even fewer mentions of the expression "reflective practice" or "reflective practitioner" (e.g., Hoben 2001). Among the members of the AICP College of Fellows—more than four hundred individuals who made exceptional contributions to the profession—only two are said to be "reflective practitioners." Most profiles of Fellows reflect an appreciation of effectiveness and expertise in rather conventional ways (AICP 2008).

Yet there are some signs that reflective practice may eventually gain in value as a norm of good planning. Judging from the contents of the *Journal of Planning Education and Research*, the main outlet for articles on professional planning education in North America, there has been a renewal of interest in practice-based teaching and in a rapprochement between academia and the profession (e.g., Wachs 1994; Baum 1997b; Shepherd and Cosgriff 1998; Brooks et al. 2002). Also, as the work of Judith Innes and other researchers indicates, planning practice seems to be evolving in ways that require practitioners to reflect-in-action and to learn from doing (Innes 1995). The increasing level of uncertainty, complexity, and conflict that characterizes collective decision making may induce planners to move away from conventional roles and to take on roles as mediators, facilitators, and advocates in collaborative processes (Healey 1997; Forester 1999; Innes and Booher 1999). This, in turn, will require the type of artful competence that Schön noted in successful professionals and the open personal stance that Schön and Argyris identified as necessary for Model II behavior.

Together with other ideas first promoted in the 1960s, the idea of reflective practice helped deflate planners' conventional claims to truth and authority. But unlike radical critiques of planning, it did so in a way that is sympathetic to individual planners, shows trust in their ability to learn from their mistakes, and lays out a path to better practice.

At its best, reflective practice is more than effective or thoughtful practice. It is characterized by a constant willingness to question one's habitual ways of doing and thinking, a readiness to eschew standard, ready-made answers for unique solutions crafted in response to specific constraints. Reflection-in-action emerges from the difficulty of coping with a new problem: "presented with a situation that troubles [them], calls a halt to action, seems to require certain transformations," Schön wrote, professionals must learn to adjust their behavior appropriately and, if that fails, to adjust their assumptions, models, and theories as well (Schön 1954, 3). As John Dewey, Schön's *maître à penser*, argued also in 1954 (in a new edition of an older work), the theory of reflective practice is not a substantive theory of action; its business is not to determine what our decisions should be.[9] Rather, reflective practice can "aid in [the] creation of methods such that experimentation may go on less blindly, less at the mercy of accident, more intelligently, so that men may learn from their errors and profit by their successes" (Dewey [1927] 1954, 34).

What makes reflective practice a powerful idea is also what makes it difficult to accept and to apply: it holds the promise of improved collective action in the future by imposing a burden of individual responsibility in the here and now. One would be "naively optimistic," a reviewer of *The Reflective Practitioner* noted, to think that all planners can readily acquire the aptitudes and attitudes that Schön discovered among the best professionals (Schwartz 1987, 616). Local culture and politics can be inimical to the development of open dialogue; institutions often keep relationships with clients and with superiors set in hierarchical patterns; traditions in many places emphasize deference and pride (Richmond 2007). Also, developing the kind of mindset and behavior that Schön found exemplary requires a certain emotional and intellectual maturity. To be reflective practitioners, professionals must be "inquisitive," "open-minded," "flexible," "willing to revise judgment," "honest," "diligent," and more (Chitty 2005, 308)—a tall psychological order for any individual.

Yet the idea of reflective practice remains appealing, particularly for professionals in the helping professions and even for private-sector managers who believe in self-improvement. Paradoxically, what may give it broader application in the years to come is a pragmatic response to changing economic conditions. Success in the postindustrial workplace will require creativity in daily practice, flexibility in job assignments, and lifelong learning in career development (Reich 1992). Knowing how to deal with surprise and failure and knowing how to handle uncertainty, complexity, and conflict will be required of all symbolic analysts, including city planners.

Notes

1. I thank John Forester for his critical and extremely helpful feedback on an earlier draft of this chapter, in particular with respect to the links between Schön's work and contemporary writings in sociology and political science. I am grateful

as well to Tony Ghaye, Langley Keyes, Jonathan Richmond, Tina Rosan, Bish Sanyal, Mary Schmidt, Larry Vale, and Dvora Yanow for sharing comments on this work, ideas on reflective practice in general, and, in some cases, unpublished writings on the subject. Finally, I wish to thank Dr. Scott Fishman and Dr. Michael Moskowitz for personifying reflective practice.

2. I was a student of Donald Schön at MIT and completed my master's thesis under his supervision. I have written about this experience in another essay (Fischler 1998).

3. Frederic Howe's *Confessions* do offer an interesting picture of a man learning from experience or, rather, "unlearning [. . .] sometimes with pleasure, sometimes with pain" what he had learned earlier in life (Howe 1925, 317).

4. It is hard to know what lines of influence there may have existed between Schön, on the one hand, and Rittel and Webber (1973) on the other. Neither party refers to the other's work. All we can say with certainty is that the authors dealt with similar issues in a shared societal and intellectual context. In general, Schön's work is part of a larger scholarly effort—which Schön does not acknowledge explicitly, or at least not systematically—to understand learning and decision making and to improve our collective capacity to learn and make decisions (e.g., Etzioni 1968).

5. The governing variables of Model II resemble the conditions that Habermas (1984) and, after him, John Forester, Judith Innes, and other planning theorists have proposed for good collective decision making (Forester 1989; Innes 1995). Argyris and Schön (1974) noted the similarity of their ideas to those of John Friedmann. A year before the former published *Theory in Practice*, the latter had called on planners to interact with others in ways that foster "self-knowledge, capacity to learn, capacity for empathy, and ability to live with conflict" (Friedmann 1973, 143).

6. Between *Theory in Practice* and *The Reflective Practitioner*, Schön co-wrote another book with Argyris. *Organizational Learning: A Theory of Action Perspective* carries their analysis of Model I and Model II behavior and of single-loop and double-loop learning from the individual level to the collective level of the organization (Argyris and Schön 1978).

7. On the other hand, the reader gets little sense of what possible conflicts or failures might have pushed Schön to question his assumptions and conclusions. Schön's ideas show remarkable consistency over time, as if their validity has never been tested by contradiction. Still, each book he published was a reflection on his own professional practice. "My basic pattern," Schön told an interviewer, "was to spend some years doing something, and then write about it" (Cruikshank 1980, 87).

8. The journal *Reflective Practice* contains articles in these and related fields. In his first editorial, founder and editor Tony Ghaye acknowledged (rather implicitly) the paternity of Donald Schön in the birth of a new field of study (Ghaye 2000)—a field in which planning is rather invisible.

9. The paraphrase is based on the following sentence: "It is not the business of political philosophy and science to determine what the state in general should or must be" (Dewey [1927] 1954, 34).

References

Altshuler, Alan A. 1965. *The City Planning Process: A Political Analysis*. Ithaca, NY: Cornell University Press.

American Institute of City Planners (AICP). 2008. AICP College of Fellows, http://www.planning.org/faicp/faicp2.htm.

Argyris, Chris, and Donald A. Schön. 1974. *Theory in Practice: Increasing Professional Effectiveness*. San Francisco: Jossey-Bass.

Argyris, Chris, and Donald A. Schön. 1978. *Organizational Learning: A Theory of Action Perspective*. Reading, MA: Addison-Wesley.

Association of Collegiate Schools of Planning (ACSP). 2011. Don Schön Award for Excellence in Learning from Practice. http://www.acsp.org/awards/donald-schon-award.

Balducci, Alessandro, and Luca Bertolini. 2007. Reflecting on Practice or Reflecting with Practice? *Planning Theory & Practice* 8 (4): 532–533.

Bassett, Edward M. 1939. *Autobiography of Edward M. Bassett*. New York: Harbour Press.

Baum, Howell S. 1983. *Planners and Public Expectations*. Cambridge, MA: Schenkman Publishing Company.

Baum, Howell S. 1990. *Organizational Membership*. Albany: State University of New York Press.

Baum, Howell S. 1995. A Further Case for Practitioner Faculty. *Journal of Planning Education and Research* 14 (3): 214–216.

Baum, Howell S. 1997a. *The Organization of Hope: Communities Planning Themselves*. Albany: State University of New York Press.

Baum, Howell S. 1997b. Teaching Practice. *Journal of Planning Education and Research* 17 (1): 21–29.

Brooks, K. R., B. C. Nocks, J. T. Farris, and M. G. Cunningham. 2002. Teaching for Practice: Implementing a Process to Integrate Work Experience in an MCRP Curriculum. *Journal of Planning Education and Research* 22 (2): 188–200.

Carson, Rachel. 1962. *Silent Spring*. Cambridge, MA: Riverside Press.

Chitty, Kay Kittrell. 2005. *Professional Nursing: Concepts and Challenges*, 4th ed. St. Louis: Elsevier Saunders.

Cruikshank, Jeffrey. 1980. Interview: Donald A. Schön. In *Plan 1980: Perspectives on Two Decades*, 84–93. Cambridge, MA: MIT School of Architecture and Planning.

Dewey, John. (1927) 1954. *The Public and Its Problems*. New York: Henry Holt. First published by A. Swallow.

Dewey, John. (1938) 1997. *Experience and Education*. New York: Touchstone Books. First published by Kappa Delta Pi.

Etzioni, Amitai. 1968. *The Active Society: A Theory of Societal and Political Processes*. New York: Colliers-Macmillan.

Filor, S. W. 1994. The Nature of Landscape Design and Design Process. *Landscape and Urban Planning* 30 (3): 121–129.

Fischler, Raphaël. 1998. Donald A. Schön: Teacher and Writer. *Journal of Planning Literature* 13 (1): 7–8.

Ford, George B. 1913. The City Scientific. In *Proceedings of the Fifth National Conference on City Planning*, 31–41. Boston.

Forester, John. 1985. Designing: Making Sense Together in Practical Conversations. *Journal of Architectural Education* 38 (3): 14–20.

Forester, John. 1987. Teaching and Studying Planning Practice: An Analysis of the "Planning and Institutional Processes" Course at MIT. *Journal of Planning Education and Research* 6 (2): 116–137.

Forester, John. 1989. *Planning in the Face of Power*. Berkeley: University of California Press.

Forester, John. 1991. Anticipating Implementation: Reflective and Normative Practices in Policy Analysis and Planning. In *The Reflective Turn: Case Studies in and on Educational Practice*, ed. Donald A. Schön, 297–312. New York: Teachers College Press.

Forester, John. 1999. *The Deliberative Practitioner: Encouraging Participatory Planning Processes*. Cambridge, MA: MIT Press.

Forester, John, Raphaël Fischler, and Deborah Shmueli, eds. 2001. *Profiles of Community Builders: Israeli Planners and Designers*. Albany: State University of New York Press.

Friedan, Betty. 1963. *The Feminine Mystique*. New York: Norton.

Friedmann, John. 1973. *Retracking America: A Theory of Transactive Planning*. Garden City, NY: Anchor Press.

Friedmann, John. 1995. Teaching Planning Theory. *Journal of Planning Education and Research* 14 (3): 156–162.

Ghaye, Tony. 2000. Into the Reflective Mode: Bridging the Stagnant Moat. *Reflective Practice* 1 (1): 5–9.

Gilroy, Peter. 1993. Reflections on Schön: An Epistemological Critique and a Practical Alternative. *Journal of Education for Teaching* 19 (4): 125–142.

Gray, Barbara. 1996. Review of *Frame Reflection: Toward the Resolution of Intractable Policy Controversies*, by Donald A. Schön and Martin Rein. *Academy of Management Review* 21 (2): 576–579.

Habermas, Jürgen. 1984. *The Theory of Communicative Action*, trans. Thomas McCarthy. Boston: Beacon Press.

Hancock, John L. 1967. Planners in the Changing American City, 1900–1940. *Journal of the American Institute of Planners* 33 (5): 290–304.

Hart, A. W. 1990. Effective Administration through Reflective Practice. *Education and Urban Society* 22 (2): 153–169.

Healey, Patsy. 1997. *Collaborative Planning: Shaping Places in Fragmented Societies*. London: Macmillan.

Hoben, James. 2001. My 30 Years at HUD: An Honest Assessment of a Reflective Federal Bureaucrat. *Planning*, August. www.planning.org.

Hoch, Charles. 1994. *What Planners Do: Power, Politics, and Persuasion.* Chicago: Planners Press.

Howe, Frederic C. 1925. *The Confessions of a Reformer.* New York: C. Scribner's Sons.

Innes, Judith E. 1992. Group Processes and the Social Construction of Growth Management: Florida, Vermont, and New Jersey. *Journal of the American Planning Association* 58 (4): 440–453.

Innes, Judith E. 1995. Planning Theory's Emerging Paradigm: Communicative Action and Interactive Practice. *Journal of Planning Education and Research* 14 (3): 183–189.

Innes, Judith E., and David E. Booher. 1999. Consensus-Building as Role-Playing and Bricolage: Toward a Theory of Collaborative Planning. *Journal of the American Planning Association* 65 (1): 9–26.

Jacobs, Allan. 1980. *Making City Planning Work.* Washington, DC: American Planning Association.

Jacobs, Jane. 1961. *The Death and Life of Great American Cities.* New York: Random House.

Kilpatrick, William Heard. 1935. The Educational Challenge. *American Journal of Nursing* 35 (7): 609–613.

Krumholz, Norman, and John Forester. 1990. *Making Equity Planning Work: Leadership in the Public Sector.* Philadelphia: Temple University Press.

Kullman, J. 1998. Mentoring and the Development of Reflective Practice: Concepts and Context. *System* 26 (4): 471–484.

Meyerson, Martin, and Edward C. Banfield. 1955. *Politics, Planning and the Public Interest: The Case of Public Housing in Chicago.* New York: Free Press.

Moskowitz, Marina. 2004. *Standard of Living: The Measure of the Middle Class in America.* Baltimore, MD: Johns Hopkins University Press.

Regional Plan of New York and Its Environs. 1929. New York Regional Plan Association, New York. Reprinted 1974 by Arno Press, New York.

Reich, Robert. 1992. *The Work of Nations: Preparing Ourselves for the 21st Century.* New York: Knopf.

Richmond, Jonathan E. D. 2007. Bringing Critical Thinking to the Education of Developing Country Professionals. *International Education Journal* 8 (1): 1–29.

Rittel, Horst W., and Melvin M. Webber. 1973. Dilemmas in a General Theory of Planning. *Policy Sciences* 4:155–169.

Sanyal, Bish. 1998. Learning from Don Schön—A Tribute. *Journal of Planning Literature* 13 (1): 5–7.

Schmidt, Mary R. 2000. You Know More Than You Can Say: In Memory of Donald A. Schön (1930–1997). *Public Administration Review* 60 (3): 266–275.

Schön, Donald A. 1954. Rationality in the Practical Decision-Process. PhD diss., Harvard University.

Schön, Donald A. 1963. *Displacement of Concepts*. London: Tavistock Publications.

Schön, Donald A. 1967. *Technology and Change*. New York: Delacorte Press.

Schön, Donald A. 1970. Notes Toward a Planning Curriculum. *Journal of the American Institute of Planners* 36 (4): 220–221.

Schön, Donald A. 1971. *Beyond the Stable State: Public and Private Learning in a Changing Society*. London: Temple Smith.

Schön, Donald A. 1978. Generative Metaphor: A Perspective on Problem Setting in Social Policy. In *Metaphor and Thought*, ed. A. Ortony, 254–283. Cambridge: Cambridge University Press.

Schön, Donald A. 1982. Some of What a Planner Knows: A Case Study of Knowing-in-Practice. *Journal of the American Planning Association* 48 (x): 351–364.

Schön, Donald A. 1983. *The Reflective Practitioner: How Professionals Think in Action*. New York: Basic Books.

Schön, Donald A. 1985. *The Design Studio: An Exploration of Its Traditions and Potentials*. London: RIBA Publications.

Schön, Donald A. 1986. Towards a New Epistemology of Practice. In *Strategic Perspectives on Planning Practice*, ed. Barry Checkoway, 231–250. Lexington, MA: Lexington Books.

Schön, Donald A. 1987. *Educating the Reflective Practitioner: Toward a New Design for Teaching and Learning in the Professions*. San Francisco: Jossey-Bass.

Schön, Donald A., ed. 1991. *The Reflective Turn: Case Studies in and on Educational Practice*. New York: Teachers College, Columbia University.

Schön, Donald A. 1994. Comments on Dilemmas of Planning Practice. *Planning Theory* 10–11:131–139.

Schön, Donald A., and Thomas E. Nutt. 1974. Endemic Turbulence: The Future for Planning Education. In *Planning in America: Learning from Turbulence*, ed. David R. Godschalk, 181–205. Washington, DC: American Institute of Planners.

Schön, Donald A., and Martin Rein. 1994. *Frame Reflection: Toward the Resolution of Intractable Policy Controversies*. New York: Basic Books.

Schwartz, Howard S. 1987. Review of *The Reflective Practitioner: How Professionals Think in Action*, by Donald A. Schön. *Administrative Science Quarterly* 32 (4): 614–617.

Shepherd, A., and B. Cosgriff. 1998. Problem-Based Learning: A Bridge between Planning Education and Planning Practice. *Journal of Planning Education and Research* 17 (4): 348–357.

Smith, Mark K. 1999. Donald Schön: Learning, Reflection and Change. *The Encyclopedia of Informal Education*. www.infed.org/thinkers/et-schon.htm.

Wachs, Martin. 1994. The Case for Practitioner Faculty. *Journal of Planning Education and Research* 13 (4): 290–296.

Weshah, H. A. 2007. Training Pre-Service Teacher Education on Reflective Practice in Jordanian Universities. *European Journal of Scientific Research* 18 (2): 306–331.

Yanow, Dvora, and Haridimos Tsoukas. 2007. What Is Reflection-in-Action? Revisioning Schön, Phenomenologically. Working paper, Department of Culture, Organization, and Management, Faculty of Social Sciences, Vrije Universiteit, Amsterdam, The Netherlands.

13
Communicative Planning: Practices, Concepts, and Rhetorics

Patsy Healey

The idea of communicative planning is by now well recognized in the planning field.[1] The claim that underlies it centers on the importance of attention to the social microdynamics of practices in all their performative dimensions. It is through such microdynamics that planning ideas and strategies are accomplished. It is within such practices that what is at stake, and what and who gets to count, is established, given concrete form, and converted into effects on material outcomes and evolving modes of thinking and acting. The development of the ideas that have come to be associated with communicative planning within the planning field thus has the quality of an intellectual project, in that it presents a way of thinking about social action in the domain of collective action, or governance.[2] But the project also has a practical implication since what goes on in these micropractices matters for public policy.

Such micropractices have become especially significant in recent years in Western Europe and North America, as mid-twentieth-century governance arrangements have been challenged and unsettled. This unsettling has fostered the emergence of new groupings and collaborations in the landscape of both formal government and wider governance arrangements. In this context, intellectual, practical, and political dimensions are wrapped together in the evolution of the idea of communicative planning.

Tentatively developed through the 1980s, communicative planning acquired its labels and stereotypical representations in the 1990s. By the 2000s, it was well established on required planning theory reading lists for students in planning programs.

This chapter tells the story of the emergence of this collection of planning ideas, considers the impact of these ideas on practice, and reviews the critical debates about them. The story is told primarily from North

American and European perspectives, as that is where most of the initial contributions came from, although ideas associated with a communicative perspective, notably collaborative governance, have been circulating vigorously in other parts of the world in recent years.[3] Western perspectives, however, though mutually referential, reflect different governance contexts. For Europeans generally, the concept of planning is strongly linked to place development and management projects and programs and, in northwestern Europe, to struggles to modify strong, welfare-oriented government. In North America, and especially in the United States, the concept of planning is linked to public policy more generally, and to the complex, diffuse governance landscape of a more decentralized, federal system. On both continents, however, by the latter part of the twentieth century, questions were being asked about how formal government could and should relate to the spheres of business and civil society, how established policy domains could be configured differently to address contemporary issues, and how policy agendas could be shaped to allow a more integrated approach to the sociocultural, environmental, and economic dimensions of human development in the natural world. The challenge became how to mobilize policy attention to new issues, new fields of governance, and newly recognized stakeholders in governance processes.

The development of ideas in any field is never a closed process. New ideas emerging from one field may inspire innovation in another, and the movements of intellectual ideas break like waves across many fields. The communicative perspective in planning needs to be situated in such an intellectual wave. But its development was deeply inspired by experiences of practical action and experimentation, and by the continuing search for new ways to push toward more progressive societal development trajectories (Healey 2010). The intellectual wave provided a vocabulary to help articulate practice experiences, and then contributed to consolidating such experiences into both practice guidance and, more generally, political agendas.

The wave reflected a philosophical effort to break from the mid-twentieth-century dominance of a positivist and individualist orientation in science to recognize that identity and knowledge are produced in social contexts and are always limited by human capacity. This shifts attention away from finding objective laws that govern social behavior and toward the social dynamics through which norms and practices are produced, legitimated, become hegemonic, and are transformed. Such ideas reverberated across all the social sciences during the 1980s and helped create an intellectual climate often referred to as postpositivist or postmodern or poststructuralist (Fischer and Forester 1993, 1). Such an intellectual climate opened the way to recognizing the significance of active agency and of micropractices. It challenged the tradition of decision making by rational procedures that had become, in the planning field, associated with a logical positivist orientation, even though its origins were in a quite different, pragmatist epistemology (Hoch 1984, 2009). The communicative perspective in planning is one response to, and development within, this wave.

The experience of working in a practice with a rationalist and positivist epistemology led many to challenge the traditional approach (see Rittel and Webber 1973; Friedmann 1973; Hillier and Healey 2008a). This experience helped foster an interest in how policies were implemented and why there were implementation gaps. The communicative perspective directed much more attention to the micropractices of how planning work was performed, and to the way planners in practice contexts actually operated. By the 1980s, planning researchers such as Donald Schön and John Forester were providing accounts of how planners actually worked, while studies were appearing in the United States and Europe on how policies were implemented and the roles of specific actors and social networks in coordinating and mobilizing the energy to get particular projects achieved and policies implemented (see Wildavsky [1979] 1987; Pressman and Wildavsky 1973; Friend, Power, and Yewlett 1974; Healey et al. 1988). These experiences and studies underlined the significance of the social relations linking actors together and of the communicative dynamics of these relations in planning work, especially that directed toward changing policy agendas and developing new directions. The limitations of basing policies just on technical analysis were beginning to show up.

Finally, the political movements of the late 1960s and 1970s— in North America and Europe, keyed to the pivotal year of 1968— reinspired a generation of people who entered planning at this time to challenge what seemed to them to be a hegemonic consensus around democracy as a technical, elite affair, honed to the needs of achieving world capitalist domination, adversely affecting communities subjected to massive urban redevelopment programs. Activists challenged the urban renewal programs and automobile-oriented transport investments that disrupted urban communities. Planning, in this perspective, seemed to have become a technical and bureaucratic tool to achieve a "modernist" and capitalist ideological program. In Europe in particular, this led to a resurgence of interest in Marxist political theory, which initially emphasized the power of economic structures and the "logic of history." Planners in practice were cast as managerial tools of the capitalist system, or at least of the mid-century welfare state settlement (Castells 1977; Harvey 1989). But this structuralist Marxism itself was increasingly challenged by the rising intellectual wave that promoted critical, constructivist perspectives in social philosophy (Bernstein 1983; Giddens 1984). Refuting the structuralist account, such perspectives emphasized instead the complex ways in which structural forces and human agency interact.

Such a focus on the interaction between structure and agency made more sense to those with experience in planning work or who had researched the microdynamics of practice. It made evident that what happened in practices could not readily be "read off" from structural assumptions. The capacity and mobilization power of agency also mattered. It mattered how the fine grain of planning work was performed and how the judgments planners made in the flow of their work contributed to whether consequences ended up advancing or diminishing the potential for more progressive outcomes. Progressive planners became interested in who got involved in setting policy agendas, and in reinterpreting agendas in implementation. They focused on the practices of building new relations and coalitions, and on the significance of the interactive practices of negotiation and persuasion. In this political orientation, some progressive planners shared a common interest in collaborative ways of involving different actors in developing policy agendas and programs and in deliberative ways of operating in practices. Such practices seemed to offer a way to reinvigorate a concept of participatory democracy, one that challenged the dominant idea of elite democracy. Studies of micropractices also disclosed some planners' efforts to counteract injustice and promote more livable and sustainable environments, often in contexts where such values were continually contested (see Krumholz and Forester 1990). In the next section I review key contributions in the planning field that helped move the idea of communicative planning forward.

Building a Perspective

Communicative planning is sometimes referred to as a theory, a kind of fully fledged package of principles, hypotheses, and prescriptions. However, most theories on close inspection are more like an association of ideas, discussions, and controversies in conversation with each other. They are perhaps better understood as a perspective and a purposive orientation from which to view an aspect of the world. In the case of the communicative planning perspective, the predominant inspiration was not initially any theory but the actual experience of doing planning work, or planning practice. It took some time to link together the different efforts of individual academics to make sense of the practices they had been engaged in or had observed in their work. As the conversations between strands developed and as critics began to probe and pick holes in arguments, there have been further developments, which have opened up new controversies and differences among those associated with the communicative planning conversation.

The Core Ideas
Before reviewing key contributions, I shall summarize the main conceptions and understandings that make up the thrust of the communicative planning perspective. I set this basic groundwork up partly as a contrast to the positivist, rationalist tradition—the primary "other" against which the developing perspective emerged—but I also note other issues that situated the developing perspective. These conceptions and understandings are not separate but overlap each other, and different authors give them different weight in their work. Overall, they lead to the insistence that the microdynamics of agency interaction matter—to the quality of planning work, but also to how governance works, and to outcomes, both material and mental. I group these core ideas into those that reflect a general perspective on social dynamics and those that are specific to the planning project.

In general, those developing a communicative perspective emphasized an ontological conception of social interaction as constituted by people in their relations with others, that is, in social contexts, as opposed to a conception of the individual with a set of autonomously formed preferences. They emphasized the intersubjective formation of consciousness, which is central to Jürgen Habermas's work (Habermas 1984), and also to many other social theorists implementing a constructivist perspective. Those known later as communicative planning theorists shared an epistemological conception of knowledge formation as an active social and performative process of learning and discovery, through social processes directed at accomplishing practical tasks, at "acting in the world," as opposed to a conception of knowledge formation as the search for objective laws of natural and human behavior.

A consequence of such an ontology and epistemology is a recognition that facts, values, and interests, cognitions and emotions, and science, craft, and practical judgment are not separate spheres but intertwined facets of how humans grasp, think, feel, act, and coevolve in the flow of life in particular cultural contexts. In such a perspective in social theory, power is understood as social energy as well as dominatory force, "power to" as well as "power over." Further, power and politics are recognized as diffused among multiple arenas and structured by several forces that interact with each other in complex ways, as distinct from a conception of power as embodied in the hierarchy of formal state administrations, or within a struggle among elites or among economic classes for formal control over the means of production, distribution, and exchange. Foucault and Giddens were significant inspirations here. These assumptions all led to the recognition that the microdynamics of social interaction are important arenas for the formation of identities, knowledge generation, and social learning and for mobilizing transformative energy, rather than background noise interfering in technical, analytic work. This implied that attention had to be paid to the qualities of the relations of interaction and to the task of building networks with mobilization potential.

Specifically, the planning project was understood as a practice of collective attention to addressing particular problems faced now, but with future potentials and challenges in mind, and with attention to impacts experienced by multiple stakeholders now and in the future. This understanding stood against the fragmented and ad hoc problem solving directed primarily at serving short-term interests and political maneuvers. Instead, the planning project was seen by most contributors to the communicative planning idea as a public policy effort to promote more just and more sustainable, as well as more effective, outcomes over the long term. Pursuing such a project in the context of established institutions and governance practices meant developing new connections between groups of people, between citizens and the state, between citizens and economic groups, and within different segments of government activity. The aim was to address previously neglected issues and problems, as opposed to the performance of routine bureaucratic and technical procedures. It also implied recognizing that planning work involves much more than just undertaking technical analyses to advise decision makers. From this perspective planning work is overtly political, as it contributes to mobilizing some issues into attention while pushing others into the background. Such a perspective stresses that communicative practices, that is, how people "make sense" (Forester 1989) and generate energy in social interaction, are critical to the quality of developing intersubjective social learning and the mobilization of attention. The quality of planning practice therefore depends not solely on competence in analytic, design, engineering, and management technique but on communicative performance and the ability to work with others with different perspectives and competences.

Early Contributions

As frequently happens, new intellectual trajectories built on a rediscovery of older strands of thought. While in Europe, and in the United States among planning scholars such as Susan and Norman Fainstein (1979, 1986), the dominant rediscovery focused on reviving conceptions of the inherent fractures and injustices of a capitalist society, two important contributions, from John Friedmann and Donald Schön in the United States, also reasserted classical pragmatist ideas. Their work took quite different directions but drew on the pragmatist understanding of the social contexts within which knowledge and values were produced and of the human limitations of what could be known. This recognition in turn emphasized learning through doing, a practical engagement in social contexts, and an insistence on moving beyond such dualistic separations as emotion and reason, humans and nature, fact and value, analysis and action (see Hoch 1984; Healey 2009; Forester 1993; Verma 1996).

In his *Re-tracking America* (1973), Friedmann reflected on his work in the 1960s advising Latin American governments on urban and regional development strategies. This exposure led him to reject the model of planning as the deployment of technical expertise. His experience taught him that "Successful planning . . . depends in large measure on the planners' skill in managing interpersonal relations. The qualities he would have to develop included a heightened knowledge of the self; an increased capacity for learning; special skills in the use of symbolic materials . . . ; a heightened capacity for empathy; an ability to live with conflict; and an understanding of the dynamics of power and the art of getting things done" (Friedmann 1973, 20). These insights led him to develop what he refers to as a theory of "transactive planning," the "life of dialogue." This idea presents planning as a project of societal guidance through mutual learning processes, in which communicative relationships through dialogue are central. In later work, Friedmann radicalizes this social learning conception into a more politicized view of transformative planning

(Friedmann 1987, 2011), but the intellectual shift is clearly signaled in his earlier account.

Donald Schön, meanwhile, became interested in how professionals could and should go about exercising their expertise. He is much more concerned with the individual professional, in contrast to Friedmann's focus on governance processes, but he too emphasizes the uncertainty of what we can know about the world and the need for experimentation and social learning. As Fischler makes clear in the previous chapter, Schön articulated this initially in *Beyond the Stable State* (1971), a book that influenced the field of organizational development as well as planning (see also Argyris and Schön 1974). This viewpoint matured in 1983 in Schön's *Reflective Practitioner*, in which he celebrates the importance of learning through doing, "knowing-in-action," and the creative work that arises as professionals experiment in meeting the challenge of new problems. Schön studied the practices of different kinds of professionals and developed a deep critique of the technical bureaucrat with which he associated planners. Quite separately, Judith Innes was doing empirical research on the interactive processes through which social indicators used in public policy were produced and used. She highlighted the complex struggles through which what came to be accepted as objective measures were actually created, emphasizing the technical uncertainties and political considerations that had to be taken into account. She showed how these measures, once produced, took on a life of their own (Innes de Neufville 1975). Republishing her book in the late 1980s, she put forward an interactive, "two-way relationship between knowledge and action" based on an

interpretive or phenomenological view of knowledge . . . more contextual, more evolutionary and more complex than the scientific model. It regards formal, identifiable decisions as only a small part of all that leads to public action . . . knowledge influences without necessarily being actively used. (Innes 1990, 3)

Critical Pragmatism
Friedmann, Schön, and Innes were all deeply influenced by their practice experiences and empirical research. So too were many of the 1970s planning academics, radicalized by the 1968 social and political movement, and specifically by the urban redevelopment practices of the 1950s and 1960s that had promoted automobile-borne, middle-class development at the expense of many poorer and marginalized groups in cities. For some, such as the Fainsteins, this experience encouraged more attention

to structuring dynamics in social organization. Others drew inspiration from German critical theory, particularly the arguments of Habermas about how to resist the encroachment of what he called the "system world" into the "lifeworld." Yet another inspiration was the work of the rediscovered classical U.S. pragmatists, who had also been very influential for both Friedmann and Schön. By the 1980s, a revival of interest in this philosophical tradition was appearing in the United States, led by the philosophers Richard Rorty, Richard Bernstein, Hilary Putnam, and Hannah Arendt (Bernstein 2010). Rorty (1980) was interested in challenging the dominance of logical positivism in U.S. philosophy and its wide-ranging influence in the social sciences. Bernstein took a broader view and was more closely connected to European philosophical developments. His project, expressed in his influential book *Beyond Objectivism and Relativism* (1983), was to move aside from dualist arguments to ways of accommodating the multiple and conflicting arguments and claims manifest in the realm of public debate of issues of collective concern.

John Forester's work, initiated during his graduate studies in the 1970s, evolved through a series of papers published during the 1980s that he collected in two books, the first of which was immediately influential.[4] *Planning in the Face of Power* (1989) considers what is involved in doing planning work in different contexts. In planning practice, Forester argues, it is not enough for a planner to rely on technical skills. Talk and argument matter, too, as does the planner's knowledge of the organizational world and ability to anticipate conflicts (Forester 1989, 5):

A critical theory of planning helps us to understand what planners do as attention-shaping, communicative action rather than as instrumental action, as means to specific ends. Planning is deeply argumentative by its very nature: Planners must routinely argue, practically and politically, about desirable and possible futures. If they fail to recognize how their ordinary actions have subtle communicative effects, they will be counterproductive. (ibid., 138)

Forester explores how skilled and morally committed planners go about such attention-shaping work and attempt to counteract "unnecessary, deeply ideological formulations of community problems" in complex political contexts (ibid., 139).

Forester's later book, *Critical Theory, Public Policy and Planning Practice* (1993), develops the intellectual arguments that underlie the conception of what doing planning work involves. What if, Forester asks, social interaction were understood . . . as a practical matter of making sense together in a politically complex world. Planning and public policy analysis would then become processes of envisioning and attending to possible futures, shaping public attention to public possibilities. Public policy itself, by patterning social interaction, could then be seen to shape not only the distribution of "who gets what," but the more subtle constitution of ways we learn about and attend to our concerns, interests and needs. (Forester 1993, ix)

For Forester, planning is not a procedure for making strategic decisions about future development destinations and how to achieve them. It is about mobilizing "attention" and about generating "hope" that it is possible, by some form of intervention directed at public purposes, to improve conditions. It is about finding ways through difficult social dilemmas that established processes and ways of thinking seem unable to address. It is a project that involves combining technical capacity with moral purpose and sociopolitical sensibility.

In his work, Forester draws on the pragmatist tradition, particularly as revived by Bernstein, to develop the idea of the active construction of knowledge and identity in social settings. In planning work, this implies more attention to developing the skills and understanding the practices of listening, learning, and "making sense together." Drawing on the work of the British social scientists Anthony Giddens and Stephen Lukes, Forester focuses particularly on the way broad structural forces are made manifest in the flow of daily governance practices. From Jürgen Habermas he develops the idea of a political practice of challenging the distortions produced by powerful forces and actors in a continual struggle to sustain more progressive potentials and dynamics against forces that would squeeze them out. He calls the approach he develops "critical pragmatism." Like Schön, he emphasizes the power of human agency, always available to planners (and to anyone) to some degree, which they could and should exploit. He highlights the ethical dimensions of the choices planners make as they perform planning work. However, his concern is directed more toward releasing planners' progressive potential than to encouraging indiscriminate forms of creativity and experimentation. Deeply committed to cultivating a progressive democratic polity, Forester thus demands a particular value orientation from planners, combined with ethical sensitivity and skill. It is this quality, as well as Forester's focus on practices—on what planners do, on what goes on in planning work—that attracted the attention of planners around the world, who read his 1989 book and the papers that led up to it. It gave inspiration to all those struggling, in often very difficult conditions, to encourage a different kind of political culture to emerge.

By the late 1980s, a group of North American scholars in the general ambit of John Forester widened their networks to include planners more interested in researching particular kinds of planning practices, notably Judith Innes in her work on the formation of planners' knowledge and on consensus-building practices, and Larry Susskind as he investigated the practice of consensus building in urban development and environmental contexts.[5] Tangentially, Tom Harper and Stan Stein were developing a "dialogical approach" that combined inspirations from Rorty and the philosopher John Rawls to produce what they refer to as a "neo-pragmatist" planning theory (Harper and Stein 2006). All these contributions were infused by a deep appreciation of what doing planning work involved, and acknowledged a constructivist perspective in the formation of identities and knowledge.

Some European scholars were also contributing to the development of the communicative perspective, although there are significant differences in the sociocultural and political worlds in different countries in Europe that affect modes of thought and empirical referents. Tøre Sager, working on transport planning practices in Norway and, like many Scandinavians of the time, aware of Habermas's ideas and Forester's work, studied controversies surrounding the introduction of road pricing in Trondheim. His *Communicative Planning Theory* draws on Friedmann's transactive planning, Lindblom's pragmatic "disjointed incrementalism," Forester's "critical pragmatism," and Habermas's work to create a formulation of a "dialogical and communicative rationality" (Sager 1994, 20). His primary concern is to develop the implications of accepting the realities of imperfect knowledge and the problems of achieving goals by rationally calculated means, especially in the practice of strategic or "synoptic" planning work. He presents the communicative model of planning as a way of combining "instrumental," goal-seeking rationality with a communicative rationality. In this way, both technical and discursive ways of establishing knowledge are brought into planning processes. Like Forester, Sager argues that this provides a critical, pragmatic perspective from which to examine planning practices.

In his study of the shaping of planning policies in the Danish city of Aalborg, Bent Flyvbjerg (1998), like Forester, argues for much more attention to what actually goes on in planning practice. However, Foucault is his inspiration rather than Habermas, and he seeks to kick modernism aside by attacking the whole project of the Enlightenment. His central argument is that what counts as rationality is defined by power, explicitly and as embedded in discourses and practices. So planners, when grounding their claims to expertise in rational technical analysis, are exercising a form of power. In a way, this supports Forester's conclusion that planners need to work in a different way if they are to challenge established power dynamics, although Flyvbjerg sees his work as critical of the communicative approach.

My own work developed from empirical studies of planning practice, mainly in the UK (see Healey 2003). I linked developments in communicative planning theory to wider shifts in political economy, and in particular to the search for new forms of governance such as consensus building, alternative dispute resolution, and all kinds of partnerships and collaboratives. My research and practice experience suggested that transformative changes did not necessarily happen through revolutionary struggles, as Marxist radicals emphasized, but through evolutionary changes in the fine grain of micropractices. This microemphasis highlighted the complex, interactive relationships through which what counts as significant—stakes, interests, arguments, claims—is forged and framed. My project then was to critique practices that narrowed the arenas and the range of voices that could be heard in establishing policy concepts and frames of reference, and to examine how different kinds of practices could open out to become more inclusive of diverse issues and values. This led me to conceive of planning as a communicative project carried forward by debate and argumentation about future possibilities. I called the overall intellectual approach "institutionalist" and the planning approach "collaborative" (Healey [1997] 2006).

The Consolidation into an Intellectual Turn
By the 1990s, others were making significant contributions, particularly through empirical analyses, but also through developing ways of undertaking policy discourse analyses (see Hillier 2000; Hajer 1995; Margerum 2002; and, later, Scholz and Stiftel 2005). There was also increasing exchange between European and U.S. contributions. The various strands were drawn together intellectually in two contributions. The first was the collection edited by policy analyst Frank Fischer with John Forester, *The Argumentative Turn in Policy Analysis and Planning* (1993), and the second was Judith Innes's paper "Planning Theory's Emerging Paradigm: Communicative Action and Interactive Practice" (1995).[6] *The Argumentative Turn* is firmly positioned in the broad intellectual wave of postmodern and postpositivist philosophy and social science. Fischer and Forester argue that

We need to understand just what policy analysts and planners do, how language and modes of representation both enable and constrain their work, how their practical rhetoric depicts and selects, describes and characterizes, includes and excludes, and more. (Fischer and Forester 1993, 2)

Policy making, in this context, becomes imagined as a practice of "constant discursive struggle" (ibid., 2) over meanings and claims.

Judith Innes, writing in the influential American *Journal of Planning Education and Research,* highlighted the communicative stream of work in planning theory as an emerging paradigm. She used the "communicative" rubric, viewing Habermas's work on communicative action theory as "likely to provide the principal framework for the new planning theory" (Innes 1995, 186). She contrasted this with the dominant planning paradigm of systematic, instrumental rationality, underpinned by a positivist philosophy. She cited a rich list of contributions that develop such an approach, while acknowledging John Forester's *Planning in the Face of Power* as the strongest exemplar of the new perspective. Her message also underlined the importance of undertaking research work on the communicative dimensions of planning practices. Her own work has since provided accounts of collaborative initiatives in different contexts, drawing significant lessons about the conditions that could lead to the realization of a governance process that would meet criteria of "authentic collaboration" (Innes and Booher 2010).

Thus, by the mid-1990s, communicative planning was no longer just a concept. It was an intellectual perspective in planning theory, with a body of adherents, rubrics, philosophical referents, and a research agenda. It was deeply infused with practice experiences and sought ways of inspiring new practice possibilities. Intellectually, its "other" was still primarily the rationalist planning paradigm in its positivist and procedural versions, along with overly structuralist accounts of government activity. The communicative perspective urged instead more attention to the significance of micropractices and structure-agency interactions. Practically, the communicative perspective challenged the idea that the core of planning practice lay in the technical tools of analysis and decision support and in the production of large-scale strategies. Instead, it emphasized the practical negotiation of how resources were actually distributed and rule systems deployed. It encouraged critical attention to the expanding experimentation in practice with new governance forms. Politically, it challenged the conception of appropriate governance arrangements centered on models of elite, paternalist technocracy, and a narrow capitalist preoccupation with individualist economic gain as the path to general societal well-being.

Debates and Critiques

For many planning academics, students, and practitioners who read work such as Forester's *Planning in the Face of Power,* the ideas associated with the communicative planning conception proved helpful in releasing them from older planning paradigms. It gave them more suitable vocabularies and concepts with which to account for and develop further the situations they actually encountered. For by the 1990s, the postmodern, postpositivist intellectual wave was penetrating the general cultural climate in North America and Western Europe, fueling much greater appreciation of the inherent uncertainty and unpredictability of human understanding and action. This emphasis on unpredictability had particular resonance in the political and economic conditions of the times. Politically, old stabilities were visibly breaking down as the cold war came to an end and new and previously suppressed forces found expression. New policy agendas were emerging and articulating difficult claims for governance attention that often cut across the politics of nation-states, such as the threats to global environmental conditions, the rise of new economic power blocks, and the stark poverty of large areas of the world, especially in exploding urban agglomerations. While philosophically, paradigm shifts in the social sciences encouraged attention to the intersubjective, relational formation of identities and values (and hence of "interests"), of understandings (ways of thinking, interpretation, meaning), and of performative practices (ways of acting), politically, attention turned to "reconfiguring governance." The reconfiguration attempts took both progressive and conservative forms. Neoliberals sought to reduce the intervention of the state and leave more to the free flow of market forces. Civic conservatives sought to restore the old values of municipal community. Progressives, meanwhile, focused on generating new forms of inclusive participatory and deliberative democracy (see Cunningham 2002).

These shifts in political ideas resulted in all kinds of initiatives to transform formal government and introduce new institutions and practices as the relations between the state, the economy, and civil society were renegotiated. Such experimentation in the United States produced the situations that researchers such as Judith Innes investigated. By the late 1980s, this experimentation in collaborative processes was accompanied by the development of techniques and process guidance. In the 1990s, similar experiments had emerged in many European countries, encouraged to an extent by the European Union. Communicative planning ideas meshed with this climate of political innovation. In Europe, experimentation with forms of collaborative work among diverse stakeholders was particularly evident in neighborhood regeneration programs, landscape improvement programs, and spatial strategy making. The academic interest in these new arenas focused attention on the problem-solving and implementation aspects of governance dynamics and their political implications rather than on abstract political ideologies and struggles between and within political parties (see also Fung and Wright 2003).

However, such planning ideas, now more clearly visible as a consequence of their description, were soon subjected to vigorous critiques from planning academics. Reflecting the success of communicative planning theory in capturing an intellectual, practical, and political mood of the times, the perspective became an arena of intense contestation in the later 1990s. The ideas attracted little attention from practitioners of the positivist, rationalist school, who in any case were shifting attention in response to the new intellectual climate. The most energetic critics were those who shared some of the intellectual perceptions and political commitments of the planners developing communicative ideas. Some of the critiques led to an oversimplified stereotyping, the same fate that befell the traditional rationalist perspective. But others raised issues that those developing the communicative perspective had to consider carefully. I won't review these critical contributions here[7] but instead will enumerate some of the key points made. I group the critiques into intellectual, practice-based, and political critiques, although often these dimensions tended to overlap.

The *intellectual* critical response identified four groups of issues. The first had to do with philosophical groundings, and here the critics accused those advancing the new perspective of merely replacing the rationalism of scientific procedure with that of communicative practices. Critics claimed that communicative practice still emphasized a rational approach, privileging the role of argument and reason in human affairs. Further, by emphasizing the social construction of understanding and arguments, the approach was antirealist and relativist. This meant that it underplayed the materiality of the issues discussed and located values as products of intersubjective debate rather than as prior commitments. The second group of issues raised in the intellectual critique had to do with the treatment of power and politics. Critics charged that the communicative approach adopted a pluralistic conception of political dynamics (as opposed to a class-based one) and assumed that power could be generated through creating arenas where previously conflicting groups could explore ways to build common ground, through participative deliberation in which initial power imbalances could be moderated. Such a concern with conflict reduction and consensus building was held to be a form of "bracketing off" power dynamics and "neutralizing" power. Third, the perspective was said to overweight process, just as the traditional rationalist approach had done, to the neglect of issues at stake and the stakeholders' interests. Finally, the communicative perspective as a theory of transformation was considered weak. Its valorization of argumentation neglected other power dynamics, such as control of the means of production and exchange or of legislative and military power. Overall, critics claimed that the perspective took too idealistic and optimistic a view of the human condition and was too narrowly focused on micropractices so that it did not see the structuring dynamics sufficiently clearly.

Several critics missed the grounding of communicative ideas in the postpositivist, pragmatist shift in philosophy. They were unaware of Richard Bernstein's encouragement to move beyond the dualistic dichotomy between objectivism and relativism and to accept that interpretations of phenomena have their own social reality and material consequences. Others mischaracterized the recognition that power was diffused among a plurality of institutional sites and that social fractures were not just those along class-based lines as a reinvention of interest-based pluralism dominant in U.S. political science in the 1960s. Many equated communicative ideas directly with Habermas's own normative hopes for the recovery of some shared sense of values across Western societies. They accused the communicative perspective holders of being committed to an idealized consensus society, in this way mistaking the pragmatic concern for seeking shared common ground in relation to specific problems and conflict issues for such an abstracted idealism (Forester 2009). This elision then set up a dualistic opposition between a Habermasian and a Foucauldian interpretation of power dynamics that has reverberated through planning theory debates, neglecting the way in which the approach combines inspirations from the two sources. Underlying this critique were assumptions about the nature of power. Many critics understood power as "power over"—power to control and dominate. Yet the communicative perspective recognized multiple relations and sources of power and focused more on "power to"—power as social energy, and the potential for the generation of such energy to challenge established patterns of domination and control.

As with all good intellectual probing, such a critique had a beneficial effect in forcing those developing the communicative perspective or working within it to think more carefully about some issues. First, it encouraged more critical attention to the theory of transformation implicit in collaborative ideas. This led to more emphasis on the institutional dynamics within which progressive collaborative practices might develop and the coevolution of such practices and wider governance dynamics. Second, those promoting more attention to collaborative practices began to explore the potential for the emergence of such practices in changes in political economy, that is, in the wider context of shifts in state-society relations. This encouraged much more empirical effort to expand the practice experiences from which the perspective drew inspiration and support. Third, while proponents of communicative ideas initially emphasized the potential for reaching agreement, as a counterblast to the attention to conflict in the more dominant perspective of adversarial politics, more attention is now being given to the positive role of conflict in keeping issues and interests in play in deliberative arenas.

Finally, those working within the communicative perspective still need to give more attention to the ways in which the issues and values at stake shape deliberative encounters, and how such encounters affect prior concerns. Although what is just, fair, sustainable, and so forth needs empirical grounding to have materiality and meaning, most progressives nevertheless would now argue that such values cannot just be left to be articulated in specific deliberative encounters. Some values and criteria are always "locked into" the wider institutional context in which specific practices are located, the result of earlier rounds of attention-shaping work. This emphasizes the significance of institutional design in governance dynamics, the interplay of hard and soft governance infrastructures, and the interaction between constitutions, legal conventions, and cultural norms, on the one hand, and the specific practices that occur in particular governance arenas on the other (Fung and Wright 2003). Thus, the intellectual critique has led to the development and refining of ideas within the communicative perspective.

A rather different line of criticism emerged from those looking at the communicative perspective from the point of view of the established *practices* of planning systems. These criticisms coalesced around three issues. First, some treated the approach as an "account" of practice, rather than as a contribution to inventing alternative practices. In the UK, with its top-down, overly bureaucratized system of land-use regulation, the approach was criticized as an inaccurate description of practice-as-it-is, and, implicitly, as it could become. Such critics in the 1990s were largely unaware of the experimental collaborative practices then going on in the United States, Canada, and other parts of the world and that were beginning to appear in the UK, particularly in urban regeneration initiatives and local environmental management. But as awareness of these experiences developed, further criticisms of the practical consequences were advanced. Second, some critics argued that such practices were too inefficient, that they took too much time, although later attention shifted, in experiments in institutional design, to whether time spent in deliberative practices establishing policy directions might actually save the time and cost of resolving conflict in adversarial arenas, such as formal inquiries and the courts. Others argued that deliberative practices could not necessarily arrive at the "right" answer. Such criticisms were heard especially from those promoting environmental agendas, who were concerned to safeguard key parameters of local and global environmental conditions. But this raises questions about who and what is right. Third, there were concerns that deliberative practices could suffer all the problems of unconstrained localism, with the potential for one group to oppress another and for wider impacts to be ignored. This criticism took aim at strategies of governance decentralization to localities and neighborhoods, widely promoted at the end of the twentieth century in many parts of the world. This critique underlines the importance of finding practical ways of combining wider considerations with releasing local energy. This led to an emerging body of work in the 2000s on combining both structuring parameters and local experimentation in the formal design of government initiatives. For example, Fung (2004) has explored what measures need to be in place in formal government systems to support the development of more active participatory modes of governance.

The final group of criticisms came from those with a progressive *political* orientation. Some progressives argued that emphasizing the development of deliberative arenas, around the margins between state and society, was merely a form of managerial co-optation. Instead, they argued, progressives should stress the importance of standing outside the state, on the margins of established values and practices, making the voices of excluded others heard and maintaining an agonistic or discordant voice in public debate. Communicative practices that connect state, economy, and civil society actors could all too easily become just another way of neutralizing conflict and reducing the struggles for justice among those marginalized and oppressed by the current dominance of corporate economic interests with their globalizing ambitions. Or such experiments could be merely tokenistic, a kind of rhetorical mask to cover business as usual. Some even accused the communicative perspective of acting as a political support for the expansion of neoliberal strategies, undermining the governance arrangements of social democracies and their ability to promote social justice and environmental sustainability.

These criticisms raised questions about how transformations in social formations are achieved. Are they the result of the struggle of revolutionary movements, or of crises internal to a particular formation, or of slow evolutions through which social formations develop and change, or of some combination of them all? Communicative planning ideas emphasize the importance of the microdynamics of slow evolutions, of the social learning processes through which societies develop and change. Although some critics consider collaborative arrangements and deliberative practices as just another way of patching the cracks in established social formations, many proponents of the progressive potential of the perspective see such practices as a way of releasing energies through enlarging social learning, with transformative possibilities.

History suggests there are no general answers to questions about how social transformations come about. Yet any planning idea that develops a profile in the field should have something to say about transformative possibilities. The communicative perspective gives significance, as arenas of learning about politics and about social formations in which they are situated, to the micropolitics of deliberative encounters where people come together to address common problems and shared conflicts. But by itself, the perspective has little to say about when, where, and how collaborative governance practices might have transformative effects. As with the other criticisms of the communicative planning perspective, this argument leads us back to the importance of locating discussion about appropriate planning practices within the specific dynamics of actual governance situations and their particular histories and geographies.

Overall, the effect of the debates over and critiques of the communicative planning perspective has been to sharpen and strengthen the claims made by proponents. It has also encouraged a significant amount of empirical work, both that designed to show the potential of the approach and that designed to highlight weaknesses. In the sense of inspiring a critical debate and a substantial body of research in the planning field, the perspective could be said to have achieved considerable intellectual success. But this is not the only reason why the perspective continues to attract so much attention. Other reasons lie in the practical experience that many planners face in the uncertain, complexly shifting, diffused, and often highly conflictual institutional contexts of the current period. Such uncertainty, complexity, and conflict have always been present as a context for planning work, and this is often used as a justification for attempting to plan. But the sense of instability has been greatly enhanced in recent years as geoeconomic and political shifts and greater awareness of environmental vulnerabilities have shaken many established twentieth-century assumptions. Building new relations and arenas, and helping groups of people develop new ways of thinking about the issues and problems they face, demand the kinds of skills that the communicative perspective emphasizes. More broadly, the perspective contributes to a wider search for ways of enriching and renewing what an inclusive, pluralistic democracy can and should mean in the twenty-first century.

The Overall Contribution

I have argued in this chapter that the idea of communicative planning needs to be situated in a broad movement in social theory and philosophy that has helped shift political and practical attention to the significance of the micropractices of collective action and, in particular, the potential of active agency within and around formal government organizations. In this intellectual shift, the perspective resists a focus on either "great men of history"—the charismatic leaders that feature in many mid-twentieth-century urban development narratives—or a focus on struggles orchestrated by political parties and interest groups, which featured strongly in urban politics studies of the 1960s, the classic "interest pluralism" accounts. Instead, it argues that the relations of micropractices, and the way broader contextual forces are made manifest in them, are not merely pregiven but are actively constructed in the flow of practicing by those involved. This places considerable responsibility on all those involved, but especially those drawn into such practices as a result of their professional skill and knowledge.

The communicative perspective places a strong emphasis, therefore, on the intertwining of multiple forms of knowledge, on moral judgment and practical skill, and on the way planning work is done, how it is performed. The perspective also parallels the classical pragmatist emphasis on developing democratic practices through learning how to reason in public, expanding the notion of reasoning from some kind of logical technique, to encompass all kinds of ways in which claims for what is at issue, at stake, who is affected, what might be done, when and by whom, are brought to attention, explained, grounded, and legitimated. Finally, the perspective makes the claim that such micropractices make a difference to what is achieved and the quality of the public realm, not just for those immediately affected by what happens in that practice but also to the evolving quality of a wider polity. In a slow, cumulative way, they carry transformative potential. This is not to deny the significance of transformative initiatives at a broader scale. As many now argue, attention is also needed to the interaction between micropractices and institutional designs in policy programs and legal interventions. But neglecting micropractices is to miss an important arena within which policy values, such as the pursuit of social justice and environmental sustainability, of economic development and livability, are combined, prioritized, and given material form and localized meaning.

But this does not imply that communicative planning as an intellectual perspective can be neatly turned into the promotion of forms of collaborative practice that will somehow move polities along a trajectory toward an ideal of a better participatory democracy. As Fung (2004) argues, the focus on micropractices should not be translated into some kind of romantic localism. Attention to micropractices needs to be combined with a recognition of the way wider forces shape and get shaped by agency. This interplay between system or structure and agency needs to retain an awareness of the specific context in which such interactions are situated. How far approaches to dispute resolution, conflict mediation, or creating new strategies collaboratively which have proved successful in one place will work in another requires careful attention to the social-political dynamics that generated the practice and its relevance in a different situation. Politically, also, it is important to remain cautious about the advocacy of collaborative governance as an attribute of government programs. The critical question in such invocations is, what political work is such a rhetoric being used to achieve?

In conclusion, the communicative idea in the planning field has opened up an important terrain of activity for critical attention. It has strengthened both analytic and normative sensibilities by directing attention to the fine grain of planning work. It has challenged broad stereotypes of what planning work is and does. It highlights the significance of communicative competence, technical skill, and ethical attention as these combine in specific social contexts to produce effects, both in shaping material products and in how issues, problems, and solutions are imagined and attended to. Once the implications of the communicative perspective have been absorbed, it should no longer be possible to view implementation gaps as simple failures in policy design or as the lack of power of one agency over another. Instead, it leads to recognition of the importance of the complex relations drawn into and generated in and around planning activity, and of the creative power of agency. The challenge for the design of policy systems is then to find ways to release that power in the service of creating futures in which there are chances for the many, not just the few, to flourish.

Notes

1. My thanks to Judith Allen, John Forester, John Friedmann, Charlie Hoch, Judith Innes, Tore Sager, Bish Sanyal, Lawrence Vale, Tina Rosan, and the discussion group at MIT on April 14, 2008, for insightful comments on earlier drafts. These comments helped me sharpen my arguments and understanding. The errors in my historical narrative and arguments are, of course, all my own.

2. I use the term "governance" here and elsewhere to refer to all forms of collective action, of which formal government activity is one (see Cars et al. 2002).

3. See the international development literature—for example, Chambers (1997), Satterthwaite (1999), Mitlin and Satterthwaite (2004), Kothari and Cooke (2001), and Hickey and Mohan (2004).

4. See Wagenaar (2011) for a review of Forester's corpus of work.

5. See Innes (1990, 1992) and Innes et al. (1994). Susskind's work is brought together in a consolidated edition, *The Consensus-Building Handbook* (Susskind, McKearnan, and Thomas-Larmer 1999).

6. The terms "argumentative" and "interpretive" were used interchangeably in the 1990s, the one centering on claims making, the other on the construction of meanings, in collaborative encounters. See Hajer and Wagenaar's edited collection (2003).

7. For reviews, see Fischler (2000), Harris (2002), and Hillier and Healey (2008b).

References

Argyris, C., and D. Schön. 1974. *Theory in Practice: Increasing Professional Effectiveness*. San Francisco: Jossey-Bass.

Bernstein, R. 1983. *Beyond Objectivism and Relativism: Science, Hermeneutics and Praxis*. Philadelphia: University of Pennsylvania Press.

Bernstein, R. J. 2010. *The Pragmatic Turn*. Cambridge: Polity Press.

Cars, G., and P. Healey, A. Madanipour, and C. De Magalhaes, eds. 2002. *Urban Governance: Institutional Capacity and Social Milieux*. Aldershot, UK: Ashgate.

Castells, M. 1977. *The Urban Question*. London: Edward Arnold.

Chambers, R. 1997. *Whose Reality Counts? Putting the First Last*. London: Intermediate Technology Publications.

Cunningham, F. 2002. *Theories of Democracy: A Critical Introduction*. London: Routledge.

Fainstein, S., and N. Fainstein. 1979. New Debates in Urban Planning: The Impact of Marxist theory in the United States. *International Journal of Urban and Regional Research* 3:381–403.

Fainstein, S., and N. Fainstein, eds. 1986. *Restructuring the City: The Political Economy of Urban Redevelopment*. New York: Longman.

Fischer, F., and J. Forester, eds. 1993. *The Argumentative Turn in Policy Analysis and Planning*. London: UCL Press.

Fischler, R. 2000. Communicative Planning Theory: A Foucauldian Assessment. *Journal of Planning Education and Research* 19:358–368.

Flyvbjerg, B. 1998. *Rationality and Power*. Chicago: University of Chicago Press.

Forester, J. 1989. *Planning in the Face of Power*. Berkeley: University of California Press.

Forester, J. 1993. *Critical Theory, Public Policy and Planning Practice: Toward a Critical Pragmatism*. Albany: State University of New York Press.

Forester, J. 2009. *Dealing with Differences: Dramas of Mediating Public Disputes*. Oxford: Oxford University Press.

Friedmann, J. 1973. *Re-tracking America: A Theory of Transactive Planning*. New York: Anchor Press.

Friedmann, J. 1987. *Planning in the Public Domain*. Princeton, NJ: Princeton University Press.

Friedmann, J. 2011. *Insurgencies: Essays in Planning Theory*. London: Routledge.

Friend, J., J. Power, and C. Yewlett. 1974. *Public Planning: The Intercorporate Dimension*. London: Tavistock Institute.

Fung, A. 2004. *Empowered Participation*. Princeton, NJ: Princeton University Press.

Fung, A., and E. O. Wright, eds. 2003. *Deepening Democracy: Institutional Innovations in Empowered Participatory Governance*. London: Verso.

Giddens, A. 1984. *The Constitution of Society*. Cambridge: Polity Press.

Habermas, J. 1984. *Reason and the Rationalisation of Society*. Vol. 1. The Theory of Communicative Action. Cambridge: Polity Press.

Hajer, M. 1995. *The Politics of Environmental Discourse*. Oxford: Oxford University Press.

Hajer, M., and H. Wagenaar, eds. 2003. *Deliberative Policy Analysis: Understanding Governance in the Network Society*. Cambridge: Cambridge University Press.

Harper, T. L., and S. M. Stein. 2006. *Dialogical Planning in a Fragmented Society*. New Brunswick, NJ: CUPR Press.

Harris, N. 2002. Collaborative Planning: From Critical Foundations to Practice Forms. In *Planning Futures: New Directions for Planning Theory*, ed. P. Allmendinger and M. Tewdwr-Jones, 21–43. London: Routledge.

Harvey, D. 1989. From Managerialism to Entrepreneurialism: The Formation of Urban Governance in Late Capitalism. *Geografiska Annaler* 71B:3–17.

Healey, P. (1997) 2006. *Collaborative Planning: Shaping Places in Fragmented Societies*. London: Macmillan.

Healey, P. 2003. Collaborative Planning in Perspective. *Planning Theory* 2:101–123.

Healey, P. 2009. The Pragmatic Tradition in Planning Thought. *Journal of Planning Education and Research* 28 (3): 277–292.

Healey, P. 2010. *Making Better Places: The Planning Project in the Twenty-first Century*. London: Palgrave Macmillan.

Healey, P., P. McNamara, M. Elson, and J. Doak. 1988. *Land Use Planning and the Mediation of Urban Change*. Cambridge: Cambridge University Press.

Hickey, S., and G. Mohan. 2004. *Participation: From Tyranny to Transformation*. London: Zed Books.

Hillier, J. 2000. Going Round the Back: Complex Networks and Informal Action in Local Planning Processes. *Environment & Planning A* 32 (1): 33–54.

Hillier, J., and P. Healey, eds. 2008a. *Critical Readings in Planning Theory*. Vol. 1. *Foundations of the Planning Enterprise*. Aldershot, UK: Ashgate.

Hillier, J., and P. Healey, eds. 2008b. *Critical Readings in Planning Theory*. Vol. 2. *Political Economy, Diversity and Pragmatism*. Aldershot, UK: Ashgate.

Hoch, C. 1984. Doing Good and Being Right: The Pragmatic Connection in Planning Theory. *Journal of the American Planning Association* 50:335–345.

Hoch, C. 2009. Planning Craft: How Planners Compose Plans. *Planning Theory* 8 (3): 219–241.

Innes de Neufville, J. 1975. *Social Indicators and Public Policy: Interactive Processes of Design and Application*. New York: Elsevier.

Innes, J. 1990. *Knowledge and Public Policy: The Search for Meaningful Indicators*. New Brunswick, NJ: Transaction Books.

Innes, J. 1992. Group Processes and the Social Construction of Growth Management. *Journal of the American Planning Association* 58:440–454.

Innes, J. 1995. Planning Theory's Emerging Paradigm: Communicative Action and Interactive Practice. *Journal of Planning Education and Research* 14:183–189.

Innes, J. E., and D. E. Booher. 2010. *Planning with Complexity: An Introduction to Collaborative Rationality for Public Policy*. London: Routledge.

Innes, J., J. Gruber, R. Thompson, and M. Neuman. 1994. *Co-ordinating Growth and Environmental Management through Consensus-building*. Berkeley: University of California Press.

Krumholz, N., and J. Forester. 1990. *Making Equity Planning Work*. Philadelphia: Temple University Press.

Kothari, V., and B. Cooke, eds. 2001. *Participation: The New Tyranny*. London: Zed Books.

Lukes, S. 1974. *Power: A Radical View*. London: Macmillan.

Margerum, R. D. 2002. Evaluating Collaborative Planning: Implications from an Empirical Analysis of Growth Management. *Journal of the American Planning Association* 68 (2): 179–193.

Mitlin, D., and D. Satterthwaite, eds. 2004. *Empowering Squatter Citizen: Local Government, Civil Society and Urban Poverty Reduction*. London: Earthscan.

Pressman, J. L., and A. B. Wildavsky. 1973. *Implementation: How Great Expectations in Washington Are Dashed in Oakland*. Berkeley: University of California Press.

Rittel, H., and M. M. Webber. 1973. Dilemmas in a General Theory of Planning. *Policy Sciences* 4:155–169.

Rorty, R. 1980. *Philosophy and the Mirror of Nature*. Oxford: Blackwell.

Sager, T. 1994. *Communicative Planning Theory*. Aldershot, UK: Hants: Avebury.

Satterthwaite, D., ed. 1999. *The Earthscan Reader in Sustainable Cities*. London: Earthscan.

Scholz, J. T., and B. Stiftel, eds. 2005. *Adaptive Governance and Water Conflict*. Washington, DC: Resources for the Future Press.

Schön, D. 1971. *Beyond the Stable State*. London: Temple Smith.

Schön, D. 1983. *The Reflective Practitioner*. New York: Basic Books.

Susskind, L., S. McKearnan, and J. Thomas-Larmer, eds. 1999. *The Consensus-Building Handbook*. London: Sage.

Verma, N. 1996. Pragmatic Rationality and Planning Theory. *Journal of Planning Education and Research* 16:5–14.

Wagenaar, H. 2011. Review Essay: "A Beckon to the Makings, Workings and Doings of Human Beings": The Critical Pragmatism of John Forester. *Public Administration Review* 17:293–298.

Wildavsky, A. (1979) 1987. *Speaking Truth to Power: The Art and Craft of Policy Analysis,* rev. ed. Boston: Little, Brown. First published 1974 by Macmillan.

14

Social Justice as Responsible Practice: Influence of Race, Ethnicity, and the Civil Rights Era

June Manning Thomas

Social justice, an important concept in planning thought, is a principle that professional, certified planners in the United States are supposed to uphold, and yet it is difficult to fully support a principle without understanding its rationale. This chapter explores the historical context in an effort to explain U.S. planners' readiness to adopt specific language regarding social justice, first in 1972 and then in succeeding versions of the American Institute of Certified Planners' (AICP's) Code of Ethics. A person who examines the main social justice provision in the U.S. code could very well question why such language is enshrined as a principle to which all certified planners should aspire. The code heavily emphasizes proper professional conduct, such as honesty and avoidance of the appearance of conflict of interest, yet as revised in recent versions it also contains a principles section that is value-driven. The principles section mentions "social justice," referring to the need to plan for the "disadvantaged" and to "urge the alteration of policies, institutions and decisions which oppose such needs" (AICP 2009). Other provisions address the need to increase opportunities for underrepresented groups in the profession. The rationale for such language apparently lies in the tumultuous period of the 1960s, when it became clear that the civil rights era and the racial crisis in cities were not aloof from urban planning. I discuss here some effects of that era on the discourse about planning practice.

The approach we use is in contrast to many other ways we could view the history of social justice as an idea in planning practice. For example, we could examine the influence of one or more heroes of this cause, such as Catherine Bauer Wurster, Paul Davidoff, Norman Krumholz, or Chester Hartman. Such people had enormous influence on planning, but our major approach here is to look at a broader array of commentators, particularly those whose remarks appear in the 1954–1971 proceedings of the annual conferences held by the American Society of Planning Officials (ASPO), which included presentations by planners, planning commissioners, scholars, and sympathetic politicians.[1] The intent here is to highlight the wide range of planning actors, scholars, and prominent citizens, not just well-known leaders of thought, who were discussing social justice ideas. For insight into scholarship, in addition, I refer to articles published in the main academic journal used by U.S. urban planners, now titled the *Journal of the American Planning Association* (*JAPA*) but previously named the *Journal of the American Institute of Planners* (*JAIP*), the title from 1944 to 1978.[2]

The dialogue I am exploring emerged in stages. I start by examining 1954–1959, actively visible years of the civil rights era, then compare this era with 1960–1966, a period that included the War on Poverty and the first part of the Model Cities era, ending just as major civil disorders were beginning; and finally the period 1967–1974, a time of social reform and political retrenchment.[3] As we will see, planners discussed very little about race, ethnicity, and social justice during the first period, when the civil rights movement and urban conditions were just gaining publicity, but much more during the second and third periods. Reviewing such a discussion—*before* the heat of the civil rights movement and just *after* the change to other forms of social protest—suggests just how influential the turmoil of the era was on planning discourse.

Concepts

The U.S. civil rights era existed well before the activism that arose so visibly in the 1950s and 1960s. Stalwart activists had fought for civil liberties for people of color for many decades before the 1950s (Greenberg 1994).[4] I begin with 1954, however, because of the major importance of the U.S. Supreme Court's opinion in *Brown v. Board of Education of Topeka* (Blaustein and Zangrando 1970, 414), which heralded the federal government's support for dismantling legally enforced racial segregation. Other key events during that time period included boycotts of public bus systems, beginning in southern cities in 1953 and 1954; the desegregation of public schools in Little Rock, Arkansas, in 1957; and passage of the Civil Rights Acts of 1964 and 1968. These events roughly define the civil rights era, but this period overlaps with the Black Power movement, associated with more radical politics and race-centered nationalism. The mid-1960s were also marked by urban "civil rebellions" or riots, protests that were in marked contrast to the nonviolent resistance that characterized civil rights activism. The era, therefore, was complicated.

Another important term is *social justice*, a pivotal concept that has many possible meanings. Social justice proponents during the civil rights era claimed that social justice required basic rights of citizenship for all citizens, regardless of race, ethnicity, or socioeconomic status. They aimed to tear down unjust laws that supported racially separate public schools and public facilities, denied blacks simple voting rights, and failed to censure discrimination in access to goods and services. As noted by Martin Luther King, Jr., "A just law is a man-made code that squares with the moral law or the law of God. . . . An unjust law is a code that a numerical or power majority group compels a minority group to obey but does not make binding on itself" (King 1991, 189). These definitions beautifully fit the civil rights context of the 1950s, when federal, state, and local laws commonly enforced racial segregation and discrimination.

For a social justice definition that relates to urban planning, I turn first to David Harvey (2002, 394), who warns of "as many competing theories of social justice as there are competing ideals of social responsibility," but suggests that plans and policies that support social justice avoid six possible forms of oppression: marginalization, powerlessness, violence, cultural imperialism, the exploitation of labor in the workplace or the home, and environmental degradation. Susan Fainstein's twofold statement is helpful as well: "A theory of the just city values participation in decision making by relatively powerless groups and equity of outcomes" (Fainstein 2003, 186). Harvey's focus on the oppressed and Fainstein's focus on relative powerlessness and outcomes define a group delimited not by race, ethnicity, or similar categorizations but by status and power. Fischer (2009, 61) echoes Harvey's warnings about the difficulty of definition: he suggests that a call for social justice is "an invitation to engage in a discourse" rather than a simple two- or three-part phenomenon. He notes that deliberative discourse could lead to anything from improved participation to social and political transformation.

The likeliest exposure of planning practitioners to discussions about social justice, however, probably occurs through their professional code of ethics rather than by way of scholarly definitions. For planners, this code includes an official "working definition" of social justice. In the late 1970s the AICP, the newly organized U.S. national body of certified professional planners, adopted the principles enumerated in its Code of Ethics, similar to the code used beginning in 1972 by professional members of the American Institute of Planners (AIP).[5] Although this code underwent constant revision, the version published in the 1972 roster for AIP members included the following "canon," or axiomatic norm not subject to disciplinary action: "A planner shall seek to expand choice and opportunity for all persons, recognizing a special responsibility to plan for the needs of disadvantaged groups and persons, and shall urge the alteration of policies, institutions and decisions which mitigate against such objectives" (American Institute of Planners [AIP] 1972, 1974, 1976). Even several decades later, the phrasing of this "working definition" seems quite remarkable, as it is both normative and activist.

The 1980 version of the AICP code also included this key provision, and noted as well that in employment decisions a planner "*shall not directly or indirectly discriminate* against any person because of said person's race, color, creed, sex or national origin" (American Institute of Certified Planners [AICP] 1980; emphasis added). The revised 1991 version contained a rule of conduct that obliged AICP planners to ensure *participation* by those without formal influence or organization, a subject not mentioned in 1980. It also required planners to expand opportunity for all persons and especially for "disadvantaged groups and persons," as above, and said they "must urge the alteration of policies, institutions, and decisions that oppose such needs," similar to the above. In addition, the 1991 code mandated that AICP planners strive to *increase the numbers of women and recognized minorities* among professional planners (AICP 1991; emphasis added). With the 2005 and 2009 revisions, the AICP's call for inclusive participation and recruitment of "underrepresented groups" (not specifically named) returned to nonbinding principles rather than binding rules of conduct, such as the following principle: "*We shall seek social justice* by working to expand choice and opportunity for all persons, recognizing a special responsibility to plan for the needs of the *disadvantaged and to promote racial and economic integration*. We shall urge the alteration of policies, institutions, and decisions that oppose such needs" (AICP 2009; emphasis added). This chapter explains some of the background necessary to understand at least the first of these definitions, from 1972 and 1980, but it is clear that expectations evolved over time.

"The disadvantaged" may aptly describe those suffering from oppression or from relative powerlessness, as presented by Harvey and Fainstein. In that era, "disadvantaged" as used in the sentence above probably also referred to those oppressed or segregated by racial or economic status. Race enters into discussions of "disadvantaged" because certain

U.S. minority-race groups are overrepresented in lower socioeconomic classes, and regardless of economic circumstance are likelier to face other forms of discrimination compared to the majority-race population. As with social justice, the term *disadvantaged* could mean many things in different circumstances, but in the context of the early 1970s in the United States, when the word "disadvantaged" first appeared in the code, we suggest a connection with the conditions facing racial minorities in central cities at that time.

Race is a social construct with little biological justification, especially in multiracial societies with a history of interracial reproduction, as in the United States. The U.S. Census Bureau has changed its definition of race frequently, but as of 2000, those counted as "white" included Irish, Italian, Arab, and other disparate groups (U. S. Census Bureau 2011).[6] Those counted as black or African American varied greatly in national origin, with those whose families had lived in the United States for many generations reflecting widely different combinations of ancestry or "ethnicity." Other major "racial" categories included American Indian and Asian, but these too are diverse; many people are multiracial or use ethnic categories such as national origin (Hirschman 2004). In this chapter I refer to race largely as a socially defined phenomenon for the era under discussion but maintain a focus on socioeconomic circumstances beyond simple minority-race or ethnic status.

Early Stage of an Era, 1954–1959

During the first stage, part of the 1950s, a number of U.S. civil rights victories took place. The Montgomery bus boycott catapulted the young minister, Martin Luther King, Jr., to prominence as an articulate voice for racial justice. Several school desegregation cases reached federal courts. *Brown v. Topeka* was decided in 1954, and the Civil Rights Act of 1957 empowered a federal commission to collect evidence on voting irregularities, an unprecedented action for the U.S. Congress (Blaustein and Zangrando 1970). Public visibility of the importance of civil rights for African Americans grew as the series of actions emerged.

The year 1954 was important as well for its planning-related legislation. The Housing Act of 1954 reauthorized the original 1949 urban redevelopment legislation, but it also facilitated an alternative approach, known as conservation (as opposed to clearance), and it required municipalities to create comprehensive municipal plans before receiving funding for redevelopment activities. The provision of Section 701 grants to fund these comprehensive plans gave a major boost to the employability of urban planners, since localities could now tap federal funds to hire them.

Racially and ethnically biased clearance and reconstruction were already visible as a result of the Housing Acts of 1937 and 1949, establishing public housing and urban redevelopment, but this situation received little attention in ASPO conference proceedings or in the organization's journal. According to Birch (1980), at this time in its organizational history the AIP focused on disseminating research, while ASPO, with its advisory service reports, was riding a wave of growing popularity among practicing planners hungry for technical information on such tasks as how to map streets and determine setbacks. Donald Krueckeberg (1980) counts these as years when *JAIP* was particularly abstract and theoretical.

A number of conference talks and articles offered some insight into the paltry state of social consciousness concerning social justice during these years. These we may group into three categories, summarized in table 14.1. A few talks and articles discussed the implications of racial contexts for cities or for planning activities. In one panel, for example, a presenter focused on analyzing how more recent black immigrants from the South compared with previous immigrant waves, in an attempt to explain lagging efforts to climb in socioeconomic status. In another talk, housing advocate Elizabeth Wood (1958), one of the original supporters of the public housing program, head of the Chicago Housing Authority from 1937 to 1954, and a visible although ultimately unsuccessful champion of public housing based on community concepts that included racial mixing (Hirsch 1983), spoke as well. She assessed the failure of planners to understand the human dimensions of redevelopment and argued that the public housing program faltered in great part because it was obliged to serve "problem families." She noted that neither planners nor social workers knew much about how to handle extensive social problems in inner-city slums.

The pages of *JAIP* reveal very little focus on topics related to race or ethnicity, the civil rights movement, or diversity. One brave practicing planner who was also a trained sociologist (Ravitz 1955) discussed the effects of racial division on efforts to redevelop central cities such as Detroit. He argued that neighborhood conservation was doomed to fail in great part because whites would refuse to continue to live in racially integrated neighborhoods, no matter how much money cities poured into them. Ravitz eventually ran for city council and became a well-known champion of open housing in Detroit (Thomas 1997). A very few *JAIP* articles described the role of racial segregation in "slums" and referred to the need for neighborhood diversity (Churchill 1954; Seeley 1959). During this time period Catherine Bauer (1957) wrote her classic critique, "The Dreary Deadlock of Public Housing," which lamented, among other things, social segregation in subsidized public housing, but she published this piece in *Architectural Forum*.

With regard to a second category summarized in table 14.1 for this era, urban renewal flaws, only one published ASPO conference paper treated the problems of relocation in any depth. At the time directing the American Council to Improve Our Neighborhoods, Martin Meyerson— who published in that same year a co-authored book concerning planning and politics in Chicago (Meyerson and Banfield 1955)—assessed the difficulty of carrying out an urban renewal "workable" program that required planners to relocate blacks, who often lived in the worst dwellings, "into districts of white residents, where the objections . . . will be very great" (Meyerson 1955, 173). Some *JAIP* articles from 1954 to 1959 suggest a small but growing awareness of the importance of relocation as part of redevelopment, but sometimes treated it as a technical matter related to budgeting. A 1954 AIP policy statement notable for its lack of substantive commentary on matters related to race, ethnicity, or poverty (AIP 1954) claimed that redevelopment needed to serve all income groups. In its list of "planners' responsibilities," the organization acknowledged the responsibility to provide for relocation of displaced families, especially those of minority-race groups, but stated without elaboration that race relations contributed to chronic housing shortages. A similar AIP policy statement on redevelopment published five years later (AIP 1959) did not mention relocation and race at all, suggesting a retrenchment in sensitivity, since problems with this aspect of redevelopment were not yet resolved. In that year planning professor and former redevelopment practitioner Herbert Gans (1959) published the initial findings of his study of the actual effects of relocation on a working-class neighborhood, inhabited by white ethnic Italian-Americans in Boston; this foreshadowed his widely read book, *The Urban Villagers*.

Pivotal Change: 1960–1966

The first portion of the 1960s saw several key victories for the civil rights movement, as well as the first glimmers of civil unrest in U.S. cities increasingly divided by class and race. It became more and more difficult to ignore the rising tide of civil disobedience associated with racial

Table 14.1
Treatment of Key U.S. Social Justice Themes in *Planning* (Yearly Proceedings of the American Society of Planning Officials, ASPO) and *Journal of the American Institute of Planning*

	Race, Ethnicity, Segregation	Other Urban Policies Besides Urban Renewal	Urban Redevelopment's Flaws of Oppression	Planning Theory, Ethics	Other
1954–1959	Very little	no	Beginning discussion of relocation	No	Some on socioeconomic diversity
1960–1966	Many conference discussions; some scholarship	Social planning, community renewal planning at ASPO	Part of ASPO discussions; increased scholarship on effects of relocation	Ethical dilemmas, responsibilities; advocacy/equal opportunity	
1967–1974	ASPO and *JAIP* focus on riots, poor, central city–suburban split	Much attention on Model Cities at ASPO, some in *JAIP*	Some direct discussion but largely implicit	Matured thinking about citizen participation, advocacy	

oppression. By 1960, Martin Luther King, Jr., and his colleagues, who formed the Southern Christian Leadership Conference (SCLC), had launched a nonviolent civil protest movement that forever changed public consciousness about the moral imperative of civil rights. Organizational efforts within the African American community flourished with the evolution of the SCLC and the Student Nonviolent Coordinating Committee, an organization of black college students dedicated to civil rights activism but soon attracted to the Black Power movement. Key events included the sit-down strike by four black students in Greensboro, North Carolina, at a whites-only lunch counter; the Civil Rights Act of 1960, which provided some federal oversight of elections in the South; King's 1963 "Letter from Birmingham Jail," addressed to America's clergy; and the Civil Rights Act of 1964, which outlawed racially based denial of voting rights or public accommodation and discrimination in employment (Blaustein and Zangrando 1970).

Civil rights activities generated massive, emotionally affecting media attention. Notable events included the 1963 March on Washington, with King's electrifying "I Have A Dream" speech soon becoming a staple of American social consciousness, and the March 1965 "Bloody Sunday" incident in Selma, Alabama, during which national press representatives photographed white police officers using tear gas, bull whips, and billy clubs to attack purposefully nonviolent marchers protesting voter disenfranchisement based on race. The shocking brutality of these scenes spurred national support for both the 1964 Civil Rights Act and the U.S. Voting Rights Act, signed into law in 1965 after U.S. president Lyndon B. Johnson addressed Congress in a stirring speech responding directly to Bloody Sunday (Johnson 2000).

Important housing and community development policies emerged as well, beginning with Kennedy's 1962 executive order outlawing racial discrimination in housing financed with federal funds. This action, combined with the Housing Act of 1959, which encouraged planners to become involved in "community renewal" based on study of social, economic, and physical problems, led to the 1963 federal decision that community renewal programs must consider the special housing difficulties faced by racial minorities in their plans. Many planners felt ill-prepared to carry out such "social" duties (Scott 1971). Yet more was to come: Johnson's Great Society initiatives included his 1964 announcement of a national War on Poverty and the formation of rural and neighborhood-based community action agencies based on a model of programmatic self-determination by low-income residents. The Housing

Act of 1964 required further shifting from slum clearance to rehabilitation respectful of social fabric, as did the 1966 Model Cities legislation, which confirmed the important role of resident-directed initiatives.

In this context, we would expect to find among planners of the period enhanced discussion of race, ethnicity, and poverty. Indeed, the many changes taking place did affect both conference proceedings and *JAIP*, as summarized in table 14.1. Beginning around 1960, the ASPO sponsored many conference sessions discussing racial segregation and the changing demographics of cities, and how this affected planning work. In 1960 the dean of the University of Pennsylvania law school (Fordham 1960) reminded the audience of the U.S. Supreme Court's lack of support for racial restrictions in housing[7] and urged them to avoid racial segregation in land use. In 1961, a special panel discussion titled "Migration, Minorities, and the Implications for Planning" included two sociologists and a representative of the U.S. Department of Labor addressing the growing importance of racial and ethnic minorities in cities and the harmful effects of racial segregation. Scott Greer (1963), who went on to publish a number of books on urban renewal, metropolitan governance, and racial ghettos, recommended improving redevelopment in the context of ethnic enclaves and the black ghetto, and several other talks discussed the implications of increasing numbers of blacks and Puerto Ricans in cities. A panel session titled "Human Renewal" discussed why assimilation that worked for other ethnic groups was not working for American blacks, and one panelist warned that failure to address the needs of this population would empower separatist black nationalists. In contrast, *JAIP* remained fairly detached from discussions related to race and demographics. The exceptions were few: Gans (1961) offered a neutral assessment of the relative merits of homogeneity versus heterogeneity in residential areas, Eleanor Wolf (1963) explored the racial tipping point in neighborhoods, and Nathan Glazer (1964) wrote about school desegregation.

Urban policy revisions, such as the Community Renewal program, spurred dialogue at the conferences. One topic was how to merge physical and social planning. Talks on human renewal at the 1963 conference referenced Ford Foundation programs in support of social planning in five cities, offering evidence that the work of a private foundation was supporting these goals. William Slayton, urban renewal commissioner of the Urban Renewal Administration, explained that society should help its "more unfortunate members" and that his agency recognized that poverty, unemployment, and inadequate education needed attention, not just physical redevelopment (Slayton 1963, 154). In a topic raised by Wood as well (1958), however, Greer (1963) at the same conference warned that planners and scholars did not understand many intricate social processes at work in cities, much less how these would respond to implementation in a plan of action. A few years later, nevertheless, the secretary of the new U.S. Department of Housing and Urban Development (HUD), Robert Weaver (1966), discussed Great Society urban proposals as if these would provide a lot of resources to planners, who would surely know how to use them.

Dominant during this period of time, however, were discussions of the two themes of redevelopment dilemmas related to relocation and the need to revise professional conduct, both of them bearing on vulnerable populations. At the ASPO conferences, several speakers began to address the human implications of urban renewal, and some pleaded for the "realization of human values" (Fordham 1960), recognition of the social significance of ethnic neighborhoods (Greer 1963), and an understanding of the negative effects of large-scale displacement, particularly of ethnic groups. In *JAIP*, articles emerged arguing that urban renewal was causing negative effects, such as Peter Marris's (1962) philosophical exploration of the social implications of urban redevelopment, short similar pieces by Charles Abrams (1963) and Nathaniel Lichfield (1961), and several articles by Chester Hartman. Hartman documented the lack of public housing alternatives for displaced working-class families (Hartman 1963), demonstrated that displaced families continued to live in substandard housing (Hartman 1964), and offered a stinging rebuke (Hartman 1965) to Boston redevelopment leader Edward Logue's claim that his city's record of relocating displaced people was good. James Q. Wilson discussed problems of power and influence for lower-income people, and warned that the capacity to organize for community-wide goals would probably be more developed among middle-class rather than lower-class citizens. He concluded that inclusion in decision making by relatively powerless people would require a fundamental reorientation of the entire system of local governance (Wilson 1963).

A parallel discourse related to planners' responsibilities under such conditions of disparity. Presenters began to consider what professional conduct would be appropriate as they became promoters of social values that were non-exclusionary and worked to solve social problems such as poverty and unemployment. A U.S. senator (Clark 1966) urged ASPO attendees to help fulfill the aspirations of all citizens without regard to their race or socioeconomic status, suggesting, by implication, that they had not been doing this.

It was in this context that *JAIP* began to publish important discussions that could begin to make sense of this very complex situation. Paul Ylvisaker (1961) used storytelling to explore the ethical dilemmas facing a planner working in a racially contentious environment. Harvey Perloff (1965) tackled the issue of social planning by looking at necessary tools and approaches, in terms of organization, substance, information, and process. Three pieces of great importance for our working definition of social justice were former *JAIP* editor Melvin Webber's (1963) "Comprehensive Planning and Social Responsibility," a piece commissioned by AIP that explored the profession's changing social responsibilities; *JAIP* editor Bernard Frieden's (1965) "Toward Equality of Opportunity," which discussed specific ways planning policies could support greater opportunity in residential choices for all groups, in frank support of open housing; and Paul Davidoff's "Advocacy and Pluralism in Planning" (1965), which argued for empowering many competing publics with their own planners. Ironically, the term "advocacy planning" soon came to suggest planning for the powerless, but Davidoff's 1965 article actually presented a more pluralistic model, granting to every interest group, including the poor, the right to planning representation. That was a step forward from the pervasive public interest model that implied planners served one public, the dominant one. Finally it was becoming clear: planning theory would have to change. First, however, events shifted to cause even more turmoil.

Paradigm Shifts: 1967–1974

The period from 1967 to 1974 witnessed a series of massive upheavals that affected the nation, its cities, and its urban professionals. In previous years the locus of civil rights activism had been in the South, where public schools, accommodations, and voting rights were most egregiously segregated and unequal. First the movement of social change shifted from the South to other parts of the United States, and then, after years of turmoil, reactionary forces simultaneously brought social order and stymied social movements on behalf of the disadvantaged.

In the mid-1960s many African Americans chafed at the SCLC nonviolent approach to civil rights. Blacks confined to inner-city ghettos experienced continuing job and housing discrimination, police harassment, and other frustrations, aggravated by marginalization. Minor confrontations with police sometimes set off violent incidents of multiday civil disorder known as race riots, the obverse of historical patterns of whites attacking blacks during the race riots of previous decades. Disaffected blacks burned down whole sections of cities, after targeting and looting, in particular, white-owned stores, and thereby subjecting their communities to retaliation and the aggressive entry of armed police and military forces, leading to the loss of life and limb as well as property. Beginning with the riots in the Watts section of Los Angeles in 1965, these incidents spread nationwide. A national advisory committee recommended federal remedies in housing, education, employment, and welfare to a nation that decided instead to buttress the criminal justice system ("Report of the National Advisory Commission on Civil Disorders" 1968).

At the same time, the Black Power movement gained followers, in secular form among groups that argued that blacks were tired of seeing civil rights protestors in the South being beaten, and in religious form among, most notably, the black Muslims. Before his 1968 assassination, King and the SCLC had broadened civil action to other locales, marching for open housing in Chicago and for garbage workers in Memphis, in an attempt to target widespread discrimination practices and impoverishment with nonviolent activism, but for many, the slogan "Black Power" had more sway (Carmichael 1966), and the response to King's assassination was another round of destructive civil disorders in U.S. cities.

Urban policy changed in response to these events. As part of President Johnson's efforts to build the Great Society, the first of two appointed task forces began work in 1964 on an initiative ultimately known as "Model Cities," designed to repair ailing cities by coordinating agency efforts, targeting distressed areas with flexible funds, and spending these in accordance with resident-driven priorities. Johnson's 1966 message to Congress urging support for this program referenced the widening gap between the suburban and inner-city minority-race poor, and he noted as well the limitations of previous urban renewal efforts. His administration supported both continued urban renewal appropriations and a city demonstration program considerably weaker than first envisioned (Frieden and Kaplan 1977), as well as several other domestic initiatives, but the Vietnam War soon absorbed Johnson's attention. When he bowed out of the 1968 election and left office, President Richard Nixon's administration supported the Model Cities program for several years, but by the early 1970s national support for this and other urban programs had dwindled considerably, partially in conservative response to the civil disorders of the 1960s. The Housing and Community Development Act of 1974 was the urban reflection of this new conservatism. Its Community Development Block Grant program ended Model Cities; spread available money to a wider range of states, cities, and suburbs; and purported to primarily benefit low- and moderate-income people, but had numerous provisions that could water down targeting.

These swings in circumstance and ideology are very much visible in the planning discourse of this time period, again as summarized in table 14.1. From 1967 to 1971, a major category of focus was the urban civil disorders, which overshadowed several ASPO conferences. At the 1967 ASPO conference Donald Elliott, chair of the New York City planning commission, called the "urban crisis" the nation's number one domestic problem and the situation facing blacks and Puerto Ricans of grave concern (Elliott 1967). Civil disorders were *the* topic of the 1968 conference, pervading that year's proceedings even when panelists were ostensibly speaking on different topics. A panel titled "City Planning and the Riot-torn City" included representatives from Newark and Detroit explaining the effects of riots and socioeconomic change on their cities. Members of the panel "Planning as an Instrument for Social Change" and of another panel on the suburbs and the central cities spoke to similar issues. The 1969 Cincinnati conference included a presentation on the National Commission on Urban Problems by urban scholar Anthony Downs (1969), concerning the need for better housing for minority-race, poor central-city residents, and the influence of the riots on domestic policy. In *JAIP*, Martin Rein (1967) published an article that probably would not have appeared without the War on Poverty, "Social Science and the Elimination of Poverty," with a supportive response from Frieden (1967). Louis Kriesberg (1968) addressed the social isolation of public housing tenants, and several 1969 articles discussed racial segregation (e.g., Mann 1969). Jack Meltzer (1968) wrote an interpretive essay on the "urban revolt," as did Richard Danforth (1970).

By 1967, the Model Cities program was a popular topic for ASPO speakers (Davidoff 1967); most saw a lot of potential for social reform, as did planning director Charles Blessing (1968), who welcomed Model Cities staff efforts after the 1967 Detroit riot. His own city's former Model Cities director, David Cason, Jr. (1970), however, frankly acknowledged the difficulty of developing a consensus among citizen groups for their efforts, and other members of his panel also offered sobering commentary about program limitations, as did Marshall Kaplan the next year (1971).

Most impressive during this time period is a third category of response: from 1967 to 1974 conference participants and scholars seemed to change, profoundly, the way they thought about themselves and their social responsibilities compared to earlier years. This is the time, 1972, when language first appeared in the professional code concerning "special responsibility" to plan for the "disadvantaged." The published ASPO conference proceedings from 1967 until 1971[8] demonstrate how fertile the context was for such a new sense of responsibility. As a corollary, planning theory changed as well, particularly concerning pluralism, participation, and social justice. Speaker after speaker during the late 1960s hammered home the point that planning would have to change. In 1967, Davidoff's (1967) talk about Model Cities also described planners' obligations to uphold racial equality and equal opportunity for all. He urged planners not to look back to past mistakes but rather to look forward to their particular charge of countering housing discrimination in the suburbs.

Attendees at the 1968 conference heard many calls to action for social justice, although not all accepted this call. For his Pomeroy Memorial Lecture, conference organizers had asked Philadelphia's Bacon (1968) to summarize and respond to conference panel discussions he was able to attend. To modern eyes, this well-known planning director's comments seem skeptical of both Model Cities and what he called advocacy planning, a skepticism shared by a few other speakers, such as New York's Roger Starr (1968), a housing and planning advocate, who chastised Harlem's Architects Renewal Committee in Harlem (ARCH) for advocacy planning that instigated unfair protests against Columbia University. ARCH's Alan Kravitz (1968) denied these charges, arguing that the problem was the way Columbia made its decisions, which riled a black neighboring community perfectly capable of organizing protest on its own. He urged planners to recognize the failures of rational planning and to support active, creative participation in ways that would redistribute power so as to promote social equity. Richard Strichartz (1968), from Detroit, stated that planners had become too bureaucratic in their traditional work; John Mauro (1968), from Pittsburgh, said that the exodus of whites to suburbia was making planning for bankrupt cities difficult even with Model Cities; the mayor of Milwaukee (Maier 1968) protested that zoning ordinances promoted American apartheid; and to varying degrees the entire "Physical Planning Standards and Social

Goals" panel pointed out that physical standards were not helping to create a peaceful society necessary because of a racial divide heightened by civil disorders.

The trend continued, in somewhat subdued form, at the 1970 and 1971 conferences, held well after the 1969 inauguration of conservative Richard Nixon as U.S. president. A series of prominent federal, state, and local officials chided conference attendees for past actions and urged changes in the planning process, as did several academics. Congresswoman Shirley Chisholm (1970) critiqued the concept that citizen participation was relevant only for War on Poverty programs, and she warned that central-city residents were struggling for survival and would no longer accept token involvement in plans for their communities. New York City mayor John Lindsay (1970) discussed the need to rethink citizen involvement, and Boston's Edward Logue (1970) urged the creation of master plans that no longer pretended that race and poverty did not matter. HUD's assistant secretary Samuel Jackson (1970) gave a spirited lecture on the exclusionary actions of suburban communities using planning tools and on the fallacy that comprehensive plans had nothing to do with class or race. He urged planners to support open housing and balance suburban resources with central-city needs. Paul Davidoff (1970) and Arthur Symes (1970) strongly criticized the new draft of New York City's master plan for ignoring social justice issues. Cleveland's mayor Carl Stokes (1971), a nationally prominent African American—as was Congresswoman Chisholm—supplemented Chisholm's remarks from the previous year by encouraging planners to take a stronger advocacy approach to planning, and wondering why the conference agenda included so little about this subject.

And then the published APSO proceedings stop. The discussions from 1967 to 1971 had been passionate, accusatory, inspirational, and a bit contentious. Starting with mutual commiseration over the civil disorders, moving on to descriptions of the War on Poverty and Model Cities, and, particularly in the 1968 conference, with much rumination, agreement, and disagreement about the changed responsibility of planners, passions appear to have abated considerably by 1971. This was, of course, the third year of the Nixon administration. It was no longer clear that federal money would be available to support planners who wished to work with Model Cities or advocacy planning and still receive salaries (Frieden and Kaplan 1977).

We see, however, in the pages of *JAIP* one of the important fruits of this time period: a profound change in planning theory. Several articles in the journal began to create an intellectual companion for the more practitioner-oriented discussions taking place at ASPO. Bernard Frieden (1967) drew on discussions of the War on Poverty and Model Cities to write "The Changing Prospects for Social Planning," which focused in particular on health care planning. Michael Brooks and Michael Stegman (1968) laid out an agenda for training more socially sensitive planners in the aftermath of the riots and in the context of racial segregation, encouraging universities to offer introductory courses in poverty and to educate advocacy planners. Walter Stafford and Joyce Ladner (1969) explained just what was wrong with traditional comprehensive plans from the perspective of oppressed racial minorities.

Two other issues emerged that would have long-lasting effects on contemporary planning: citizen participation and advocacy planning. With their discussions of citizen participation, Melvin Mogulof (1969), Sherry Arnstein (1969), and Neil Gilbert and Joseph Eaton (1970) all drew on pivotal examples from Model Cities and the War on Poverty's programs to offer a revised view of the responsibility of the planner in relation to the citizenry. Mogulof's commentary used three federal Great Society programs to describe varying effects on neighborhood involvement, and Gilbert and Eaton's research report was an intelligent discussion of the limitations of such involvement, but it is Arnstein's ladder of citizen participation that has gained lasting fame for describing the widely varying levels of citizen involvement possible in public decision making. The examples she used in the article linked directly with the Model Cities program, born in the context of civil rights activism and civil disorder, both of which sprang from racial inequality.

The second theory of lasting influence was advocacy planning. Many social activists and others adopted this term as a way to describe professional representation of the oppressed, and the concept gained credibility in academia as well, as we can see from Lisa Peattie's cautionary remarks (1968), Marshall Kaplan's classificatory description (1969), Frances Piven's use of the term in connection with urban management and with the activist group Planners for Equal Opportunity (1969), and most especially Paul Davidoff, Linda Davidoff, and Neil Gold's (1970) "Suburban Action: Advocate Planning for an Open Society."

With this last article, we see the remarkable results of Paul Davidoff's own evolving intellectual journey. He had co-authored a *JAIP* article about planning process published eight years earlier (Davidoff and Reiner 1962) that had little to do with social justice or advocacy. His article on advocacy (Davidoff 1965), however, drew direct connections to work being done to rebuild inner-city ghettos. With the last of this series (Davidoff, Davidoff, and Gold 1970), it became clear that, as Davidoff had noted in ASPO conference talks, the issue was not simply rebuilding the ghetto but also opening up the suburbs to everyone, regardless of race, ethnicity, or socioeconomic class.

Intellectual Heritage

Looking at two major sources reflecting the evolution of ordinary planning officials' and planning scholars' thinking about race, ethnicity, and social justice during the civil rights era helps illuminate the context in which a professional code of ethics emerged. Given this context, it is not surprising that ethical conduct among U.S. planners became associated with subsequent statements about opportunity for the disadvantaged. Both the ASPO conference proceedings and the pages of *JAIP* from 1960 to 1974 reveal a passionate dialogue about urban context, urban policy, and planners' and planning officials' responsibilities, with ASPO conference proceedings proving to be particularly sensitive barometers of the times, unfettered by the time lag associated with academic journal publishing. The civil rights era, apparently, left its mark.

What survived decades later? In addition to the AICP's Code of Ethics, I suggest two things in particular, concerning theories of citizen participation and advocacy. An activist tradition has lingered as well, sometimes known as "radical planning," as exemplified by Chester Hartman (2002). As for the theoretical legacy in mainstream planning, disenchantment with citizen participation as a strategy for social justice grew somewhat after the civil rights era, when it became clear that such participation was not the solution to the problems of inner-city poverty and that middle-class populations were adept at using participation as a way to protect their own interests, as Wilson (1963) had predicted. However, the current communicative planning tradition owes much to the concepts first verbalized during the discussions about citizen participation in planning during the Model Cities era, and the best of the communicative genre includes considerations about class and poverty (Healey 2003).

Advocacy planning as a concept has held sway; the attractiveness of the idea that planners could focus on providing planning services to powerless groups also lingers in other ways as well, as with universities that set up outreach partnerships working with nearby communities as learning laboratories that also allow students to provide low-income communities with planning-related research. But the concept of professional advocacy planners suffered greatly in the United States with the demise of federal programs such as Model Cities, and for practical reasons advocacy planning did not always work because of lack of a permanent organizational vehicle (Genovese 1983) and lack of funding (Davidoff and Davidoff 1978), as well as other problems of implementation (Heskin 1980). As Davidoff worked to open suburban borders, he continued to fight for the right of central-city low-income populations to have access to full-time professional planners and architects who worked for their benefit. Some planning organizations based on advocacy, however, encountered difficulties in contexts plagued by problematic questions about professionals' roles and responsibilities (Heskin 1980; Corey 1972).

Offshoots of the advocacy planning idea include Krumholz's concept of equity planning (Krumholz 1982). Equity planning is an especially intriguing concept dating from this era because it approached the problem of the planners' role in cities fraught with social justice problems in a slightly different way than did advocacy planning. Both equity planning as described by Krumholz (1982) and advocacy planning as promoted by Davidoff, Davidoff, and Gold (1970) were concerned with social justice for disadvantaged urban populations, and called on planners to assist such populations by planning on their behalf. Krumholz's concept, however, built largely on just one of five approaches to advocacy planning that Corey had identified, the one labeled "inside-nondirected advocacy planning" (Corey 1972).[9] Unlike allied advocacy planning efforts, which required a planner to work outside government in independent or citizen-driven organizations or to educate citizens to plan for themselves, this branch of advocacy planning entailed a professional planner working in government but committed to "the interests of a perceived constituency" (Corey 1972, 55). Krumholz explicitly called on professional planners in government positions to support policies and programs based on one overriding goal: to provide the widest possible choices for those citizens who had the fewest choices, in frank support of social equity (Krumholz 1982). Krumholz and Pierre Clavel demonstrated that planners in many U.S. cities adopted this approach for at least some of their activities (Krumholz and Clavel 1994), and conversations about topics such as inclusionary and exclusionary zoning and spatial rights remain alive (Soja 2010).

Nevertheless, a nagging concern is whether these ideas have led to practical results in the everyday life of current practitioners. A real issue is whether, absent the pressing context of the 1960s and early 1970s,

U.S. planners feel committed to related ideals exhorted in the AICP Code of Ethics, and whether they act on what commitment they do have. Dilemmas of social inequality continue, in problem areas ranging from lack of access to good public education and employment opportunities to inadequate housing, and many people remain trapped in marginalized central-city ghettoes. In the 1960s, one commentator noted that no one understood the social forces taking place in central cities, much less whether they would yield to a plan of action (Greer 1963); today we understand the forces better, having analyzed them with reams of reports and data and maps, but apparently we still have neither the tools nor the social will to resolve them.

Exhortations for planning for social justice continue, such as in the 2009 AICP Code of Ethics, and in planning classrooms that prepare students for practice, but the political structure of metropolitan areas encourages severe stratification, disunity, and isolation for the most vulnerable populations, and graduating planning students very likely go to work as practitioners in a singular municipality, a cell within the subdivided whole metropolis. Social justice options for the cell exist but may seem limited in a metropolitan context, and methods for carrying out effective strategies as described by Fischer (2009), Fainstein (2010), and Soja (2010) are not always readily apparent. It may be time to reintroduce into planning discourse about both practice and scholarship more purposeful solution building concerning social justice, although this would probably never match the passionate self-examination so characteristic of the era reviewed in this chapter.

Notes

1. The American Institute of Planners also held conferences during many of these years; see the Cornell University finder's guide: http://rmc.library.cornell.edu/EAD/htmldocs/RMM04007.html.

2. Although *JAPA* is now mostly composed of scholarly reports on empirical research, for many years *JAPA* and its precursors also published reflective essays by practitioners. See Krueckeberg (1980).

3. The chapter examines the ASPO proceedings from 1954 to 1971 and the journal publications from 1954 to 1974. See Worsham (1979).

4. With apologies: I do not discuss Native American battles for their sovereign rights or other major civil rights concerns of, for example, the Latino or Asian community simply because of time and space. The focus here is on the civil rights movement led by African Americans.

5. The canon that follows was in use as early as 1972 in the code governing members of the professional American Institute of Planners, according to the version published with the 1972 roster (AIP 1971, 1972, 1974, 1976). This canon was not evident in the code published with the 1971 roster. No provisions concerning social equity appeared in the canon for the years dating from 1959 to 1966.

6. Gibson and Jung (2005) review the evolution of racial categories in the United States. For varying classifications of groups, see Roediger (2005).

7. *Shelley v. Kraemer,* 334 U.S. 1 (1948), was a U.S. Supreme Court ruling that declared racially restrictive residential covenants unenforceable.

8. The AIP and ASPO may have held joint conferences thereafter; the two groups merged to form the American Planning Association in 1978.

9. Corey (1972) studied seven major advocacy planning operations and classified their activities and policies into five major types of advocacy planning: inside-nondirected, which I define in the text; outside-directed, in which a planner may be under contract with a client group; educational, focused on learning by students or residents; ideological, in which the planner himself or herself is the only client; and indigenous-liberation advocacy planning, in which community residents plan for themselves.

References

Abrams, Charles. 1963. The Ethics of Power in Government Housing Programs. *Journal of the American Institute of Planners* 29 (3): 223–224.

American Institute of Certified Planners. 1980. *American Institute of Certified Planners Code of Ethics and Rules of Procedure. AICP 1980 Roster.* Washington, DC: American Institute of Certified Planners.

American Institute of Certified Planners. 1991. American Institute of Certified Planners Code of Ethics and Professional Conduct. http://www.planning.org/ethics/conduct1991.html.

American Institute of Certified Planners. 2009. American Institute of Certified Planners Code of Ethics and Professional Conduct. http://www.planning.org/ethics/conduct.html.

American Institute of Planners. 1954. Statement of Policy on Urban Redevelopment. *Journal of the American Institute of Planners* 20 (1): 53–56.

American Institute of Planners. 1959. Urban Renewal: A Policy Statement of the American Institute of Planners. *Journal of the American Institute of Planners* 25 (4): 217–221.

American Institute of Planners. 1971. *Roster.* Washington, DC: American Institute of Planners.

American Institute of Planners. 1972. *Roster.* Washington, DC: American Institute of Planners.

American Institute of Planners. 1974. *Roster*. Washington, DC: American Institute of Planners.

American Institute of Planners. 1976. *Roster*. Washington, DC: American Institute of Planners.

Arnstein, Sherry. 1969. A Ladder of Citizen Participation. *Journal of the American Institute of Planners* 35 (4): 16–24.

Bacon, Edmund. 1968. Pomeroy Memorial Lecture. In *Planning 1968: Selected Papers from the ASPO National Planning Conference*, 1–12. Chicago: American Society of Planning Officials.

Bauer, Catherine. 1957. The Dreary Deadlock of Public Housing. *Architectural Forum* 105 (5): 140–141.

Birch, Eugenie. 1980. Advancing the Art and Science of Planning: Planners and Their Organizations 1909–1980. *Journal of the American Planning Association* 46 (1): 22–49.

Blaustein, Albert, and Robert Zangrando. 1970. *Civil Rights and the Black American: A Documentary History*. New York: Simon and Schuster.

Blessing, Charles. 1968. America's Riot-Torn Cities. In *Planning 1968: Selected Papers from the ASPO National Planning Conference*, 23–28. Chicago: American Society of Planning Officials.

Brooks, Michael, and Michael Stegman. 1968. Urban Social Policy, Race, and the Education of Planners. *Journal of the American Institute of Planners* 34 (5): 275–286.

Carmichael, Stokely. 1966. What We Want. In *Civil Rights Since 1787: A Reader on the Black Struggle*, ed. Jonathan Birnbaum and Clarence Taylor, 599–605. New York: New York University Press.

Cason, David Jr. 1970. A Brief Critique of the Model Cities Program. In *Planning 1970: Selected Papers from the ASPO National Planning Conference*, 63–71. Chicago: American Society of Planning Officials.

Chisholm, Shirley. 1970. Planning with and Not for People. In *Planning 1970: Selected Papers from the ASPO National Planning Conference*, 1–5. Chicago: American Society of Planning Officials.

Churchill, Henry. 1954. Planning in a Free Society. *Journal of the American Institute of Planners* 20 (4): 189–191.

Clark, Joseph. 1966. Planning for People. In *Planning 1966: Selected Papers from the ASPO National Planning Conference*, 119–124. Chicago: American Society of Planning Officials.

Corey, Kenneth. 1972. Advocacy in Planning: A Reflective Analysis. *Antipode* 4 (2): 46–63.

Danforth, Richard. 1970. The Central City and the Forgotten American. *Journal of the American Institute of Planners* 36 (6): 426–428.

Davidoff, Paul. 1965. Advocacy and Pluralism in Planning. *Journal of the American Institute of Planners* 31 (4): 331–338.

Davidoff, Paul. 1967. A Rebuilt Ghetto Does Not a Model City Make. In *Planning 1967: Selected Papers from the ASPO National Planning Conference*, 187–192. Chicago: American Society of Planning Officials.

Davidoff, Paul. 1970. John Lindsay, Why Do Your Words Exceed Your Plan? In *Planning 1970: Selected Papers from the ASPO National Planning Conference*, 184–187. Chicago: American Society of Planning Officials.

Davidoff, Paul, Linda Davidoff, and Neil Gold. 1970. Suburban Action: Advocate Planning for an Open Society. *Journal of the American Institute of Planners* 36 (1): 12–21.

Davidoff, Paul, and Linda Davidoff. 1978. Advocacy and Urban Planning. In *Social Scientists as Advocates: Views from the Applied Disciplines*, ed. George Weber and George McCall, 99–120. Beverly Hills, CA: Sage.

Davidoff, Paul, and Thomas Reiner. 1962. A Choice Theory of Planning. *Journal of the American Institute of Planners* 28 (2): 103–115.

Downs, Anthony. 1969. Urbanization Policies Recommended by the National Commission on Urban Problems. In *Planning 1969: Selected Papers from the ASPO National Planning Conference*, 20–32. Chicago: American Society of Planning Officials.

Elliott, Donald. 1967. Top Priority Problems and Their Effect on Planning and Urban Policies. In *Planning 1967: Selected Papers from the ASPO National Planning Conference*, 34–39. Chicago: American Society of Planning Officials.

Fainstein, Susan. 2003. New Directions in Planning Theory. In *Readings in Planning Theory*. 2nd ed., ed. Scott Campbell and Susan Fainstein, 173–195. Malden, MA: Blackwell.

Fainstein, Susan. 2010. *The Just City*. Ithaca, NY: Cornell University Press.

Fischer, Frank. 2009. Discursive Planning: Social Justice as Discourse. In *Searching for the Just City: Debates in Urban Theory and Practice*, ed. Peter Marcuse, et al., 52–71. New York: Routledge.

Fordham, Jefferson. 1960. Planning for the Realization of Human Values. *Planning 1960: Selected Papers from the ASPO National Planning Conference*, 1–7. Chicago: American Society of Planning Officials.

Frieden, Bernard. 1965. Toward Equality of Opportunity. *Journal of the American Institute of Planners* 31 (4): 320–330.

Frieden, Bernard. 1967. The Changing Prospects for Social Planning. *Journal of the American Institute of Planners* 33 (5): 311–323.

Frieden, Bernard, and Marshall Kaplan. 1977. *The Politics of Neglect: Urban Aid from Model Cities to Revenue Sharing*. Cambridge, MA: MIT Press.

Gans, Herbert. 1959. The Human Implications of Current Redevelopment and Relocation Planning. *Journal of the American Institute of Planners* 25 (1): 15–26.

Gans, Herbert. 1961. The Balanced Community: Homogeneity or Heterogeneity in Residential Areas. *Journal of the American Institute of Planners* 27 (3): 176–184.

Genovese, Rosalie. 1983. Dilemmas in Introducing Activism and Advocacy into Urban Planning. In *Professionals and Urban Form*, ed. Judith Blau, Mark La Gory, and John Pipkin, 320–339. Albany: State University of New York Press.

Gibson, Campbell, and Kay Jung. 2005. Historical Census Statistics on Population Totals by Race, 1790 to 1990, and By Historical Origin, 1970 to 1990, for Large Cities and Other Urban Places in the United States. Populations Division, Working Paper No. 76. Washington, DC: U.S. Census Bureau. http://www.census .gov/population/www/documentation/twps0076.pdf.

Gilbert, Neil, and Joseph Eaton. 1970. Research Report: Who Speaks for the Poor? *Journal of the American Institute of Planners* 36 (6): 411–416.

Glazer, Nathan. 1964. School Integration Policies in Northern Cities. *Journal of the American Institute of Planners* 30 (3): 178–189.

Greenberg, Jack. 1994. *Crusaders in the Courts: How a Dedicated Band of Lawyers Fought for the Civil Rights Revolution*. New York: Basic Books.

Greer, Scott. 1963. Key Issues for the Central City. In *Planning 1963: Selected Papers from the ASPO National Planning Conference*, 123–139. Chicago: American Society of Planning Officials.

Hartman, Chester. 1963. The Limitations of Public Housing: Relocation Choices in a Working-Class Community. *Journal of the American Institute of Planners* 29 (4): 283–296.

Hartman, Chester. 1964. The Housing of Relocated Families. *Journal of the American Institute of Planners* 30 (4): 266–286.

Hartman, Chester. 1965. Rejoinder by the Author. *Journal of the American Institute of Planners* 31 (4): 340–345.

Hartman, Chester. 2002. *Between Eminence and Notoriety: Four Decades of Radical Urban Planning*. New Brunswick, NJ: Center for Urban Policy Research Press.

Harvey, David. 2002. Social Justice, Postmodernism, and the City. In *Readings in Planning Theory*. 2nd ed., ed. Susan Fainstein and Scott Campbell, 386–402. Malden, MA: Blackwell.

Healey, Patsy. 2003. The Communicative Turn in Planning Theory and its Implications for Spatial Strategy Formation. In *Readings in Planning Theory*, 2nd ed., ed. Susan Fainstein and Scott Campbell, 237–255. Malden, MA: Blackwell.

Heskin, Allan. 1980. Crisis and Response: A Historical Perspective on Advocacy Planning. *Journal of the American Planning Association* 46 (1): 50–63.

Hirsch, Arnold. 1983. *Making of The Second Ghetto: Race and Housing in Chicago, 1940–1960*. Cambridge: Cambridge University Press.

Hirschman, Charles. 2004. The Origins and Demise of the Concept of Race. *Population and Development Review* 30 (3): 385–415.

Jackson, Samuel. 1970. The Role of Planning in Meeting the Nation's Housing Call. In *Planning 1970: Selected Papers from the ASPO National Planning Conference*, 31–37. Chicago: American Society of Planning Officials.

Johnson, Lyndon B. 2000. Address on Voting Rights. In *Civil Rights Since 1787: A Reader on the Black Struggle*, ed. Jonathan Birnbaum and Clarence Taylor, 546–550. New York: New York University Press.

Kaplan, Marshall. 1969. Advocacy and the Urban Poor. *Journal of the American Institute of Planners* 35 (2):96–101.

Kaplan, Marshall. 1971. The Relevance of Model Cities. In *Planning 1971: Selected Papers from the ASPO National Planning Conference*, 28–35. Chicago: American Society of Planning Officials.

King, Martin Luther, Jr. 1991. Letter from a Birmingham Jail. In *A History of Our Time: Readings on Postwar America*, 3rd ed., ed. William Chafe and Harvard Sitkoff, 184–197. New York: Oxford University Press.

Kravitz, Alan. 1968. Advocacy and Beyond. In *Planning 1968: Selected Papers from the ASPO National Planning Conference*, 38–45. Chicago: American Society of Planning Officials.

Kriesberg, Louis. 1968. Neighborhood Setting and the Isolation of Public Housing Tenants. *Journal of the American Institute of Planners* 34 (1): 43–49.

Krueckeberg, Donald. 1980. The Story of the Planner's Journal, 1915-80. *Journal of the American Planning Association* 46 (1): 5–21.

Krumholz, Norman. 1982. A Retrospective View of Equity Planning: Cleveland 1969–1979. *Journal of the American Planning Association* 48 (2): 136–152.

Krumholz, Norman, and Pierre Clavel. 1994. *Reinventing Cities: Equity Planners Tell Their Stories*. Philadelphia: Temple University Press.

Lichfield, Nathaniel. 1961. Relocation: The Impact on Housing Welfare. *Journal of the American Institute of Planners* 27 (3): 199–203.

Lindsay, John. 1970. The New Planning. In *Planning 1970: Selected Papers from the ASPO National Planning Conference*, 17–20. Chicago: American Society of Planning Officials.

Logue, Edward. 1970. Pomeroy Memorial Lecture: Urban Policies for the 1970s. In *Planning 1970: Selected Papers from the ASPO National Planning Conference*, 21–30. Chicago: American Society of Planning Officials.

Maier, Henry. 1968. The Open Metropolis. In *Planning 1968: Selected Papers from the ASPO National Planning Conference*, 232–235. Chicago: American Society of Planning Officials.

Mann, Lawrence. 1969. The New, Black and White, Urbanism. *Journal of the American Institute of Planners* 35 (2): 121–131.

Marris, Peter. 1962. The Social Implications of Urban Redevelopment. *Journal of the American Institute of Planners* 28 (3): 180–186.

Mauro, John. 1968. Social Change in Pittsburgh. In *Planning 1968: Selected Papers from the ASPO National Planning Conference*, 59–66. Chicago: American Society of Planning Officials.

Meltzer, Jack. 1968. A New Look at the Urban Revolt. *Journal of the American Institute of Planners* 34 (4): 255–259.

Meyerson, Martin. 1955. Urban Renewal. In *Planning 1955: Selected Papers from the ASPO National Planning Conference*, 169–175. Chicago: American Society of Planning Officials.

Meyerson, Martin, and Edward Banfield. 1955. *Politics, Planning, and the Public Interest: The Case of Public Housing in Chicago*. Glencoe, IL: Free Press.

Mogulof, Melvin. 1969. Coalition to Adversary: Citizen Participation in Three Federal Programs. *Journal of the American Institute of Planners* 35 (4): 225–232.

Peattie, Lisa. 1968. Reflections on Advocacy Planning. *Journal of the American Institute of Planners* 34 (2): 80–88.

Perloff, Harvey. 1965. New Directions in Social Planning. *Journal of the American Institute of Planners* 31 (4): 297–304.

Piven, Frances. 1969. Advocacy as a Strategy of Political Management. *Prospecta* 12:37–38.

Ravitz, Mel. 1955. Urban Renewal Faces Critical Roadblocks. *Journal of the American Institute of Planners* 21 (1): 17–21.

Rein, Martin. 1967. Social Science and the Elimination of Poverty. *Journal of the American Institute of Planners* 33 (3): 146–163.

Report of the National Advisory Commission on Civil Disorders. 1968. Excerpted in *Civil Rights Since 1787: A Reader on the Black Struggle*, ed. Jonathan Birnbaum and Clarence Taylor, 619–656. New York: New York University Press.

Roediger, David R. 2005. *Working Toward Whiteness*. New York: Basic Books.

Scott, Mel. 1971. *American City Planning Since 1890*. Berkeley: University of California Press.

Seeley, John. 1959. The Slum: Its Nature, Use, and Users. *Journal of the American Institute of Planners* 25 (1): 7–14.

Slayton, William. 1963. Urban Renewal Philosophy. In *Planning 1963: Selected Papers from the ASPO National Planning Conference*, 154–159. Chicago: American Society of Planning Officials.

Soja, Edward. 2010. *Seeking Spatial Justice*. Minneapolis: University of Minnesota Press.

Stafford, Walter, and Joyce Ladner. 1969. Comprehensive Planning and Racism. *Journal of the American Institute of Planners* 35 (2): 68–74.

Starr, Roger. 1963. Learning about the Community. In *Planning 1963: Selected Papers from the ASPO National Planning Conference*, 246–250. Chicago: American Society of Planning Officials.

Starr, Roger. 1968. Advocates and Adversaries. In *Planning 1968: Selected Papers from the ASPO National Planning Conference*, 33–37. Chicago: American Society of Planning Officials.

Strichartz, Richard. 1968. The Failure of Planning. In *Planning 1968: Selected Papers from the ASPO National Planning Conference*, 29–32. Chicago: American Society of Planning Officials.

Stokes, Carl. 1971. On Reordering the Priorities of the Planning Profession. In *Planning 1971: Selected Papers from the ASPO National Planning Conference*, 1–6. Chicago: American Society of Planning Officials.

Symes, Arthur. 1970. The New York City Master Plan. In *Planning 1970: Selected Papers from the ASPO National Planning Conference*, 183–184. Chicago: American Society of Planning Officials.

Thomas, June M. 1997. *Redevelopment and Race: Planning a Finer City in Postwar Detroit*. Baltimore, MD: Johns Hopkins University Press.

U.S. Census Bureau. 2011. State and County Quick Facts. http://quickfacts .census.gov/qfd/meta/long_RHI125200.htm.

Weaver, Robert. 1966. Planning in the Great Society: A Crisis of Involvement. In *Planning 1966: Selected Papers from the ASPO National Planning Conference*, 6–13. Chicago: American Society of Planning Officials.

Webber, Melvin. 1963. Comprehensive Planning and Social Responsibility: Toward an AIP Consensus on the Profession's Roles. *Journal of the American Institute of Planners* 29 (4): 232–241.

Wilson, James Q. 1963. Planning and Politics: Citizen Participation in Urban Renewal. *Journal of the American Institute of Planners* 29 (4): 242–249.

Wolf, Eleanor. 1963. The Tipping-Point in Racially Changing Neighborhoods. *Journal of the American Institute of Planners* 29 (3): 217–222.

Wood, Elizabeth. 1958. Public Housing. In *Planning 1958: Selected Papers from the ASPO National Planning Conference*, 198–204. Chicago: American Society of Planning Officials.

Worsham, John P. 1979. *Planning: An Author and Subject Index to the Selected Papers from the American Society of Planning Officials National Planning Conference, 1960–71*. Monticello, IL: Vance Bibliographies.

Ylvisaker, Paul. 1961. Diversity and the Public Interest: Two Cases in Metropolitan Decision-Making. *Journal of the American Institute of Planners* 27 (2): 107–117.

Index

Note: Italicized page numbers indicate figures.